Willamette Management Associates

GUIDE to ESOP VALUATION

and Financial Advisory Services

Robert F. Reilly and Robert P. Schweihs

Willamette Management Associates Partners

Chicago • New York • Westport • Washington, DC
Atlanta • San Francisco • Portland

This publication is intended to provide accurate and authoritative information regarding the subject matter. It is not intended to offer legal, accounting, or other advice. If legal or other expert advice is required, the services of a competent professional should be sought.

Willamette Management Associates Guide to ESOP Valuation and Financial Advisory Services
Robert F. Reilly and Robert P. Schweihs

Book design by Charlene M. Blalock
Cover Photo: comstock.com

ISBN: 0-9767683-0-5

Printed in the United States of America
First printing: March 2005

Willamette Management Associates Partners
111 SW Fifth Avenue
Suite 2150
Portland, Oregon 97204
(800) 241-3939
www.willamette.com

We dedicate this book to our children:

Ashley Reilly
Brandon Reilly
Cameron Reilly
Patrick Schweihs
Mary Katherine Schweihs
Bridget Schweihs
Ann Marie Schweihs

No matter what we have (or ever will) accomplish professionally, our children are the greatest source of pride and joy in our lives.

Contents

Section IV ESOP Financial Adviser Issues

Section V ESOP Trustee Issues

Section VI ESOP Stock Valuation Case Study

Section VIII ESOP Bibliography

Introduction

This book is intended to present a consensus of the current thinking with regard to employee stock ownership plan (ESOP) stock valuation, transaction structure, acquisition financing, independent financial adviser, and trustee fiduciary issues. This book describes the practical applications of ESOP valuation, financing, taxation, and transaction structuring. This book does not focus on the theory of ESOP stock valuation or corporate finance issues. There are numerous textbooks already published that address the topics of closely held business valuation and security analysis. This book is not designed to be a "how to value ESOP stock" text. Rather, it is designed to explore (and, when possible, resolve) the practical issues currently facing ESOP valuation analysts and financial advisers.

This book is intended to benefit practicing ESOP valuation analysts and ESOP transaction financial advisers, ESOP trustees, ESOP legal counsel, ESOP accountants and auditors, ESOP administrators, and other ESOP professionals. Accordingly, this book assumes that the reader already has a basic working knowledge of generally accepted business valuation approaches, methods, and procedures (or is in a position where such a working knowledge is not needed). Due to the practical nature of the discussions, this book is also intended to benefit (1) the managers and non-ESOP stockholders of ESOP sponsor companies, (2) the current ESOP participants of employer corporations, and (3) the management and stockholders of companies that are considering an initial ESOP formation.

For the most part, the discussions in this book were adapted from articles that originally appeared in the Willamette Management Associates client publication *Insights*. *Insights* is a quarterly publication with a special topic annual edition. Over the decades, the *Insights* special topic annual edition has often focused on ESOP valuation issues and related ERISA issues. For this book, we selected "the best of" the ESOP valuation articles published in *Insights* during the last decade. In each case, we thoroughly edited and updated the original article so that the discussions presented in this book are both timely and topical.

We hope this book presents clear, convincing, and cogent discussions of the current issues facing the ESOP valuation practitioner. This is the first edition of this book. We hope to periodically update this book. Accordingly, we hope that future editions of this book will be of even greater practical use both to ESOP professionals and to the general ESOP community.

Acknowledgements

As with any project of this magnitude, there are numerous people to whom we would like to express our sincerest gratitude.

First, we would like to thank our families for their patience and understanding. By now, our wives and children are used to the periodic monastic sequestration that we go through during these publication projects.

Second, we thank several Willamette Management Associates colleagues who were essential to the production of this book, particularly:

- Hale Chan, director of marketing and communications, who conceived, defined, and refined this project,
- Mary McCallister, administrative assistant, who typed and proofread the entire manuscript, and
- Charlene Blalock, research associate, who is the person most responsible for making this book (and all of our other books) come to fruition.

Third, we acknowledge Jeffrey Tarbell, Portland office principal, and Malcolm (Mike) Hartman, Atlanta office principal. Jeff and Mike edited this manuscript and provided invaluable technical advice and assistance to this project.

Fourth, we appreciate the efforts of the following Willamette Management Associates colleagues who edited and updated individual chapters in this book:

- Gregg Gaffen, senior manager, Chicago office
- Malcolm Hartman, principal, Atlanta office
- Curtis Kimball, principal, Atlanta office
- Tim Meinhart, senior manager, Chicago office
- Thomas Millon, principal, Washington, DC, office
- James O'Sullivan, senior manager, New York office
- Jeffrey Tarbell, principal, Portland office

- Daniel VanVleet, principal, Chicago office
- Charles Wilhoite, principal, Portland office

Fifth, we particularly thanks:

- Pamela Garland, senior manager, Chicago office, and Ashley Reilly, research intern, Chicago office, for conducting the Willamette Management Associates discount for lack of voting rights study discussed in Chapter 13.
- James Rabe, principal, Portland office, and Aaron Rotkowski, senior associate, Portland office, for preparing the Employer, Inc., sample ESOP valuation report.
- Dan Van Vleet, principal, Chicago office, for the conceptual development of the SEAM model and for his work on Chapter 15.
- Charlene Blalock, research associate, Portland office, and Victoria Platt, director of research, Chicago office, for preparing the bibliography chapter.

Sixth, and most importantly, we express our appreciation to the following ESOP trustees and ESOP/ERISA attorneys who originally authored the *Insights* articles from which we adapted chapters for this *Guide to ESOP Valuation*. These individuals are all prominent and eminent ESOP professionals. We are most appreciative that they spent the time and effort to share their experience and expertise. In particular, we want to thank these individuals for their continued support of Willamette Management Associates and our ESOP practice financial advisory services. Their integrity and professionalism benefit the entire ESOP community.

- David Ackerman, Esq., Morgan Lewis & Bockius, LLP
- John Banasek, GreatBancTrust Company
- Keith Butcher, Esq., Morgan Stanley ESOP Transaction Services Group
- E. Vaughn Gordy, LaSalle Bank N.A.
- John Kober, Esq., Morgan Lewis & Bockius, LLP
- Marilyn Marchetti, GreatBanc Trust Company
- William Merten, Esq., McDermott, Will & Emery
- Danielle Montesano, GreatBancTrust Company

- Stephen D. Smith, Esq., Krieg DeVault Alexander & Caphart, LLP
- James Staruck, GreatBanc Trust Company

Each of the above-mentioned individuals contributed to the positive aspects of this book. We alone are responsible for any of the deficiencies of this text.

Robert F. Reilly
Robert P. Schweihs
Chicago, Illinois
March 2005

About the Authors

ROBERT F. REILLY

Robert Reilly is a managing director of Willamette Management Associates. Before joining the firm in 1991, he was a partner and national director of valuation services at accounting firm Deloitte & Touche. Before that, he was a vice president at the consulting firm Arthur D. Little Valuation, Inc.

Robert's practice focuses on the valuation of businesses, securities, and intangible assets for transaction, financing, litigation, bankruptcy, licensing, strategic planning, income tax, gift and estate tax, and ad valorem property tax purposes.

Robert has served as an expert witness in well over 100 litigation matters related to business and security valuation, economic damages and lost profits, economic event analysis, transfer price and royalty rate analysis, and financial adviser due diligence procedures. He has been accepted as an expert in various international, federal, state, and local courts. Robert has served as an expert witness in ESOP and ERISA disputes in Federal District Court and in the Court of Federal Claims.

Robert performed his first ESOP stock valuation in 1981, and has been actively involved as an ESOP valuation analyst ever since.

Robert holds a B.A. in economics from Columbia College and an M.B.A. in finance from the Columbia University Graduate School of Business. He is a certified public accountant/accredited in business valuation, certified management accountant, accredited tax adviser, enrolled agent to practice before the IRS, and chartered financial analyst. He is a certified business appraiser, certified real estate appraiser, certified review appraiser, accredited senior appraiser, and state certified general appraiser in numerous states from Virginia to California.

He is the co-author of seven valuation textbooks, including *The Handbook of Business Valuation and Intellectual Property Analysis*. He is the author of over 300 articles published in professional journals. He currently serves as a valuation editor of the *American Bankruptcy Institute Journal* and *The Journal of Valuation and Property Taxation*. He also serves as the intellectual property editor for the RIA journal *Valuation Strategies*.

ROBERT P. SCHWEIHS

Bob Schweihs is a managing director of Willamette Management Associates. Before joining the firm in 1991, Bob was a partner and national director of valuation services at accounting firm Deloitte & Touche. Before that, he was a regional manager for the consulting firm Arthur D. Little Valuation, Inc.

Bob's practice focuses on the valuation of business and securities and on the transfer price, and remaining useful life, and economic damages analysis of intangible assets and intellectual properties. In addition to private/public company financial advisory services, Bob provides business/security valuation services related to federal income, gift, and estate taxation; state/local property taxation; reorganization and restructuring; financial accounting; and ESOP stock transactions and ERISA compliance.

Bob has served as an expert witness on well over 50 occasions regarding the valuation of businesses, securities, and intangible assets and intellectual properties. He has testified in numerous federal, state, and local courts and tribunals. Bob has been actively involved in performing ESOP stock valuation and ESOP financial adviser services for over 20 years.

Bob holds a B.S. degree in engineering from Notre Dame University and an M.B.A. in finance from the University of Chicago Graduate School of Business. He is a certified business appraiser and an accredited senior appraiser.

Bob is the co-author of seven valuation textbooks, including *The Handbook of Business Valuation and Intellectual Property Analysis*. And, Bob has authored well over 100 technical articles related that have been published in numerous professional journals. These articles relate to the valuation of various types of business interests and to the analysis of economic damages and lost profits. Bob currently serves as an editor of the Institute of Business Appraisers journal, *Appraisal Practice*.

Bob is frequently asked to speak before the professional organization conferences and seminars, including proceedings of the Institute for Professionals in Taxation, the National Center for Employee Ownership, the Institute of Business Appraisers, The ESOP Association, and the American Society of Appraisers.

Over the years, he has served on numerous committees of the American Society of Appraisers and of other professional organizations. In addition, Bob has served the maximum limit of two three-year terms as a Trustee of The Appraisal Foundation.

About Willamette Management Associates

EXPERIENCE, CREATIVITY, AND RESPONSIVENESS IN ESOP VALUATION AND FINANCIAL ADVISER SERVICES

Our valuation consulting services include:

- valuations of closely held businesses
- valuations of securities and fractional business interests
- valuations of restricted stock of public corporations
- valuations of thinly traded stock of public corporations
- valuations of stock options, warrants, grants, and rights
- valuations of intangible asset and intellectual properties

Our economic analysis services include:

- lost profits/economic analysis of breach of contract or noncompete agreement, intellectual property infringement, lender liability damages, shareholder dispute, and other litigation claims
- event analysis, including the effect on the security price of a government regulation, of governmental expropriation, of a particular transaction, or of a failure to disclose reportable information
- reasonableness of executive owner/employee, or professional practitioner compensation
- intercompany transfer pricing for tangible and intangible assets
- royalty rate and license analysis of intangible assets and intellectual properties
- remaining useful life analysis for tangible and intangible assets

Our financial advisory opinion services include:

- fairness opinions, solvency opinions, and adequate consideration opinions
- insolvency opinions for bankruptcy and taxation purposes
- financing fraudulent conveyance opinions
- opinions for fiduciaries regarding related-party transactions
- equity allocation opinions related to business mergers
- asset allocation opinions related to business dissolutions

Willamette Capital, our specialized investment banking firm, provides a full range of private company investment banking and business brokerage services, with particular emphasis on:

- employee buyouts of private companies and business units of public companies, both with and without the leveraged ESOP acquisition structure
- private placement of debt and equity securities of middle-market companies
- debt restructuring of troubled companies, both with and without a recapitalization or reorganization

ESOP INDEPENDENT FINANCIAL ADVISORY SERVICES

The Employee Retirement Income and Securities Act (ERISA) and the Internal Revenue Code require special consideration with regard to the formation and financing of an employee stock ownership plan (ESOP) and with regard to transactions between the ESOP and the employer corporation. In these situations, prudent ESOP fiduciaries seek the advice of independent financial advisers. This is because ESOP transactions are often the focus of ex post facto scrutiny by the U.S. Department of Labor and by the Internal Revenue Service.

In leveraged and nonleveraged ESOP transactions, Willamette Management Associates has served as an independent financial adviser to plan fiduciaries related to the purchase or sale of employer corporation securities in closely held businesses and in publicly traded corporations.

Our independent financial advisory services to ESOP fiduciaries include:

- ESOP formation feasibility studies
- leveraged ESOP debt capacity studies
- transaction negotiation and structuring on behalf of ESOPs
- financing negotiation and structuring on behalf of ESOPs
- design of multiple security classes and instruments
- equity allocations in multiple-investor transactions
- adequate consideration opinions on ESOP formations, financings, and recapitalizations
- adequate consideration opinions for ESOP stock tender offers
- analysis of repurchase liability and other risk factors
- periodic ESOP employer corporation stock valuations
- analysis of ESOP termination and distributions
- analysis of employer corporation S election or conversion
- audit support during regulatory challenges
- litigation support/expert testimony during regulatory challenges

Section I

Structuring the ESOP Transaction

Chapter 1

Structuring the Leveraged ESOP Stock Purchase Transaction

INTRODUCTION

This discussion explains the general structure of a leveraged employee stock ownership plan (ESOP) stock purchase transaction. This discussion also summarizes the circumstances in which an ESOP can be used for successful ownership transition of a closely held business. A leveraged ESOP is an ownership succession strategy that allows the selling stockholder to cash out a significant portion of equity while maintaining control of the employer corporation. This discussion also considers procedures for managing the ESOP after the operational leveraged stock purchase transaction. And, this discussion considers the use of a leveraged ESOP as part of an estate planning strategy.

TYPICAL LEVERAGED ESOP STOCK PURCHASE STRUCTURE

A leveraged ESOP transaction involves the purchase of the stock of a private or a public company by the employees with the use of borrowed funds through a qualified defined benefit retirement plan. The benefits of an ESOP are similar to the benefits of other qualified plans—including profit sharing plans—except that the ESOP benefits are distributable in employer corporation stock. Unlike other qualified plans, an ESOP may borrow money and enter into related party transactions to acquire the employer corporation stock. Therefore, the ESOP can function as a financing vehicle to accomplish the ownership transition of a closely held corporation.

Since the ability of any business to service debt is limited, the size of the ESOP stock purchase transaction is limited to the employer corporation's debt-carrying capacity. This limitation occurs unless other equity investors are included in the stock purchase transaction. A multi-investor leveraged

ESOP transaction is defined as a transaction in which more than one investor (exclusive of the senior lender) provides financing for the employer corporation stock purchase.

The basic leveraged ESOP transaction is illustrated in Figure 1. In the basic ESOP stock purchase transaction, the employer corporation enters into a loan agreement with an outside lender or lenders (the "bank loan"). The employer corporation lends the proceeds from that bank loan to the ESOP (the "ESOP loan"). The ESOP uses the cash it receives from the employer corporation to purchase stock from the selling stockholders.

Figure 1

Basic Structure of a Leveraged ESOP Stock Purchase Transaction

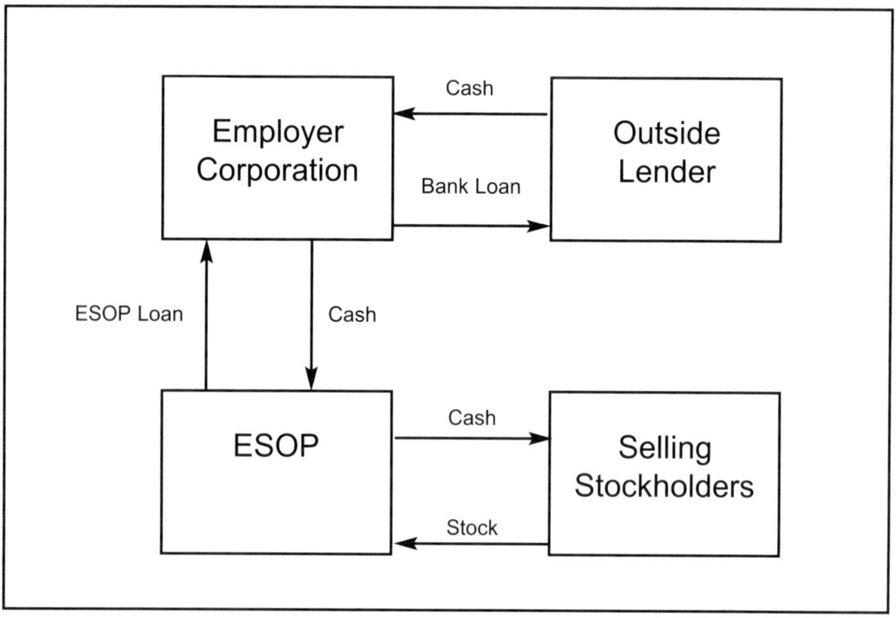

Each year, the employer corporation makes contributions of cash to the ESOP. These contributions of cash are used by the ESOP to amortize the ESOP loan. First, the employer corporation receives the cash payments of the ESOP loan from the ESOP. And, second, the employer corporation uses the cash to make payments on the bank loan. This typical cash flow structure of a leveraged ESOP stock purchase transaction is illustrated in Figure 2.

Figure 2

Typical Cash Flow Structure of a Leveraged ESOP Stock Purchase Transaction

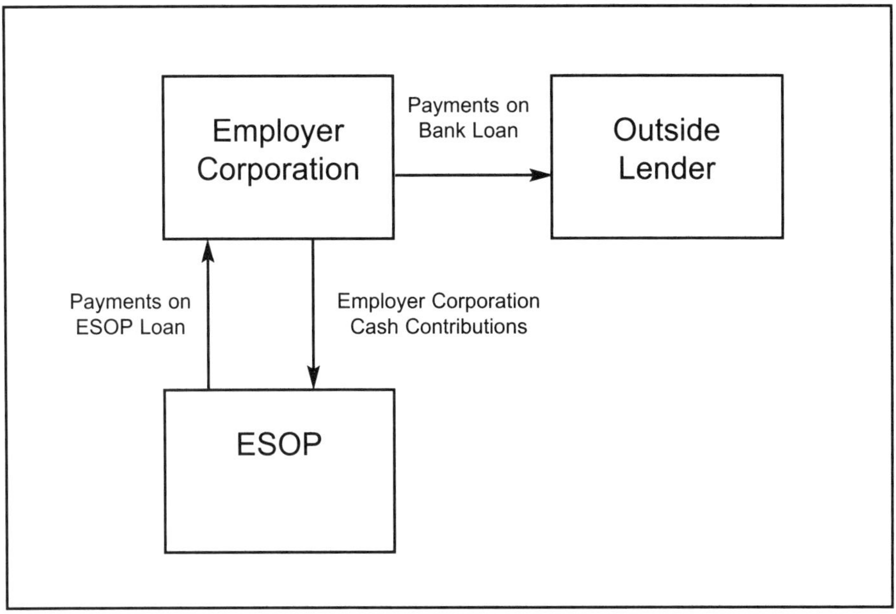

ECONOMIC BENEFITS OF A LEVERAGED ESOP STOCK PURCHASE TRANSACTION

If properly structured, the leveraged ESOP provides economic benefits to all parties to the stock purchase transaction. The structure of the leveraged ESOP transaction must comply with the specific rules and guidelines of both (1) the Internal Revenue Service and (2) the U.S. Department of Labor (DOL). In addition to income tax benefits, there are other economic benefits associated with a leveraged ESOP transaction. If properly structured, the leveraged ESOP stock purchase transaction can achieve many, if not all, of the available economic benefits.

Economic Benefits to the Selling Stockholders

The typical objectives of the selling stockholder are to achieve liquidity and diversification. These objectives are accomplished through the sale of the closely held corporation stock to the ESOP. Typically, a large proportion of the business owner's wealth is invested in the closely held business. If the closely held business were to decline in value, the business owner's retirement could be impaired. As a closely held business owner reaches retirement age, he or she often desires to diversify previously concentrated wealth. The proceeds form the sale of the closely held business owner's stock to an ESOP provides the opportunity to diversify. If the closely held business owner sells less than 50 percent of the company stock to the ESOP, the stockholder can maintain ownership control of the company. Accordingly, the selling stockholder can (1) achieve diversification and liquidity and (2) still maintain ownership and operational control of the family-owned business.

The major income tax benefit to the selling stockholder relates to Internal Revenue Code Section 1042. Under Section 1042, an individual business owner can elect to defer the payment of capital gains taxes on the sale of employer corporation to an ESOP. The requirements for this Section 1042 tax deferral include the following:

1. Immediately after the stock sale to the ESOP, the ESOP must own at least 30 percent of the voting stock of the employer corporation or 30 percent of the value of the employer corporation.
2. Qualified replacement property (QRP) must be purchased with the stock sale proceeds within a 15-month period beginning three months prior to the stock sale to the ESOP. QRP is generally defined as stocks and bonds of domestic operating corporations.
3. The selling stockholder must have owned the employer corporation stock sold to the ESOP for at least three years prior to the sale.

If a closely held business owner is contemplating a sale of the business, a sale to an ESOP will often generate greater net proceeds to the selling stockholder. This is because no income tax will be due at the time of the sale to the ESOP. Another economic benefit to the Section 1042 requirement is that the QRP stock is the type of investment that the business owner would typically select as a retirement investment. Therefore, the leveraged ESOP may be an attractive exit vehicle for the closely held business owner.

Economic Benefits to the Employer Corporation

The employer corporation objectives in a leveraged ESOP transaction include: (1) enhancing cash flow, (2) obtaining financing, (3) increasing productivity, (4) motivating employees, and (5) attracting employees. The

ESOP participant account balances will increase with the value of the employer corporation and provide a strong financial incentive to join and stay with the employer corporation. In addition, employees of ESOP-owned companies typically generate higher productivity rates than comparable employees of non-ESOP-owned companies.

The ESOP income tax advantage for the employer corporation is that the repayment of ESOP acquisition debt is tax deductible. The employer corporation payments to the ESOP are employer contributions. These contributions are tax deductible under Section 404. These same payments are used to pay the stock acquisition debt. Accordingly, the principal on the bank loan is effectively tax deductible to the employer corporation.

In addition, dividends paid on employer corporation stock or that are distributed to the ESOP participants are also tax deductible. The effect on the employer corporation is that there is a significant tax savings. This income tax savings results in improved employer corporation cash flows. Since the net cash flow on a leveraged ESOP transaction is greater than on other acquisition financing, the leveraged ESOP structure has less financial risk. In addition, ESOP financing is often easier to obtain than conventional acquisition financing.

Economic Benefits to the ESOP Participants

Employees typically desire increases in their compensation and continued employment. The value of any going-concern company depends on its financial performance. The ESOP ties the employee retirement benefits with the success of the employer corporation. Accordingly, the objectives of the employees are more closely aligned with the objectives of the stockholders. Some leveraged ESOP transactions provide economic benefits to employees in excess of 30 percent of their annual compensation. Typically, economic incentives increase employee morale and employee retention rates. ESOP-owned company employees often feel like they have more control over their own employment destiny.

Economic Benefits to the ESOP Lender

Since most ESOP stock purchase transactions involve leverage, a lender is typically involved. The major objectives of the ESOP lender are (1) to be paid back by the employer corporation and (2) to earn a fair rate of return during the loan amortization period. As mentioned above, principal payments on the ESOP loan are tax deductible. Therefore, employer corporation cash flow is enhanced due to a decrease in federal income taxes paid.

Accordingly, the probability that the ESOP lender will be paid back is enhanced with an ESOP stock acquisition loan as compared to a conventional acquisition loan.

The typical lender analyzes a credit by considering the two sources of funds from which the lender can be paid back. The first source of funds is from cash flow from company operations. The second source of funds is from a liquidation of the company assets. The enhancement of employer corporation cash flow in an ESOP stock purchase transaction increases the creditworthiness of the sponsor company. In addition, the selling stockholders QRP often serves as collateral in the case of a liquidation of the company assets. If the employer corporation borrowing ability does not support the size of the ESOP stock purchase transaction, the selling stockholder may often pledge the QRP as loan collateral. The ESOP lender perceives this pledge as an enhancement in the collateral position it takes—further increasing the employer corporation creditworthiness.

Economic Benefits to Third-Party Investors

Third-party investors in ESOP stock purchase transactions often take the form of subordinated lenders, venture capital groups, public stockholders, or other equity investors. Each investor's objective is to earn a fair rate of return, consistent with the degree of investment risk that it assumes. There are also subordinated debt funds that finance ESOP leveraged buyouts (LBOs). These funds fill the need for capital by offering unsecured subordinated debt instruments with equity risk enhancements.

The income tax benefits associated with the tax deductibility of principal payments on ESOP debt are shared by all investors. The increased employer corporation cash flow increases the equity rate of return. The leveraged ESOP transaction also provides an economic benefit to the current stockholders by serving as an exit vehicle. The ESOP gives current stockholders the opportunity to liquidate their investment position.

FEASIBILITY OF A LEVERAGED ESOP STOCK PURCHASE TRANSACTION

Although there are numerous economic benefits of the leveraged ESOP stock purchase transaction, not every company should implement an ESOP. The first step in assessing a leveraged ESOP transaction is to analyze whether it is feasible, given the employer corporation specific facts and circumstances. The employer corporation characteristics discussed below are intended to indicate successful ESOP implementation attributes.

The Valuation of the Employer Corporation Stock

The first step in assessing whether an ESOP transaction is feasible is to estimate the value of the employer corporation stock. All other ESOP financial analysis variables depend on the employer corporation stock valuation. These other financial analysis variables include: (1) the employer corporation debt capacity, (2) the benefit to the employees, (3) the cash flow available to amortize the ESOP debt, and so forth. An ESOP may not pay more than adequate consideration for the employer corporation stock. Adequate consideration is defined by the DOL Proposed Regulation 29.C.F.R. 2510.3-18(b).

The DOL requires that the ESOP valuation analyst be a person who normally engaged in valuation activity, preferably on a full-time basis. The consensus of ESOP professionals is that valuation analysts should have specific experience with ESOP appraisals, be members of relevant professional organizations, and have achieved relevant professional certifications.

The Employer Corporation Debt Capacity

After the employer corporation stock value is estimated, the analyst should consider the sponsor company's debt capacity. The stock price paid by the ESOP will be financed by the operating cash flow of the employer corporation. The employer corporation should be capable of generating adequate cash flow to satisfy the ESOP debt, and any other debt service. If the employer corporation has no outstanding debt prior to the ESOP stock purchase transaction, then the new ESOP debt will be easier to amortize. Accordingly, it is more difficult to finance ESOP stock purchase transactions in capital-intensive businesses that already service large amounts of outstanding debt.

Most ESOP lenders have guidelines for the minimum level of earnings before interest, taxes, depreciation, and amortization (EBITDA) relative to the annual amounts of debt service. Typically, the employer corporation should have a "cushion" in its operating cash flow amount after meeting all of its debt service obligations. A cash flow cushion of 20 percent to 50 percent over annual debt service requirements is typical.

ESOP lenders also assess the availability of loan collateral before issuing a commitment to lend. Advance rates are applied to each class of collateral asset. These advance rates are based on the relative amount of expected risk associated with receiving full value for the collateral in a liquidation. For example, manufacturing companies typically have larger investments in real estate and tangible personal property that can be used to collateralize loans. Also, operating companies that own real estate have a greater ability to collateralize debt. Service companies that own small amounts of tangible assets should have income and cash flows adequate to service the ESOP loan.

Another loan collateral enhancement available in ESOP stock purchase transactions is the pledge of QRP by the selling stockholders. Advance rates are also applied to the QRP to determine the amount of the loan collateral value. This selling stockholder QRP pledge is typically limited both in amount and in duration. Of course, the income on the pledged securities continues to be earned by the selling stockholders.

Not every employer corporation can finance a 100 percent ESOP stock purchase with its operating cash flow. Often in 100 percent acquisitions, another equity investor is brought in to the transaction to provide the additional equity required by the senior lender. The additional equity can be provided through various direct equity securities and derivative securities. This additional equity may include: subordinated debt with warrants, management stock, preferred stock, third party investors, and so on. Several equity investors may be needed in leveraged ESOP stock purchase transactions depending on (1) the percentage of the employer corporation stock the ESOP purchases and (2) the employer corporation debt capacity.

Employee Benefit Plan Contribution Limitations

Another limitation of the employer corporation ability to implement an ESOP transaction is the Section 415 limitations on "annual additions" to qualified plans. Employer contributions to qualified plans are also limited by Section 404. Section 415 generally provides that annual additions may not exceed the lesser of (1) 25 percent of employee compensation or (2) $30,000 per employee. Annual additions include employer corporation contributions that are used to pay interest on the ESOP loan, which are excluded from the Section 415 limitations.

Since there is a limit to the amount of tax deductible employer corporation contributions based on payroll, the level of total qualified payroll is important in assessing ESOP feasibility. In the case where a significant percentage of the employer corporation stock is sold to an ESOP, a large payroll base better allows the sponsor company to repay the ESOP debt principal with tax deductible contributions. In the case where the sponsor company has a small payroll base, the leveraged ESOP transaction may be designed to include a dividend preference stock. A dividend preference stock could be either (1) a convertible preferred or (2) a common stock with a dividend preference. Such dividend preference common stock is commonly called super common stock.

The employer corporation is recapitalized so that the super common stock or convertible preferred stock is sold to the ESOP. The dividends on these dividend preference stocks are then tax deductible under Section 404(k). And, the dividends on these stocks are not included in the definition of annual additions under Section 415. The use of a super common or convertible preferred stock in a leveraged ESOP transaction allows the total contribution to the participant accounts to exceed the 25 percent limitation under Section 415. In addition, the full amount of the principal payment on the ESOP loan is fully tax deductible to the employer corporation.

If the employer corporation has an existing profit sharing or pension plan, these other plan provisions should be considered when installing an ESOP. In some ESOP stock purchase transactions, the existing plan benefits need to be frozen or terminated. This is because the ESOP will use the entire Section 415 limitation amount. All qualified plan benefits are combined for purposes of assessing the Section 415 limitation. Just as with other qualified plans, the sponsor company management needs to make decisions about coverage, vesting, distributions, and so on when implementing an ESOP plan. In addition, the employer corporation should consider the interactive effect of all of its employee benefit plans.

Other ESOP Feasibility Considerations

With the Section 1042 election, the selling stockholders can defer the capital gain on the sale to the ESOP in certain circumstances. These income tax benefits are more valuable if the selling stockholder has a low tax basis in the employer corporation stock sold to the ESOP. If the selling stockholder tax basis is at or near the employer stock fair market value, then the income benefit of the Section 1042 deferral is less significant.

Employer corporations with larger revenue or substantial tangible assets are often better candidates for a leveraged ESOP transaction. This is because larger companies can typically attract more favorable financing. And, such companies typically have a lower cost of debt. In addition, the cost of completing the transaction as a percentage of the total sale proceeds is relatively lower for larger employer corporations. Although small dollar value ESOPs can be implemented, the transaction structure should remain simple in order to reduce the total transaction costs.

The employer corporation has to service the new ESOP debt. Therefore, a competent management team is important for a successful leveraged

ESOP transaction. The ESOP is a passive investor, and the ESOP trustee is not involved in day-to-day management decisions. In cases where the previous management team is exiting after the company ESOP transaction, the expertise of the new management team becomes even more important. Some ESOP lenders require employment contracts or noncompete agreements with the sponsor company senior management in leveraged ESOP transactions. If the previous management team is not exiting the company, then effective operational control of the employer corporation remains with the existing management.

ATTRIBUTES OF A SUCCESSFUL LEVERAGED ESOP STOCK PURCHASE TRANSACTION

Closely held companies are bought and sold every day. There are many seller motivations that drive these business sale transactions. The closely held business owner invests in the company to earn (1) interim returns and (2) a terminal return at the time of the business sale. The following listing describes several situations in which a leveraged ESOP stock purchase transaction may be a strategic exit vehicle for the closely held company owner (or, in some cases, for the publicly traded company owner).

- a privately held company where the stockholders want or need liquidity for their estate, their retirement, etc.;
- a private or public corporation that is looking to divest business units that no longer fit its strategic or financial objectives;
- a privately held company that wants to offer additional incentives to management and employees;
- a "going private" transaction for a publicly traded company that seeks to avoid the regulatory costs of a public corporation;
- a management group that desires to buy out the existing owner; or
- the buyout of one or more investor groups where the investor objectives/expectations are no longer in line with management objectives/expectations.

All of the above-described economic benefits may or may not be available in each of these situations. However, income tax benefits are not always the principal factor behind an ESOP stock purchase transaction. When an ESOP is implemented, a new culture is typically created within the employer corporation. Ideally, this new culture results in an alignment of management, stockholders, and employee objectives.

PROCEDURES IN IMPLEMENTING THE LEVERAGED ESOP STOCK PURCHASE TRANSACTION

The decision to implement an ESOP should consider the collective objectives of the employer corporation, management, employees, the selling stockholder, and any third-party investors. If the feasibility analysis indicates that a leveraged ESOP is financially feasible, then the employer corporation should follow very specific procedures with regard to the ESOP implementation and stock purchase transaction. The following list summarizes the typical procedures that should be followed for a successful implementation of a leveraged ESOP:

- Complete the feasibility study to determine if the leveraged ESOP will achieve the objectives of the principal participants in the stock sale/purchase transaction. This procedure includes a preliminary valuation of the employer corporation stock.
- Develop a transaction structure that meets the objective of all the principal participants in the transaction. In order to satisfy the differing investment objectives, a complex transaction structure may be necessary.
- Select an individual or financial institution to act as an independent trustee to represent the employees on behalf of the ESOP. The ESOP trustee will typically retain independent legal counsel to act on behalf of the trustee in reviewing the legal framework of the transaction.
- Complete a comprehensive valuation of the employer corporation common stock (or other classes of stock), based on the transaction structure. The ESOP trustee will typically retain an independent financial adviser to assist in this process.
- Review the existing employer corporation qualified plans and integrate the ESOP design with the existing benefit plans. Consider the total compensation (salary plus benefits, including ESOP contributions) to be paid to employees and determine if that compensation is commensurate with the subject industry.
- Negotiate financing for the stock purchase transaction from qualified lenders or third-party investors, if necessary.
- Determine whether the employer corporation will be able to accommodate the expected cash flow requirement due to the ESOP stock repurchase liability.
- Prepare ESOP plan administration statements that include the number of shares allocated to participant accounts and the value of those shares

at the end of the plan year. Other plan administration information may be disclosed at the discretion of the employer corporation.

- Develop a company-wide communication program to deliver the employee ownership message to the employee/ESOP participants. The ESOP is a significant benefit for employees, and ESOP transactions can enhance the wealth of individual employees. An effective company-wide communication program is essential to the success of the ESOP.
- Coordinate and file the required election for the reinvestment in QRP for the selling stockholders, if necessary.

Many of these procedures may be performed concurrently. And, some procedures require continuous attention. The ESOP feasibility, structuring, valuation, plan design, and financial procedures may be performed simultaneously. These procedures also interact with one another and may need adjustment as the ESOP stock purchase transaction progresses. For example, if the design of the stock purchase transaction requires the creation of a new class of employer corporation security, the valuation of that security should reflect all subsequent changes.

The ESOP trustee should be selected before the principal terms of the ESOP stock purchase transaction are negotiated. The ESOP trustee represents the interests of the employee/plan participants. The ESOP trustee is a fiduciary with respect to the transaction. Therefore, involvement on the part of the ESOP trustee helps to protect the transaction from contrarian challenge by the DOL. It is prudent to involve the ESOP trustee in the transaction as soon as possible. It is prudent to ensure that the ESOP trustee has enough time to conduct a thorough examination of (1) the terms of the transaction and (2) the employer corporation. Since the ESOP trustee will typically retain an independent financial adviser and independent legal counsel, these advisers also need time to conduct a thorough due diligence.

Management of the repurchase liability, plan administration, and communication programs are ongoing tasks that should become part of the management culture of the sponsor company. If effectively managed, the ESOP can provide employees with the incentive to increase productivity and profitability. In addition, if the ESOP purchases closely held company stock, then the employer corporation stock must be valued at least annually. Therefore, an annual stock valuation must be completed for purposes of communicating to the ESOP participants the value of their plan account balances.

PROTECTING THE LEVERAGED ESOP STOCK PURCHASE TRANSACTION

Every qualified ESOP is part of a trust that is covered by the Employee Retirement Income Security Act of 1974 (ERISA). The trust is governed by the trust document that specifies the duties and responsibilities of the ESOP trustee. Under ERISA Section 404(a)(1), a fiduciary—that is, the ESOP trustee—must approach the transaction "with the care, skill, prudence, and diligence under the circumstances then prevailing that a prudent man acting in a like capacity and familiar with such matters would use in the conduct of an enterprise of a like character and with like aims."

The employer corporation should carefully select the ESOP trustee, as this fiduciary obligation is significant. The ESOP trustee may be a "party in interest"—generally defined as corporate officers, employees, and more than 10 percent shareholders—but that is not advisable. This is because fiduciaries can be held personally liable for their actions. Many sponsor companies retain institutional trustees for independence. Ultimately, it is the ESOP trustee's responsibility to make the decision to purchase the employer corporation stock ESOP on behalf of the ESOP.

Section 401(a)(28)(C) provides that, after 1986, all valuations of employer corporation securities that are not readily tradable must be conducted by an independent appraiser. Therefore, the financial adviser to the ESOP trustee must be independent of all parties to the leveraged ESOP stock purchase transaction. The financial adviser must be hired by and report directly to the ESOP trustee. The agreement between the ESOP trustee and its financial adviser should define the types of opinions that the financial adviser will provide.

The following sections summarize the types of opinions that the financial adviser typically provides to the ESOP trustee.

Adequate Consideration

The first and most important opinion is whether the price paid by the ESOP for the employer stock exceeds adequate consideration. Adequate consideration is defined by ERISA Section 3(18)(B) as "the fair market value of the asset as determined in good faith by the trustee or named fiduciary . . . pursuant to the terms of the plan and in accordance with regulations promulgated by the Secretary of Labor."

Fair market value is defined by the DOL proposed regulations as the amount at which the company stock would change hands between a willing buyer and a willing seller, each having reasonable knowledge of all relevant facts, neither being under any compulsion to act, and with equity to both. The independent financial adviser must conduct a thorough and well supported valuation analysis that (1) incorporates all of the appropriate methods and (2) provides the ESOP trustee with the necessary justification for the adequate consideration opinion.

Fairness from a Financial Point of View

The adequate consideration test is sometimes referred to as the absolute fairness test. The adequate consideration question is: Does the price paid by the ESOP exceed some benchmark that represents fair market value? The "fairness from a financial point of view" opinion incorporates the concept of relative fairness. The independent financial adviser must also advise the ESOP trustee as to whether the price paid by the ESOP for the employer stock is fair relative to prices paid by any other investor.

The essence of the relative fairness test is a comparison of (1) the relative investment risk accepted by each investor and (2) the expected return associated with that risk. In the basic leveraged ESOP stock purchase transaction where a senior lender provides all of the financing, the concepts of relative and absolute fairness converge. Since there are no parties to the transaction other than the senior lender, the determination of relative fairness is based on whether the terms of the senior financing are fair relative to the ESOP.

In a multi-investor ESOP structure, relative fairness may become a significant issue. The allocation of equity to the various transaction participants in the leveraged ESOP can affect the internal rate of return (IRR) earned by each participant. The relative IRRs can affect whether the transaction is fair from a financial point of view. Accordingly, in transactions with more than one investor, the ESOP trustee must be actively involved in structuring the stock purchased by the ESOP and also the stock purchased by each of the transaction participants.

Measuring the IRR for each investor is one way to measure the fairness to the transaction to each of the transaction participants. As investment risk increases among the various employer corporation debt and equity securities, the expected rate of return should increase. The relative investment IRRs can be compared to empirical market returns of publicly traded securities with similar investment risk characteristics.

Reasonableness of the Stock Conversion Premium

If (1) the ESOP purchases a security other than a common stock and (2) that security has a dividend preference, then the ESOP trustee may require an opinion as to the reasonableness of the conversion premium. The conversion premium is measured as the premium paid by the preferred dividend security over the value of the common stock. The value of a dividend preference security is typically equal to (1) the value of the employer corporation common stock plus (2) the value of the dividend preference. Therefore, the premium paid by the preferred security is typically related to the value of the dividend preference.

To assess the reasonableness of the conversion premium, the financial adviser typically considers guideline publicly traded securities with similar investment characteristics and risk attributes. A comparison can be made of the (1) dividend coverage ratio, (2) capitalization ratio, (3) fixed charge coverage ratio, and (4) debt to equity ratio—between the employer corporation security and the guideline publicly traded securities. This comparison is made in order to assess the relative risks applicable to the employer corporation security, and therefore, the reasonableness of the conversion premium.

Reasonableness of the ESOP Acquisition Debt Terms and Conditions

Since the terms of the stock purchase transaction can also affect the purchase price, the financial adviser should also review the terms of the ESOP acquisition debt. The major terms of the ESOP acquisition debt that affect price are (1) the interest rate and (2) the term of the financing. A comparison of the ESOP debt terms with empirical debt market evidence can indicate whether these terms are reasonable in the existing economic environment. An analysis of current market interest rates will illustrate whether the interest rate on the ESOP debt is market-related.

The financial adviser should also consider the implied quality rating on the ESOP debt, so that a comparison can be made with the appropriately rated public debt. For example, if the ESOP debt represents 80 percent of the total invested capital value of the employer corporation, that debt may be rated lower than if the ESOP debt only represented 20 percent of the total invested capital value of the employer corporation.

MULTI-INVESTOR ESOP STOCK PURCHASE TRANSACTIONS

If the objective of the ESOP transaction is a complete transition of ownership control, other equity investors may be needed to complete the stock sale transaction. It is often difficult for the employer corporation to finance 100 percent of its value without additional equity investments. Debt holders typically view their credit as a short-term investment. Equity investors typically view their investment as a long-term investment. In order to protect the debt holder, the ESOP lender typically requires an employer corporation capital structure that includes adequate equity capital.

Since multi-investor transactions involve more complex capital structures, the ESOP financial adviser should apply greater due diligence to the terms and conditions of the stock purchase transaction. This due diligence should ensure that the relative and absolute fairness tests are met. In addition, the financial adviser should be involved in the transaction process in negotiating terms and conditions. The ESOP trustee should also be assured that procedural prudence is followed. That is, the ESOP trustee is concerned that its legal and financial advisers have taken all of the proper precautions to ensure that the ESOP is treated fairly. Multiple-investor transactions typically receive greater scrutiny by regulators due to their complexity. Regulatory authorities often review multi-investor transactions from the perspectives of security features such as equity and/or dividend preferences, redemption provisions, put and call provisions, liquidation preferences, the terms of shareholder agreements, registration rights, employment contracts, and earn-out provisions.

In structuring multi-investor ESOP transactions, each of the transaction participants will hold a debt or equity position. Some investors may hold a security that has both debt and equity features. The risk tolerances and investment objectives of these various transaction participants will differ significantly.

THE ESOP REPURCHASE LIABILITY

Code Section 409(h) provides that an ESOP plan participant has the right to require the employer corporation to repurchase its stock under a fair market value valuation formula at the time of the required distribution. This stock repurchase liability is an employer corporation obligation. It is typically called the "repurchase liability." In order to satisfy the repurchase liability, the employer corporation may transact with the plan participant directly in a "redemption" transaction. Alternatively, the ESOP trust may repurchase the shares in a "repurchase" transaction. Each of these transaction types results in different economics for (1) the non-ESOP stockholders and (2) the remaining ESOP participants.

First, the stock repurchase transaction is a transaction between the ESOP trust and the plan participant. Repurchase transactions can be dilutive to the other stockholders. This is true to the extent cash that could be used for other purposes is used to fund the repurchase liability. The repurchased stock terminates the ownership interest held by the existing employee. Then, that same stock is reallocated to the other ESOP participants and remains outstanding. Repurchases by the ESOP trust are tax deductible as an employer corporation contribution. These income tax benefits help offset any cash constraints on the stock repurchase.

Second, the stock redemption transaction is a transaction between (1) the employer corporation and (2) the ESOP participant. A redemption transaction is nondilutive to the other stockholders if the redemption occurs at fair market value. The aggregate size of the employer corporation is reduced by the cash used to finance the purchase. However, since the shares are also canceled, there is no effect on per share value. The redeemed employer corporation stock terminates the ownership interest held by the existing employee. The redemption does not create any additional ownership interest as in the repurchase transaction. Redemptions by the employer corporation are not tax deductible. And, the employer corporation needs to carefully plan to be sure the ESOP can meet the cash requirements.

The employer corporation must purchase the ESOP shares at the time of a required distribution. The rules governing qualified plans require that an ESOP participant must receive a distribution at the time of retirement, death, disability, or termination of the participant. However, distributions to terminated participants in a leveraged ESOP can be suspended during the term of the securities acquisition loan. The securities acquisition loan is the loan that is used by the trustee to acquire the ESOP stock. The purpose of this provision is to allow the employer corporation to use as much of its cash flow as possible for the amortization of the ESOP loan.

ESOP participants who die, retire, or become disabled must begin receiving distributions no later than one year from their separation from service. Older ESOP participants are also allowed to diversify their holdings in an ESOP as they near retirement age. Repurchase liability studies that incorporate employee turnover, actuarial assumptions, and the estimated future value of the employer corporation stock may be used to estimate the dollar amount and timing of the required distributions.

The level of the ESOP repurchase liability is typically low during the ESOP loan amortization period. This is due to the suspension of certain distributions. This period is the period in which distributions are required for those participants who die, retire, or become disabled. These stock repurchases are typically not significant. These repurchases can be funded out of the current employer corporation cash flow. In addition, the vesting schedule may make the distributions requirement nominal.

Once the employer corporation has paid off the ESOP acquisition debt, there may be additional borrowing capacity to assist with the repurchase obligation. The Internal Revenue Code allows distributions to be in the form of a note. That option can alleviate the repurchase liability burden.

If the employer corporation management makes a decision to redeem stock to satisfy the ESOP repurchase obligation each year, the ESOP contracts in size. This is because the redeemed shares are canceled. Continuous redemptions can be planned based on the timing of the distributions from the plan. Eventually all of the ESOP shares will be extinguished. At the time, the ESOP will hold no stock if the employer corporation makes redemptions for all the required distributions.

If the employer corporation management decides to repurchase stock to satisfy the ESOP repurchase obligation each year, the size of the ESOP or the amount of shares held by the ESOP does not change. As the shares are repurchased by the ESOP trust, the shares are reallocated to the remaining plan participants. These reallocated shares also have repurchase obligation on them. Therefore, when the shares are put back to the trust, the employer corporation must repurchase the shares. This "recycling" of shares creates a perpetual repurchase program as long as the shares are not redeemed and canceled.

Since a repurchase of shares also provides a compensation benefit to the plan participants that the shares are reallocated to, the compensation and benefits structure of the employer corporation should be analyzed periodically. The employer corporation needs to consider what level of benefits it will provide to employees.

If a repurchase of shares in one year would mean the employer corporation provides benefits in excess of the targeted level of benefits, then the sponsor company may redeem some of the shares to keep benefits paid commensurate with the market. If a repurchase of shares in one year would mean the employer corporation provides benefits below the targeted level, then the sponsor company may consider additional contributions to a qualified plan or the ESOP. If a repurchase of shares in one year would mean that the employer corporation provides benefits at the targeted level of benefits, then the sponsor company can repurchase all the shares without increasing the benefit level.

An employer corporation can use any combination of redemptions, repurchases, and additional cash contributions in any given year to manage the repurchase liability. The objective is to plan around the statutory obligation in order to provide liquidity to the terminating ESOP participant. The ESOP can solve a transition of ownership issue for the selling stockholder. However, as in any ownership transition, as one transition is solved, another transition is created. This is because every equity owner needs an exit vehicle. The obligation to honor the ESOP participant's put right regulates the timing for the next ownership transition. Planning for this obligation may become an annual analysis once the ESOP is implemented.

THE USE OF AN ESOP IN ESTATE PLANNING

The primary goal of many privately held business owner estate plans is to transfer the value of the family-owned enterprise to the next generation. Individuals who have a significant portion of their estates tied up in a privately held business risk losing the business at the death of the owner. Since combined federal and state estate tax rates approach 50 percent, the estate tax liability related to a privately held business may exceed the company's borrowing capacity.

Typically, an ESOPs is implemented in a leveraged stock purchase transaction. Since additional leverage can reduce the subsequent value of the employer corporation equity, an ESOP is also a valuable estate planning alternative.

Illustrative Example

Let's assume a hypothetical Sponsor Company. Sponsor Company has pretax earnings of $2 million in an industry with a four to six times invested capital valuation earnings pricing multiple. Accordingly, the Sponsor Company equity value would be approximately $10 million (i.e., $2 million earnings x 5 times industry average pricing multiple).

This value estimate concludes the value of the company's total invested capital (i.e., the long-term debt plus the owners' equity). If Sponsor Company has no long-term debt, then the Sponsor Company equity value would be $10 million. However, if Sponsor Company has $6 million in outstanding debt, then the value of the Sponsor Company equity is approximately $4 million. This illustrative example is summarized in Exhibit 1.

If the ESOP purchases 60 percent of the common stock of the unlevered Sponsor Company in a leveraged ESOP stock purchase transaction, then the value of the Sponsor Company equity would decrease immediately. Of course, the decrease in the company equity value is not exactly 60 percent. This is because the cost of debt capital is typically lower than the cost of equity capital.

Exhibit 1

The Effect of Leverage on Equity Value

Valuation Analysis	Sponsor Company with no debt	Sponsor Company with debt
Pretax earnings	$2 million	$2 million
Industry average valuation pricing multiple	x 5	x 5
Indicated invested capital value	$10 million	$10 million
Less: Long-term debt	$0 million	$6 million
Equals: Indicated equity value	$10 million	$4 million

If the remaining 40 percent of the Sponsor Company common stock is gifted by the funding stockholder to the family children, then this gift would be a transfer of a noncontrolling ownership interest in employer corporation common stock. Accordingly, the value of the gifted shares would be subject to a discount for lack of control. Since the employer corporation is assumed to be a privately held corporation, the value of gifted shares would also be subject to a discount for lack of marketability.

Let's assume that the appropriate discount for lack of marketability is 40 percent, and that the appropriate discount for lack of control is 40 percent. Based on these assumed valuation adjustments, the indicated fair market value of the gifted shares (after the sale of 60 percent of the employer corporation stock to the ESOP) is as presented in Exhibit 2.

Exhibit 2

Fair Market Value of the Gift of Sponsor Company Common Stock

Valuation Analysis		Sponsor Company
Indicated invested capital value		$10,000,000
Less:	ESOP acquisition loan	6,000,000
Equals:	Marketable, controlling interest equity value	4,000,000
Less:	Discount for lack of control (at 40%)	1,600,000
Equals:	Marketable, noncontrolling interest equity value	2,400,000
Less:	Discount for lack of marketability (at 40%)	960,000
Equals:	Indicated equity value on a nonmarketable, noncontrolling ownership interest basis, for federal gift tax purposes	$1,440,000

In addition, if the ESOP-owned stock is redeemed and cancelled in the future, then the percent of the employer corporation common stock owned by the ESOP will decrease. Accordingly, the percent of the employer corporation common stock owned by stockholders increases (as the ESOP ownership percentage decreases). Therefore, ownership control of the privately held company can remain with the 40 percent (second-generation) family stockholder through a series of ESOP stock redemptions.

SUMMARY AND CONCLUSION

The leveraged ESOP stock purchase transaction can provide a means to a successful ownership transition. This is more likely to occur if all the objectives of all of the parties to the stock sale/purchase transaction are considered. An ESOP offers (1) significant income tax benefits to the transaction participants and (2) qualitative productivity benefits to the employer corporation. The various aspects of ESOP feasibility and employer security design flexibility can allow most companies to implement an ESOP. This conclusion is true as long as all of the various legal and regulatory requirements of ESOPs are understood. Since an ESOP is a qualified retirement plan, certain fiduciary requirements must also be met.

Some ESOP stock purchase transactions may involve the investment return objectives and investment risk tolerances of various equity participants. Greater financial adviser due diligence is required for these multi-investor ESOP stock purchase transactions. This enhanced due diligence is due to the need for relative fairness to the ESOP.

The employer corporation should perform the necessary procedures to measure and manage the ESOP repurchase liability after the ESOP acquisition loan is paid off. The ESOP repurchase liability is another ownership transition planning for the next generation of equity holders. The ESOP also provides the selling stockholder with an estate planning opportunity. If the ESOP is properly structured, the founding family generation can transfer significant value to the next generation, without losing ownership control of the family business. And, if the ESOP is property structured, the founding family generation can transfer significant value to the next generation, while incurring a minimum of estate tax liability.

Chapter 2

ESOP Stock Purchase Transaction Structure

INTRODUCTION

An ESOP is often a versatile and effective vehicle for structuring (1) the sale of a closely held business; (2) the divestiture of a division or subsidiary of a publicly traded company; (3) the restructuring of a closely held or family-owned business where the current owners desire liquidity and a partial ownership transition; or (4) the recapitalization and reorganization of the subject business. This reorganization transaction objective may apply to both financially sound businesses and financially distressed businesses. The economic advantages of an ESOP structure in acquisitions, divestitures (partial and complete), and refinancings result primarily from numerous income taxation benefits that are available to ESOPs.

ESOP stock purchase/sale transactions encompass business valuation, legal and regulatory, plan administration, financing, and fiduciary concerns. This discussion presents these multidisciplinary concerns from the perspective of structuring either: (1) a business purchase or sale transaction or (2) a business recapitalization or reorganization transaction.

GENERAL ESOP FRAMEWORK

The starting point for understanding the complexities of ESOP acquisition, financing, or reorganization transactions is an understanding of the general ESOP framework. An ESOP serves the dual purpose of meeting corporate finance and employee compensation objectives. The following list presents some of the common purposes for implementing an ESOP:

- liquidity for shareholders,
- estate planning,

- management succession planning,
- capital for expansion,
- acquisitions,
- LBO by management,
- divestiture,
- recapitalization,
- takeover defense,
- motivating employees,
- employee benefit,
- privatization,
- charitable giving, and
- going private transaction.

TYPES OF ESOPS

Nonleveraged ESOPs

The nonleveraged ESOP transaction structure does not use debt to purchase the employer corporation securities. The nonleveraged ESOP acquires the employer corporation securities through (1) tax-deductible stock contributions or (2) tax-deductible cash contributions. Thus, debt financing is not necessary. The employer corporation stock is purchased gradually each year based on the company's annual contribution amount. The ESOP percentage ownership of the employer corporation stock increases with each annual contribution.

Leveraged ESOPs

The typical leveraged ESOP stock purchase transaction is accomplished through a series of steps that are best illustrated by the diagram presented in Exhibit 1. Let's assume that Sponsor Company ("Sponsor") borrows money from the bank (the "Bank Loan"). Sponsor then loans the proceeds from the Bank Loan to an ESOP, evidenced by the "ESOP Loan." The ESOP purchases Sponsor stock from existing shareholders in return for the cash from the proceeds of the ESOP Loan.

Exhibit 2 illustrates the cash flow effects of the leveraged ESOP transaction on an annual basis. Annually, Sponsor Company makes tax-deductible

Exhibit 1

Typical Leveraged ESOP Structure
Purchase of Employer Corporation Stock

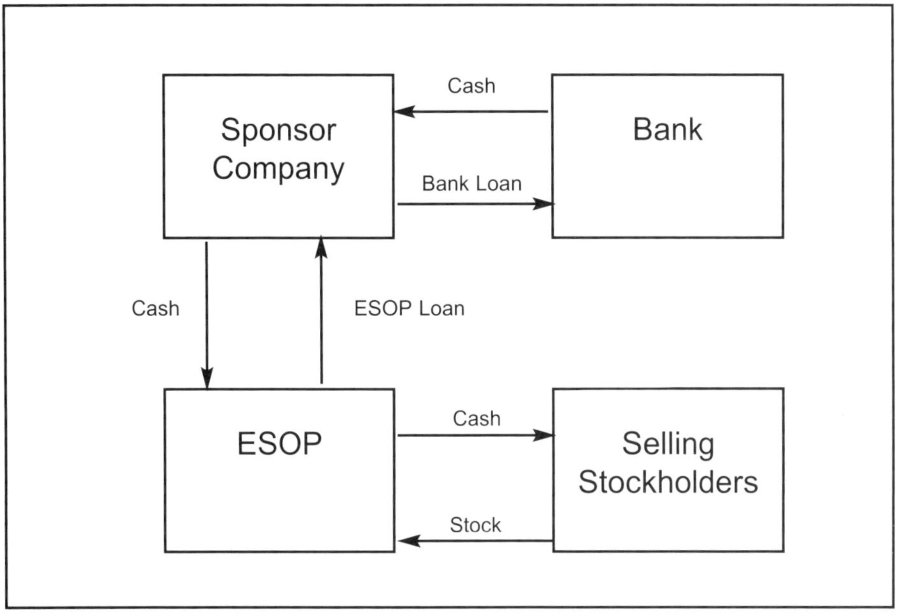

Exhibit 2

Typical Leveraged ESOP Structure
Repayment of ESOP Acquisition Loan

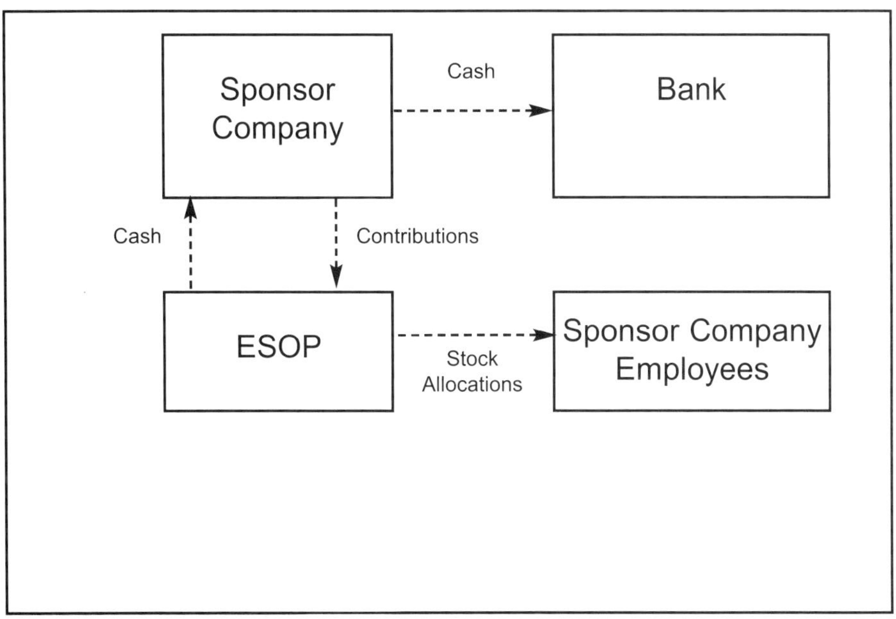

employer contributions to the ESOP (or pays dividends on the ESOP stock). The ESOP uses its cash from these employer contributions to make principal and interest payments on the ESOP Loan. As a result, Sponsor Company can now use the tax-sheltered cash to make payments on the Bank Loan. As the ESOP Loan is paid back, the employer corporation securities are allocated to ESOP participant accounts.

All Parties to a Leveraged ESOP Transaction Benefit

The income tax and other economic advantages of a leveraged ESOP transaction typically benefit all parties to the transaction, including the employer corporation, the selling stockholders, the retained management, the sponsor company employees, and the ESOP lenders. The economic benefits to these various parties in interest are explained below.

The Employer Corporation

The most significant benefit for the employer corporation is the ability to effectively deduct the principal payments on the ESOP acquisition loan. The employer corporation also may experience productivity gains due to employee ownership. In addition, the ESOP should be helpful in attracting and retaining talented employees.

The Selling Stockholders

The most significant benefit for the selling stockholder is the availability of the "1042 election." Under Internal Revenue Code Section 1042, the selling stockholder can defer the capital gains tax on the sale of the employer corporation stock to the ESOP. Therefore, the selling stockholder would realize greater net after-tax proceeds when selling employer corporation stock to an ESOP. It is important to note that the ESOP stock purchase/sale transaction is a liquidity event for the selling stockholder. In addition, an ESOP sale can be beneficial to the individual shareholder's estate plan.

The Retained Management

Additional equity incentives for retained management are available in the ESOP-owned company. In fact, equity-based incentive compensation plans for retained management are common in ESOP-owned companies.

The Employer Corporation Employees

The major benefit for employees is the ability to share in the equity growth of the sponsor company. And, just as in other qualified retirement plans, the employee does not recognize taxable income in the year the shares are allocated to the employee accounts. Rather, taxable income is recognized when the plan participant receives a distribution from the ESOP, unless proceeds are rolled into an individual retirement account. During the period that the employer corporation stock is held by the ESOP, the appreciation in value is also not currently taxed.

The ESOP Lenders

The major benefit for the lenders in ESOP transactions is the reduced credit risk associated with the sponsor company. This is due to the sponsor company ability (1) to reduce income taxes and (2) to deduct debt principal payment. The income tax savings increase after-tax cash flow and provide a greater probability that the sponsor company can meet its debt obligations.

An ESOP stock purchase/sale transaction can also enhance credit through a pledge of the qualified replacement property (QRP) purchased by the selling stockholder in a Section 1042 rollover transaction. This is because the QRP is pledged as collateral for the ESOP acquisition bank loan.

VALUATION OF THE EMPLOYER CORPORATION FOR ESOP FORMATION PURPOSES

The first step in assessing the feasibility of an ESOP is to estimate the business value of the subject employer corporation stock. An ESOP adds some complexity to the typical business valuation process. The following section describes the valuation issues related to ESOP-owned employer corporation securities.

Adequate Consideration

ERISA requires that an ESOP pay no more than "adequate consideration" when investing in employer corporation securities. Adequate consideration generally follows the specific guidelines for the definition of fair market value under Internal Revenue Service Revenue Ruling 59-60. On May 17, 1988, the Department of Labor (DOL) issued the "Proposed Regulation Relating to the Definition of Adequate Consideration" for ESOP transactions. The full contents of the adequate consideration regulations are available on the Department of Labor web site at www.dol.gov.

For purposes of ERISA and the adequate consideration regulations, fair market value is defined as:

> The price at which an asset would change hands between a willing buyer and a willing seller when the former is not under any compulsion to buy and the latter is not under any compulsion to sell, and both parties are able, as well as willing, to trade and are well informed about the asset and the market for such asset.[1]

An employer corporation stock valuation is required (1) when the ESOP makes an acquisition of employer corporation securities, (2) at least annually thereafter (although some sponsor companies routinely have their stock appraisals updated semiannually or quarterly), (3) whenever there is a transaction between the plan and a party in interest, and (4) if the ESOP sells out of its stock position.

The DOL adequate consideration regulations provide that the written document include an assessment of all "relevant factors" including (1) generally those factors listed in Revenue Ruling 59-60 and (2) the following additional factors:

1. The marketability, or lack thereof, of the employer corporation securities. Where the plan is the purchaser of securities that are subject to "put" rights and such rights are taken into account in reducing the discount for lack of marketability, such assessment should include consideration of the extent to which such rights are enforceable, as well as the sponsor company's ability to meet its obligations with respect to the "put rights" (taking into account the company's financial strength and liquidity).
2. Whether or not the seller would be able to obtain an ownership control price premium from an unrelated third party with regard to the block of securities being valued, provided that in cases where a control price premium is taken into account:
    a. Actual control (both in form and in substance) passes to the purchaser with the sale, or will pass to the purchaser within a reasonable time pursuant to a binding agreement in effect at the time of the sale, and
    b. It is reasonable to assume that the purchaser's control will not be dissipated within a short period of time subsequent to acquisition.[2]

INDEPENDENCE OF THE APPRAISER AND THE APPRAISER'S ROLE

The DOL adequate consideration regulations require that someone who is independent of all parties to the ESOP stock purchase/sale transaction conduct the employer corporation stock appraisal. The DOL notes that under Internal Revenue Code Section 401(a)(28)(C), ESOP fiduciaries must employ an independent appraiser meeting requirements similar to Regulation 1.170A-13(c)(5). That Regulation relates to independent appraisals of property donations made to charitable organizations.

REPORTING REQUIREMENTS

The DOL proposed adequate consideration regulations also address the ESOP stock valuation reporting requirements. In order to comply with the regulations, the ESOP stock valuation report should contain the following information:

- a summary of the qualifications of the person making the valuation to evaluate assets of the type being valued;
- a statement of the employer corporation stock value, a statement of the methods used in estimating that value, and the reasons for the valuation in light of those methods;
- a full description of the employer corporation stock being valued;
- the factors taken into account in making the valuation, including any restrictions, undertakings, agreements, or obligations limiting the use or disposition of the employer corporation stock;
- the purpose for which the valuation was made;
- the relevance or significance accorded to the valuation methods taken into account;
- the effective date of the valuation; and
- in cases where a valuation report has been prepared, the signature of the person or firm making the valuation and the date the report was signed.[3]

BUSINESS VALUATION APPROACHES AND METHODS

The generally accepted business valuation approaches are the income approach, the market approach, and the asset-based approach. While all of these approaches may be used to value shares of sponsor company stock held by an ESOP, the asset-based approach is used less often than the other two business valuation approaches.

OWNERSHIP CONTROL PRICE PREMIUMS

Valuation analysts generally agree that the level of value for the employer stock valuation will differ depending on whether the ESOP-owned block of stock carries elements of ownership control. Generally, a buyer will pay more for a controlling ownership block of stock. Most valuation analysts take the position that the ESOP should be able to pay whatever a hypothetical third-party buyer would pay for the block of stock being purchased, including an ownership control price premium.

If the ESOP purchases ownership control over a period of time instead of in one transaction, the issue of whether a control price premium applies is more complex. Evidence in the public marketplace generally suggests that control price premiums are paid along the entire spectrum of "creeping control." Consistency in this regard among employer stock valuations from year to year is important.

DISCOUNT FOR LACK OF MARKETABILITY

There is some controversy surrounding the extent to which a discount for lack of marketability should be applied in employer corporation valuations. Marketability is the ability of the stock to be sold and turned into cash quickly. On the one end of the marketability spectrum, there are relatively few potential buyers for shares in most closely held companies. On the other end of the marketability spectrum, shares in publicly traded corporations have almost instant marketability on an organized stock exchange.

Put Option and Repurchase Liability

The economic factor that generally distinguishes ESOP-owned shares from other shares of a closely held corporation is that a "put option" is required to be attached to the ESOP-owned stock. Without this put option, employees could be forced to hold employer securities for extended periods of time. The put option requires the employer corporation to provide the needed liquidity by repurchasing the distributed employer corporation securities. This employer corporation obligation to purchase shares is referred to generally as the *repurchase obligation.*

The DOL proposed regulations guide the analyst to consider (1) the extent to which the put rights are enforceable and (2) the sponsor company's ability to meet its obligation. Most ESOP valuation analysts "interpret the ESOP put right as substantially mitigating, if not eliminating, any marketability discount that would otherwise apply."[4]

The principal economic factors that influence the magnitude of the discount for lack of marketability with regard to ESOP-owned employer securities are as follows:

- the provisions of the ESOP plan documents, including the put rights;
- the financial strength and solvency of the employer corporation;
- the size of the share block owned by the ESOP;
- the degree of liquidity in the ESOP trust and the sponsor company;
- the extra borrowing capacity of the employer corporation;
- the repurchase liability and the expected funding requirements;
- the extent to which the sponsor company has planned and managed the repurchase liability;
- past practices in repurchases by the sponsor company;
- the form and timing of payments to selling stockholders and ESOP lenders; and
- the overall priority of acknowledged and contingent claims that may conflict with achieving liquidity for plan participants over time.

The ESOP-owned company can best plan for the repurchase liability by setting corporation policies regarding how repurchases will be handled. These policies will aid the valuation analyst in assessing the appropriate amount (if any) for the discount for lack of marketability.

POST-TRANSACTION EQUITY VALUE IN LEVERAGED ESOPS

The post-transaction fair market value of ESOP-owned stock is affected by the debt used to finance the ESOP stock acquisition transaction. The "tax shield" created by the ESOP debt mitigates the reduction in employer corporation stock value. This ESOP tax shield can be quantified by computing the present value of the income tax savings over the period of the ESOP stock acquisition loan. If the value for the company does not change over the period the ESOP stock acquisition loan is amortized, this reduction in value is recovered.

LEGISLATIVE AND REGULATORY ISSUES IN ESOPS

The analyst conducting an ESOP valuation needs to have a general understanding of the legislative and regulatory issues that impact ESOPs. The following is a general discussion of some of the legislative rules regarding ESOPs.

Section 1042 Rollover

Internal Revenue Code Section 1042 generally provides that, if certain requirements are met, no gain will be recognized by the selling stockholder upon the sale of the employer corporation stock to an ESOP. The requirements of this tax deferral include:

- Immediately after the stock sale to the ESOP, the ESOP must own (1) at least 30 percent of the voting stock of the business or (2) 30 percent of the value of the business.
- Qualified replacement property (QRP) must be purchased with the proceeds within a 15-month period beginning three months prior to the sale of the ESOP. QRP is generally defined as stocks and bonds of domestic operating corporations.
- The selling stockholder must have owned the employer corporation securities sold to the ESOP for at least three years prior to the sale.

The gain is deferred until the sale of the QRP. And, if the selling stockholder holds the QRP in his estate, the gain is never taxed. This is due to the step-up in basis allowed upon the selling stockholder's death.

Section 409(1) Employer Securities

The ESOP must purchase an employer corporation security that meets the requirements of Internal Revenue Code Section 409(1). This Section generally provides that the employer corporation security purchased by the ESOP be (1) the highest voting common stock, or (2) convertible into the highest voting common stock.

Loan Principal Deductibility and Section 415

The sponsor company may deduct dividends paid on employer corporation securities held by a leveraged ESOP, provided that the dividends paid are reasonable and are either (1) paid in cash directly to the participants after receipt by the ESOP trust, or (2) used to make payments on the ESOP stock acquisition loan. At times, the valuation analyst may be asked to opine on the reasonableness of the ESOP dividend.

Dividends used to make payments on the ESOP stock acquisition loan are not included in ESOP participants' annual additions for purposes of the Section 415 contribution limitations. This provision allows an ESOP design that provides for a dividend-paying security to enhance the debt payment abilities under the ESOP stock acquisition loan without the constraints of the 25 percent of compensation limitations under Section 415.

THE IRS AUDIT GUIDELINES

The Service audits ESOPs from time to time. Internal Revenue Service Announcement 95-33 contains finalized examination guidelines for (among other things) audits of ESOPs. Familiarity with these guidelines will assist the valuation practitioner when analyzing the ESOP (1) transaction structure and (2) stock valuation issues. Familiarity with these audit guidelines should help the analyst protect the transaction structure and employer stock valuations from attack by the Service. These audit guidelines address the issues of:

1. how much is "primarily invested,"
2. the ESOP exempt loan,
3. the Section 1042 rollover,
4. the Section 415 limitations,
5. dividends paid on ESOP stock,

6. the ESOP put option,
7. voting rights,
8. the date of the appraisal,
9. adequate consideration,
10. the independence of the appraiser,
11. appraisal conclusions,
12. subsequent events, and
13. proceeds from the sale of unallocated shares.

SPECIFIC ESOP PLAN ADMINISTRATION ISSUES

The following discussion summarizes some of the plan administration issues related to an ESOP. An ESOP is a qualified plan and must therefore meet the minimum coverage, distribution, vesting, and participation requirements under ERISA.

A general understanding of ESOP plan administration issues is important for the ESOP valuation analyst. This is because the plan administration issues impact the size and timing of the sponsor company's repurchase obligation.

Allocations to Participant Accounts

The ESOP plan document governs the operation of the ESOP. The sponsor company gathers certain demographic data on employees. The plan administrator then determines who among the employees is eligible to participate in the ESOP stock allocations.

The number of shares that are released annually from the plan is determined based on a choice between two methods. The first method is an allocation based on the ratio of principal paid in the current year over the total principal obligation. The second method is similar, except that principal and interest are considered.

Dividends are allocated in a different manner. Dividends on allocated shares that are not used to make payments on the ESOP debt are allocated to respective accounts of the participants to whom the shares are allocated. When dividend payments on allocated shares are used to repay an ESOP loan, shares (1) will be released from the suspense account based on their current fair market value and (2) will replace the cash dividend allocated to the plan participant's account.

Distribution Policy

Distribution of benefits from an ESOP must commence no later than one year after the close of the plan year (1) in which the participant terminates employment due to reaching normal retirement age, disability, or death or (2) which is the fifth plan year following the plan year in which the participant separates from service with the employer.

Distributions of securities acquired with the proceeds of an ESOP loan may be delayed until the loan is repaid. Benefits to the ESOP plan participants may be distributed in installments over five years (up to 10 years where the benefits exceed $710,000).

Diversification

Qualified ESOP participants may elect to diversify their accounts. A qualified ESOP participant includes an individual who (1) has attained age 55 and (2) has at least 10 years participation in the ESOP. The election period is a six-year period that begins with—or in—the plan year during which the participant becomes qualified. The first five elections are limited to 25 percent of the participant's account balance. The final year, the qualified participant may diversify up to 50 percent of the account balance attributable to such participant.

FINANCING ISSUES IN A LEVERAGED ESOP

Other qualified retirement plans are prohibited from borrowing funds under the prohibited transaction rules. ERISA Section 408(b)(3) and Internal Revenue Code Section 4975(d)(3) contain the provisions that exempt the ESOP from this prohibited transaction rule.

The leveraged ESOP stock purchase transaction is significantly different from conventional financing. An inexperienced ESOP lender may be concerned with the accounting provisions that can result in negative equity on the ESOP employer corporation balance sheet. The ESOP lender also must consider the enhanced cash flow associated with the deductibility of principal payments in order to be competitive. In addition, the pledge of Section 1042 QRP securities is a typical procedure in the ESOP stock acquisition financing that can make up for collateral shortfalls.

If the valuation analyst is issuing a fairness opinion, a review of the credit agreement is necessary in order to understand the significant terms of the financing.

REPURCHASE LIABILITY

The repurchase liability is created by the employer corporation's obligation to purchase shares from the ESOP trust at the time the participant receives a distribution. There are two methods that can be used by the sponsor company to satisfy the obligation.

The first method is called a repurchase, or recycling, transaction. In a "repurchase," the ESOP trust purchases the shares of withdrawing participants and recycles them to other ESOP participants in the plan. The trust's cash for the purchase comes from the sponsor company in the form of a deductible employer contribution.

The second method is called a redemption transaction. In a "redemption," the shares are purchased directly by the sponsor company and then canceled. Redemptions do not use tax-deductible contributions, since the shares are no longer considered outstanding. However, the immediate effect on fair market value should be negligible if the transaction occurs at fair market value.

FIDUCIARY ISSUES IN ESOPS

The independent financial adviser is hired directly by the ESOP fiduciary or trustee. Thus, an ESOP independent financial adviser needs an understanding of (1) the role of the ESOP trustee and (2) how the employer stock valuation assignment interfaces with that role.

General fiduciary duties that apply to ESOP fiduciaries are outlined in ERISA (the Overriding ERISA Fiduciary Standards). These duties apply to all trustee actions. ERISA requires the fiduciary to manage and administer the ESOP trust:

1. solely in the interests of plan participants and beneficiaries;
2. for the exclusive purpose of providing benefits to plan participants and their beneficiaries and defraying reasonable expenses of administering the ESOP trust;
3. with the care, skill, prudence, and diligence that, under the circumstances then prevailing, a prudent man or woman acting in like capacity and familiar with such matters would use in the conduct of an enterprise of a like character and with like aims;
4. in accordance with the plan and trust agreement in most circumstances; and
5. in accordance with applicable requirements of the law.

STEPS TO IMPLEMENTING AN ESOP

The following list summarizes some of the steps involved in implementing the typical leveraged ESOP stock purchase transaction.

1. Retain qualified advisers with the areas of expertise described in this discussion.
2. Conduct a feasibility study to see if an ESOP makes sense from a financial point of view.
3. Design and structure the stock purchase transaction.
4. Estimate the value of the sponsor company stock.
5. Consider the design of the plan and trust provisions.
6. Obtain financing for the stock purchase transaction.
7. Estimate the repurchase liability.
8. Close the stock purchase transaction.
9. Use an effective communication program to inform employees about the benefits and limitations of the ESOP.

SUMMARY AND CONCLUSION

This discussion summarized the issues related to a sale of a privately owned company to an ESOP. The ESOP structure is, in many instances, beneficial to: (1) closely held business owners seeking a sale of all or part of their ownership interest, (2) managers of public companies considering the strategic divestiture of a division or subsidiary, (3) investors analyzing the leveraged acquisition of a business enterprise, and (4) business owners pursuing a recapitalization or financial restructuring of the company.

Notes:

1. Proposed Regulation Relating to the Definition of Adequate Consideration, 53 Fed. Reg. 17,632 (1988), P. 17,634.
2. Ibid., pp. 17,637–38.
3. Ibid.
4. J. Michael Julius, "ESOP Appraisals and Non-ESOP Shareholders," *CPA Litigation Service Counselor*, July 1998, p. 9.

Chapter 3

An ESOP as a Corporate Planning Tool

INTRODUCTION

An ESOP is a special type of qualified retirement plan that can serve as a vehicle to:

1. provide retirement benefits to employees and management of a privately held or a publicly traded corporation,
2. provide a market for capital stock of a privately held corporation (and serve as an alternative to a going public transaction),
3. provide a vehicle for buying out dissident corporate stockholders and facilitating divorce settlements (where the stock of a closely held corporation is a primary asset of the marital estate),
4. provide a corporate finance vehicle for the employer corporation to expand its business on a pretax basis,
5. provide a vehicle for company management, venture funds, and others to make acquisitions of other companies on a pretax basis, and
6. provide creative solutions to the estate-planning problems that typically confront the owners of successful privately owned businesses.

This discussion summarizes the economic benefits related to ESOP formation at a typical privately owned corporation.

EMPLOYEE RETIREMENT BENEFITS AND MANAGEMENT INCENTIVES

An ESOP is a defined contribution plan that provides retirement benefits to eligible employees of a sponsor company. The most important difference between an ESOP and any other type of defined contribution plan is that the ESOP is designed to: (1) invest primarily in stock of the employer corporation, and (2) borrow money for the sole purpose of using the loan proceeds to purchase the stock of the employer corporation. As a result, employees are given the opportunity (1) to own all or part of the employer corporation and (2) to participate in the growth and success (as well as the downside) of the employer corporation.

Although the formation of an ESOP may provide substantial motivational incentives to all eligible employees of the employer corporation, the company may need to adopt a nonqualified equity-based plan (1) to further motivate key management and (2) to increase benefits to key management. This type of compensation plan is often used because the individual allocation limits applicable to ESOPs may restrict the allocation of the stock of the employer corporation to the key employees participating in the ESOP.

Most ESOP-owned companies, in conjunction with the adoption of an ESOP, also adopt a nonqualified equity plan. The objective of the nonqualified equity plan is to retain and further motivate existing key management and attract key personnel.

MARKET FOR CLOSELY HELD CORPORATION STOCK

An ESOP may serve as a vehicle to create a market for the stock held by stockholders of a closely held corporation. The ESOP is the mechanism that enables these stockholders to sell all or a portion of their shares to management and to the employees. These individuals are often the most logical buyers if they can obtain the necessary stock acquisition financing. The selling stockholders have the flexibility to integrate their estate planning and personal financial planning needs as they sell all or part of their equity holdings to an ESOP.

This is an important consideration for selling stockholders (1) who have management responsibilities and (2) who are key employees of the sponsor company. The ESOP stock purchase/sale transaction benefits:

1. the selling stockholders—by allowing them to cash out their interests in the corporation in a tax advantaged way (provided the requirements of Code Section 1042 are satisfied),
2. the key management executives and the rank and file employees—by allowing them to purchase employer corporation stock through the ESOP in a tax advantaged way, and
3. the employer corporation—by creating a market for all stockholders who desire to retire their stock in the future.

Another advantage of this type of stock purchase/sale transaction is that it provides for the continuity of management. The ESOP enables new employees to acquire stock as older employees and shareholders retire, without diluting the equity of the remaining stockholders.

The tax-free rollover provisions of Section 1042 provide some of the best tax and financial planning opportunities available for shareholders of closely held corporations. Under Section 1042, a number of common business planning problems can be addressed on a tax-favored basis.

SECTION 1042 TAX-FREE ROLLOVER EXAMPLE

The typical potential ESOP transaction involves a successful business owner that has most of his or her wealth tied up in the capital stock of a privately held corporation. The business owner has reached the stage in life when he or she needs to consider estate planning and personal financial planning. This planning involves the desire of the business owner, or need of the business owner, to diversify his or her investment portfolio.

The closely held business owner is confronted with the following choices:

1. sell his or her business to a third party for cash, stock of the acquirer corporation, installment note, or a combination thereof,
2. sell a portion of the stock of the closely held corporation to the public (assuming the company is large enough and the business will be able to liquidate his or her stock in the future),
3. sell his or her business to the management group—typically structured with the business owner receiving some cash and an installment note,
4. sell his or her stock to an ESOP, or
5. do nothing and let his or her beneficiaries deal with a potentially significant problem.

If the stockholder sells the employer corporation to an ESOP, he or she may elect Section 1042 treatment on the proceeds. Upon the sale of the employer corporation stock to the ESOP, the stockholder must invest the proceeds in qualified replacement property (QRP).

If the requirements of Section 1042 are satisfied, the selling stockholder can postpone the capital gains taxation on the sale of his or her stock until disposition of the QRP. The use of an ESOP and QRP effectively allows the stockholder to diversify his or her wealth from a single holding in a closely held company into a liquid market portfolio—without triggering capital gains tax.

In addition to the advantages to a selling stockholder resulting from a stock sale to the ESOP, the employer corporation also benefits. This is because: (1) the employer corporation is purchasing the stock from the business owner with pretax dollars and (2) it is easier for the parties to reach an agreement as to (a) the terms of the stock sale and (b) the ability of the sponsor company to borrow funds for an ESOP stock purchase transaction. This is because the stock purchase is conducted on a tax-advantaged basis, which will also facilitate the financing of the stock purchase transaction.

If a business owner fails to take advantage of the tax benefits available for the sale of the stock to an ESOP, the opportunity to use an ESOP may still exist after his or her death. Where an estate owns stock of a closely held company, the executor may need to raise cash to pay estate taxes. The estate executor may have to sell a portion of the closely held stock in order to pay the estate taxes. The executor could sell the closely held stock back to the employer corporation. This would cause the employer corporation to purchase the stock with after-tax dollars. Such a purchase (i.e. with after-tax dollars) reduces the value of the closely held corporation and, therefore, reduces the value of the estate bequeathed to the children.

Alternatively, an ESOP may serve as an effective vehicle to provide a mechanism for the employer corporation to redeem the stock held by the estate on a pretax basis. Such a transaction benefits the beneficiaries of the estate. The employer corporation purchases the stock with tax-deductible contributions to the ESOP. This enables the ESOP to pay for the purchased stock with before-tax dollars—rather than to use after-tax dollars to redeem the shares directly from the estate.

DISSIDENT STOCKHOLDERS AND DIVORCE OF A STOCKHOLDERS

An ESOP may also serve as a useful vehicle for buying out a dissident stockholder. Because of the income tax benefits, the dissident stockholder may be willing to sell his or her stock to the sponsor company at a reduced price. This is because the dissident stockholder has the opportunity to postpone the capital gains tax on the sale of the stock to the ESOP (assuming the requirements of Section 1042 are satisfied). In addition, the employer corporation can reduce the stock purchase cost to the corporation and the remaining stockholders. This is because the employer corporation can finance the buy-out of the dissident shareholder through the ESOP with income tax-deductible dollars.

Similarly, an ESOP may also serve as a useful vehicle for facilitating a divorce settlement where stock of a closely held corporation constitutes a primary asset of the marital estate. In both of the situations, an ESOP buy-out makes it easier for the parties to reach an agreement as to the terms of the stock sale. And, an ESOP makes it easier for the employer corporation and the remaining stockholders to borrow the funds necessary to consummate the stock purchase transaction.

In most dissident stockholder and stockholder divorce situations, after the separation or divorce, the stockholders (or both spouses) are likely to want to liquidate their stock in the closely held company.

The stockholder or the spouse who continues to work in the business will not want the dissident stockholder, or his or her ex-spouse, as a stockholder. In addition, the dissident shareholder or the spouse who does not work in the business will not desire to hold stock in a closely held corporation that he or she does not control.

Disputes are likely to develop (1) over whether dividends should be declared and (2) over whether the active stockholder or the working spouse's compensation is excessive. In addition, the active stockholder, or spouse working in the business, is likely to prefer the value of the stock to increase, to reinvest earnings in the business, and to expand operations.

AN ESOP AS A CORPORATE FINANCE MECHANISM

An ESOP may serve as a financing vehicle to expand the business or to purchase capital assets in a tax-advantaged manner. Under conventional financing, a company that needs to raise money for working capital or expansion purposes may borrow the funds from a financial institution or another lending source. Then, the company repays the loan with after-tax dollars. Although the interest component of each loan payment is a tax deductible expense to the corporation, the loan principal payment is not tax deductible for federal corporate income tax purposes.

While conventional loans require repayment of principal with after-tax dollars, ESOP financing enhances the ability of the borrowing company to meet debt service requirements with pretax dollars. By using the ESOP as a corporate finance vehicle, the repayment of both the principal and interest are tax deductible by the employer corporation.

Under this type of corporate financing structure:

1. Either the ESOP borrows money or (more commonly) the employer corporation borrows money from the lending institution and then the corporation loans the proceeds to the ESOP.
2. The ESOP then purchases newly issued stock from the sponsor company.

As a result, the proceeds from the sale of the newly issued stock are used by the employer corporation to finance the acquisition of capital assets, to expand the business, or to refinance existing corporate indebtedness.

Each existing stockholders' ownership percentage is diluted because of the ESOP purchasing new shares of stock. However, the stockholders' ESOP value may be increased because of the savings and use of money (typically paid in corporate income taxes) to expand the business. As loan payments become due to the financial institutions, the employer corporation makes a tax-deductible contribution to the ESOP consisting of:

1. an amount of up to 25 percent of covered payroll for the purpose of repaying the loan principal, plus
2. an unlimited amount used to pay interest on the stock acquisition loan.

ESOP CORPORATE FINANCING EXAMPLE

Let's assume a company borrows $1,000,000 to expand its business. The conventional loan is repayable over 10 years in equal annual installments of principal plus interest at the annual rate of 8 percent. Further, let's assume that the fair market value of the company's stock is $10.00 per share and the company is in the 34 percent corporate income tax bracket. Over the 10-year period, the company must earn $1,340,000 in order to pay the lender $1,000,000 in principal.

If the company uses an ESOP to finance the expansion, the sponsor company will (1) borrow the $1,000,000 from the financial institution, (2) loan the proceeds to the ESOP, (3) sell newly issued stock in the sponsor company to the ESOP for $1,000,000, and (4) use the $1,000,000 to finance the sponsor company's expansion.

The ESOP stock purchase loan is repaid as follows:

1. The employer corporation makes a contribution to the ESOP equal to the principal and interest payment due to the financial institution.
2. The ESOP makes a payment on the loan between the employer corporation and the ESOP in same amount.
3. The employer corporation uses the repayment proceeds made by the ESOP to repay the loan with the financial institution.

Over the 10-year period, the sponsor company's annual cost is $660,000 plus the interest amount. Compared to direct borrowing by the sponsor company to finance its expansion, ESOP financing results in substantial savings and added value to the stockholders.

AN ESOP USED TO ACQUIRE OTHER COMPANIES

An ESOP may serve as a vehicle to acquire on a pretax basis: (1) the stock of another corporation or (2) the assets of another corporation. If the employer corporation acquirer is purchasing the stock of another company, the transaction can be structured to satisfy the requirements of Section 1042. This Section permits the selling stockholders to postpone the capital gains created by the stock sale transaction.

The target company acquisition transaction is typically structured as follows:

1. The acquiring employer corporation borrows money from a financial institution necessary to acquire another company ("Target").
2. The ESOP uses the loan proceeds to acquire newly issued stock of the purchasing employer corporation.
3. The employer corporation uses the proceeds from the sale of the sponsor company stock to acquire either the stock of Target or the assets of Target.
4. The employer corporation makes tax-deductible contributions to the ESOP which are used to repay the indebtedness.

Another structure that enables the selling stockholder to postpone the capital gains tax on the stock sale is structured as follows:

1. The employer corporation and Target merge.
2. The merged employer corporation borrows the money from a financial institution which is necessary to acquire the stock of the selling stockholder(s).
3. The ESOP uses the loan proceeds to acquire the stock of the selling stockholders.
4. The employer corporation makes tax-deductible contributions to the ESOP which are used to repay the acquisition indebtedness.

AN ESOP AS AN ESTATE PLANNING MECHANISM

An ESOP may serve as a vehicle to provide creative solutions to the estate planning problems that typically confront the owners of successful closely held corporations. Many stockholders' estates consist primarily of the value of the stock of the closely held corporation. If the value of that stock is not established before the owner's death, an arbitrary figure (one based on a compromise of an Internal Revenue Service valuation engineer and the estate's valuation analyst) may be used to determine the amount of estate taxes due.

The formation of an ESOP before the stockholder's death may ease this burden on the estate. This is because the fair market value of the stock acquired by the ESOP would be determined by an independent appraiser beforehand. This reduces the chances of a dispute with the Internal Revenue Service.

The ESOP can also provide cash to pay the estate taxes and administration expenses of a deceased majority stockholder. The estate tax laws provide various solutions to the liquidity problems of an estate that consists mostly of the stock of a closely held corporation.

Accordingly, an ESOP formation may serve to accomplish the following estate planning objectives:

- shareholder liquidity,
- diversification of the shareholder's wealth,
- estate liquidity,

- equalization of inheritances,
- enhancement of charitable gifting through a charitable remainder trust,
- maximization of gifts to family members, and
- maximization of the use of family limited partnerships.

Each of these estate planning objectives will be summarized below.

Stockholder Liquidity

If the requirements of Section 1042 are satisfied, the owners of a closely held corporation can sell some or all of their company stock to an ESOP and postpone all of the capital gains tax. Section 1042 provides a tax-favored means for a business owner to convert a non–income producing and illiquid investment into a diversified income-producing marketable investment portfolio.

As part of an estate planning tool, an ESOP can be used to purchase all or a part of the business owner's interest. And, an ESOP may serve as an attractive alternative (1) to a corporate redemption or to selling the business to outsiders. This is especially true when the selling stockholder desires to keep control of the business within a founding family or key-employee group.

In either case, if the funds required to purchase the business owner's stock must be borrowed by the sponsor company, an ESOP can be used to reduce the financing cost.

Diversification of the Stockholder's Wealth

A selling stockholder has the ability to diversify his or her wealth through an ESOP formation:

1. to protect the spouse of the business owner and his or her family investment by investing the stock sale proceeds in a diversified investment portfolio;
2. to fund all or part of the payment of estate taxes by investing the stock sale proceeds in a diversified investment portfolio (or use of the earnings on the investments to purchase additional life insurance through an irrevocable life insurance trust for the purpose of replenishing the estate); and

3. to convert an illiquid, non-income-producing stock investment into a marketable, income-producing diversified stock investment portfolio, this conversion reduces the business owner's investment risk.

Estate Liquidity

The bulk of the investment holdings of most successful entrepreneurs consists of some cash and the value of the stock of the privately held company. Without adequate estate planning, it may be necessary for the entrepreneur's heirs to sell the business in order to (1) continue the company and (2) generate the funds needed to pay the estate taxes.

If the owner sells at least 30 percent of his or her stock in the privately held company (assuming the other requirements of Section 1042 are satisfied), the business owner can create a source of estate liquidity on a tax-deferred basis. At the same time, the selling stockholder may retain control of the sponsor company and continue to manage it on a day-to-day basis.

As long as he or she retains more than 50 percent of the outstanding stock, the business owner can maintain control of the closely held business. Unlike virtually any other prospective buyer of an ownership interest in a closely held corporation, an ESOP is satisfied to be a noncontrolling owner.

Equalization of Inheritances

Another ESOP-related wealth diversification benefit for a business owner is that properties other than stock of the family business can be designated for inheritance by family members who are not employed by the business.

Let's consider, for example, a business owner with two children, one employed in the business and the other employed elsewhere. In order to avoid giving an equal interest in the business or making unequal bequeaths, the stocks and bonds (the investments with the ESOP proceeds) can be used to provide the child who is not employed in the business with an equal amount. As a result, the selling stockholder can treat the children "equally" without treating them "identically."

Owners of closely held companies often fail to diversify their wealth. This is because it is difficult to find buyers for a noncontrolling ownership interest in a private held company. This is also because, typically, a large capital gains tax must be paid in connection with a sale of the closely held company stock.

These problems can be avoided with the formation of an ESOP. An ESOP can serve as a willing buyer of a noncontrolling ownership interest in a closely held company. And, the sale of a noncontrolling ownership interest in a privately held company to an ESOP can be arranged on a tax-deferred basis.

Enhance Charitable Gifting through a Charitable Remainder Trust

One procedure to permanently avoid the capital gains tax on the ESOP stock sale proceeds is to (1) purchase stocks and bonds that satisfy the definition of "qualified replacement property" (QRP) for purposes of Section 1042 and (2) then donate the QRP to a charitable remainder trust. Although most dispositions of QRP will trigger income tax, an exception is provided for charitable gifts.

This structure allows for (1) the active trading and continued diversification of the ESOP sale proceeds investment portfolio and (2) the purchase of life insurance to replenish the assets gifted to charity. The charitable remainder trust typically would be designed to pay an annual income from its earnings (1) for the remainder of the business owner's life or (2) for the remaining lives of his or her spouse. In addition, the business owner will be entitled to an income tax deduction in the amount of the present value of the gift to the charity. In addition, a substantial deferred benefit may be provided for the charitable beneficiary.

Any QRP that is donated to a charitable trust will escape federal estate tax. And, the family members receive life insurance proceeds that replace the property gifted to charity.

Maximize Gifts to Family Members

Gifts of the QRP

QRP can be transferred to children, grandchildren, and other relatives without triggering the recognition of income. Subject to annual and lifetime limits, the transfer of property other than stock of the family-owned company often is preferable to a transfer of interests in a family-owned business. All of the traditional procedures for leveraging gifts are available with respect to transfers of QRP, including:

1. the use of the annual and lifetime gift-tax exclusions and
2. the use of various kinds of trusts, including grantor retained annuity trusts.

Gifts of Remaining Stock

If the ESOP stock purchase transaction involves the ESOP's purchase of less than all of the outstanding shares of the employer corporation, there is an important element of estate planning for a business owner with respect to how to deal with the remaining stock. The business owner may consider one or more strategies for making gifts of stock of the employer corporation to his or her children or grandchildren.

The period immediately following an ESOP stock purchase transaction (the company has obtained a loan and the loan proceeds have been used by the ESOP to purchase the stock) is an ideal time to make a gift of company stock. This is because the value of the employer corporation stock will be reduced due to the ESOP acquisition indebtedness.

In addition, if the business owner owns less than 51 percent of the stock of the employer corporation after the ESOP transaction, the valuation of the employer corporation stock for gift tax purposes will be based on a noncontrolling ownership interest. The value of the employer corporation stock will be likely to appreciate rapidly as the ESOP indebtedness is paid down and the sponsor company grows.

By making a gift immediately after the ESOP transaction, a business owner can transfer a larger percentage ownership interest at the same gift tax cost than he or she could transfer immediately prior to the transaction. And, all future appreciation in the value of the transferred stock can be shielded from tax in his or her estate.

Family Limited Partnerships

An ESOP can be combined effectively with a family limited partnership. The proceeds from a tax-deferred sale to an ESOP cannot be transferred directly to a family limited partnership. This is because a partnership interest does not constitute QRP.

However, let's assume (1) a family limited partnership is created prior to an ESOP transaction and (2) shares of stock of a closely held C corporation are transferred to the family limited partnership. Then, the family limited partnership can (1) sell the stock of the company to the ESOP and (2) postpone the capital gains incurred on the transaction (assuming the requirements of Section 1042 are satisfied).

The family limited partnership would be required to purchase QRP within one year. And, those replacement properties could be retained in the family limited partnership. The result of this transaction that the tax on the gain realized in connection with the sale to the ESOP could be deferred indefinitely.

Another way to combine an ESOP with a family limited partnership is to (1) sell the employer corporation stock to the ESOP in a seller financing transaction using a long-term floating-rate bond, (2) purchase stock, bonds, treasury bills, real estate, or other assets as the ESOP pays off the seller financing notes, and then (3) transfer those assets to a family limited partnership.

SUMMARY AND CONCLUSION

This discussion summarized many of the ways that an ESOP can be used as (1) an effective estate planning mechanism and (2) an efficient intergenerational wealth transfer mechanism for a closely held business owner.

This discussion was originally authored by John A. Kober, Esq. John Kober is a partner with Morgan Lewis & Bockius, LLP. He can be reached at (214) 438-1552 or at jkober@morganlewis.com.

The original version of this article appeared in the Spring 2001 issue of Willamette Management Associates Insights. *This discussion was substantially edited and updated by Thomas Millon. Tom is a principal in the suburban Washington, D.C., office of Willamette Management Associates.*

Chapter 4

Using an ESOP and Stock-Based Compensation for Business Ownership Succession

INTRODUCTION

Recent returns to high stock prices and the cyclical volatility of both stock and bond markets have prompted many closely held business owners to review their financial goals in light of two issues. First, how much longer can the current slow but steady U.S. economic expansion continue? Second, should closely held business owners hold onto their stock with the hope that the economy will continue to improve or should they monetize all or part of their ownership interests through a sale of company stock?

The decision to sell the company is often difficult for a business owner who is confronted with conflicting concerns. The business owner's entire persona or self-image may be tied to his or her business. If the business is sold to achieve personal financial worth, the owner may diminish his or her self-worth. And, the selling business owner may deprive his or her descendents of the family business legacy. A business owner who decides not to sell the family-owned company may forego the potential for financial security and, at the same time, risk (1) a decrease in the value of the company stock or (2) a significant estate tax liability.

This discussion summarizes how the closely held business owner can remain tied to his or her company, preserve the legacy of a family owned business for descendents, and attain both liquidity and personal financial security.

A CREATIVE SOLUTION

A creative and effective solution to this family control/investment liquidity dilemma involves the use of both (1) an ESOP and (2) stock-based compensation planning. A leveraged ESOP transaction can be used to permit a closely held business owner to:

1. sell a portion of the family-owned business in a tax-advantaged sale,
2. allow the funding family to retain actual or operational ownership control of the sponsor company, and
3. significantly reduce the selling stockholder's gift and/or estate tax liability.

Following a leveraged ESOP employer stock purchase transaction, stock-based compensation planning can be accomplished on a tax-advantageous basis. The use of stock-based compensation strategies accomplishes two goals: (1) transferring stock to the retained employee/stockholder and to other employees who are effectively unable to receive shares under the ESOP and (2) attracting and retaining key employees. By adopting an ESOP and implementing stock-based compensation, a closely held business owner can:

1. achieve personal financial security by liquidating a portion of the family's single largest asset,
2. keep the family-owned business within the founding family's control, and
3. assure that the types of employees needed to help the business expand are attracted to—and motivated to remain with—the sponsor company.

The selling stockholder's enhanced liquidity and diversification (due to the leveraged ESOP stock purchase transaction) can provide the founding family with greater real value measured in terms of risk-adjusted investment returns.

THE TAX ADVANTAGED ESOP PURCHASE/SALE

Most leveraged ESOP stock purchase transactions are based, in part, on the provisions of Section 1042. Section 1042 states generally that, as long as an

ESOP purchases at least 30 percent of a closely held company's stock (measured in terms of value or of share ownership), the selling stockholder who has held shares purchased by the ESOP for at least three years can defer the payment of their transaction-related capital gains taxes.

To defer the capital gains tax, the selling stockholder must reinvest the stock sale proceeds within 12 months in stocks or bonds of domestic operating entities—U.S. domiciled companies generating no more than 25 percent of their earnings from passive investments.

Because the selling stockholder's "qualified replacement securities" will take the basis the selling stockholder had in his or her company shares, deferred capital gains taxes (that would have otherwise been payable in connection with the sale) will become due only when the stockholder sells some (or all) of the replacement securities. Under current tax laws, if the selling stockholder's replacement securities are held until death, the heirs' cost basis in the securities will then be stepped up to fair market value.

AN ESOP FORMATION AND ESTATE PLANNING

Let's consider an illustrative example. Cal Miller founded Codemaster (the "Company") in the late 1960s. Cal has a zero income tax basis in his Company stock. Cal has paid himself a relatively modest salary as the Company's president, as he reinvested most of the Company's profits back into the business. Cal's financial adviser estimates the fair market value of the Codemaster stockholder's equity to be $20 million.

With this business value estimate in mind, Cal is considering the sale of 51 percent of his stock in a leveraged ESOP transaction for $10.2 million. Cal intends to elect Section 1042 rollover treatment with respect to the stock sale transaction. The Section 1042 capital gains tax deferral will permit Cal to receive net sale proceeds of $10.2 million. And, Cal will still retain a 49 percent ownership interest in Codemaster.

By making the Section 1042 election, Cal can reinvest the entire $10.2 million stock sale proceeds in qualified replacement securities. These securities will generate investment returns on a tax-deferred basis until the securities are sold.

Although an ESOP can never pay more than the fair market value of the employer corporation shares that are purchased, the Codemaster ESOP will acquire more than 50 percent of the Company's outstanding stock. Therefore, the ESOP can pay a purchase price reflecting the stock's ownership control value. The payment of an ownership control premium is based on the fact that investors generally assign significant value to the ability to control a company's assets. Empirically observed ownership control price premiums tend to fluctuate (with significant variation) around 35 percent.

THE EFFECTS OF A LEVERAGED ESOP TRANSACTION ON GIFTING STRATEGIES

When an ESOP uses debt to finance the purchase of employee corporation stock, the transaction is typically referred to as a leveraged transaction. The ESOP stock acquisition indebtedness is generally recorded on the employer corporation's balance sheet. This recognition of the acquisition debt recognition of the acquisition debt generally causes the value of the sponsor company's equity to decline. In this illustrative example, let's assume that the stock purchase transaction is fully leveraged. On a preliminary basis, we may assume that Codemaster's $20 million pretransaction equity value will decline by as much as the $10.2 million amount of the assumed debt.

Of course, this assumption would oversimplify the stock valuation process. The decrease in a sponsor company's post-transaction equity value is typically less than the amount of ESOP stock purchase indebtedness for two reasons: (1) debt financing usually has a lower cost of capital than equity financing and (2) the ESOP stock purchase indebtedness can receive preferential income tax treatment. This is because both the interest and the principal on the stock acquisition indebtedness are tax-deductible to the employer corporation.

Although the ESOP acquisition indebtedness does not result in a dollar-for-dollar equity value reduction, post-leverage equity value reductions provide excellent gift and estate planning opportunities for selling stockholder who continues to own company shares.

Now, let's assume that Cal has decided to sell 51 percent of Codemaster to the ESOP for $10.2 million in a Section 1042 rollover transaction. By selling ownership control, Cal has reduced his interest in Codemaster to a noncontrolling ownership position. Even if he continues to serve as the Company's president and maintains effective control of the Company, Cal no longer owns a controlling equity interest. At this point. Cal is in an excellent position to gift all or a portion of his remaining Codemaster shares to his two children.

Let's assume that Cal implements a gifting program. Under this program, each child will receive a 24.5 percent interest in the Company stock. The fair market value of each child's interest will be determined on a nonmarketable, noncontrolling ownership interest basis. This "level of value" is significant for both gift and estate planning purposes. This is because this "level of value" permits the application of discounts for both (1) lack of control and (2) lack of marketability in the employer corporation stock valuation.

The discount for lack of control is typically estimated as the inverse of a calculated ownership control price premium. The discount for lack of marketability, in turn, reflects the fact that the stock of a closely held company is less valuable than stock of a similar publicly traded company. The market pays a price premium for liquidity or, conversely, demands a price discount for lack of liquidity. Consequently, business interests that lack ready marketability generally are worth less than otherwise comparable business interests that are readily marketable. Two well-known studies quantifying the discount for lack of marketability for closely held stock generally indicate that such discounts are often in the range of 35 to 50 percent.

Going back to our illustrative example, if we use a 25 percent discount for lack of control and a 45 percent discount for lack of marketability, then the fair market value of the Codemaster stock gifted to Cal's children will be as presented in Exhibit 1:

Exhibit 1

Fair Market Value of 49 Percent Ownership Interest in Codemaster Stock

Valuation Analysis		Codemaster
Fair market value of the total business enterprise		$20,000,000
Less:	ESOP stock purchase loan	10,200,000
Add:	ESOP debt income tax benefit	2,000,000
Ownership control value of the total company equity		11,800,000
Less:	Discount for lack of control @ 25 percent	2,950,000
Marketable, noncontrolling ownership value of total equity		8,850,000
Less:	Discount for lack of marketability @ 45 percent	3,982,500
Equals:	Indicated fair market value of the total company equity for federal gift and estate tax purposes	$4,867,500
Indicated fair market value of Cal's 49% retained—or gifted—ownership interest (rounded)		$2,385,000

If he wants to, Cal can transfer his 49 percent ownership interest to his two children at an aggregate fair market value of only $2,385,000. Let's assume that Cal and his wife do so, and that each spouse will use his or her entire available gift tax credit. In 2005, each taxpayer has a gift tax exclusion of $1,000,000.

Accordingly, the stock transfer to Cal's children would result in a minimal gift tax of approximately $130,000 [($2,385,000 fair market value of the gifted stock – $2,000,000 combined gift tax exclusion) x 34% approximate gift tax rate].

Tacking this gifting strategy to his Section 1042 sale transaction would permit Cal to (1) liquidate 51 percent of his ownership interest in Codemaster for $10.2 million (with no resulting immediate capital gains taxes) and (2) transfer a 49 percent ownership interest in the family-owned business to his children with a gift tax liability of only about $130,000.

Alternatively, Cal and his wife can transfer their entire remaining 49 percent of Company interest to their children through a staggered gift program over a period of years. The $11,000 gift tax exclusion per taxpayer/per donee in 2005 will permit them to make joint annual gifts of up to $22,000 per child on a gift tax-free basis.

If Cal and his wife implement this gifting program, the value of the stock being gifted, together with the resulting gift tax, will likely increase as the ESOP acquisition loan is paid off. The impact of the increased gift tax that will be payable under such a staggered gift program may nonetheless be palatable from a cash flow standpoint. This is because Cal can now pay the gift tax using interest and dividend income earned on his qualified replacement securities.

Whether Cal decides to make a lump-sum gift of his 49 percent ownership interest or to transfer it in a staggered gift program, his gift tax liability can be further reduced or eliminated. This would happen if (1) he places the 49 percent interest in a family limited partnership and (2) then gifts limited partnership interests to his children. Since limited partnership interests represent nonmarketable, noncontrolling ownership interests, the interests warrant additional discounts (although the additional valuation discounts may be lower than the valuation discounts previously applied).

Had Cal foregone his leveraged ESOP transaction and gifted his entire Codemaster ownership interest to his children, his estate would have incurred gift taxes of approximately $8.6 million [($20 – $2) x 48% approximate gift tax rate]. His net gift to his children would effectively be worth $11.4 million.

Similarly, had Cal died owning all of his Codemaster stock, his estate would likely have had to sell the Company in order to satisfy the resulting federal estate tax liability. After the company sale and estate tax payment, the estate would wind up with approximately half of Codemaster's $20 million total equity value.

Clearly, Cal's decision to follow his ESOP stock sale with an aggressive gifting program will enable him to make a greater transfer of wealth to the younger generation than if he only (1) gifted Company shares to his children or (2) sold his Company shares.

STOCK-BASED COMPENSATION

Stock-based compensation can be used to transfer stock to Section 1042 selling stockholders, 25 percent stockholders, and certain related employees who are effectively unable to receive shares under the ESOP (because of the "prohibited group" rules). Stock-based compensation can also be used if the sponsor company desires to transfer a greater number of shares to certain key employees than may otherwise be allocated to them under the sponsor company's ESOP allocation.

For example, let's assume that Cal wanted to receive shares under the ESOP because he was going to continue working for the Company until his retirement. What if Cal also wanted to attract key executives to the Company? And, what if the ESOP lender wanted to retain some of the better executives already working at the Company?

The Company could adopt a stock-based compensation plan or arrangement on a post-transaction basis. Such a plan would permit Cal to receive a Company stock grant corresponding in size to the number of shares he would have been able to receive under the ESOP (but for the prohibited allocation rules). The same arrangement could also provide for grants and/or vesting that would be partially or wholly dependent on the attainment of Company and/or individual performance objectives.

Like Cal's remaining 49 percent ownership interest, the Company's treasury shares will decrease in value following the ESOP stock purchase transaction. This stock value decrease is due to the ESOP stock purchase indebtedness. For several reasons, stock-based compensation planning can be accomplished after Cal's ESOP transaction on a more tax-advantageous basis than would have been possible before the ESOP transaction. Most stock-based compensation arrangements include a compensatory element. That compensatory element is measured partially or wholly on the value of the sponsor company stock. If that stock value is lower, the compensatory element will be smaller.

In addition, some compensation arrangements either:

1. wholly or partially determine the amount of a required accounting expense by reference to grant date fair market value or
2. require that the compensatory piece (e.g., a share of stock purchased by exercising an option) be purchased at its fair market value on the grant date.

In these cases, stock-based compensation planning will generally be easier following a leveraged ESOP stock purchase transaction.

COMMON TYPES OF STOCK-BASED INCENTIVE COMPENSATION PLANS

The following discussion summarizes the income tax and other characteristics associated with several of the more common types of stock-based incentive compensation plans. These plans can be implemented by an employer corporation to provide stock-based compensation (1) for the Section 1042 selling stockholders and (2) for key company employees.

Incentive Stock Option Plan

Under an incentive stock option (ISO) plan, a company grants a right to a key employee to buy the company's stock. The employee has the right, during a stated period of time, to buy the stock at a price equal to, or based on, its per share value. Such an ISO plan can be designed to restrict the stock purchased. That way, the key employee receiving the stock can only sell it to the company—and only upon termination of employment—at a price equal to the value of such stock at the time of the sale.

If the key employee exercises an ISO at a time when the value of the stock exceeds the purchase price, then he or she will receive an immediate benefit in the form of a bargain purchase. If the stock's value continues to increase, he or she will receive a further benefit. This is because the employee can sell the stock to the company on the termination of employment at a price that takes into account the increased value.

In order for an option to quality as an ISO, the option must satisfy a number of requirements set forth in Section 422. Each ISO must be granted in connection with the optionee's employment, under a plan that details both:

1. the aggregate number of shares that may be issued upon the exercise of the ISOs and
2. the employees (or class of employees) who are eligible to receive the ISOs.

In addition, ISOs may only be granted with an exercise term of 10 years or less. And, the ISO exercise price may not be less than the stock's fair market value.

Where these requirements are satisfied, the ISO issuance constitutes a nontaxable event for federal income tax purposes. The company granting the ISO receives no income tax deduction either (1) on the date the ISO is granted or (2) on the date the ISO is exercised. Similarly, no amount is generally included in taxable income by the employee optionee on either date.

However, the potential for income recognition exists on the date of exercise for an ISO. This is because the difference between (1) the value of the stock received on the exercise of the option and (2) the option price constitutes an item of tax preference for purposes of the alternative minimum tax.

Absent income recognition by the optionee under applicable alternative minimum tax rules, gain or loss will be recognized by the employee receiving an ISO only upon his or her sale of the stock. The amount of gain or loss will equal the difference between (1) the sum realized on the sale of the stock and (2) the sum of (a) any amount paid for the option (presumably zero) plus (b) the amount paid for the stock upon the exercise of the option.

Nonqualified Stock Option Plan

Like ISOs, nonqualified stock options (NSOs) are contractual rights to buy stock from the stock issuer at a specified price. Unlike ISOs, the NSO grant is not restricted to company employees. And, NSOs are not required to meet specific income tax requirements.

Accordingly, a good deal of flexibility is available in designing NSOs. For example, the price of NSOs that are granted need not bear any relationship to the price of the stock being optioned. Nor must NSOs be exercised within any particular time frame.

Whether the granting of an NSO constitutes a taxable event depends principally on whether the NSO has a "readily ascertainable fair market value" at the time it is granted. Because NSOs are normally nontransferable and are not immediately exercisable in full, they generally do not have an ascertainable fair market value. For this reason, the exercise of an NSO will generally constitute a taxable event.

The amount that will be included in income by the NSO recipient will be the excess of (1) the fair market value of the stock over (2) the sum of (a) any amount paid for the NSO (presumably zero) plus (b) the amount paid for stock. The amount taken into income by the individual recipient will be characterized as ordinary income. The company granting the NSO will generally be entitled to a tax-deduction equal to the amount that is included in the individual's income.

If the optionee continues to hold the stock after exercise, and he or she eventually sells the stock for a gain, the additional tax due on the gain will be taxed at capital gains rates. The capital gains tax rate will be applied to the difference in value from the date of exercise to the date of sale.

Restricted Stock Plan

Under a restricted stock plan, an employee is generally granted shares of stock that are subject to: (1) a substantial risk of forfeiture, and (2) transfer restrictions that lapse only if he or she remains in the employ of the company for a specified period. If the employee terminates employment prior to the restriction period expiration, then he or she forfeits the shares to the company.

If the employee remains employed by the company until the end of the restriction period, then the forfeiture provision will lapse and the employee will own the stock. A restricted stock plan may also provide that the employee (1) can only sell the stock to the company and (2) will have to sell the stock to the company when his or her employment terminates.

Section 83(a) indicates that an employee receiving stock under such a plan will not realize income for federal income tax purposes at the time of the grant. This statement is true unless the employee files an election pursuant to Section 83(b). Rather, the employee will realize income when the restriction or forfeiture provision lapses. That realized income will be an amount equal to the then value per share multiplied by the applicable number of shares.

The company issuing the shares will be entitled to a compensation expense deduction equal to the amount taken into income by the employee (to the extent that the amount constitutes reasonable compensation). Upon the employee's sale of the shares to the company, the employee will also realize income or loss.

Phantom Stock Plan

Under a "phantom stock" plan, hypothetical shares of a company's stock are allocated by book entry to the account of an employee. No actual cash or shares of stock are set aside by the company to fund future distributions.

If the employee remains with the company until the end of the restriction period, then the phantom shares are converted into actual shares or cash, or both. Again, the company may use a restriction period to prevent any employee from leaving within a set period of years from receiving any stock or cash.

To the extent that the phantom shares are distributed in cash, they are valued using the existing value per share of the company's stock. Shares distributed to an employee may be restricted so that they may be sold only to the company. And, phantom shares must be sold to the company when the employee's employment terminates.

An employee receiving a phantom stock grant realizes no taxable income at the time of the award. The employee is taxed at ordinary income tax rates when distributions are made from the phantom stock account.

At the date of distribution, the company is entitled to a tax deduction for the amount distributed (to the extent it constitutes reasonable compensation). If distributed shares are later sold to the company, then the employee will realize income or loss, as the case may be. The employee will pay capital gains tax on any income so realized.

Stock Appreciation Rights Plan

A stock appreciation rights (SAR) plan is another type of management compensation plan. An SAR plan operates in a manner similar to that of a phantom stock plan, and it has similar income tax characteristics. However, in contrast to distributions from a phantom stock plan, distributions from an employee's SAR account are based only on the increase, if any, in the value per share between (1) the date of the award and (2) the date of distribution. While some SAR plans use a maturity date as a time for distribution, other SAR plans allow an employee to choose—within a prescribed period—the timing of distributions from his or her account.

Stock Bonus Plan

Under a stock bonus plan, an employee's bonus is contingent upon the issuing company's earnings exceeding a stated level for a specified period. Bonuses under the plan may be contingent on the financial or earnings performance of the company. A stock bonus plan allows a company great flexibility in compensating key employees. For instance, such a plan can provide that if earnings increase above a certain minimum level, the bonus amounts will also increase. This feature provides the company employees an incentive to maximize company earnings. The bonuses may be paid in the form of the company's stock or cash, or both.

A stock bonus plan can provide that the stock received under the plan can only be sold to the company and/or must be sold to the company when employment terminates. The stock would be sold at a price equal to the value per share at the time of transfer.

An employee receiving shares under a stock bonus plan realizes no taxable income at the time he or she is awarded bonus credits. When the amount of the stock bonus is paid, then the employee will realize ordinary income. The ordinary income is (1) an amount equal to the value per share multiplied by the number of shares he or she receives plus (2) the amount of any cash received.

The company awarding the bonus credits is entitled to a tax deduction equal to such amount (to the extent it constitutes reasonable compensation). When the employee sells the stock to the company, he or she realizes income or loss, as the case may be.

STOCKHOLDER APPROVAL

An ISO must be granted pursuant to a plan that is approved by the sponsoring company's stockholders within 12 months before or after the adoption of the plan. The approval by the stockholders of a stock option plan must comply with all applicable provisions of the corporate charter, bylaws, and the law of the state of incorporation.

Although the other stock-based incentive plans described herein may generally be put into effect by the board of directors of the ESOP employer corporation without stockholder ratification, such ratification is desirable:

1. if the company officers and directors are participants in these arrangements or
2. if the preemptive rights of the existing shareholders are affected.

Ratification of any stock incentive plan by the stockholders may insulate the arrangement from any complaint by a minority shareholder. This statement is true except for a complaint of fraud, illegality, or waste of corporate assets. Therefore, it is typically recommended that the company obtain stockholder ratification of any stock-based incentive plan.

SUMMARY AND CONCLUSION

The sale of closely held company stock to an ESOP, followed by stock-based incentive compensation planning, can achieve the following economic benefits to the selling stockholder:

1. creation of personal wealth and estate liquidity,
2. creation of investment diversification,

3. significant gift tax savings on assets bequeathed to children or other beneficiaries,
4. transition of sponsor company stock to key employees,
5. an employee reward for increased share value,
6. assurance of the ultimate success of the ESOP through additional stock incentives at key management levels.

The current federal gift and estate tax rates are significantly higher than capital gains and even ordinary income tax rates. Therefore, combining an ESOP stock sale transaction with established estate planning procedures can augment the income tax benefits associated with the ESOP stock sale alone.

Ultimately, significant gift tax savings on assets bequeathed to children or other beneficiaries may also be achieved. In total, an ESOP, combined with other estate planning strategies, may benefit all parties involved in the ownership of the privately held company.

This discussion was authored by William W. Merten, Esq. Bill Merten is a partner with the law firm of McDermott, Will & Emery, where he concentrates on business succession planning and executive compensation. Bill can be contacted at (312) 984-7647 or wmerten@mwe.com.

The original version of this article appeared in the Spring 1999 issue of Willamette Management Associates Insights.

This discussion was edited and updated by Malcolm Hartman. Mike is a principal in the Atlanta, Georgia, office of Willamette Management Associates.

Chapter 5

Using 401(k) Assets to Purchase Employer Corporation Stock

INTRODUCTION

Closely held business owners often find an ESOP to be an attractive mechanism (1) for providing current stockholders with liquidity and investment diversification and (2) for implementing and financing an ownership transition strategy. Creative transaction structuring procedures —including the use of innovative tax and legal structures—allow for a variety of opportunities for closely held business owners to implement an ESOP. One transaction structure provides an opportunity for employees to use their existing 401(k) assets to purchase the employer corporation stock through an ESOP formation.

For purposes of this discussion, we will refer to such acquisitive transactions as K-ESOPs. However, some ESOP practitioners use this phrase to refer to various different types of ESOP acquisition transactions.

The K-ESOP transaction structure has been used to implement employee acquisitions of employer corporation stock for some time. However, current income tax regulations permitting S corporations to sponsor ESOPs have generated renewed interest in this acquisition financing structure. This discussion summarizes (1) the current trends in K-ESOP stock purchase transactions, (2) how these stock purchase transactions are structured, and (3) the specific valuation issues that arise in K-ESOP transactions.

TRENDS IN ESOP TRANSACTIONS

In general, current interest in an ESOP as a tax-advantaged employee acquisition vehicle remains strong. Closely held corporation owners continue to deal with ownership liquidity events and management succession planning. For many of these companies, the economic benefits of implementing an ESOP are severalfold. First, the selling stockholder enjoys a capital gains tax deferral by electing Section 1042 treatment. This election is available if the selling stockholder sells at least 30 percent of the company stock to the ESOP. Second, many closely held company founders—and their family members—have a strong desire for the family-owned company to remain closely held and locally owned. Third, an ESOP provides an opportunity for loyal employees to participate in the long-term value appreciation and wealth creation of a successful company.

An important factor that affects both current ESOP-owned companies and potential ESOP company acquisition is the ability of an S corporation to sponsor an ESOP. In an S corporation, the corporation does not pay federal income taxes. Instead, the individual shareholders pay income taxes on their pro rata share of the S corporation's taxable income. Generally, S corporation shareholders must be individual taxpayers, and not other corporate entities.

However, due to legislation that was passed in 1998, an ESOP trust, although it is not an individual, may hold stock in an S corporation. Furthermore, since a trust is not a taxable entity, the ESOP trust does not pay federal income taxes on its share of the S corporation taxable income. As a result, if an S corporation is 100 percent owned by an ESOP trust, then that corporation effectively has a zero federal income tax liability.

Willamette Management Associates has served as the financial adviser in several K-ESOP stock purchase transactions. In some of these stock purchase transactions, the ESOP acquired the equity interest of an outside equity investor, such as a private equity firm. In other K-ESOP transactions, both the ESOP and the company management jointly participated in the acquisition of a subsidiary of a larger company. And, in other cases, the K-ESOP participated in a traditional leveraged buyout of the employer corporation founding family.

However, in the majority of these ESOP stock purchase transactions, the transaction was structured so that (1) the ESOP would own 100 percent of the outstanding stock of the employer company and (2) the employer corporation would elect S corporation tax status immediately after the completion of the ESOP stock acquisition. Such an acquisition structure creates very compelling income tax savings for the employer corporation on a post-transaction basis.

Another trend in K-ESOP stock purchase transactions is that many of the employer corporations are highly leveraged on a post-transaction basis. If the ESOP purchases a significant block of stock (often 100 percent of the employer corporation stock), then the only company equity is owned by the employees' 401(k) plan assets. The ESOP stock purchase is typically financed through new acquisition loans to the sponsor company. Lenders will accept this highly leveraged structure because the income tax savings to the 100 percent ESOP-owned S corporation provide (1) enhanced cash flow/debt payment capacity to the sponsor company on a post-transaction basis and (2) improved debt coverage ratios that provide comfort to the lenders.

Even with the enhanced cash flow from the income tax savings in a 100 percent ESOP-owned S corporation, many ESOP transactions are so highly leveraged that the sponsor company borrows both (1) traditional senior debt and (2) mezzanine (or subordinated) debt. The senior acquisition debt is typically collateralized with all of the employer corporation fixed assets, accounts receivable, and inventory. Therefore, the mezzanine (or subordinated) acquisition debt is considered to be a "cash flow" collateral loan. The subordinated acquisition debt only has a secondary claim (if any) on the employer company's collateral assets.

By its very nature, the mezzanine (or junior) debt has a greater degree of risk to it. Therefore, the mezzanine level of acquisition commands higher total financing costs. These total financing costs may be structured in a variety of ways, including annual coupons, warrants, and exit fees. In such highly leveraged transactions, the "all-in" interest rate on these debt instruments may range from 10 to 20 percent or more, depending on (1) the specific transaction structure, (2) the credit worthiness of the employer corporation, and (3) the current capital market conditions at the time of the deal.

Another significant trend in K-ESOP stock purchase transactions is that most involve some type of equity incentive plan for the retained company management. Since so many of these K-ESOP transactions are structured to achieve both (1) 100 percent ESOP ownership and (2) S corporation income tax status, these types of equity incentive plans are often "phantom" plans.

Typical phantom management incentive plans include (1) stock appreciation rights (SAR) plans or (2) phantom stock ownership plans. These plans create incentives for retained sponsor company management, based on improvements in the equity value of the employer company. But, these plans typically do not award actual shares of stock to any individuals. Because no actual shares of stock are issued to management, the employer company preserves the income tax benefits of the 100 percent ESOP-owned S corporation structure.

When a transaction is structured to allow employees to invest all or a portion of their 401(k) plan account balances in company stock through the ESOP, the company generally determines what limits, if any, will be placed on the plan participants' ability to invest in the employer corporation stock.

For many company acquisitions to work, a minimum amount of equity must be raised from the 401(k) plan assets. In general, the minimum required amount is often a relatively low percentage of the total 401(k) plans assets, in the range of 10 to 35 percent.

Based on a review of the plan participants' age distribution, a determination is made whether or not to place limits on the employees' ability to invest in the employer securities. Some transactions allow no more than 50 percent of an employee's 401(k) account balance to be invested in the employer corporation stock. Other transactions do not place any individual limits. However, these transactions often do place a limit on the total maximum amount of employee 401(k) plan assets that may be invested in employer securities through the ESOP. In that case, if some employees subscribe for more than the maximum allowable investment amount, all employees' investments are scaled back on a pro rata basis.

In general, there are two areas of concern in K-ESOP stock purchase transactions: (1) the employer corporation's repurchase obligation and (2) employee investment diversification.

When employees invest in an ESOP using their 401(k) plan assets, the employer corporation has a high immediate repurchase obligation. This is because those same investment funds have to be available to be paid out to employees upon any termination event. Although raising a significant amount of acquisition financing from the 401(k) plan can be interpreted as a sign of employee support in the company, and can ultimately provide for less leverage in the acquisition transaction, there is an offsetting constraint. That is, K-ESOP-owned companies should be aware of the increased employer corporation repurchase obligation associated with the use of 401(k) funds to finance the ESOP acquisition.

Also, employer corporations should assess the plan participants' ages before implementing a K-ESOP stock purchase transaction. This consideration relates to the lack of investment diversification of the ESOP. An ESOP is designed "to invest primarily in employer corporation securities." Therefore, the ESOP does not have to have any investments other than the employer company stock. The only diversification requirement is that the ESOP must provide diversification for sponsor company employees who have (1) attained age 55 and (2) completed 10 years of service.

For any ESOP-owned company where the average age of the plan participants is high, allowing employees to invest previously diversified 401(k) plan assets in the employer company stock can be problematic. This problem is due to the lack of investment diversification for those older plan participants.

However, even in these instances, an ESOP stock purchase transaction may still work. This is because the employee's 401(k) plan may have enough total assets that only a small percentage of the plan assets is required to make the ESOP acquisition work. In such an instance, the ESOP stock purchase transaction will not severely limit the 401(k) plan participants' overall investment diversification.

STRUCTURING A K-ESOP STOCK PURCHASE TRANSACTION

Structuring a K-ESOP stock purchase transaction can be complex and time consuming. A stock purchase transaction of this type, in its most simplified form, is typically completed through the following procedures:

1. First, each individual 401(k) participant must make an investment decision to transfer some portion of his or her total 401(k) plan assets into the ESOP trust.
2. Second, once the elections are tabulated, the 401(k) assets are liquidated and cash is transferred into the ESOP trust. At the same time, the employer corporation also arranges for the necessary acquisition financing from outside lenders.
3. Third, the employer corporation loans the stock acquisition funds to the ESOP in an amount (together with the 401(k) investment transfer money) sufficient to purchase all of the outstanding sponsor company shares.
4. Fourth, the ESOP uses both the funds from the sponsor company acquisition financings and the funds from the 401(k) investments to purchase the employer corporation stock (1) from the selling shareholders and/or (2) from the sponsor company itself. At the same time, any new management incentive plans are implemented.
5. Fifth, the newly ESOP-controlled employer corporation elects S corporation status for federal income tax purposes.

Of course, the above-described steps to complete a K-ESOP stock purchase transaction are intentionally simplified for discussion purposes. In reality, this type of K-ESOP acquisition transaction can take between 6 to 12 months to complete. This K-ESOP acquisition process can be broken down into several phases. In the preliminary phase, the employer corporation structures a transaction with the interested selling parties, identifying parameters such as (1) target stock price, (2) estimated new financing sources and amounts, (3) estimated investment from the 401(k) plan, and (4) estimated final transaction structure.

Then, legal and financial advisers are retained to advise the various parties as to the feasibility of the proposed stock purchase transaction. In general, due to the complexity of this type of transaction, an external independent ESOP trustee is retained, along with independent financial and legal advisers to the trustee.

During the second phase, intense negotiations often take place as the specific parameters of the proposed stock purchase transaction are determined. And, each interested party identifies its legal and financial issues. In addition, during this time period, the employer corporation (1) identifies all required lending, (2) secures bids for the new debt, and (3) selects the lenders. These lenders also become involved in the transaction negotiations, particularly if there is mezzanine or subordinated debt used to finance the stock purchase transaction.

During this second phase, many of the specific details of the design of the new ESOP plan are also finalized. These design features include decisions by the sponsor company on the distribution rules, matching formulas, protected benefits, and other features that must be determined to finalize the plan design.

These first two phases, which incorporate (1) general transaction structuring and (2) specific price/structure negotiations between the various parties, can take anywhere from one to six months to complete.

Once the transaction structure has been negotiated and the transaction specifics have been analyzed by all parties, then the employer company enters into the process of notifying employees of the opportunity to invest in the company. Since each 401(k) plan participant is making an investment decision to invest funds in employer corporation securities, the participants must receive full disclosure about (1) the employer corporation, (2) its financial performance, (3) the terms of the proposed transaction, and (4) the risks associated with an investment of this type.

This information is distributed to employees in the form of a Disclosure Memorandum, which is similar to—albeit shorter than—a securities registration on SEC Form S-1.

The Disclosure Memorandum typically contains information on (1) the terms of the stock purchase transaction, (2) the risks of the employer corporation, the industry, and the particular employer corporation securities, (3) an overview of the company, its history, its products/services, markets, and outlook, (4) historical financial statements, including a management discussion and analysis, (5) financial projections, (6) information on the going-forward management team and the board of directors, (7) a summary ESOP plan description, and (8) an investment election form.

The Disclosure Memorandum is prepared by the employer corporation and by its legal advisers. In addition, the Disclosure Memorandum is typically reviewed by many of the parties involved in transaction prior to its release in final form to the 401(k) plan participants.

In general, most companies prepare the Disclosure Memorandum, send it out to all employees, and then plan for a one to two week period of employee meetings (depending on the size of the employer corporation and the location of all participants). During these employee meetings, sponsor company management (1) makes presentations about the sponsor company and the proposed stock purchase transaction and (2) answers questions from employees about the investment process.

The 401(k) participants have a set time period to return an investment election form to the sponsor company (or to its plan administrator). This election form indicates whether the participant is investing some, all, or none of the 401(k) account balance in the employer corporation stock through the ESOP. Finally, once all the employee election forms are returned and tabulated, the process of (1) liquidating assets in the 401(k) plan and (2) transferring the cash to the ESOP trust can begin. And, the K-ESOP stock purchase transaction can be completed.

STOCK VALUATION ISSUES

There are many valuation issues in K-ESOP stock purchase transactions. Some of these valuation issues emerge due to the significant amount of leverage the employer corporation assumes in order to complete the buy-out. Of course, the leverage may be necessary in order for the K-ESOP to achieve 100 percent ownership by the ESOP and, thereby, obtain the S corporation income tax status and related income tax benefits.

Because these K-ESOP transactions often include mezzanine or subordinated debt, these debt instruments often require some form of detachable equity interest in the employer corporation, such as warrants. These equity interests can result in dilution to the ESOP's economic interest in the employer corporation.

In addition, although it may be desirable to implement a new management equity incentive plan (phantom or otherwise), this equity position may also dilute the ESOP's ownership position. If the ESOP's ownership position is excessively diluted on a post-transaction basis, then the financial fairness of the stock purchase transaction can be jeopardized. In general, it is often possible to structure an acquisition that accommodates all of these different interests. However, in many cases, each party to the transaction may have to compromise somewhat on its position.

Another valuation issue that emerges in these K-ESOP transactions is the repurchase liability obligation associated with the transferred 401(k) assets.

Since these 401(k) assets are fully owned by the participants, they have immediate withdrawal rights (for termination, death, disability, and retirement) on a post-transaction basis. Therefore, it is important for the sponsor company to assess (1) the age of the participants, (2) the account balances, and (3) the expected sponsor company employee turnover prior to implementing the K-ESOP stock purchase transaction.

Although no one can precisely predict stock repurchases in the future, the employer corporation, the ESOP trustee, and the lenders should understand the parameters of the employee census. Based on such an understanding, the various parties can develop a comfort level as to the most likely stock repurchase scenarios.

A third valuation issue is whether future share repurchases (1) will be recycled through the ESOP or (2) retired into treasury. In most cases, it is desirable (1) to recycle the shares through the ESOP and (2) to contribute those shares to all employees. However, depending on the amount, such a contribution can be more than the typical amount the company spends on retirement plan contributions.

In this case, the equity ownership interests other than the ESOP (such as the mezzanine lenders that have warrants) may object. However, the ESOP trustee will want to prevent dilution to the ESOP ownership position that would result from retiring the repurchased shares into treasury. Again, it is important for all parties to assess the likely repurchase scenarios and the expected amounts of share repurchases in the first five years after the acquisitive transaction. Based on such an analysis, all parties can assess the impact of this issue on the employer corporation stock valuation.

SUMMARY AND CONCLUSION

In summary, many closely held companies have implemented K-ESOP stock purchase transactions. The time commitment and complexity involved in these K-ESOP stock purchase transactions indicate that such companies should rely on experienced legal and financial advisers to ensure that the transaction is successful. When properly structured, using 401(k) plan assets to implement an ESOP stock acquisition provides a tax-advantaged ownership transition from the founding family to the employee owners.

Chapter 6

Using an ESOP as a Corporate Acquisition Vehicle

INTRODUCTION

The use of an ESOP as a corporate acquisition vehicle reflects the multidimensional nature of the leveraged ESOP within the context of corporate finance. In addition to using an ESOP to raise capital, refinance existing debt, create a market for non-publicly-traded stock, and acquire significant blocks of employer corporation stock from stockholders, an ESOP can be used to finance the acquisition of a target corporation ("Target") with tax-deductible funds.

The key financial advantage of the use of an ESOP in connection with a corporate acquisition in which debt will be used is essentially the same as its advantage over conventional financing in other transactions. The ability of the employer corporation to amortize acquisition debt with (1) tax-deductible contributions to its ESOP and (2) tax-deductible cash dividends (in the case of a C corporation) on stock held by the plan generally results in enhanced cash flow and a more easily financed transaction.

This discussion constitutes a summary of a complex topic that involves issues under the Internal Revenue Code, the Employee Retirement Income Security Act, state and federal securities laws and state corporate laws. This discussion is not intended to be exhaustive in its treatment of the subject matter. Rather, this discussion is intended to provide the reader with a starting point for further study and analysis. Nevertheless, the use of an ESOP is often an attractive alternative to the "standard" form of acquisition, and it is particularly useful in connection with the acquisition of a subsidiary.

ILLUSTRATIVE EXAMPLE

For example, let's assume Acquirer Corporation ("Acquirer") normally pays federal and state income tax at a marginal rate of 40 percent. Let's assume

Acquirer desires to acquire Target for $6 million. Acquirer would have to earn, on an pretax basis, approximately $10 million to fund the acquisition (without taking into account the interest on its acquisition debt). On the other hand, if Acquirer uses a leveraged ESOP to facilitate the acquisition, it would need to generate pretax acquisition funds of $6 million. As discussed below, in the case of an S corporation, the transaction economics can be even more favorable.

The enhanced motivation and productivity of employees that can occur as a result of their ownership of Target can also constitute a significant advantage over conventional acquisition procedures. Depending on the structure of the acquisition, individual Target stockholders may be eligible to defer the recognition of capital gain realized on the sale of their Target stock if, within a specified replacement period, "qualified replacement property" is purchased.

In addition to simply using an established ESOP to facilitate the acquisition of Target, Acquirer may use an ESOP in a variety of leveraged buy-out (LBO) transactions, including: (1) the acquisition of a subsidiary or division of the corporation and (2) going private transactions. In deciding whether an ESOP should be used to acquire a Target or effect an LBO, the following crucial issues should be considered:

1. Economic issues:
   a. Whether the transaction will be dilutive or accretive to the ESOP and the other Acquirer stockholders.
   b. The financial feasibility of the transaction, taking into account the economics of scale to be achieved, including:
      (1) the extent to which the Acquirer ESOP, and Acquirer itself, are currently leveraged;
      (2) the post-transaction cash flow and debt load of Target;
      (3) the level of employer corporation contributions that can be made to the ESOP to pay acquisition debt;
      (4) in the case of an S corporation, the level of Acquirer's post-transaction "tax dividends" or distributions to the ESOP and other shareholders; and
      (5) the effect of the transaction on Acquirer's (or the ESOP's) repurchase liability (if Acquirer stock is not publicly traded).
   c. The ability of Acquirer to pay a "strategic buyer" price for Target.
   d. The effect of converting Target's contributions to its retirement plan to ESOP debt payments.

   e. The potential use of a Section 1042 gain deferral transaction by Target prior to the acquisition.
   f. The effect of income tax and federal and state securities laws on the parties to the transaction.
2. Other issues:
   a. All acquisitions involve multiple legal issues with regard to the disposition of Acquirer's and Target's qualified plans. Typically, there are several alternatives for the disposition of Target's plans. For example, Target's plan may be merged into the Acquirer ESOP or into another plan sponsored by Acquirer. Alternatively, the plan could be terminated and participants' benefits distributed and rolled over to the Acquirer plan or to an IRA.
   b. The effect of the fiduciary responsibility rules contained in the Employee Retirement Income Security Act of 1974, as amended (ERISA), on the plan fiduciaries must also be considered.
   c. The extent to which Target employees will (or must) be covered by the ESOP is a critical issue for Target's employees.

The use of an ESOP in connection with an acquisition is not without its economic disadvantages, including the following:

- The ESOP may achieve a superior equity position as compared to other shareholders.
- Additional complexity and cost, both initial and ongoing, will be incurred whenever an ESOP is involved in an acquisitive transaction.
- The integration of Target employees into Acquirer "employee/owner" culture always presents a challenge.

STRUCTURE OF ACQUISITIVE TRANSACTIONS WITH THE USE OF AN ESOP

The Basic ESOP Acquisition Format

In its most basic form, an acquisitive transaction in which an ESOP is utilized involves the acquisition of Target stock or Target assets for cash. Under this format, the acquisition can generally be structured as (1) an outright purchase of stock or assets, (2) a merger of Target into Acquirer or its subsidiary ("Acquisition Subsidiary") (in a "forward" merger), or (3) a merger of Acquirer or its Acquisition Subsidiary into Target (in a "reverse" merger). The following discussion summarizes the major elements of a basic ESOP-facilitated acquisitive transaction:

Procedure One

A definitive agreement is negotiated between Acquirer and Target pursuant to which Acquirer agrees to pay cash for the Target stock or the Target assets. This procedure is illustrated in Figure 1.

Figure 1

Acquisition Procedure One Illustration

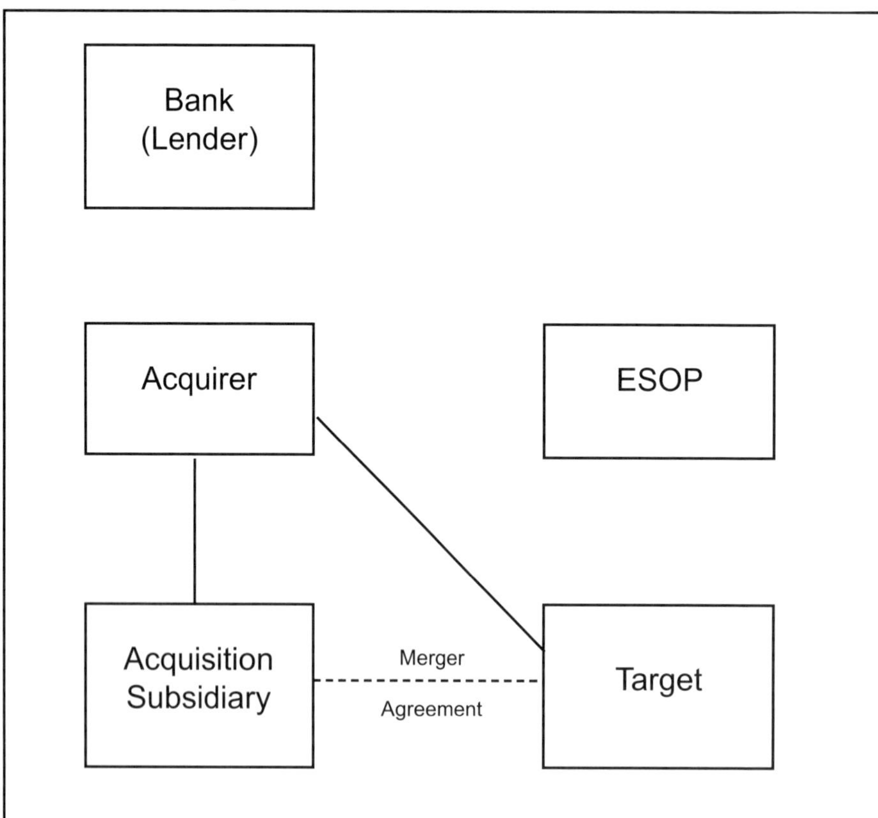

Procedure Two

Acquirer borrows sufficient funds from a lender to make the acquisition. Acquirer lends the borrowed funds to its ESOP, in an "inside loan." The ESOP uses the loan proceeds to purchase authorized but unissued stock directly from Acquirer. This procedure is illustrated in Figure 2.

Figure 2

Acquisition Procedure Two Illustration

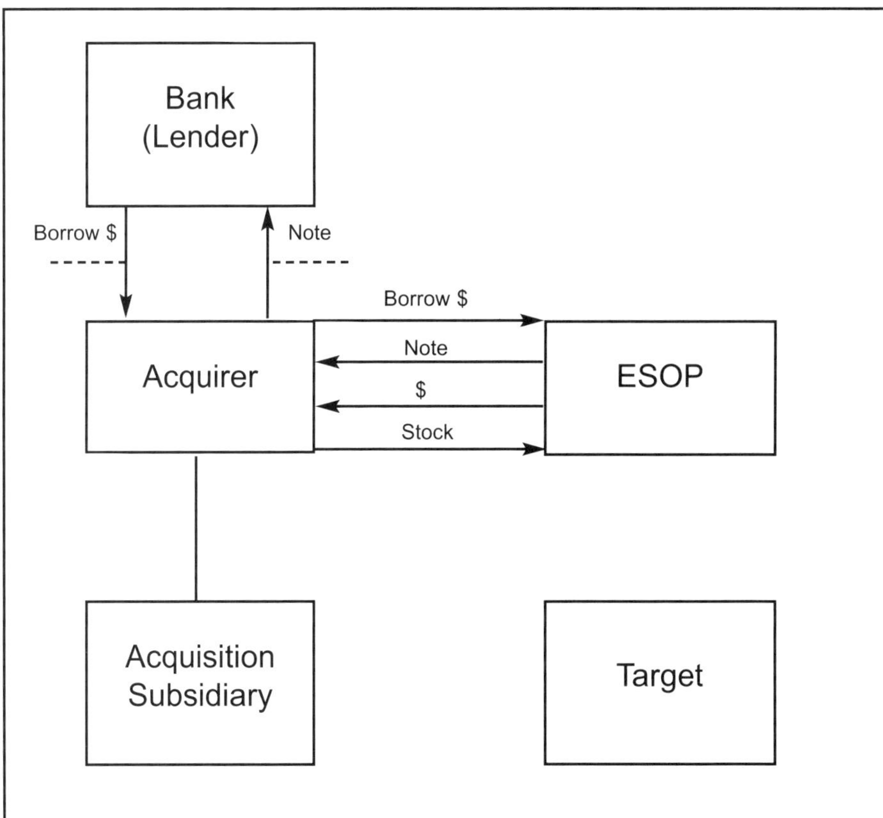

Procedure Three

Acquirer uses the proceeds of the stock sale to the ESOP to acquire Target. Acquirer then makes annual tax-deductible contributions to the ESOP. The ESOP, in turn, uses the contributions to repay the loan.

In the case of a C Corporation, cash dividends on shares held by the ESOP may be used to pay the loan. Such dividends are generally tax deductible by Acquirer. In the case of an S corporation that is partially owned by an ESOP, the ESOP may use its share of Acquirer's "tax dividends" paid with respect to unallocated shares to pay the acquisition debt.

Target can be merged into Acquisition Subsidiary (treated as an acquisition of assets for federal income tax purposes) or Acquisition Subsidiary can be merged into Target (generally treated as a purchase of stock for income tax purposes). This procedure is illustrated in Figure 3.

Figure 3

Acquisition Procedure Three Illustration

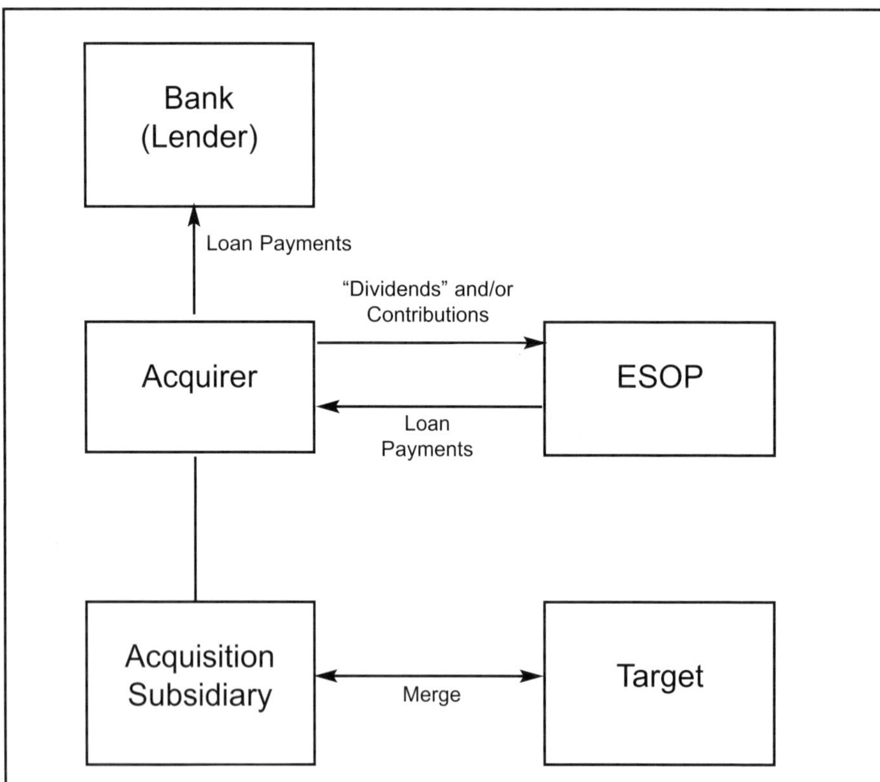

If Acquirer sponsors a 401(k) plan or the ESOP includes a 401(k) feature, Acquirer's matching contributions may also be used by the ESOP to pay the acquisition debt.

Variation of Basic Acquisition Format—Use of Section 1042 Tax Deferral Feature

If the Target is a C corporation with one or more individual stockholders, the acquisition may be structured to allow Target stockholders to defer recognition of gain on the transaction under Section 1042

In this instance, the following additional procedures are involved:

- Target forms an ESOP (or uses an existing ESOP) to purchase, for cash, at least 30 percent of Target's stock from individual shareholders in a transaction that qualifies for gain deferral under Section 1042.
- Acquirer issues its shares for the shares of Target, including shares acquired by the ESOP in the Section 1042 transaction.
- Target is merged into Acquisition Subsidiary or vice versa, in a tax-free reorganization; Target's ESOP is then merged into the Acquirer's ESOP.
- The Acquirer's ESOP succeeds to Target's ESOP debt from Section 1042 transaction through the ESOP merger and services the debt with contributions and/or dividends.
- As an alternative, Target's ESOP may issue notes to the selling stockholders to avoid time and expense of borrowing.
- Acquirer consummates the transaction, leverages its ESOP and, within 12 months after Target's ESOP issued its notes, uses the stock sale proceeds to pay the notes.
- The Target ESOP is then merged into the Acquirer ESOP.

A note of caution regarding the Section 1042 transaction is in order. If the transaction is not properly structured, the Internal Revenue Service could take the position (under the "step transaction" or the "substance over form" doctrine, or both) that the transaction should be judged, from a federal income tax standpoint, as a sale by Target's stockholders of their Target stock to Acquirer's ESOP. Such a sale may or may not qualify under Section 1042.

Assessment of Economic Benefits of an ESOP to Acquire Target

In deciding whether to use its ESOP to acquire Target, Acquirer should consider the following factors:

- the cost of using an ESOP versus the cost of using conventional borrowing based on financial projections, including the effect on the Acquirer's financial statements;
- use of Acquirer cash rather than borrowing and comparison of "opportunity cost" to cost of borrowing;
- the amount of contributions/dividends necessary to amortize acquisition debt compared to the Acquirer historical level of contributions/dividends to its ESOP, and Target's contributions to its plan(s);
- the effect of contributions/dividends on "compensation expense" and level of benefits to employees; and
- the involvement of the ESOP financial adviser and the ESOP trustee at an early stage and throughout the process.

Variation of Basic Acquisition Format; Creation of New Corporations and ESOP to Acquire Target Corporation

The acquisition of Target by an investor or group of investors with borrowed funds can be achieved, on a pretax basis, through the use of an ESOP. Under this format, the procedures involved are quite similar to the procedures under the basic ESOP acquisition format described earlier, with the addition of the following procedures:

- Acquirer and Acquisition Subsidiary are organized by the investor group as the stockholders of Acquirer. Acquirer may have a separate class of stock to be owned by the investor group and/or members of management.
- Acquirer implements an ESOP that will cover Target's employees. The ESOP then purchases "qualifying employer securities" from Acquirer (which may be a different class of voting stock than the stock held by the investors and/or management) in exchange for the ESOP note. The amortization schedule under the note coincides with the amortization schedule under the Acquirer loan.
- Acquirer acquires Target for cash which has been borrowed by Acquirer and, in turn, has been used to capitalize Acquisition Subsidiary. The capital of Acquisition Subsidiary is used as the acquisition currency.

BASIC MULTI-INVESTOR ESOP LBO TRANSACTION

The acquisition of Target is often structured as a multi-investor LBO. In such a transaction, an ESOP constitutes the major source of financing. In many cases, Target's management initiates and takes an active role in the LBO and constitutes the only other participant. In other cases, management is joined by an investor group, the employees of Target, or both. Many multi-investor ESOP LBOs also involve the use of mezzanine (i.e., secondary) financing.

The following discussion summarizes a typical format for an ESOP/management LBO of a subsidiary corporation:

Procedure One

The management group arranges primary and mezzanine financing, which may include borrowing from either the primary or mezzanine lender by management. Management also implements a leveraged ESOP that is designed to invest primarily in the stock of Target. This procedure is illustrated in Figure 4.

Figure 4

LBO Transaction Procedure One

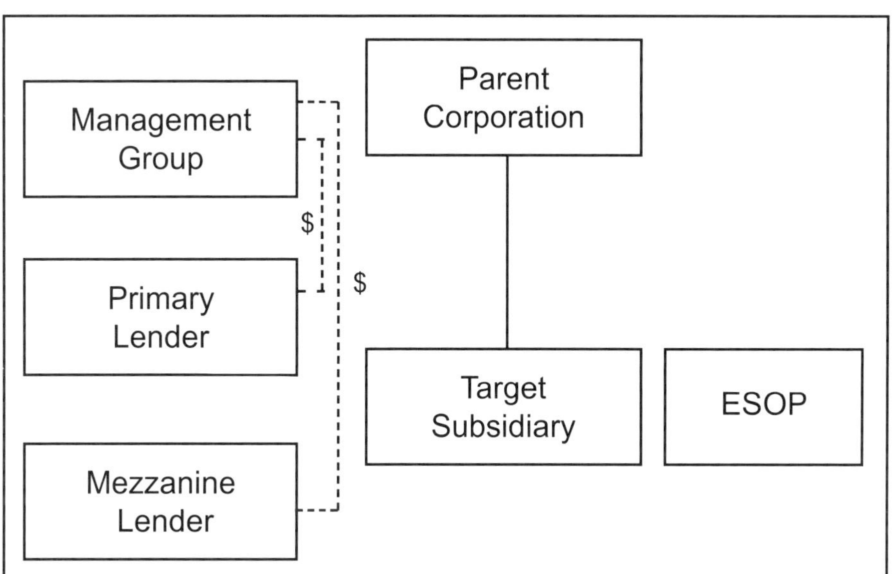

Procedure Two

The primary and mezzanine financing sources loan the acquisition funds to Target in exchange for a note, in the case of the primary lender, and a note or other form of debt security—such as warrants—in the case of the mezzanine lender. Management may also purchase a portion of the Target stock. This procedure is illustrated in Figure 5.

Figure 5

LBO Transaction Procedure Two

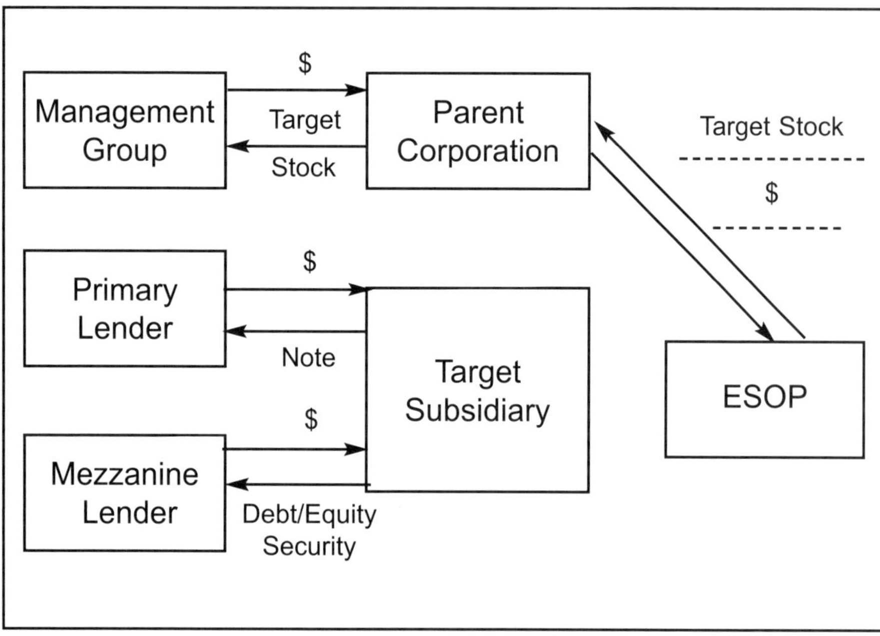

Procedure Three

Target, which is now held by management and the ESOP, makes tax-deductible contributions to the ESOP. These contributions are, in turn, used by the ESOP to repay its note to Target. Finally, Target uses the payments by the ESOP to pay the primary lender (and the mezzanine lender—depending upon the nature of the debt security issued by Target to the mezzanine lender). This procedure is illustrated in Figure 6.

Figure 6

LBO Transaction Step Three

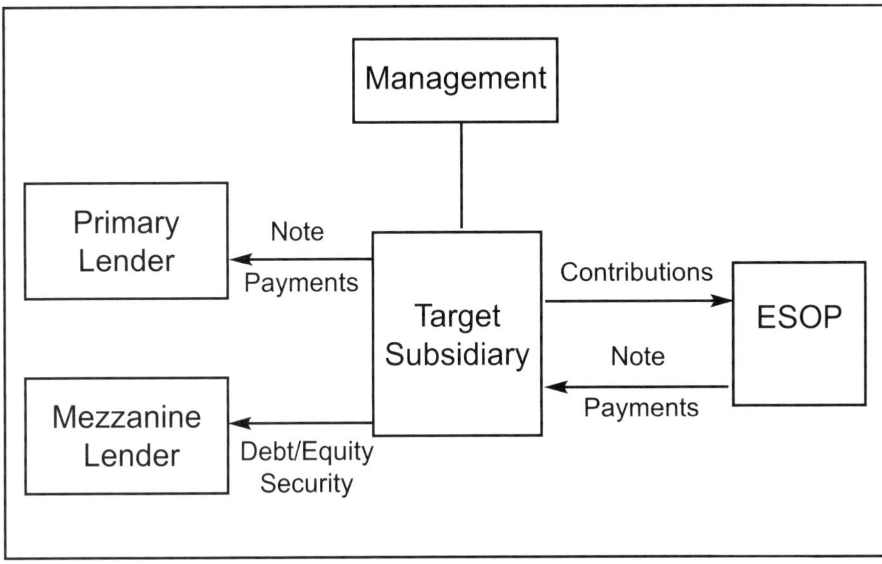

Typical Variations of a Multi-Investor ESOP LBO Transaction

Just as every ESOP is unique, virtually every ESOP LBO transaction is characterized by its own set of facts and circumstances. However, multi-investor LBOs often have the following common elements:

- The mezzanine lender may require a particular form of debt or equity security. If a form of equity is issued to the mezzanine lender, warrants are often used.
- The Target stockholders or Parent Corporation may participate in the LBO by holding back some of the Target stock or by reinvesting a portion of the sales proceeds in Target. The new securities issued by Target to the selling stockholders are often a form of preferred stock. The preferred stock may be accompanied by warrants.
- If Target sponsors a tax-qualified plan, its disposition in connection with the transaction may include the use of its assets by its members to participate with the ESOP in the LBO.
- If Target has union employees, then the transaction may involve the equity participation of the employees. This participation may be through

the employees' collectively bargained benefit plan assets or through direct participation—or both.

Key Issues in a Multi-Investor ESOP LBO

A multi-investor ESOP LBO transaction presents a variety of critical issues that should be addressed and resolved prior to commencing the transaction. As is the case with respect to any ESOP transaction, the issues include ERISA fiduciary, tax, federal and state securities law, corporate governance, and other concerns.

- Consideration paid by the ESOP for the Target stock, as compared to the consideration paid by management and other investors, is always a key issue. The ESOP financial advisers must ensure that the plan pays no more than adequate consideration for Target's stock. And, the ESOP financial adviser must ensure that the price paid by the ESOP is fair in relation to the consideration paid by the other participants. Resolution of the fairness issue is often complicated (1) by the different types of securities held by the participants after the transaction or (2) where management expects to receive "sweat" equity in Target in consideration of initiating and implementing the transaction.
- Where more than one class of Target stock will be issued, the stock held by the ESOP must satisfy the requirements applicable to "qualified employer securities."
- In those cases where employee funds, particularly assets held in employee benefit plans, will participate in the LBO, significant ERISA fiduciary and federal and state securities law issues will apply.
- Whether the Department of Labor should be notified of the proposed transaction and the effect of such notification on both the structure and timing of the transaction must be addressed.

This discussion was originally authored by Stephen D. Smith, Esq. Stephen Smith is a partner in the Indianapolis law firm of Krieg DeVault Alexander & Capehart, LLP. He practices primarily in the area of employee stock ownership plans and equity-based incentive compensation plans. He chairs the firm's Employee Benefits and Executive Compensation Practice Group. Mr. Smith can be reached at (317) 238-6218 or at ssmith@kdlegal.com.

The original article upon which this discussion is based first appeared in the Spring 2001 issue of Willamette Management Associates Insights.

This discussion was edited and updated by James G. Rabe. Jim is a principal of Willamette Management Associates and director of the firm's Portland, Oregon, office.

Section II

General ESOP Valuation Issues

Chapter 7

Current Issues in the Valuation of ESOP-Owned Stock

INTRODUCTION

The purpose of a business valuation assignment often has a material impact on the estimated value conclusion. For example, the valuation of an employer corporation performed for an ESOP should consider several special factors.

This discussion summarizes the special factors related to the valuation of employer corporation stock. Specifically, this discussion will focus on the recent developments that impact the valuation of ESOP-owned employer corporation stock.

THE ESOP STOCK PURCHASE DEBT "TAX SHIELD"

ESOP purchases of employer corporation stock are often leveraged transaction. This means that the employer corporation stock purchased by the ESOP is financed with debt that the sponsor company is obligated to repay. The impact of this acquisition debt generally reduces the equity value of the employer corporation on a post-transaction basis.

However, there is an income tax benefit available to the leveraged ESOP that partially offsets the value decrement caused by the ESOP debt. Specifically, principal payments made on the ESOP loan—as well as interest payments on the ESOP loan—are deductible by the employer corporation for federal income tax purposes. This tax deduction treatment is different from other forms of debt, which only allow interest (and not principal) payments to be deductible for determining federal income taxes.

An example of the impact of the ESOP debt and the corresponding ESOP debt "tax shield" is presented in Table 1. In this transaction, let's assume that the ESOP acquired a 30 percent common stock ownership interest in Employer Company.

The ESOP debt "tax shield" is calculated as the present value of future income tax savings associated with the tax deductibility of the ESOP debt principal payments. It is important to note that the ESOP debt "tax shield" declines over time as the ESOP stock purchase debt is repaid.

Table 1

Employer Company
Total Equity Valuation

Valuation Analysis	Before ESOP Stock Purchase Transaction	After ESOP Stock Purchase Transaction
Total Business Enterprise Value	$50,000,000	$50,000,000
Less: Interest-Bearing Debt	—	(15,000,000)
Add: ESOP Debt "Tax Shield"	—	2,500,000
Equals: Total Equity Value	$50,000,000	$37,500,000

Note: Total business enterprise value includes both interest-bearing debt and all classes of stockholders' equity.

PRICE PROTECTION IN SECOND-STAGE ESOP STOCK PURCHASE TRANSACTIONS

Many ESOP transactions are consummated for less than 100 percent of the employer corporation stock, for a number of reasons. First, the selling stockholder may be reluctant to give up total control of his or her company. Second, the employer corporation may not be able to finance a 100 percent stock acquisition transaction. As a result, an ESOP often acquires employer corporation stock in more than one purchase transaction.

These multi-stage transactions create a challenge related to the valuation of the different tranches of ESOP stock. This is because the debt created in a subsequent ESOP transaction is dilutive to the original ESOP and to its participants. Those original ESOP participants who terminate their employment before the new ESOP debt is totally repaid risk having their shares redeemed at a price that is less than the fair market value indicated if the second ESOP transaction had not occurred.

ESOP plan documents are often amended to provide the ESOP participants in the original ESOP with a floor value or price protection. This ESOP plan contractual price protection offsets dilution caused by the new ESOP. The floor value can be a fixed price. This fixed price is generally equal to the pretransaction value prior to the second stage stock purchase transaction.

However, this "floor value" is sometimes considered to be an unfair solution. This is because the original ESOP stockholders would not be subject to future business risk. And, this future business risk could reduce the value of all of the stockholders' ownership interest over time.

A more appropriate way to treat the dilution caused by the second stage ESOP transaction is to value the original ESOP stock excluding the impact of the new ESOP debt. This procedure is dilutive to the new ESOP's ownership interest. This is because some original ESOP participants will have their shares redeemed at a price that is above current fair market value.

However, this solution is considered to be the most fair treatment of all ESOP participants. Accordingly, in determining the financial fairness of a pending second-stage ESOP stock purchase transaction, the financial adviser should consider the dilution caused by the price protection as part of its analysis.

It is important to note that the dilution caused by the price protection only affects those original ESOP participants who terminate their employment during the time period that the new ESOP debt exists. After the new ESOP debt is totally repaid, all ESOP participants are treated on an equal basis for valuation purposes.

As presented in Table 2, the impact of price protection is indicated for both (1) the original pretransaction ESOP and (2) the new second-stage ESOP on the one-year anniversary of the second-stage stock purchase transaction.

Employer Company had no debt prior to the second-stage ESOP transaction. In the second-stage stock purchase transaction, the ESOP acquired an additional 50 percent ownership interest in Employer Company.

Table 2

Employer Company
Equity Valuation

Valuation Analysis	After the Stock Purchase Second Stage ESOP Transaction	Before the Stock Purchase First ESOP Transaction
Total Business Enterprise Value	$50,000,000	$50,000,000
Less: Interest-Bearing Debt	—	(22,500,000)
Less: Price Protection Liability [a]	—	(1,000,000)
Equals: Total Equity Value	$50,000,000	$26,500,000

[a] Price protection liability for the shares owed by the ESOP prior to the second-stage stock purchase transaction estimated based on (1) straight line amortization of the employer corporation debt obligations and (2) a repurchase liability study prepared by company management.

Note: Total business enterprise value includes both interest-bearing debt and all classes of stockholders' equity.

DISCOUNT FOR LACK OF MARKETABILITY

There is a significant difference between the employer corporation stock held in an ESOP, and otherwise identical closely held employer corporation stock. One difference is that there is a mandatory repurchase obligation (often referred to as a "put" option) related to ESOP stock.

This put option requires the sponsoring company to repurchase an ESOP participant's shares upon certain events (such as retirement, death, or disability). Generally, a put option requires the sponsoring company to repurchase the ESOP shares at the current fair market value.

The effect of a put option is that it greatly improves the marketability of the underlying closely held employer corporation shares. Therefore, the put option greatly improves the liquidity of a retirement ESOP plan's participant investment. Hence, the existence of a put option will reduce—or often eliminate—the otherwise appropriate discount for a lack of marketability.

The selection of an appropriate discount for a lack of marketability for ESOP shares subject to a put option depends on several factors, including:

1. the payment terms of the put option,
2. the ESOP sponsor company's historical record of redeeming ESOP shares,
3. studies related to the future repurchase of ESOP shares (the "repurchase obligation"), and
4. the employer corporation's financial ability to redeem the shares.

However, the ultimate selection of a discount, if any, is often based on an analyst's professional judgment and practical experience.

It is more likely today that a discount for lack of marketability will be applied to ESOP-owned stock. This conclusion is the result of certain court cases as well as communications from the U.S. Department of Labor (the "DOL"). The DOL has indicated its preference that a discount for a lack of marketability should apply when an ESOP purchases employer corporation stock.

The effect of the sponsor company's repurchase obligation should be considered in the valuation of ESOP-owned stock. ESOP financial advisers should, at a minimum, consider management's actions to make sure that the employer corporation has adequate funds to repurchase the ESOP-owned stock. The ESOP financial adviser may recognize the effect of the repurchase obligation by selecting a higher discount for lack of marketability in the ESOP-owned stock valuation.

ACQUISITIONS BY ESOP-OWNED COMPANIES

In an effort to increase revenue and profitability, ESOP-owned companies often grow through acquisition. Generally, if the acquisition transaction is completed (1) between independent parties subject to arm's-length negotiations and (2) within a reasonable time period of the valuation date (less than one year), the transaction should have a neutral impact on the value of the company. This conclusion is based on the assumption that the value of the assets acquired is equal to the value of the cash paid and the liabilities assumed.

Accordingly, the acquisition transaction has a neutral impact on the value of an employer corporation as of the date of the transaction. After a certain period of time however, the acquired company will be valued either (1) separately or (2) as part of the combined company. The valuation should be performed using generally accepted business valuation approaches and methods.

This treatment is appropriate even if the ESOP-owned acquirer is an S corporation. An S corporation ESOP provides an attractive ownership structure to facilitate acquisitions. This is because ESOP-owned companies as tax exempt entities can acquire pretax dollars at after-tax costs.

However, based on the fair market value standard, the unique benefits to an ESOP-owned company should not be considered in the valuation analysis. The real economic benefit that accrues to the employer corporation in the form of incrementally higher cash flow is accounted for within future valuations as the income tax benefit is realized.

The impact of acquisitions made by ESOP-owned companies with regard to a variety of financial issues was highlighted in the recently decided *Armstrong v. Amsted Industries* case (No. 01 C 2963, 2004 U.S. Dist. LEXIS 14776 (N.D. Ill. July 29, 2004). This will likely continue to be a key issue for ESOP trustees and for their financial and legal advisers.

STOCK OPTIONS AND OTHER TYPES OF MANAGEMENT INCENTIVE COMPENSATION

The employer corporation management is often the single biggest factor that determines changes in the value of the ESOP's ownership interest in the sponsor company. Therefore, it is important the sponsor company management is provided with appropriate incentives to increase the business for all stockholders, including the ESOP.

Since participation in the ESOP alone does not generally provide appropriate incentives, stock options or other forms of management perquisites are used to compensate employer corporation management for developing the business. The valuation issue that needs to be considered with regard to management incentives is (1) the dilution, if any, caused by the management incentives and (2) how to quantify it.

The question of dilution is relatively straightforward. If the management incentives are not performance-based, then there is dilution that needs to be factored into the valuation analysis. For example, if stock options vest based solely on the passage of time, management will be entitled to this additional form of compensation regardless of the sponsor company's change in value. However, if the options vest based on the achievement of certain performance targets (which generally are equal to or exceed current financial projections), then the value of the sponsor company will increase. This will benefit all employer corporation stockholders, including the ESOP.

The dilution in ownership percentage will generally be more than offset by the increased value. And, the management incentives will therefore not dilute the value of the ESOP stock.

If the analysis determines that the management perquisites are dilutive, the most accepted basis for quantifying their value is via a theoretical option pricing model such as Black-Scholes. A detailed explanation of Black-Scholes is beyond the scope of this discussion. However, the variables used to determine the value of stock options (as well as other forms of compensation based on the underlying value of the sponsor company) include:

1. current fair market value of sponsor company stock,
2. option price,
3. time to option expiration,
4. volatility of sponsor company stock, and
5. current interest rates.

SUMMARY AND CONCLUSION

The valuation of ESOP-owned employer corporation stock is a complicated process. The ESOP-owned stock valuation should consider several special factors that may not be considered in other business valuation assignments.

Accordingly, it is important that ESOP-owned companies and ESOP trustees retain valuation analysts with specific expertise in the valuation of employer corporation securities.

Chapter 8

Perennial Issues in the Valuation of ESOP-Owned Stock

INTRODUCTION

This discussion is adapted from an article that was originally published in the Spring 1995 issue of Willamette Management Associates *Insights*. Therefore, it presents a perspective on ESOP valuation practices that is now about a decade old. Surprisingly, many of the valuation issues that were timely in 1995 are still timely in 2005. This discussion has been edited and updated, particularly with regard to regulatory, legislative, and taxation changes that occurred during the last decade.

The mid-1990s experienced a number of recent trends with regard to employee stock ownership plan (ESOP) formation, ESOP financing and refinancing, and ESOP employer corporation restructuring. These recent trends have both direct and indirect impacts (1) on ESOP employer corporation stock valuations and (2) on ESOP valuation analysts.

These recent ESOP trends are summarized below:

1. smaller, less leveraged ESOP formation transactions—as compared to the larger highly leveraged ESOP transaction of the late 1980s;
2. more seller-provided financing than the typical ESOP stock purchase transaction—in exchange for the favorable Section 1042 "rollover" provisions to the selling shareholder;
3. a significant number of refinancings and restructurings of the highly leveraged ESOP employer corporation acquisitions of the late 1980s;
4. greater recognition of the enhanced competitive economic position associated with employee-owned companies;
5. increased awareness of the economic and legal liability associated with the sponsor company ESOP stock repurchase obligation;

6. enhanced awareness of employee ownership-related corporate governance issues, particularly in cases where the ESOP has a controlling ownership interest in the employer corporation;
7. augmented recognition of the need for all parties to an ESOP ownership transaction to comply with the ERISA-mandated fiduciary rules, particularly (1) in light of a number of milestone judicial decisions and (2) in light of the recent willingness of the U.S. Department of Labor to vigorously pursue alleged fiduciary obligation violations; and
8. increased union awareness of, and support of, ESOP ownership—with regard to both (1) financially healthy unionized companies and (2) financially distressed unionized companies.

This discussion is presented in light of these recent trends (1) with respect to employee corporate ownership and (2) with respect to ESOP formations, financings, and restructurings.

ESOP BASIC ECONOMIC BENEFITS

The Employee Retirement Income Security Act of 1974 (ERISA) classified an employee stock ownership plan (ESOP) as a statutorily defined employee pension benefit plan. According to ERISA, an ESOP is defined as a qualified retirement plan designed to invest primarily in the employer's securities, thus providing a means for employees to have an ownership interest in the company for which they work.

There are numerous taxation, financing, and organizational benefits to ESOP ownership of employer companies. The primary economic and organizational benefits of ESOP corporate ownership include the following:

1. an ESOP provides a means for employees to share in the direct ownership of the employer corporation;
2. an ESOP provides a means of liquidity for closely held corporation stockholders and for their beneficiaries;
3. an ESOP is an effective transactional vehicle for corporate financing and refinancing:
   a. for raising new capital, and
   b. for financing a leveraged buyout (involving either the sale of the entire sponsor company or of a partial interest in the sponsor company);

4. an ESOP involves numerous federal income tax advantages to the employer corporation sellers, to the ESOP participants, and (as of the mid-1990s), to certain sources of financing for leveraged ESOP transactions; and
5. an ESOP has been demonstrated to promote improved employee relations and employee productivity.

BASIC FEATURES OF AN ESOP

Under ERISA, an ESOP is a qualified employee benefit plan designed to invest primarily in employer corporation securities. However, neither the ERISA nor the relevant Treasury regulations adequately define the term *primarily*. While most ESOPs are invested entirely in the employer corporation securities, various interpretations have suggested that the plan may need to only be invested over 50 percent in such employer corporation securities.

The eligible employer corporation securities can be either:

1. common stock or
2. preferred stock that is convertible into common stock.

While most ESOPs are invested in common stock, there are certain income tax advantages to the ESOP ownership of convertible preferred stock.

ESOP INCOME TAX INCENTIVES

Under the Internal Revenue Code, several attractive taxation incentives are available to both employer corporations and to selling stockholders in connection with ESOP formations, ESOP contributions, and ESOP financing. The primary ESOP-related income taxation incentives are as follows:

1. Periodic contributions to the ESOP are a tax-deductible expense to the employer corporation, whether the contributions are made in the form of cash or employer corporation stock.
2. Selling stockholders can "roll over" the proceeds of the sale of the employer corporation stock to the ESOP tax free, deferring the capital gains tax on the sale until the qualified replacement securities purchased with the ESOP sale proceeds are ultimately sold; this is often called the Section 1042 "rollover."

3. Dividends paid on ESOP-owned employer corporation securities can be tax-deductible to the paying employer corporation.
4. As of 1995, under certain conditions, certain lenders recognized only half the interest received on an ESOP acquisition loan as taxable income; this tax attribute historically resulted in below-market interest rate loans on ESOP employer stock acquisitions.

Periodic Contributions to the Plan Are Tax Deductible

Employer corporation contributions to an ESOP are a tax-deductible expense to the corporation, regardless of whether the contribution is made in cash or in employer corporation stock.

Cash contributions can be used to buy employer corporation stock from existing stockholders or, in the case of a leveraged ESOP, to make payments on the ESOP stock acquisition debt. In the latter case, the economic effect is that the acquisition loan principal payments, as well as the loan interest payments, become tax-deductible expenses to the employer corporation.

If the periodic contribution to the ESOP is made in employer corporation stock (either treasury stock or authorized but unissued shares of stock), then there is some dilution to the existing stockholders—but the effect on company cash flow generally is positive. As the ESOP contribution is a deduction from taxable income, it usually results in a lower employer corporation effective income tax expense—with no corresponding cash outlay.

The annual employer contribution limitation normally is 15 percent of eligible employer corporation payroll. In some cases, it may be as high as 25 percent of employer corporation annual payroll.

Tax-Free Rollover on the Sale of Stock to an ESOP

An employer corporation stockholder selling stock to an ESOP can reinvest the proceeds on a Section 1042 tax-free "rollover"—if the ESOP owns at least 30 percent of the employer corporation's stock immediately after the sale. In order to qualify for the tax-free "rollover," the selling stockholder must invest the sale proceeds in stock, debt, or options of one or more domestic operating corporations within a 15-month period—beginning three months before the date of the sale.

Further, notice of the Section 1042 election must be filed on the appropriate income tax return during the taxable year of the stock sale.

As long as the ESOP maintains its 30 percent ownership of the outstanding stock of the employer corporation, additional sales of stock to the ESOP—in any amounts—are eligible for the Section 1042 tax-free "rollover" treatment.

Dividends Tax Deductible to the Employer Corporation

Dividends paid on the employer stock held by an ESOP are a tax-deductible expense to the employer corporation—either (1) if they are paid directly to the plan participants or (2) if they are paid to the ESOP and then distributed to the plan participants or to their beneficiaries no later than 90 days after the close of the plan year.

Dividends distributions also qualify as a tax-deductible expense if the dividends are used to make the debt service payments of principal and/or interest on the loan that was used by the ESOP to acquire the employer corporation stock. This tax attribute, of course, greatly enhances the stock acquisition ability of leveraged ESOPs. This is because such tax-deductible dividends can be paid in addition to the maximum contributions allowed on the basis of a percentage of eligible payroll.

Also, the ability to use tax-deductible dividends to service ESOP stock acquisition debt enhances the attractiveness of using convertible preferred stock (which normally would carry a slightly higher dividend rate than common stock) instead of using common stock as the equity security in an ESOP.

ESOP Loan Interest Excluded from Taxable Income

In the mid-1990s, under certain circumstances involving the purchase of a controlling interest in the employer corporation by an ESOP, commercial lenders—such as banks, insurance companies, and regulated investment companies—excluded from their taxable income 50 percent of the interest they received on ESOP stock acquisition loans. Such loans were made either directly to the ESOP or to the employer corporation, which in turn lent the loan proceeds directly to the ESOP.

As a result of this 1990-era income tax attribute, some financial institutions were more inclined to seek ESOP loan business. In addition, ESOP loans were used as a tool for either corporate leveraged buyouts or for raising capital for the employer corporation. This was because ESOP debt could typically be borrowed at interest rates below those that the sponsor company would have paid for conventional debt financing.

EMPLOYER CORPORATION VALUATION ISSUES

ERISA requires ESOPs to pay no more than "adequate consideration" when investing in qualifying employer corporation securities. This means that plan trustees and fiduciaries must estimate, in good faith, the fair market value of employer corporation securities (1) pursuant to the terms of the plan and (2) in accordance with regulations issued by the Secretary of Labor and the Internal Revenue Service.

On May 17, 1988, the DOL issued the "Proposed Regulation Relating to the Definition of Adequate Consideration." While the DOL never finalized—and ultimately withdrew—the proposed regulation, valuation analysts still refer to the "proposed regulations" for professional guidance.

As a reference source, the Valuation Advisory Committee of The ESOP Association has provided important guidance with respect to the valuation of ESOP employer corporation stock. This valuation guidance is relevant to ESOP fiduciaries, to sponsoring employer corporations, and to financial adviser and other professionals rendering advice to these plans. This guidance is in the form of the publication *Valuing ESOP Shares* and *An Introduction to ESOP Valuations* book published by The ESOP Association. The ESOP Association publications generally discuss the following valuation topics:

1. the DOL proposed regulation and its implications for employer corporation security valuation,
2. commonly accepted practices for estimating the fair market value of closely held employer corporation stock for ESOP purposes, and
3. four special valuation positions adopted by the Valuation Advisory Committee of The ESOP Association:
   a. discount for lack of marketability,
   b. repurchase liability,
   c. price premium for control, and
   d. effects of leverage.

Reference to *Valuing ESOP Shares* and *An Introduction to ESOP Valuations*, and to any other published positions of The ESOP Association Valuation

Advisory Committee, is highly recommended to ESOP advisers, to ESOP trustees, and to ESOP participants.

ESOP EMPLOYER CORPORATION STOCK VALUATION FACTORS

The DOL proposed regulation defined fair market value as:

> . . . the price at which an asset would change hands between a willing buyer and a willing seller when the former is not under any compulsion to buy and the latter is not under any compulsion to sell, and both parties are able, as well as willing, to trade and are well informed about the asset and the market for such asset. (Proposed Regulation Relating to the Definition of Adequate Consideration, 53 Fed. Reg. 17,632 (1988)(to be codified at 29 CFR Part 2510, p. 17634.)

The DOL proposed regulation requires the fair market value of an employer corporation security:

1. to be estimated as of the date of the transaction involving the subject security;
2. to be estimated without considering transactions resulting from other than arm's-length negotiations, such as distressed sales;
3. to reflect the application of "sound business principles of evaluation"; and
4. to be recorded in a document meeting the reporting requirements of the proposed regulation.

This value definition and these analytical requirements, with the exception of the requirement for written report documentation, follow the guidance for estimating the fair market value of closely held corporation securities found in Internal Revenue Service Revenue Ruling 59-60.

Written Valuation Report

When the subject security is the stock of a closely held employer corporation, the DOL proposed regulation requires that the written valuation report include an assessment of all "relevant factors" plus an assessment of the following specific factors:

1. the nature of the business and the history of the enterprise from its inception;
2. the economic outlook in general, and the condition and outlook of the specific industry in particular;
3. the book value of the securities and the financial condition of the business;
4. the earnings capacity of the company;
5. the dividend-paying capacity of the company;
6. whether or not the enterprise has goodwill or other intangible value;
7. the market price of securities of corporations engaged in the same or a similar line of business, which are actively traded in a free and open market, either on an exchange or other-the-counter;
8. the marketability, or lack thereof, of the securities; where the plan is the purchaser of the securities that are subject to "put" rights and such rights are taken into account in reducing the discount for lack of marketability, such assessment shall include consideration of the extent to which such rights are enforceable, as well as the company's ability to meet its obligations with respect to the 'put' rights (taking into account the company's financial strength and liquidity); and
9. whether or not the seller would be able to obtain a control premium from an unrelated third party with regard to the block of securities being valued, provided that in cases where a control premium is taken into account:
    a. actual control (both in form and in substance) is passed to the purchaser with the sale, or will pass to the purchaser within a reasonable time pursuant to a binding agreement in effect at the time of the sale, and
    b. it is reasonable to assume that the purchaser's control will not be dissipated within a short period of time subsequent to acquisition (Proposed Regulation Relating to the Definition of Adequate Consideration, p. 17638).

The requirement to assess factors (1) through (7) as well as all relevant factors, such as the definition of fair market value, is consistent with Revenue Ruling 59-60. Factors (8) and (9) are additional factors with specific application to ESOP-owned employer corporation securities.

Requirement of Independent Annual Stock Appraisal

The Tax Reform Act of 1986 mandated that ESOP-owned employer corporation securities that are not readily traded on organized exchanges must be appraised annually by a qualified, independent appraiser. A form stating the appraised value, signed by the independent appraiser, must be filed with the Service.

The DOL proposed regulation provides guidelines as to what constitutes "adequate consideration." The proposed regulation says that in order for plan fiduciaries to meet the requirement of estimating fair market value in good faith, the valuation must be performed by someone who is independent of all parties to the transaction. The DOL proposed regulation also requires a written valuation report and specifies its minimum content.

An appraisal of ESOP-owned employer corporation stock is required:

1. when the ESOP makes its first acquisition of employer corporation stock,
2. at least annually thereafter (although some ESOP-owned companies routinely have their stock appraisals updated semiannually or even quarterly),
3. whenever there is an employer corporation stock sale transaction with a controlling stockholder or with a member of a control group, and
4. if the ESOP sells out its stock position.

Qualifications of an Independent Appraiser

With regard to who qualifies as an "independent appraiser," the DOL notes that under Section 401(a)(28)(C), ESOP fiduciaries must employ an independent valuation practitioner meeting requirements similar to the requirements of the regulations under Section 170(a)(1). Section 170 relates to independent appraisals of donations to charitable organizations.

A qualified valuation analyst—according to these regulations—is a person who, among other qualifications:

1. is not a party to the transaction, is not related to any party to the transaction, is not married to any person with a relationship to the transaction, is not regularly used by any of the parties to the transaction, and who does not perform a majority of appraisals for these persons;
2. holds himself out to the public as a valuation practitioner or who performs appraisals on a regular basis;

3. is qualified to make appraisals of the type of property being valued including, by background, experience, education, and memberships, if any, in professional associations;
4. understands that an intentionally false or fraudulent overstatement of value may subject the valuation practitioner to a civil penalty; and
5. receives an appraisal fee that is not based upon a percentage of the appraised value of the property.

As stated in the DOL proposed regulation, each valuation report prepared in compliance with the fair market value requirement must contain the following information:

1. a summary of the qualifications to evaluate assets of the type being valued of the person making the valuation;
2. a statement of asset's value, a statement of methods used in determining that value, and the reasons for the valuation in light of those methods;
3. a full description of the asset being valued;
4. the factors taken into account in making the valuation, including any restrictions, understandings, agreements or obligations limiting the use or disposition of the property;
5. the purpose for which valuation was made;
6. the relevance or significance accorded to the valuation methodologies taken into account;
7. the effective date of valuation; and
8. in cases where a valuation report has been prepared, the signature of the person making valuation and date the report was signed (Proposed Regulation Relating to the Definition of Adequate Consideration, pp. 17637-38).

OWNERSHIP CONTROL VERSUS LACK OF OWNERSHIP CONTROL FOR EMPLOYER STOCK VALUATION

Valuation analysts generally agree that the employer corporation valuation procedures will differ depending on the appropriate level of value—that is whether the ESOP owns: (1) a noncontrolling ownership interest or (2) a controlling ownership interest. Typically, a buyer will pay a price premium for a controlling ownership interest in a business enterprise if the buyer expects to make changes that will:

1. enhance the economic income–generating aspects of the subject business, or
2. in some other way will improve the economic situation for the subject business.

This additional value is evidenced by a higher price relative to the price that would be paid for a noncontrolling ownership interest in the same business.

However, ESOP valuation analysts sometimes differ in their application of an ownership control premium to the employer corporation stock purchased by an ESOP. Most analysts agree that an ESOP should be able to pay whatever a hypothetical third-party willing buyer would pay for the subject block of employer corporation stock.

In other words, most analysts recognize that the estimation of fair market value is not dictated by arbitrary percentage limitations (e.g., greater than or less than 50 percent equity ownership). Rather, fair market value is estimated by what an independent, willing buyer would pay to an independent, willing seller.

Notwithstanding differences of opinion among ESOP valuation analysts, certain general factors should be considered when valuing a block of employer corporation stock that carries elements of control. The ESOP Association Valuation Advisory Committee suggests the following as factors to consider when estimating the appropriate ownership control price premium, if any:

1. the elements of ownership control inherent in the particular block of stock;
2. the degree of ownership control—effective, operating, and absolute;
3. the aggregate percentage interest purchased or held by the ESOP—regardless of whether the sellers constituted noncontrolling or control interests;
4. the potential for control, such as binding agreements with other shareholders that result in the passing of ownership control to the ESOP;
5. the distribution of the total stock ownership;
6. any empirical evidence of ownership control premiums actually paid in similar transactions;

7. any value enhancements that may result from the passing of ownership control (e.g., effective use of leverage elimination of excess compensation paid to selling shareholders, sale of undervalued assets, etc.);
8. any value enhancement due to a put right; and
9. the rights and obligations under the employer corporation's articles of incorporation and state law.

DISCOUNT FOR LACK OF MARKETABILITY

Another issue in employer corporation stock valuations is whether, or the extent to which, some valuation adjustment should be applied for the lack of marketability of the ESOP-owned stock. Certainly, the fair market value of ESOP-owned employer stock is dependent, in part, on its marketability. Marketability, of course, is the ability of the investor to sell the stock and turn it into cash quickly.

On one end of the marketability spectrum, there are relatively few potential buyers for shares in most closely held corporations (especially for noncontrolling ownership interests). It may take months to market these shares and to receive payment. On the other end of the marketability spectrum, shares in publicly traded corporations have almost instant marketability on an organized securities exchange. Shares of publicly traded companies have high liquidity since the seller can receive cash within a few business days.

Clearly, the economic feature of marketability adds value. Several empirical studies have indicated that the value of shares with restricted marketability is substantially less than the value of actively traded shares in the same corporation. Thus, relative to the value of the actively traded shares, the value of the restricted shares suffers from a discount for lack of marketability.

In many ESOP-owned stock valuations, the fair market value estimate is based on market comparisons to securities of publicly traded guideline companies. The value conclusion estimated from this valuation method is on a marketable, noncontrolling ownership basis. This level of value is sometimes referred to as an "as if freely traded value" or a "publicly traded equivalent value." If this is the preliminary basis of value, then some discount for lack of marketability may be appropriate in order to estimate the fair market value of shares in a typical closely held corporation.

The ESOP Put Option

The economic factor that generally distinguishes ESOP-owned shares from non-ESOP-owned shares in a closely held corporation is the put option associated with the ESOP-owned shares. A put option requires the employer corporation to repurchase the distributed employer securities (1) unless the ESOP distributes benefits in cash or (2) unless the ESOP repurchases the distributed shares.

Under Section 409(h)(1)(B), employer corporation securities that are acquired by an ESOP after December 31, 1979, must be subject to a put option. This is true if the securities are not readily tradable on an organized market at the time of distribution to the plan participants. Employer corporation securities acquired with the proceeds of an ESOP stock purchase loan after September 30, 1976, must also be subject to a put option. Again, this rule applies if the shares are not readily tradable upon distribution.

For employer corporation securities not subject to these mandatory put option requirements, a voluntary put option may be provided by the employer corporation.

Written Assessment of Stock Marketability

In the DOL proposed regulation, a written assessment of the marketability of the shares held by the ESOP is required. The proposed regulation states the following with respect to a discount for lack of marketability:

> Where the plan is the purchaser of securities that are subject to "put" rights and such rights are taken into account in reducing the discount for lack of marketability, such assessment shall include consideration of the extent to which such rights are enforceable, as well as the company's ability to meet its obligation with respect to the "put" rights (taking into account the company's financial strength and liquidity). (Proposed Regulation Relating to the Definition of Adequate Consideration, p. 17638.)

The effect of the ESOP put option is to generally enhance the marketability and the liquidity of the plan participant's ownership interest. Therefore, the effect of the put option is to reduce (or perhaps to eliminate) the appropriate discount for lack of marketability. ESOP valuation analysts may also evaluate the features of the subject put option, including payment terms, as well as the employer corporation's record in redeeming shares.

Ultimately, the estimation of the appropriate amount of the valuation discount to conclude, if any, is a function of the professional judgment of the ESOP valuation practitioner.

The ESOP Repurchase Liability

Another economic feature unique to an ESOP is the repurchase liability that stems from the ESOP put option. The repurchase liability tends to increase over time (1) as the ESOP shares vest and (2) as the value of employer corporation increases.

The repurchase liability arising from the terms of the ESOP is normally not considered to significantly affect the discount for lack of marketability. This is true unless the ability to repurchase the stock is impaired or the employer corporation's ability to honor the put option is in question. The DOL proposed guidelines make it clear, however, that the employer corporation's financial ability to meet its put obligations should be considered when assessing an appropriate discount for lack of marketability.

The financial position of the ESOP trust should also be considered with regard to this lack of marketability issue. If the ESOP trust has excess cash, then it may repurchase the shares distributed to participants—rather than having the shares repurchased by the employer corporation.

In summary, the principal economic factors that influence the discount for lack of marketability with regard to ESOP-owned employer corporation stock are summarized below:

1. the provisions of the ESOP plan documents, including the put rights,
2. the financial strength and the solvency of the employer corporation,
3. the size of the block of employer corporation securities owned by the ESOP,
4. the degree of liquidity of the particular securities,
5. the borrowing capacity of the employer corporation,
6. the repurchase liability and the funding thereof,
7. any past repurchase experience of ESOP shares by the employer corporation,
8. the form and timing of the payment by the employer corporation to the selling shareholders, and
9. the overall priority of acknowledged and contingent financial claims that may conflict with achieving liquidity for plan participants over time.

SUMMARY AND CONCLUSION

This discussion explained how the use of an ESOP can provide financial incentives for employer corporations and for selling stockholders. However, in order to achieve these economic benefits, employer corporations should follow strict and complex rules to protect the interests (1) of the ESOP plan participants and (2) of their beneficiaries.

The employer corporation stock valuation is an important component of ESOP compliance. And, unsupported (or unsupportable) ESOP valuations have been the source of a significant proportion of ESOP compliance problems.

Many ESOP employer stock valuation problems have occurred because:

1. the valuation was lacking in independence, objectivity, or an understanding of valuation principles and/or regulatory or legal guidelines, or
2. of a lack of adequate written documentation of the stock valuation process and employer corporation stock value conclusion.

Chapter 9

Valuation Issues Related to Mature ESOPs

INTRODUCTION

ESOPs have been used during the past 30 years to provide (1) an ownership transition mechanism for closely held business owners, (2) a source of retirement benefits to sponsor company employees, (3) an internal market for the sale of employer corporation securities, and (4) a source of low-cost financing for corporate expansion (or other purposes). The sale of employer corporation stock from closely held business owners to an ESOP became particularly advantageous during the 1980s. This was due to favorable federal income tax laws related to both (1) the selling stockholders and (2) the employer corporation.

Historically, many ownership transition transactions involving the creation of new ESOPs were driven by the income tax advantages to the selling stockholders, to the financing sources, and to the employer corporation. Frequently, the longer-term ESOP funding requirements—related to both (1) ESOP share purchase requirements and for (2) sustaining the level of benefits for newer employees—received considerably less attention in the ESOP formation and implementation stage.

Also, historically, the concept of an ESOP as long term employee benefit plan—and as a potential tool for improvement of management/employee relationships and of employee productivity—often was given less consideration.

As many of the ESOPs that were formed in the 1980s have matured, the longer-term attributes of these plans are becoming more apparent. Employer corporation management, participating employees, and ESOP practitioners have become increasingly focused upon the effects of the ESOP's maturity (1) on the sponsor company's financial position and (2) on the annual per share value of the employer corporation stock.

In addition, certain ESOP stock valuation issues are avoidable when sponsor companies, ESOP fiduciaries, and valuation analysts understand the most appropriate valuation methods and the most appropriate means of dealing with these issues.

This discussion focuses on the valuation issues that specifically affect mature ESOPs. We will consider alternative ways that ESOP valuation practitioners may deal with these issues. And, we will consider when employer corporation management and ESOP plan fiduciaries should know about these issues in order to effectively communicate with the valuation analyst.

VALUATION ISSUES WITH REGARD TO MATURE ESOPS

Certain employer corporation valuation issues are more pronounced with regard to mature ESOPs. For purposes of this discussion, mature ESOPs include ESOPs with mature employer corporation stock acquisition debt. Some of these employer corporation stock valuation issues include the following:

1. the treatment of employee benefit plan expenses (both on a historical and on a prospective basis), including the level of ESOP contributions and/or ESOP dividends—relative to the analysis of the earnings fundamentals;
2. the treatment of the ESOP stock acquisition debt, along with the employer corporation's regular interest bearing debt, in the calculation of residual business enterprise equity value;
3. the effect of the employer corporation's capital structure (i.e., the company's debt/equity mix), both on the estimation of the appropriate equity risk component (of the required rate of return on equity capital) and on the fair market value of the employer securities;
4. the impact of volatility in the employer corporation's earnings, of the pricing of guideline publicly traded companies in the industry, and of the current capital market price/performance trends upon the estimation of the value of the ESOP-owned stock; and
5. the determination of the level of investment liquidity possessed by the ESOP-owned shares, including a consideration of the ESOP share repurchase liability under the put option provisions of the ESOP trust plan.

ESOP-RELATED FAIRNESS ISSUES

The way in which each of these issues is treated during the valuation process of the ESOP-owned shares will influence the estimation of fair market value of those shares. And, the fair market value of the ESOP-owned shares affects the degree of fairness and equity accorded to the ESOP participants. Over time, the prices paid for the employer shares purchased from departing ESOP participants will impact the value of the residual equity that is available for those ESOP participants who remain with the employer corporation.

Certainly, sponsor company employees with 20 or more years until retirement should anticipate per share values at retirement that are not adversely influenced by the per share values that were paid to those employees who departed during prior periods.

CONSIDERATION OF THESE ESOP-RELATED ISSUES

Serious consideration of these ESOP-related valuation issues should begin during the ESOP feasibility and implementation phase for new ESOPs. And, serious consideration of these valuation issues should continue during the life cycle of the ESOP.

Consideration during the ESOP feasibility phase should influence both the ESOP plan design and the stock purchase transaction structure. For mature ESOPs, the valuation issues mentioned above change in relative importance over time. Accordingly, these valuation issues should be examined each year. This annual examination should consider their effect, if any, on the fair market value of the employer corporation stock.

Several means of dealing with these valuation issues are summarized in the following paragraphs.

Employee Benefit Plan Expense—Including the Annual ESOP Contribution

Typically, the employer corporation reported income fundamentals are adjusted or normalized in the ESOP stock valuation process. In this normalization procedure, an adjustment is made to add back most or all of the annual ESOP contribution in order to estimate normalized earning power for the employer corporation.

In leveraged ESOP situations, this procedure is performed as an earnings adjustment in order to reflect that the ESOP contribution is actually a component of the ESOP financing strategy. In nonleveraged ESOPs, a similar earnings adjustment may be made in order to reflect the noncash nature of a stock contribution.

This "adding back" of the annual ESOP contribution to the employer corporation earnings measures implies that the employer corporation will require no cash benefit plan contributions after:

1. the repayment of the ESOP debt, or
2. the completion of the planned stock contributions to the ESOP trust.

These normalization adjustments to reported income fundamentals imply that the employer corporation may achieve these normalized earnings levels (both in terms of dollars and of percentages of revenue) indefinitely.

This normalization procedure in the valuation process will produce a material change in concluded fair market value in the first year after:

1. the ESOP stock acquisition debt is repaid, or
2. the ESOP stock contributions are replaced by cash contributions to the ESOP (or by another employee benefit plan).

In each of the above-described situations, the appropriate employee benefit plan expense level in the annual employer corporation stock valuation should be estimated by considering:

1. the industry employee benefit expense norms,
2. the company-specific benefit expense experience, and
3. management estimates of sustainable employee benefit plan expense.

Based on consideration of these three factors, the analyst may make an appropriate normalization adjustment to the reported employer corporation income measures.

Interest-Bearing Debt—Including the ESOP Share Acquisition Debt

The ESOP stock acquisition debt is either a direct or a contingent obligation of the employer corporation. And, as such, along with other forms of interest-bearing debt (IBD), it has a measurable impact on the overall equity value of the employer corporation.

Consideration of the impact of IBD on the employer corporation stock value often requires the use of invested capital (i.e., total IBD and stockholder's equity) valuation procedures. In the valuation of most non-financial business entities, these invested capital valuation procedures are used for a proper estimation of the net cash flow claim priority and other risk-related attributes of the employer corporation.

The application of invested capital valuation procedures is an effective way of dealing with this valuation issue. Invested capital valuation procedures are based on performance measures and earnings fundamentals that consider the total of the employer corporation IBD and stockholders' equity.

The estimation of the market value of the employer corporation stock begins with the calculation of the total invested capital value of the sponsor company (i.e., the value of an operating business asset, regardless of the sponsor company debt and equity structure). Total invested capital value may be estimated by capitalizing debt-free income, cash flow, revenue, or other financial fundamentals.

The deduction of the estimated market value of IBD, including the ESOP debt, from total invested capital value estimates the residual value of the employer corporation stockholders' equity. Since ESOP debt is repaid through pretax contributions to the ESOP, the present value of the income tax benefits may be added to the residual value estimate of the employer corporation stockholders' equity.

Invested Capital Composition

The invested capital composition is one of the financial attributes which may impact the equity value of the employer corporation. At the same time, highly leveraged corporations may have greater equity return potential, higher levels of stock value volatility, and greater equity risk attributes. Accordingly, it is important that the employer corporation stock valuation analysis incorporate the balance sheet attributes of the sponsor company.

The employer corporation's balance sheet reflects its invested capital components on a book value basis. In most cases, the sponsor company's balance sheet provides a guideline as to the employer corporation's additional debt capacity. Also, the company's balance sheet is an integral component to a net cash flow analysis. Invested capital valuation procedures, including analysis of the company's balance sheet strength, the collateral value of its assets, and the market values of its interest-bearing debt, provide the necessary foundation for estimating the impact of the company's capital structure on the ESOP share value.

ESOP Employer Corporation Share Value Volatility

Annual variations in reported income (however defined) are common for all businesses, whether publicly traded or privately held. In many instances, however, this periodic variation in earnings is temporary. And, the periodic variation in company income may not be a good barometer of longer-term value of the subject business enterprise. As an employee benefit plan, an ESOP is a long-term equity investor—rather than a short term market trader.

Other than to accommodate the account diversification provisions, an ESOP must remain invested in employer corporation securities. Accordingly, it is appropriate for the valuation analyst to consider a long-term investor's investment time horizon in the ESOP stock valuation process.

A long-term investment time horizon perspective will consider that variations in year-to-year ESOP stock values will be principally affected by the following factors:

1. changes in the sponsoring company's longer-term financial performance fundamentals,
2. sustainable alterations in the pricing of "guideline" publicly traded company industry participants, and
3. long-term changes to other material external economic variables or capital market pricing variables.

Long-Term Investment Perspective

In order to reflect the ESOP share value volatility that would be considered by a long-term investor, the employer stock valuation should examine guideline pricing evidence on both a current and a longer-term perspective.

This analysis is performed in order to determine if current market pricing is reasonably in line with normal, long-term security pricing norms—that is, such price/financial fundamental relationships as: (1) price/net income, price/book value, and market value of invested capital (MVIC) to EBIT, EBITDA, debt-free cash flow, and so forth.

The valuation analyst may consider longer-term security pricing data where they are more reflective of the guideline industry long-term security pricing relationships. It may also be appropriate for the valuation analyst to consider both the current and the longer-term financial fundamentals of the employer corporation. Typically, the appropriate historical period subject to analysis is a function of industry characteristics such as cyclicality, raw materials pricing, acquisition/divestiture activity, changes to competitive dynamics/efficiencies, and so forth.

It is also appropriate for the valuation analyst to consider several employer corporation performance measures and invested capital financial fundamentals in order to develop value indications. The valuation analyst will typically consider (1) various income measures, such as earnings before interest and taxes (EBIT), earnings before depreciation, amortization, interest, and taxes (EBITDA), and (2) various measures of invested capital, such as stockholders' equity, total invested capital (long-term debt and stockholders' equity), or tangible net asset value.

And, it is appropriate for the valuation analyst to analyze the employer corporation's business plan, operating forecast, or financial projections in order to develop value indications. The valuation analyst will perform appropriate due diligence projections to determine that the plan assumptions and variables are reasonable and supportable. Traditional security analysis and investment theory emphasize the importance of future expectations with regard to the estimation of equity value.

Estimation of the Liquidity (or Illiquidity) of the ESOP Employer Corporation Shares

The proposition that fractional equity ownership interests in closely held corporations have limited liquidity is well documented by empirical evidence that has been gathered over the past 30 years. This evidence, as applied by valuation analysts, supports discounts for a lack of investment liquidity (sometimes called lack of marketability) that often fall in the range of 25 percent to 45 percent.

These valuation adjustments are applied to the indicated market values of closely held corporations that are estimated by reference to (1) public market pricing of guideline companies and/or (2) empirical evidence of longer-term equity returns derived from guideline public market evidence.

The closely held corporation ESOP holds shares of stock that possess these same illiquidity attributes, except for the "internal market" created by the ESOP put option.

Therefore, the valuation analyst will typically consider the capacity of the employer corporation to meet its put option obligations—in order to assess the level of liquidity provided by the employer corporation (relative to the public capital markets that were used as guidance for price/performance evidence).

The assessment of the employer corporation's capacity to meet its share repurchase obligations under the ESOP put option is also suggested in the DOL Proposed Regulation relating to adequate consideration. For any particular employer corporation, the impact of the ESOP repurchase obligation will vary based on:

1. internal company-specific factors, such as the projected level of sponsor company share repurchase requirements, the existing and projected employer corporation capital structure and balance sheet, and the degree of operating leverage in the employer corporation's expense mix, and
2. external factors, including the level of industry volatility and current capital market price/performance evidence.

SUMMARY AND CONCLUSION

The periodic valuation of employer corporation shares in a mature ESOP affects the ability of both the sponsor company and its shareholders to achieve their stated objectives. There are many company-specific factors and external factors that should be given special attention with regard to the valuation of employer corporation shares owned by the mature ESOP.

The factors that should be considered with regard to the valuation of employer corporation shares in the mature ESOP include: (1) incorporating a longer-term ESOP investment time horizon, and (2) considering the impact of the ESOP repurchase liability on the investment marketability of the ESOP-owned employer shares.

In summary, the analysis and appraisal of the employer corporation securities held by the mature (or "seasoned") ESOP require the experience, expertise, and judgment of the mature (or "seasoned") valuation analyst.

Chapter 10

The ESOP Long-Term Investment Perspective and Stock Valuation

INTRODUCTION

Employer corporation stock valuations are an important component of the administration of an ESOP. The employer stock valuation is an important component in the ESOP formation. The valuation influences how much the ESOP will pay for the initial employer corporation stock purchase transaction. In addition, in the case of an ESOP that owns the stock of a closely held corporation, annual employer stock appraisals are required by the Internal Revenue Service and the U.S. Labor Department. An important consideration in the ESOP valuation process is that the valuation analyst recognize the specific characteristics that differentiate an ESOP from other types of equity investors.

For example, investors in public securities have a relatively short-term investment time horizon perspective. However, ESOP participants, by both choice and necessity, have a long-term investment time horizon perspective. ESOP participants are interested in long-term returns, long-term capital appreciation, and the accumulation of wealth for employee retirement purposes. Since ESOP-owned employer corporation stock is usually not subject to the vagaries of capital market pricing and yield variability, some ESOP valuation procedures reduce the effects of these short-term effects in the valuation of employer corporation stock.

The estimation of employer stock fair market value will typically focus on (1) the normalized or long-term expected performance of the employer securities and (2) the long-term required rates of return on similar investment opportunities. That focus tends to reduce the effects of short-term fluctuations in market-derived yield or capitalization rates.

An employer corporation stock valuation that does not consider the ESOP long-term investment time horizon may appraise the employer securities in a vacuum. An employer stock valuation should consider the long-term historical investment performance—and the long-term investment potential—of the employer corporation. An employer stock valuation should not unduly focus on short-term capital market dynamics, including fluctuating pricing multiples of guideline publicly traded companies or fluctuating capital market debt and equity yields.

The effect of a short-term investment perspective is that ESOP-owned employer stock values may vary significantly from one valuation date to the next. In fact, due to the highly leveraged nature of some ESOP-owned companies, loans on a short-term investment horizon may cause ESOP share values to fluctuate more than some capital market indicators (i.e., stock prices, valuation pricing multiples, debt and equity rates of return, etc.). Unpredictable variability in share values adds a degree of investment risk to the ESOP-owned employer stock investment. This investment risk, in turn, further reduces the value of the employer corporation stock, as well as the benefits to the parties to the ESOP stock purchase a transaction.

A secondary effect of a short-term investment perspective is an employer stock value indication that is counter-intuitive. For example, a valuation process that ignores the investment time horizon may conclude a declining employers stock value when the employer corporation financial and operating results are improving. This phenomenon may occur when a temporarily depressed stock market valuation pricing multiple more than offsets the positive employer corporation financial fundamentals.

EMPLOYER CORPORATION BUSINESS VALUATION APPROACHES AND METHODS

The common ESOP-owned employer corporation stock valuation approaches and methods are described below.

The market approach, guideline publicly traded company method—This method values the employer corporation stock by reference to market-extracted valuation pricing multiples of guideline publicly traded companies. The more common market-derived pricing multiples include: price to earnings before interest and taxes (EBIT), price to earnings before interest, taxes, depreciation, and amortization (EBITDA), price to net income, price to net cash flow, price to revenue, and others. This valuation method typically produces a marketable, noncontrolling ownership interest level of value for the subject employer stock.

The market approach, guideline merged and acquired company method—This method estimates value based on extracting valuation pricing multiples from completed merger and acquisition (M&A) transactions of companies in the same or similar business as the employer corporation. Based on the available data regarding the guideline M&A transaction, the analyst will calculate price to revenue, price to cash flow, and/or price to net income valuation multiples. This method typically concludes a marketable, controlling ownership interest level of value.

The income approach, discounted cash flow method—This method estimates value as the present value of the subject company's prospective net cash flow generating capacity. It typically combines an analysis of a discrete net cash flow projection period (e.g., a five-year projection period) and an analysis of the residual value of the subject company (often based on the direct capitalization of net cash flow as an annuity in perpetuity). This method may conclude either a marketable, controlling ownership interest level of value or a marketable, noncontrolling ownership interest level of value.

The asset-based approach, asset accumulation method—This method estimates value based on (1) the fair market value of all of the subject company assets less (2) the current value of subject company liabilities.

The asset accumulation method involves:

1. appraising the fair market value of the sponsor company's financial assets, e.g., securities, receivables inventory, etc.;
2. appraising the fair market value of the sponsor company's real estate and tangible personal property, e.g., land, buildings, and equipment;
3. identifying and appraising the fair market value of the sponsor company's off-balance-sheet intangible assets, such as leases, patents, trademarks, going-concern value, goodwill, etc.; and
4. subtracting the current value of (1) the sponsor company's short-term and long-term liabilities, e.g., bonds, notes, mortgages and debentures, and (2) the sponsor company's off-balance-sheet continent liabilities, e.g., environmental liabilities and litigation claims.

This method typically concludes a marketable, controlling ownership interest level of value.

These valuation methods typically estimate the value of the employer corporation total common equity. The ESOP typically owns a nonmarketable, noncontrolling ownership interest in one class of the employer corporation voting stock.

That distinction is a fundamental difference between an overall business valuation and a valuation analysis of the ESOP-owned employer corporation stock. While the ESOP trustee and the plan beneficiaries are interested in the employer corporation overall business value, they are more keenly interested in the fair market value of the stock owned by the ESOP.

To value the ESOP-owned common stock, the analyst typically starts with the employer corporation business enterprise value or total invested capital value. From this business enterprise value, the analyst subtracts the value of employer corporation long-term debt securities, convertible securities, and preferred stock. The residual amount represents the value of all classes of employer corporation common stocks. If the ESOP owns all of the employer corporation common stock, this class of stock is valued in its entirety. To complete the stock valuation process, the analyst identifies and quantifies any valuation adjustments associated with the ESOP-owned shares. These security analysis valuation adjustments may reflect some discount for lack of marketability, if appropriate, and some discount for lack of control, if appropriate.

Market Approach—Guideline Publicly Traded Company Method

Arguably, the guideline publicly traded company valuation method is most subject to the short-term variations in the capital markets. A simplistic application of this valuation method may result in an unreasonable value conclusion (1) if the employer corporation earnings are either temporarily depressed or temporarily inflated or (2) if the capital-market-derived pricing multiples are either temporarily depressed or temporarily inflated. To mitigate these temporary highs and lows in the market-derived pricing multiples, several investment time horizon valuation procedures may be considered.

First, the market-derived valuation pricing multiples may be applied against long-term averages of the employer corporation financial fundamentals. Of course, the market-derived valuation pricing multiples should be based on similar long-term time periods. The financial fundamental benchmarks may be three-year or five-year averages of earnings, net cash flow, dividends, and so on. And, the financial fundamentals may be presented as either arithmetic means or weighted averages. The objective is to focus on the long-term financial performance of the employer corporation so as to mitigate the short-term effects of cyclical earnings aberrations.

Second, the market-derived valuation pricing multiples may be based on periodic price averages, as opposed to being based on a single date price estimate. For example, the selected valuation pricing multiples, such as the price to earnings multiple, may be calculated from the average closing price of the selected publicly traded guideline companies over a period of 90 days prior to the valuation date. That price averaging procedure mitigates the effect of short-term stock market peaks or valleys that may occur around the valuation date.

Third, the market-derived valuation pricing multiples applied in the analysis may be ex ante multiples, as opposed to ex poste multiples. Ex ante pricing multiples are derived from the current stock prices of the guideline publicly traded companies compared to published security analysts' projections of the prospective financial performance of the selected guideline companies. Ex ante valuation pricing multiples are often more reflective of market watchers' and market makers' expectations of "normal" or sustainable pricing multiples than ex poste pricing multiples. This is because ex poste pricing multiples are based on current stock prices compared to published, historical earnings. The market-derived ex ante valuation pricing multiples may be applied against employer corporation management's projection of future results for the ESOP-owned company. Such projections often reflect management's expectations of a return to "normal" or sustainable earnings, after a period of abnormally high or low earnings.

These valuation procedures indicate an estimate of the fair market value of the ESOP-owned stock based on the normalized or long-term financial performance of the employer corporation—as opposed to an estimate of value based on short-term (and perhaps aberrational) influences on company performance or in stock market pricing multiples.

Market Approach—Guideline Merged and Acquired Company Method

The guideline merged and acquired company method also may be subject to the effects of short-term anomalies in employer corporation performance and short-term aberrations in the merger and acquisition market. Several investment time horizon valuation procedures may be appropriate to mitigate short-term variations in employer corporation stock values.

The market-derived merger and acquisition valuation pricing multiples may be applied against long-term averages in the employer company's financial fundamentals, provided the pricing multiples are based on similar long-term periods. The long-term financial fundamentals include three-year or five-year averages of assets, net book value, revenue, net income, and so on, that are either arithmetic means or weighted averages. Again, the objective of using multi-year financial fundamental averages is to emphasize the long-term investment characteristics of the employer corporate and to mitigate any unusual or nonrecurring short-term performance statistics.

An alternative procedure derives valuation pricing multiples from merger and acquisition transactions that span several years prior to the valuation date, as opposed to focusing on deals consummated just before the valuation date. While there is no absolute right or wrong observation period, an observation period of one to two years prior to the valuation date may help mitigate any short-term aberrations in acquisition pricing multiples.

The result of these valuation procedures is an estimate of the fair market value of the ESOP-owned employer stock from a longer-term investment time horizon perspective—as opposed to a value estimate based on (1) the short-term financial performance of the employer corporation or (2) the short term influences in the M&A market.

Income Approach—Discounted Cash Flow Method

Generally, the discounted cash flow valuation method is less susceptible to the effects of short-term aberrations in employer corporation performance or in investment market dynamics. The DCF method is a common ESOP stock valuation method given the long-term investment time horizon perspective of the plan participants. The DCF method tends to mitigate short-term aberrations because:

1. it is a prospective, or forward-looking, analysis involving a long-term cash flow projection;
2. net cash flow projections generally predict a return to normalized financial performance, even if recent performance has been unusually superior or inferior compared to the normal; and
3. the longer projection period, often five years or longer, will better reflect the earnings capacity, cash flow capacity, and dividend-paying capacity of the employer corporation over a long-term investment horizon.

But normalization procedures should still be considered in the discounted cash flow method. The base period on which the cash flow projections are made should be a normalized period. Trending off of a particularly depressed or inflated performance period may produce unrealistic cash flow projections.

In addition, the residual value analysis—the valuation of the employer corporation at the end of the discrete projection period—should consider a long-term investment time horizon. For example, residual value multiples based on a perpetuity capitalization of the terminal year's cash flow are less affected by short-term anomalies than residual value multiples based on current capital-market-derived pricing multiples.

Finally, the investment yields used to estimate an appropriate present value discount rate should be derived from long-term investment returns. A common discount rate method involves using the weighted average cost of capital, which blends the cost of debt and the cost of equity. Given the ESOP participants' long-term investment time horizon, capital costs based on long-term investment returns for debt and equity are the most appropriate.

The discounted cash flow method value indication should be a value of the ESOP-owned securities that is consistent with its long-term financial performance and the long-term investment objectives (i.e., risk tolerance and return preference) of the ESOP participants.

Asset-Based Approach—Asset Accumulation Method

Like the discounted cash flow method, the asset accumulation method is fairly resistant to the effects of short-term aberrations in employer company performance or in investment market price indices. Therefore, this valuation method tends to mitigate any short-term value aberrations because it requires discrete valuations of the sponsor company:

1. financial assets, such as cash receivables, prepared expenses, inventory, etc.;
2. real estate and tangible personal property assets, such as land, buildings, and equipment;
3. intangible assets, such as favorable leases, favorable supplier contracts, customer contracts and relationships, patents and proprietary know-how, trademarks and trade names, a trained and assembled work force, goodwill, going-concern value, etc; and
4. liabilities such as bonds, notes, mortgages, and debentures. (However, the current value of the long-term liabilities may be somewhat affected by the current trends in long-term investment rates as of the valuation date.)

Nonetheless, there are several valuation procedures within the asset accumulation method that are appropriate to the long-term investment time horizon perspective of most ESOP participants.

First, the valuation method should be applied consistently from one valuation date to another. Generally, the same assets, tangible and intangible, should be subject to appraisal. And, the same individual asset valuation approaches—such as the cost approach, market approach, and income approach—should be applied consistently over time.

In addition, the discrete valuations of individual categories of assets may reflect a long-term investment time horizon. If a cost approach is used to value certain assets (e.g., equipment, computer software, engineering drawings and documentation), the particular cost approach method may be based on long-term creation times and development costs. If a market approach is used to value other assets (e.g., land, buildings, leases, trademarks and trade names), long-term market comparable transactional data may be used. If the income approach is used to value certain assets (e.g., customer relationships, going-concern value, goodwill), the income approach method may be based on capitalization (1) of long-term average historical economic income or (2) of a long-term projection of prospective economic income. Additionally, the capitalization rate and/or the present value discount rate may be based on long-term or normalized indications of the cost of debt and the cost of equity.

The income approach normalization procedure is important in the valuation of goodwill and customer-related intangible assets. Some income approach method is typically used in the discrete valuation of the employer company's goodwill or of its customer-related intangible asset.

Valuation Adjustments

As mentioned above, one of the ways to convert the business enterprise valuation to a value of the specific security interests owned by the ESOP is by the analysis and application of valuation discounts and premiums.

Common valuation discounts reflect the illiquid nature of a closely held employer corporation, the lack of marketability of the actual block of stock owned by the ESOP (after consideration of the positive effects of the ESOP put option), the lack of control of the ESOP-owned stock (if applicable), and the security's preference (or lack thereof) on dividend distribution and liquidation proceeds.

Common valuation premiums reflect (1) the controlling ownership interest of the ESOP-owned stock (if applicable) and (2) the security's preference with regard to voting and preemptive rights, dividend and profit distributions, and liquidation proceeds.

Valuation methods to quantify discounts and premiums are typically grouped in two categories: empirical models and theoretical models.

Empirical models are based on measurable empirical evidence regarding the subject valuation discount or premium. These models often rely on published studies of discounts and extrapolation of the results of these studies to the particular ESOP-owned securities. Theoretical models construct an algorithmic relationship to quantify a discount or premium. The quantitative model is based on micro-economic data specific to the subject employer corporation. Both models attempt to isolate and quantify a specific non-systematic risk factor (or, in some cases, a specific non-systematic return factor) associated with a particular block of securities.

When the securities are owned by an ESOP, the analyst may consider a long-term investment time horizon. This consideration may affect both the selection of—and the derivation of—the models used to quantify valuation discounts and premiums. For example, whether an empirical or a theoretical model is selected, it should be based on a long-term investment trend and risk/return investment tradeoff, rather than on a short-term orientation.

SUMMARY AND CONCLUSION

The consideration of investment time horizons are intended to conclude the fair market value of the ESOP-owned employer corporation securities as of a particular valuation date. That valuation date may be the date the ESOP was formed, the date employer corporations securities were sold to or bought from the ESOP, the date the employer corporation contributed securities to the ESOP trust, or any other significant date of a transaction involving employer corporation securities and the ESOP.

Normalization procedures are not intended to distort ESOP share values or to provide hypothetical values not consistent with the actual fair market value of the employer corporation securities. Rather, normalization procedures are intended to mitigate the effects of short-term trends in capital market or merger and acquisition market indicators and short-term aberrations in the employer company's financial fundamentals.

Active capital market investors and portfolio managers may be influenced by the effects of such short-term investment phenomena. However, long-term strategic investors are much less influenced by the effects of short-term aberrational company-specific or market performance indicators. Such strategic investors take a long-term investment perspective. They consider the long-term trends in the subject company's financial and operational performance. And, they consider the long-term security yields and expected risk and rate of return tradeoffs of the organized investment markets.

Certainly, ESOP participants have a long-term investment time horizon perspective that is analogous to that of strategic investors. Accordingly, it is appropriate to consider that long-term investment perspective in estimating the fair market value of the employer corporation securities. It is appropriate to consider procedures that minimize the short-term variability of employer stock values and that quantify employer corporation stock values by reference to longer-term financial performances and investment trends.

Section III

Special ESOP Valuation Issues

Chapter 11

ESOP Valuation Discounts and Premiums

INTRODUCTION

When the ESOP owns something less than 100 percent of the stock of the employer corporation, the valuation of a fractional (or partial) ownership interest is part of the employer stock valuation process. This discussion summarizes an important component in the valuation of a fractional (i.e., less than 100 percent) ownership interest in the employer corporation stock. That component is the identification and quantification of valuation adjustments. The term "valuation adjustments" includes both valuation discounts and premiums.

One advantage of using the term "valuation adjustment" is that unsophisticated readers of ESOP stock valuation reports will often correctly interpret this procedure as an adjustment required in order to get to (or arrive at) the appropriate standard of value. On the other hand, unsophisticated readers of ESOP stock valuation reports will often incorrectly interpret the term discount or premium as an adjustment performed to get from (or after) the appropriate standard of value in order to get to (or arrive at) a "discounted" valuation conclusion. This discussion uses the terms valuation "discounts and premiums" and valuation "adjustments" interchangeably.

There are at least three circumstances when it is appropriate for the analyst to consider the application of valuation adjustments in an employer stock valuation performed for ESOP purposes:

1. when the ESOP-owned stock is other than a marketable, absolute controlling ownership interest in the employer corporation;
2. when the subject employer corporation securities are materially different in any way from the guideline publicly traded companies and/or

guideline merger and acquisition transactions used to develop any of the valuation variables used in the analysis; and

3. when the employer corporation is subject to any nonsystematic risk or expected return features that would make it materially different from the typical business entity in the employer corporation's industry.

The identification and quantification of valuation adjustments is common in the ESOP employer corporation stock valuation process. For example, in the typical employer corporation valuation engagement, the subject ESOP ownership interest is rarely an absolute controlling ownership interest, nor is it often readily marketable. Even if the ESOP-owned stock is a controlling ownership interest in a closely held employer corporation, that ownership position may not represent absolute control. Therefore, valuation adjustments—that is, valuation discounts and premiums—are often a necessary consideration in most closely held employer corporation valuations.

MODELS COMMONLY USED TO ESTIMATE VALUATION ADJUSTMENTS

There are four models (or methods) that are typically used to estimate valuation adjustments. They are:

1. *Theoretical models*—that is, methods based on (1) the identification and isolation of one adjustment factor in the business valuation process and (2) the application of deductible reasoning to the generally accepted business valuation approaches and methods.
2. *Original empirical models*—that is, methods in which the valuation analyst gathers and synthesizes empirical valuation pricing data in order to quantify the effects of the valuation adjustment factor on valuation pricing multiples—or on some other market-derived value indicator.
3. *Inferential empirical models*—that is, methods that rely on the results of published research regarding the particular valuation adjustment factor relevant to the subject closely held employer corporation valuation analysis; in this method, the published research itself is based on actual empirical valuation pricing data.
4. *Precedential models*—that is, methods that rely on published judicial precedent (or administrative rulings) with regard to the description and the quantification of the relevant valuation adjustment.

The following discussion briefly introduces these four categories of models. This discussion summarizes the theoretical strengths and weaknesses and the practical applications and limitations of each model—particularly with regard to employer corporation stock valuations.

Theoretical Models

These quantitative models are typically one procedure in, or a variation of one procedure in, the actual business valuation method. Theoretical models sometimes use the generally accepted business valuation method to (essentially) estimate the value of the subject closely held employer corporation both with and without the relevant adjustment factor. In that case, the difference between the two employer corporation value estimates is the valuation impact of the relevant adjustment factor.

One example of the use of theoretical models is the quantification of the key-person dependence adjustment. While there are many procedures available to quantify this valuation adjustment, the two most common procedures include:

1. Capitalize the expense of key-person life insurance premiums for an insurance policy large enough to cover the value of the key person to the subject closely held employer corporation, or
2. Capitalize the compensation expense of an additional executive employee who could replace or succeed to the key executive, if needed.

The result of either incremental expense capitalization procedure would indicate the value decrement—or adjustment—associated with the key-person dependence.

These theoretical models are particularly applicable when: (1) there are no relevant published studies or other empirical data available to quantify the particular valuation discount or premium and (2) the effect of the adjustment factor can be estimated by adjusting individual identifiable line items in a generally accepted business valuation method (e.g., insurance expense, executive salary expense, etc.).

A caveat regarding the use of theoretical models is that there should be some empirical basis for the theoretical adjustment. For example, the above theoretical analyses regarding key person life insurance premiums and/or executive compensation expense should be based on actual empirical data gathered from, for example, commercial insurances agents or executive search firms.

Original Empirical Models

As introduced above, these methods are typically comparative in nature. Original empirical models often involve two sets of empirical market data: (1) one set of empirical data that exhibit the relevant valuation adjustment factor and (2) one set of empirical data that do not exhibit the relevant factor. The empirical market data subject to this comparative analysis could include: guideline publicly traded companies, guideline merger and acquisition transactions, and so forth. The empirical pricing evidence could include: valuation pricing multiples, direct capitalization rates, and present value discount rates.

What is significant about these methods is that the analyst performs original research—as compared to relying on published secondary research—to quantify the specific valuation adjustment. And, the analytical procedures should be applied to data that are as representative as possible of the relevant adjustment factor at the employer corporation.

One example of the use of original empirical models is the quantification of the key customer dependence adjustment. While there are many procedures available to quantify this phenomenon, one common procedure is to analyze the differences in valuation pricing multiples between two sets of guideline publicly traded companies:

1. guideline publicly traded companies do not experience significant key customer dependence (i.e., there is no disclosure of such key customer dependence in the guideline company Form 10-K) and
2. guideline publicly traded companies that do experience significant key customer dependence (i.e., there is a disclosure of key customer dependence in the guideline company Form 10-K).

The valuation analyst then calculates the difference in the observed valuation pricing multiples (e.g., price to cash flow multiple) for the two sets of guideline companies. This observed difference is applied to the appropriate employer corporation financial fundamental (e.g., cash flow) in order to estimate the valuation adjustment for key customer dependence.

Two strengths of this method are (1) the data used in the analysis are current (e.g., based on current date stock prices and pricing multiples) and (2) the data are specifically appropriate to the employer corporation (e.g., all of the selected guideline companies are in the same industry as the subject company).

Since the empirical data are original, timely, and subject-specific, this valuation adjustment method is particularly persuasive in controversy valuation assignments, such as ESOP valuations subject to IRS or DOL review. Some of the practical limitations of this method are that:

1. There is substantial effort associated with designing and conducting an original research study.
2. It may be difficult to isolate only the one economic influence related to the relevant valuation adjustment factor.

Inferential Empirical Models

These methods are also comparative in nature. However, these valuation adjustment methods rely on secondary published studies, as compared with primary—or original—empirical data. The published studies are typically based on actual empirical valuation data. However, the data in the studies are not directly related to the valuation subject employer corporation, so the methods are "inferential." That is, the analyst has to infer the valuation adjustment relevant to the subject closely held employer corporation from the results of generalized published studies.

Inferential empirical models are frequently used by valuation analysts. Accordingly, many of the published studies upon which these valuation adjustments are based are often quoted (and sometimes misquoted) in the valuation profession. There are several practical limitations of these methods:

1. The empirical studies typically only quantify the most common valuation adjustments, such as the ownership control premium, discount for lack of control, and discount for lack of marketability.
2. The empirical studies may include dated data.
3. The empirical studies may include data that are not related to the subject employer corporation industry.

Accordingly, particularly in controversy matters (such as ESOP valuations subject to IRS or DOL review), it is important for the analyst to clearly and convincingly explain the relevance of the selected published studies to the specific valuation adjustment.

Precedential Models

These methods are based on published judicial decisions that involve the explanation and quantification of valuation adjustments. Decisions of the

U.S. Tax Court, U.S. Court of Federal Claims, Federal District Courts, and U.S. Bankruptcy Courts, are commonly cited as precedents for valuation adjustments.

When using this method, it is important that the valuation analyst:

1. Be aware of the facts and circumstances of each judicial decision.
2. Compare and contrast the facts and circumstances in the subject employer stock valuation to the facts and circumstances in the cases relied on as precedents.

In controversy valuation matters, one strength of this method is that the analyst can (in effect) remind the court of previous decisions related to the relevant valuation adjustment. One limitation of this method is that no two sets of facts and circumstances are ever identical enough for the results of this method to be considered scientific. And, in controversy matters (such as litigated ESOP valuations), judges are more interested in the facts and circumstances of the subject closely held business than in comparisons to historical judicial precedent.

Accordingly, this method is most effectively used to provide mutually supportive evidence of the valuation adjustment (i.e., to demonstrate the reasonableness of the valuation adjustment estimated by one of the other methods).

SUMMARY AND CONCLUSION

The identification and quantification of valuation adjustments is a common procedure in many closely held business valuations—and particularly in employer corporation valuations performed by ESOP stock purchase/sale purposes. Most valuation analysts rely on the inferential empirical models to quantify these valuation adjustments. While this reliance is not inappropriate, valuation analysts involved in ESOP stock sale/purchase transactions should be aware of all of the models or methods available to quantify valuation discounts and premiums.

Chapter 12

Valuation Adjustments in ESOP Valuations

INTRODUCTION

The application of valuation adjustments (i.e., discounts and premiums) is a common procedure in many ESOP employer corporation stock valuation analyses. There are level of value valuation adjustments that analysts routinely consider in many valuation analyses. These level of value adjustments include consideration of (1) the degree of control or lack of control and (2) the degree of marketability or lack of marketability of the subject employer corporation stock.

Consideration of these level of value valuation adjustments is a common analytical procedure in an ESOP stock valuation. This is because different valuation approaches and methods typically conclude different levels of value. These valuation adjustments are called systematic adjustments. This is because they often apply across industries and across company types and sizes. The application of systematic valuation adjustments is influenced by:

1. the legal/economic characteristics of the subject employer stock (e.g., does the ESOP-owned stock represent operational/ownership control or not?);
2. the selected standard of value (e.g., fair market value in the case of ESOP stock valuations); and
3. the selected premise of value (e.g., what premise of value represents the highest and best use of the employer stock?).

This discussion does not emphasize these systematic (or level of value) adjustments. Rather, this discussion focuses on nonsystematic valuation adjustments. As the name implies, these adjustments do not apply across the board to all business interests of the same level of value. While nonsystematic adjustments should be considered in all employer stock valuation analyses, they are probably applied less often than not.

Nonsystematic valuation adjustments typically fall into the following four categories:

1. company-specific adjustments
2. security-specific adjustments
3. contract-imposed adjustments
4. multitier adjustments

These four categories are described in greater detail later in this discussion. As an introduction, these adjustments relate to some factors that are specific to the individual valuation subject (i.e., the particular ESOP-owned block of employer stock) that would cause the analyst to apply a valuation discount or premium.

An example of a company-specific adjustment may be key customer dependence. Let's assume that 90 percent of the subject employer corporation revenue comes from one customer/client. An example of a security-specific adjustment may be super-voting rights. Let's assume the valuation subject is class B common stock that enjoys 100 votes per share, compared to the one vote per share enjoyed by the employer corporation class A common stock. An example of a contract-imposed adjustment may be if the employer stock (but probably not the ESOP-owned stock) is subject to a mandatory shareholder agreement. Let's assume that agreement allows the employer corporation to call the subject stock at any time at a call price equal to accounting net book value. An example of a multitier adjustment may be a family limited partnership (FLP) interest that owns the remaining nonmarketable, noncontrolling stock of a closely held employer corporation. Let's assume the corporation owns marketable securities but neither (1) the subject FLP interest nor (2) the subject closely held stock interest has the right to demand an income distribution or asset liquidation.

These illustrative nonsystematic valuation adjustments do not relate to the subject stock level of value. And, these illustrative adjustments do not apply across a broad range of valuation subjects. Rather, the application of nonsystematic valuation adjustments is specific to the facts and circumstances of each individual subject business interest. In contrast, while the quantification of nonsystematic adjustments is unique to each specific valuation subject, the application of systematic valuation discounts and premiums is common across a broad range of ESOP valuation subjects.

First, this discussion describes various nonsystematic valuation adjustments. This discussion presents a representative (but nonexhaustive) list of the various types of nonsystematic adjustments. Second, this discussion considers when the application of nonsystematic valuation adjustments is appropriate. Third, this discussion explains the common procedures for identifying the factors or conditions that indicate the need for a nonsystematic valuation adjustment. Fourth, this discussion explains the common procedures for quantifying nonsystematic valuation adjustments. This explanation includes several simplified illustrative examples. Fifth, this discussion considers the appropriate sequencing of nonsystematic adjustments, particularly in a multitier business interest environment.

Finally, this discussion concludes with a summary of caveats regarding the identification and quantification of nonsystematic valuation adjustments in ESOP stock valuation analyses. However, it is noteworthy to mention a few valuation adjustment general caveats in this introduction.

GENERAL CAVEATS REGARDING VALUATION ADJUSTMENTS

First, regarding both systematic and nonsystematic adjustments, adjustments are always made *to reach* a conclusion of value. Adjustments are not made *from* a conclusion of value. Novice valuation analysts (and many other ESOP practitioners) are often confused by this very important distinction. They believe that analysts first reach a conclusion of the correct value for the subject ESOP-owned business interest. Then, the analyst applies a discount or premium to the concluded value in order to arrive at a discounted value—or an inflated value.

This misconception is both procedurally and conceptually incorrect. In fact, analysts apply valuation methods to conclude value indications. Each business valuation method involves numerous analytical procedures. The various methods provide preliminary indications of value—until all of the requisite procedures are performed. And, one of the requisite procedures in all business valuation methods is to consider (and apply, when appropriate) valuation discounts and premiums. So, valuation adjustments are applied to preliminary value indications to arrive at a final value conclusion. Valuation adjustments are not applied to a final value conclusion to arrive at a discounted or inflated value conclusion.

Second, regarding both systematic and nonsystematic adjustments, the application of adjustments—and the magnitude of adjustments—may vary by valuation approach and method. And, there are two components to this caveat: (1) implicit level of value, systematic adjustments and (2) implicit/explicit quantification of nonsystematic adjustments.

Some valuation approaches and methods automatically conclude a certain level of value. Typically, the market approach/guideline publicly traded company method concludes a marketable, noncontrolling ownership interest level of value. Typically, the asset-based approach/asset accumulation method concludes a marketable, controlling ownership interest level of value. Typically, the income approach/discounted cash flow method can conclude either (1) a controlling ownership interest level of value or (2) a noncontrolling ownership interest level of value; the concluded level of value depends on the individual valuation variables selected for both (1) the cash flow projection and (2) the present value discount rate.

In each of these instances, the application of a systematic, level of value adjustment will depend on both (1) the level of value typically concluded by the selected method and (2) the individual valuation variables used in the specific analysis of that method. Therefore, within the same valuation assignment, systematic adjustments may apply to some valuation methods and not to others. And, depending on the individual variables used within the method, different magnitudes of the same valuation adjustment (e.g., discount for lack of marketability) may apply between the different valuation methods used in the overall analysis.

Regarding nonsystematic valuation adjustments, sometimes the analyst may make an adjustment implicitly within an individual valuation method analysis. And, sometimes, the analyst may apply an explicit adjustment to the value indication concluded by the individual valuation method.

For example, let's consider a discount for key person dependence. The key person could be the employer corporation chief executive, chief salesperson, chief design engineer, or any other senior—and strategically important—executive. If the analyst uses the income approach/discounted cash flow method, the analyst could quantify a key person dependence discount either implicitly or explicitly.

Implicitly, the analyst could adjust the cash flow projection for the cost to recruit, hire, train, and maintain a hypothetical replacement executive (e.g., a first lieutenant for the key executive). Explicitly, the analyst could conclude an unaffected preliminary business enterprise value indication—and then subtract either a discrete percentage discount or a discrete dollar discount (for key person dependence) from the preliminary value indication.

As another example, let's consider a discount for lack of voting rights in the valuation of the employer corporation class B nonvoting common stock (e.g., a class of stock retained by the founding family). Again, the analyst may quantify this valuation adjustment either implicitly or explicitly. If the analyst uses the market approach/guideline publicly traded company method, the valuation adjustment could be made within the analytical procedures—to conclude an implicitly discounted value indication. Or, the valuation procedures could be performed on an unaffected basis, and the preliminary value indication could be explicitly adjusted for the discount.

Implicitly, the analyst could select only nonvoting guideline company stocks from which to extract market-derived valuation pricing multiples. The application of such pricing multiples would conclude a final value indication that is implicitly affected by a lack of voting rights. Alternatively, the analyst could select voting guideline company stocks from which to extract market-derived valuation pricing multiples. The application of such pricing multiples would conclude a preliminary value indication that would need to be explicitly adjusted by a percentage discount for lack of voting rights.

Third, regarding both systematic and nonsystematic adjustments, the application of adjustments is directly affected by the standard (or definition) of value sought in the valuation assignment. If the assignment standard of value is fair market value (as it is in ESOP stock valuations), then most valuation adjustments will typically apply. This is because the marketplace of willing buyers and willing sellers will generally recognize all valuation discounts and premiums.

However, if the assignment standard of value is fair value (as in a statutory dissenting shareholder rights case or a shareholder oppression case), then certain systematic, level of value adjustments may not apply. In many states (by statute or by judicial precedent), fair value is synonymous with pro rata business enterprise value (BEV). This type of analysis concludes a value that is legally "fair" to all parties to the subject litigation. That is, business enterprise value is the only level of value where all shares of stock in the subject company have the same value per share—regardless of whether they are owned by a 90 percent stockholder or by a 10 percent stockholder. Therefore, the controlling stockholder receives no economic reward for squeezing out or oppressing the noncontrolling stockholder.

For example, under this interpretation of fair value, the controlling stockholder is not allowed to pay a "discounted" price of $10 per share to the noncontrolling stockholder for shares that are worth a pro rata BEV of $20 per share to that controlling stockholder. Therefore, in many fair value assignments, systematic, level of value discounts are legally not applicable—even if the subject block of stock is a nonmarketable, noncontrolling ownership interest.

Similarly, in an investment value assignment, the analyst may not apply a nonsystematic discount for a suboptimal product distribution function at the subject employer corporation. If the current corporate owner wants to quantify the value to itself (given its specific corporate investment criteria) of a certain subsidiary, a discount for the lack of a distribution function may not be relevant.

Let's assume that the corporate parent is a company like Procter & Gamble, a company that is recognized for its world class product distribution function. Let's assume that the current corporate parent manages the subject company to be a manufacturing subsidiary that effectively sells to a market/distribution subsidiary. For such an investment value analysis, the lack of the subject company's distribution system would not represent a value penalty to the current owner. Therefore, the analyst may not apply a nonsystematic lack of distribution function discount in an investment value analysis for a Procter & Gamble-like corporate owner.

As another example, let's assume an acquisition value assignment for a corporate acquirer. Let's assume the subject target company clearly suffers from key person dependence. The target company founder is a key person who will retire at the time that the company is sold. The potential acquirer is a large, publicly traded corporation that has several tiers of mid-level executives who are qualified to (and waiting for the opportunity to) manage a company the size of the target company.

The acquisition value standard of value indicates what a specific buyer would be willing to pay to a specific seller for the subject business interest. Given (1) the acquisition value standard of value and (2) the fact that the target's key person dependence does not represent a deficiency to the specific corporate acquirer, the analyst may not apply a nonsystematic key person dependence discount in the acquisition value assignment for this particular acquirer.

NONSYSTEMATIC VALUATION ADJUSTMENTS

Something that is nonsystematic is not orderly, regular, or consistent. Nonsystematic valuation adjustments are discounts or premiums that may be considered—but are typically not applied—in all valuation assignments. Rather, they are specific to the individual facts and circumstances of a particular valuation subject employer corporation/security.

Nonsystematic valuation adjustments generally fall into the following four categories:

1. company-specific
2. security-specific
3. contract-specific
4. multitier

Each of these four categories of nonsystematic valuation adjustments is discussed below.

Company-Specific Adjustments

Company-specific valuation adjustments relate to facts and circumstances that are specific to the subject employer corporation. Common examples of company-specific valuation adjustments include:

1. discount for key person dependence,
2. discount for key customer dependence,
3. discount for key supplier dependence,
4. discount for key product/technology dependence,
5. discount for suboptimal capital structure, and
6. discount for suboptimal cost of capital.

These company-specific valuation factors can be either controllable or noncontrollable. The subject employer corporation management may decide to employ a 100 percent equity capital structure because of its aversion to financial risk. However, that is a controllable decision. On the other hand, there may be only one domestic supplier for a subject company's key production component. In that case, management's reliance on the key supplier is an example of an uncontrollable decision.

In any event, all of these factors first affect the valuation at the employer corporation business enterprise level. These factors are not related to the level of value of the subject ownership interest. And, these factors typically do not affect one class of the company's security differently than another class of the company's security. And, each of the factors in this category makes the subject employer corporation different (from an investment risk and/or expected return perspective) from the typical company in the subject industry or peer group. Accordingly, this category of valuation adjustments is typically made at the employer corporation (invested capital or total equity) level.

Security-Specific Adjustments

Security-specific valuation adjustments relate to facts and circumstances that are specific to the subject security interest or block of stock. Common examples of security-specific valuation adjustments include:

1. discount for lack of voting rights,
2. premium for supervoting rights,
3. blockage discount, and
4. discount for lack of preemptive rights.

All of these factors first affect the valuation at either (1) the class of security level (e.g., a discount for lack of voting rights may be applied to all of the employer corporation nonvoting common stock) or (2) the specific subject security level (e.g., a blockage discount may be applied to a 25 percent block of stock in an inactively traded public company). And, each of the factors in this category makes the subject security interest different (from an investment risk and/or expected return perspective) from either (1) the typical security in the subject employer corporation or (2) a guideline or benchmark security used for comparative pricing purposes.

In any event, this category of valuation adjustments is typically applied at the subject security level (e.g., per share of stock level) and not at the employer corporation level.

Contract-Specific Adjustments

Contract-specific valuation adjustments relate to facts and circumstances that are imposed on the subject security by the influences of a contract, agreement, regulation, or covenant. Common examples of contract-specific valuation adjustments include:

1. stock subject to the buy-sell provisions of a shareholder agreement;
2. restricted publicly traded stock;
3. founder, letter, or other unlisted stock of a listed company; and
4. partnership units subject to a partnership agreement; limited liability company (LLC) units subject to an LLC agreement.

All of these factors affect the valuation of the individual subject ownership interest as the result of an exogenous influence. That exogenous influence is the result of a particular ownership interest being subject to the terms and conditions of some type of contract or agreement. This is often the case with employer corporation stock owned by a private equity investor. The contract terms may involve put, call, transfer, or ownership restrictions of a stockholder, LLC, or family limited partnership (FLP) agreement. The contract terms may affect the income distribution or asset liquidation proceeds rights of the subject ownership interest. In some cases, the contract terms may positively enhance the transferability of the subject ownership interest—such as the put option on ESOP-owned common stock that is a contractual condition of most ESOP trust agreements.

The exogenous influence may be the result of an employment agreement. Such an employment agreement may prohibit an executive from selling the subject employer stock (1) while he or she remains an employee or (2) for a specified number of years. The exogenous influence may be the result of (1) an agreement with security underwriters or (2) a requirement of the Securities Exchange Commission (SEC) or an individual stock exchange. Unlisted shares of stock of a publicly traded company (e.g., founder stock, letter or legend stock, or stock subject to SEC Rule 144) are subject to contractual and/or regulatory transferability restrictions.

Each of the factors in this category makes the subject ownership interest different (from an investment risk and/or expected return perspective) from either (1) the typical security of the subject employer company that is not subject to the contractual/regulatory influence or (2) a guideline or benchmark security used for comparative pricing purposes. In any event, this category of valuation adjustments is typically applied at the subject ownership interest level (e.g., the particular block of stock or other equity units).

Multitier Adjustments

Multitier valuation adjustments relate to facts and circumstances that are specific to the ownership structure of the subject security interest. Common examples of multitier valuation adjustments include:

1. closely held corporation (CHC) stock owned by an FLP;
2. nonconsolidated CHC stock owned by a CHC;
3. any multitier ownership where a distribution will trigger the recognition of capital gains; and
4. a fractional or partial property ownership interest inside a CHC or FLP.

Multitier valuation adjustments are sometimes referred to as inside/outside valuation adjustments. In these instances, asset A is owned by asset B, which may itself be owned by asset C. Asset C is the valuation subject. Typically, in order to receive income distributions, the owner of asset C must first liquidate assets A and B. Accordingly, there is a series of security-specific and/or contract-specific adjustments that should be applied in the multitier ownership interest valuation.

In multitier ownership interest valuations, questions arise not only as to the magnitude of the appropriate valuation adjustments. Questions also arise as to the sequencing (and relative magnitude) of the appropriate valuation adjustments. Typically, the lower level/inside adjustments are applied first, and the higher level/outside adjustments are applied second. That is, adjustments are applied to asset A, and an asset A cash equivalency value is estimated. Then, adjustments are applied to asset B, and an asset B cash equivalency value is estimated. Finally, adjustments are applied to asset C, and an asset C value is concluded.

SYSTEMATIC VALUATION ADJUSTMENTS

Systematic events affect a broad population and occur with regularity and order. This statement is also true of systematic valuation adjustments. They affect a broad range of employer corporation business valuation assignments. And, the requirement to apply systematic valuation adjustments occurs with great regularity. In fact, depending on the valuation methods used, virtually all CHC business/stock valuations involve either implicit or explicit systematic valuation adjustments. Accordingly, analysts should consider the appropriateness of systematic valuation adjustments in virtually all employer corporation valuations.

Although the category of systematic adjustments is not limited to level of value adjustments, level of value adjustments are the most common type of systematic adjustments. There are two reasons for this. First, virtually every business valuation assignment involves a specified level of value. And, second, alternative valuation methods typically produce value indications at different levels of value.

Therefore, if the analysis involves two or more valuation methods, the analyst will typically have to apply some systematic adjustment in order to conform all of the value indications to the same level of value. All value indications have to be stated on the same level of value (typically, the level of value consistent with the valuation assignment) before a meaningful valuation synthesis and conclusion can be reached.

The most common systematic valuation adjustments include:

1. discount for lack of marketability (related to any ownership interest less than an overall business enterprise);

2. discount for illiquidity (related to the analysis of the overall closely held business enterprise);
3. discount for lack of ownership/operational control;
4. premium for ownership/operational control; and
5. premium for strategic/synergistic benefits.

The above-listed common systematic adjustments relate to the level of value of the subject ownership interest. Many inexperienced valuation analysts (and many ESOP practitioners who rely on valuation opinions) believe that there are only three or four discrete levels of value. In fact, there is a virtually continuous spectrum of levels of value. And, the spectrum itself has two axes: (1) ownership control elements and (2) marketability elements.

There is a broad spectrum of value influences ranging from (1) absolute ownership/operational control with immediate synergistic opportunities to (2) absolute lack of ownership/operational control. For example, an owner of a 30 percent block of CHC stock may have significant elements of operational control if there are 70 other unrelated stockholders, each of whom owns only one percent of the CHC stock. As another example, the owner of a two percent block of CHC stock can experience the swing vote value influences of control if there are two other unrelated stockholders, each of whom own 49 percent of the CHC stock.

The owner of 51 percent of a CHC stock has one level of ownership control. The value of that block of employer stock would likely deserve some level of control premium. However, in many states, a two-thirds vote is legally required for many corporate "control events" (e.g., a corporate liquidation or a sale of substantially all of the company assets). Therefore, the owner of a 67 percent block of stock may deserve a greater control premium than the owner of a 51 percent block of employer stock.

Likewise, the ownership of 80 percent of a company is required to consolidate a subsidiary for both financial accounting and income tax reporting purposes. That's why many acquirers won't pursue a target company unless they are sure of buying at least 80 percent of the stock. Therefore, the owner of an 80 percent block of stock may deserve a greater control premium than the owner of a 79 percent block of employer stock.

The owner of a 95 percent block of CHC stock still has fiduciary obligations to the employer company's minority stockholders. The elimination of minority stockholders eliminates both this fiduciary duty and the possibility of nuisance litigation claims from minority stockholders. Therefore, the owner of a 100 percent block of CHC stock may deserve a greater control premium than the owner of a 95 percent block of stock.

There is also a continuing spectrum of value influences with regard to marketability elements. This broad spectrum of value influences ranges from (1) absolute liquidity (equivalent to that enjoyed by actively traded stock listed on a public stock exchange) to (2) virtually absolute illiquidity (imposed by FLP, stockholder, buy-sell agreement, or by an other contract/agreement that restricts transfer, limits potential buyers, and dictates sale price). The multitier ownership structure of the subject security (e.g., a security owned by an entity that is owned by another entity) may also have marketability implications that influence value.

While it may be impossible for analysts to conceptualize all of the discrete steps along the control/marketability continuum, these two elements really represent a continuous spectrum of combined valuation adjustment possibilities. However, for visualization and illustrative purposes only, Figure 1 represents several of the common levels of value with regard to business/security valuation. Where applicable, Figure 1 also presents simplified indications of the valuation discount/premium relationships between the common levels of value.

Nonsystematic valuation discounts and premiums may be quantified as either (1) a percentage adjustment or (2) a dollar amount adjustment. When both percentage and dollar amount adjustments are appropriate, the analyst should carefully consider the appropriate sequence for applying the adjustments.

However, systematic valuation discounts and premiums (particularly level of value adjustments) are typically quantified as percentage adjustments. Therefore, if both control influence and marketability influence discounts/premiums are applied as percentage adjustments, then the mathematical sequencing of the application of systematic adjustments is irrelevant. That is, as long as they are all expressed on a percentage discount or premiums basis, the systematic valuation adjustments can be applied in any order.

WHY VALUATION ADJUSTMENTS ARE INTEGRAL TO THE VALUATION PROCESS

Experienced analysts understand that the concept of valuation adjustments is meaningless without a clear answer to the question: adjustment to what? The analyst first has to understand the baseline or benchmark against which any valuation discount or premium is contemplated. In other words, the application of any valuation discount or premium is fundamentally inappropriate unless the benchmark (against which the adjustment is compared) is clearly defined.

For example, it may be inappropriate to apply a discount for lack of marketability to a value indication that is already stated on a nonmarketable basis. Likewise, it may be inappropriate to apply an ownership control premium to a value indication that is already stated on a controlling ownership interest basis.

Figure 1

Business Valuation Adjustments
Simplified Illustration of the Common Levels of Value

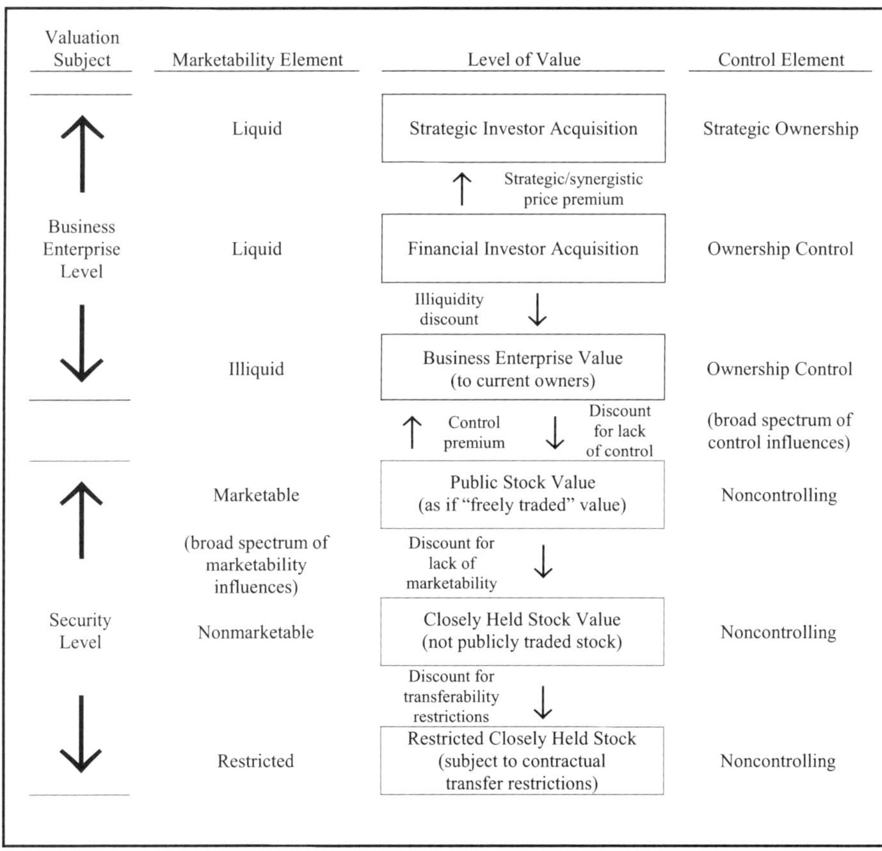

The first question for the analyst to ask with regard to valuation adjustments is: What do I have? This question relates to what systematic and nonsystematic elements exist in:

1. the valuation approaches and methods selected,
2. the valuation variables used,
3. the guideline or other transactional data extracted, and
4. the valuation indications derived.

These elements (that either are present or are absent) represent the baseline or benchmark of the valuation analysis.

The second question for the analyst to ask with regard to valuation adjustments is: what do I want? This question relates to what systematic and nonsystematic elements exist in:

1. the subject employer corporation and/or
2. the subject security/ownership interest.

In particular, the analyst is looking for operational, financial, contractual, and regulatory features of the subject company/security that are different from those of the benchmark analysis. These selected features should make the subject company/security different from the benchmark analysis from an investment risk/expected return perspective.

It should be obvious why the analyst should thoroughly understand the benchmark analysis first. At this point in the valuation, the benchmark analysis is what the analyst has. Ideally, the benchmark analysis should perfectly match the subject company/security from an investment risk/expected return perspective. This is because an analysis of the subject company/security is what the analyst wants. If the elements in the benchmark analysis perfectly matches up with the elements in the subject company/security, then no valuation adjustments are needed. Of course, that is rarely the case.

Therefore, the third question for the analyst to ask with regard to valuation adjustments is: how is the subject company/security different from the benchmark analysis? When answering this question, the analyst identifies all of the systematic and nonsystematic elements in the subject that are not in the benchmark analysis—and vice versa.

Finally, the fourth question for the analyst to ask with regard to valuation adjustments is: how do I get to what I want from what I have? In other words, what valuation adjustments are needed to make the value indications/conclusions of the benchmark analysis more applicable to the valuation subject? Alternatively, what valuation adjustments are needed to minimize the systematic and nonsystematic element differences between the benchmark analysis and the valuation subject?

It is noteworthy that this fourth question helps the analyst identify valuation adjustments that make the investment risk/expected return features of the benchmark analysis look more like the valuation subject. It is not the objective of valuation adjustments to make the investment risk/expected return features of the subject company/security look more like the benchmark analysis.

In summary, valuation adjustments are only applicable to make the benchmark or baseline analysis look more like the subject company/security from an investment risk/expected return perspective. Therefore, it is important that the analyst fully understand the systematic and nonsystematic elements of the benchmark analysis before any valuation adjustments are considered. In addition, the selection of valuation adjustments will be influenced by (1) the specific valuation approaches, methods, and procedures performed and (2) the purpose and objectives of the analysis, including the standard of value and the premise of value appropriate of the individual assignment.

ILLUSTRATIVE LISTING OF VALUATION ADJUSTMENTS

Table 1 on the following page presents a noncomprehensive listing of common valuation discounts and premiums. Table 1 does not distinguish between systematic (or level of value) adjustments and nonsystematic adjustments. While Table 1 is not intended to be comprehensive, it may provide a convenient valuation adjustment checklist or reminder list for analysts performing ESOP stock valuation assignments.

METHODS TO QUANTIFY VALUATION ADJUSTMENTS

There are numerous analytical procedures that may be used to quantify individual valuation adjustments. When considered conceptually, all of these individual procedures may be grouped into four categories of methods:

1. comparative empirical data regarding the valuation subject,
2. comparative income data regarding the valuation subject,
3. published empirical data regarding valuation guidelines/benchmarks, and
4. reliance on judicial/administrative guidance.

Table 1

Business/Security Valuation Adjustments
List of Common Valuation Discounts and Premiums

Valuation Discounts Related to	Valuation Premiums Related to
Assignee ownership interest	Ownership/operational control
Blockage (size of public stock)	Put options
Built-in capital gains taxes	Strategic/synergistic benefits
Call options	Superliquidation preference
Founder/letter/legend stock	Supervoting rights
Illiquidity (at business enterprise level)	
Key customer dependence	
Key person dependence	
Key supplier dependence	
Key technology dependence	
Lack of dividend rights	
Lack of marketability (at security level)	
Lack of ownership/operational control	
Lack of preemptive rights	
Lack of voting rights	
Multitier ownership structure	
Partial/fractional ownership interest	
Right of first refusal	
SEC Rule 144	
Suboptimal capital structure	
Suboptimal cost of capital	
Transferability restrictions (contractual)	
Unlisted stock of public company	

Each of these four categories of methods is described below.

The first two above-listed methods use data extracted directly from the subject company/security. If such data are available, then these methods provide valuation adjustment indications that are specifically derived from the valuation subject.

In the first method, the analyst compares the valuation subject to a benchmark or baseline that does not have the discount/premium value influence. Based on this comparison, the analyst extracts pricing metric data that are used to quantify the specific valuation adjustment. In the second method, the analyst compares some measure of the valuation subject income to the same income measure, adjusted to exclude the effect of the valuation discount/premium. The capitalization of this income differentiate provides an indication of the appropriate amount of the valuation adjustment.

Using the comparative empirical data method, the analyst typically looks for comparative sales involving the subject security, where (1) one sale doesn't have the particular discount/premium feature and (2) the otherwise comparable sale does have the particular discount/premium feature.

For example, let's assume that there were historical sale transactions involving two classes of the employer company stock (one class with voting rights and one class without voting rights). The analyst could examine these transactions and extract a discount for lack of voting rights. Likewise, let's assume that there were historical sale transactions involving (1) employer company stock subject to a right of first refusal and (2) otherwise comparable employer company stock not subject to a right of first refusal. Again, the analyst could examine these transactions and extract a discount related to a contractual agreement right of first refusal.

Using the comparative income data method, the analyst typically identifies revenue, expense, or investment differences that are attributable to the particular discount/premium feature. The analyst attempts to quantify how the subject revenue, expenses, or investment would change if the particular discount/premium feature changes. The analyst then capitalizes the expected income change over the remaining useful life (RUL) of the income change. The present value of the projected income difference provides an estimate of the amount of the valuation discount/premium.

For example, let's assume that Mr. Founder is the controlling stockholder at Employer Corporation, a CHC. As controlling stockholder, Mr. Founder pays himself a salary that is $1 million per year greater than a reasonable salary level for a comparable executive at a comparable company. The analyst is attempting to quantify the ownership control premium associated with the Mr. Founder stock ownership interest. The analyst could isolate the economic benefit associated with the Founder ownership control (i.e., his excess compensation) and capitalize that benefit at an appropriate capitalization rate. The capitalized excess compensation is one indication of the amount of the Founder ownership control premium.

All of the procedures related to the empirical data and the empirical income methods ultimately involve three types of analyses:

1. estimate of the income shortfall related to the valuation discount; estimate of the income excess related to the valuation premium;
2. estimate of the cost to cure the deficiency feature; and
3. paired sales analysis of (1) transactions with the subject discount/premium feature and (2) transactions without the subject discount/premium feature

The empirical data and empirical income methods rely on income, cost, or sales data extracted from the subject employer corporation in order to quantify the systematic or nonsystematic valuation adjustment.

The published empirical data method is the most commonly used method to quantify valuation discounts and premiums. Arguably, it is also the most commonly misused method.

Many analysts rely on published studies of empirical data to derive level of value adjustments, such as a discount for lack of marketability or a premium for ownership control. There are also numerous published studies with regard to nonsystematic valuation adjustments as well, such as a discount for lack of voting rights. Most published empirical studies rely on the paired sales analysis procedure. That is, they analyze (1) one set of sale transactions that are not affected by the subject feature and (2) one set of sale transactions that are affected by the subject feature. The percentage difference in transaction prices (or the percentage difference in transaction pricing multiples) provides an indication of the amount of the individual valuation discount or premium.

The difference in this third method (compared to the first two methods) is that both sides of the paired sales analysis comparison relate to guideline company/security transactions. In other words, none of the data analyzed in these published studies actually comes from the subject company/security. This factor should not invalidate this method however.

The concern regarding the use of this valuation adjustment quantification method is not the data source. The concern is how analysts rely on the published study results in order to select subject-specific valuation adjustments. Analysts often naively rely on the more popular published empirical studies (1) without understanding the procedural mechanics of the published study, (2) without understanding the type (e.g., industry, size, etc.) of transactions analyzed in the published study, and (3) without considering the time period of the published study (compared to the subject assignment valuation date).

In addition, many analysts naively select the mean or median conclusion from the published study as the appropriate valuation discount or premium in every business/security valuation assignment. These analysts often do not study the range of results indicated by published studies—such as the interquartile conclusions, the standard deviations, and the high/low observations. And, these analysts often do not consider (qualitatively or quantitatively) exactly what valuation adjustment would be appropriate to the unique factors of the specific subject company/security—given the range of data reported in the published empirical study.

The fourth method for quantifying valuation adjustments relies on published judicial precedent and administrative rulings (e.g., Internal Revenue Service audit settlement agreements) for guidance. While this method is sometimes used by inexperienced analysts, it is not recommended by experienced analysts. This method does provide the analyst with very useful information as to the reasonable range of valuation discounts and premiums that courts and regulators have found acceptable. However, these data do not provide a particularly useful source of information from which to select a particular valuation adjustment related to a specific business valuation assignment.

Judicial precedent, IRS letter rulings and settlement agreements, and other administrative rulings are always fact-specific. By definition, they only apply to the specific facts and circumstances of the matter and/or taxpayer to which they apply. They are not intended to provide general professional guidance with regard to the appropriate level of valuation discounts and premiums. Published judicial decisions (and other rulings) are only applicable to the extent that the subject company/security facts and circumstances are identical to the published decision facts and circumstances. And, that is hardly ever the case.

VALUATION ANALYST CAVEATS

Table 2 on the following page presents a nonexhaustive listing of ten caveats that valuation analysts should consider with regard to the identification and quantification of valuation discounts and premiums. These "top ten" caveats apply to all four methods for quantifying valuation adjustments.

SUMMARY AND CONCLUSION

This discussion focused on the identification and quantification of nonsystematic and multitier valuation adjustments. This discussion also touched on the identification and quantification of systematic (level of value) valuation adjustments. This discussion considered both (1) when and (2) why valuation adjustments are applicable in the employer corporation stock valuation process. This discussion presented an illustrative (but nonexhaustive) listing of common business valuation discounts and premiums.

In particular, this discussion presented (1) the four common methods for quantifying valuation adjustments and (2) the three common procedures for quantifying valuation adjustments. Comparative conceptual/practical strengths and weaknesses of the various valuation adjustment methods were discussed. And, this discussion presented a nonexhaustive listing of top ten caveats that ESOP valuation analysts should consider when selecting specific business/security valuation discounts and premiums.

Table 2

Business Valuation Adjustments
List of "Top Ten" Analyst Caveats
Regarding Valuation Discounts and Premiums

1. Analysts should thoroughly understand the valuation analysis baseline or benchmark before applying any valuation adjustments.
2. Analysts should thoroughly understand the economic influences of the specific systematic or nonsystematic feature considered; does it actually affect the investment risk and/or expected return of the subject employer company/security?
3. Analysts should be careful not to "double count" valuation adjustments. For example, a valuation discount for the BIG tax may be a component of an overall discount for lack of marketability—and not a separate, discrete valuation adjustment.
4. Typically, when analysts use alternative procedures to quantify valuation adjustments (e.g., income shortfall/excess, cost to cure, paired sales analysis), the lowest valuation adjustment indication is the most appropriate valuation adjustment conclusion.
5. Analysts should not directly rely on published judicial precedent as the basis of selecting specific valuation adjustments, unless the facts and circumstances in the subject assignment are identical to those in the published decision.
6. Analysts should be aware that not all valuation methods/indications may be subject to the same valuation adjustment—or to the same magnitude (either dollar amount or percentage) of valuation adjustment.
7. Analysts should recognize that the application of valuation adjustments is influenced by the purpose and objective of the analysis (e.g., assignment standard of value, premise of value, etc.) as well as by the specific features of the subject employer company/security.
8. Analysts should be sufficiently familiar with the content and intent of published empirical valuation adjustment studies before relying on such published studies as the basis of selecting a specific valuation discount or premium.
9. Analysts should carefully consider the time period covered in any published empirical valuation adjustment study before relying on that published study for use as of a specific valuation date.
10. Analysts should carefully consider the dispersion of the results reported in published empirical valuation adjustment studies. Analysts should avoid the naïve reliance on the mean or median results of such published studies without considering whether such conclusions are applicable to the specific facts and circumstances of the particular ESOP stock valuation assignment.

Chapter 13

Voting-Related Adjustments in ESOP Valuations

INTRODUCTION

The valuation of employer corporation securities without voting rights or with supernormal (i.e., superior) voting rights is a common ESOP valuation assignment. This is particularly true in the case of a multi-investor ESOP stock purchase transaction. In such a transaction, it is not uncommon for the ESOP to own one class of employer corporation stock while the management group, the founding family, and a private equity investor may all own different classes of stock.

While they may differ with regard to other ownership attributes, these different classes of employer corporation stock often differ with regard to voting rights. Accordingly, the quantification of voting-related valuation adjustments (i.e., discounts and premiums) is a common procedure in an ESOP stock valuation.

Empirical evidence indicates that the public stock exchange market price for voting common shares is generally greater than the stock market price for comparable nonvoting common shares. Empirical evidence also indicates that the stock market price for super-voting common stock is generally greater than the stock market price for comparable normal-voting common stock.

These empirical data indicate that shareholders pay a price premium for voting privileges related to publicly traded common shares. These empirical data also indicate that shareholders will extract a price discount for the lack of voting privileges related to publicly traded common shares. While there are not sufficient empirical transaction pricing data to quantitatively prove this hypothesis, valuation analysts generally agree that this relationship also holds for shares of privately held employer corporations.

VOTING RIGHTS

For purposes of this discussion, we define voting common stock as having (1) one vote per share or (2) a fraction of a vote per share while another class of stock has one vote per share. We define super-voting common stock as having either (1) a greater number of votes per share than the voting common stock or (2) the ability to elect a disproportionately high number of board of directors members. Therefore, this class of stock has greater than normal voting rights in a corporation that has at least two classes of common stock outstanding.

For purposes of this discussion, we define nonvoting common stock as having no voting rights per share. Therefore, this class of stock has less than normal voting rights in a corporation that has at least two classes of common stock outstanding.

Our categories of "voting" stock and "nonvoting" stock are not absolute. That is, we did not strictly limit our analysis to a comparison of stock with one vote per share and stock with no votes per share. Rather, our analysis considers the general pricing differences between three voting rights-related conditions: (1) stock with normal voting rights, (2) stock with greater than normal voting rights, and (3) stock with less than normal voting rights.

Voting shares enable stockholders to vote on certain corporate matters. These corporate matters include electing the corporation's board of directors (who oversee the management of the corporation). Nonvoting shares do not allow stockholders to vote on certain corporate matters. In some cases, the voting power of nonvoting shares may be limited to those corporate matters that are minimally required specifically by state corporation law. Other than voting rights, the voting shares and nonvoting shares of the corporations considered in our analysis are typically comparable with regard to the shareholder investment risks and expected returns.

Super-voting shares have more than one vote per share and typically elect the majority of the corporation's board of directors. Other than voting rights, the voting and super-voting shares of the corporations considered in our analysis are typically comparable with regard to stockholder investment risks and expected returns.

OBJECTIVES OF THE VOTING RIGHTS STUDY

This discussion presents the results of recent empirical research regarding the market-derived price discount regarding the lack of voting rights (or of inferior voting rights) and the market-derived price premium for voting rights (or of superior voting rights). First, we will summarize the recent professional literature with regard to discount for lack of voting rights/premium for voting rights (DLVR/PVR) studies. Second, we will report the results of a DLVR/PVR study recently performed by Willamette Management Associates (WMA).

This WMA DLVR/PVR study considered both (1) price discounts and price premiums related to voting rights on a per share basis and (2) the allocation of a corporation's total equity value between (a) stockholder voting rights only and (b) all other stockholder ownership rights.

The principal research objectives of the WMA DLVR/PVR study were to quantify the market-derived price discount associated with the lack of voting rights (or inferior voting rights) of common stock and to quantify the market-derived price premium associated with the voting rights (or super voting rights) of common stock.

The second research objective of the DLVR/PVR study was to identify any corporate attributes/factors that affect the magnitude of the DLVR/PVR. The corporate attributes/factors considered in the study include: (1) company size, (2) stock exchange listing, (3) subject industry, (4) stock classes (voting/nonvoting versus supervoting/voting), and (5) concentration of stock owned by founders/insiders. The third research objective of the study was to quantify the value of voting rights only as a percent of the total bundle of legal rights associated with common stock ownership.

The WMA DLVR/PVR study analyzed these three research objectives using empirical stock market data as of two time periods: (1) as of December 30, 1994, and (2) as of December 31, 1999.

We selected December 31, 1999, as the most recent analysis date for two related reasons. First, that date includes most of the stock price "irrational exuberance" of the late 1990s and early 2000. It is the last calendar year end before the dot-com and general stock market price increase "bubble" burst. Second, after the stock market "bubble" burst in 2000, the market experienced a severe price correction period through most of 2002.

After the correction period, the market experienced a period of price increases in 2003 and early 2004. However, the market did not return to the "irrational exuberance" prices of 2000. This recent period of price correction/price increase may have caused a short term aberration in the relationship of voting/nonvoting stock prices. Accordingly, we selected an analysis date prior to this potentially aberrational period.

We selected December 31, 1994, as the first analysis date simply because it represents the middle of the decade of the 1990s. The decade of the 1990s experienced a fairly consistent trend of stock market price increases. We selected December 30, 1994, to represent (1) a period of normalcy within a longer term market cycle and (2) a period before the influence of the rapid dot-com and general stock market increase.

Many valuation analysts have quantified the DLVR/PVR over different time periods. As part of our analysis, we reviewed recent published DLVR/PVR studies. We reviewed these published studies looking for both (1) trends in the empirical DLVR/PVR conclusions and (2) consistencies/inconsistencies with the WMA DLVR/PVR study conclusions.

RELATIONSHIP BETWEEN DLVR AND PVR

Most empirical DLVR/PVR studies directly quantify the price premium for voting rights. This relationship is quantified as follows:

$$PVR = \frac{P_S - P_I}{P_I}$$

where: P_S equals the price of the stock with superior rights, and
P_I equals the price of the stock with inferior voting rights.

For instance, if the Public Company voting stock sells for \$22 per share and the otherwise comparable Public Company nonvoting stock sells for \$20 per share, the PVR is calculated as follows:

$$PVR = \frac{\$22 - \$20}{\$20}$$

$$= \frac{\$2}{\$20}$$

$$= 10\%$$

Likewise, most empirical DLVR/PVR studies indirectly quantify the price discount for lack of voting rights. That is, the DLVR is calculated based on the previously determined PVR. This DLVR relationship is quantified as follows:

$$DLVR = 1 - \left(\frac{1}{1 + PVR} \right)$$

For instance, if the Public Company PVR is determined (from the above example) to be 10 percent, the DLVR is calculated as follows:

$$\text{DLVR} = 1 - \left(\frac{1}{1+10\%} \right)$$

$$\text{DLVR} = 1 - 0.9091$$
$$\text{DLVR} = 9.1\%$$

Therefore, a 10 percent PVR implies a 9.1 percent DLVR. And, a 9.1 percent DLVR implies a 10 percent PVR.

This relationship is the methodology the WMA study used to extract the DLVR from the calculated PVR. First, we calculated the PVR from the empirical stock market price data. Second, we quantified the DLVR (using the above-indicated formula) from the calculated PVR.

Review of Published DLVR/PVR Studies

Previously published DLVR/PVR studies have covered the time period of 1940 through 1994. There is a diverse range of both nations and stock exchanges covered by these DLVR/PVR studies, including: the United States, Canada, Italy, Great Britain, Switzerland, Sweden, and Israel. The results of several recently published DLVR/PVR studies are presented in Table 1 at the end of this article.

Many of the DLVR/PVR studies listed in Table 1 are not directly applicable to U.S. corporations. This is because there are significant differences between various countries with regard to (1) securities laws (particularly with regard to stockholder rights), (2) stock exchange listing and regulation requirements, (3) public reporting and stockholder disclosure requirements, and (4) the relative rights of nonvoting stockholders versus voting shareholders.

Even within the same country (e.g., within the United States), federal securities laws and stock exchange regulations have changed over time. For that reason, the market-derived DLVR/PVR may have changed since the above-listed studies were performed. Accordingly, the results of DLVR/PVR studies encompassing earlier time periods may no longer be applicable as of the current date.

The DLVR/PVR studies performed by (1) O'Shea and Siwicki and (2) Houlihan, Lokey, Howard, & Zukin, appear to be the most relevant to current domestic corporations. This is because these two DLVR/PVR studies (1) are the most recent and (2) pertain to the U.S. securities markets. The results of both of these two studies conclude both a mean and a median price PVR of under 5 percent.

The following discussion summarizes the methodology, data sources, and conclusions of the WMA DLVR/PVR study. The study (1) updates (and confirms) the results of the two aforementioned studies, (2) reaches independent conclusions regarding the DLVR/PVR for the subject time periods, and (3) quantifies the value of voting rights alone as a percent of the total bundle of legal rights associated with common stock ownership.

The WMA DLVR/PVR

In the DLVR/PVR study, first, we identified corporations with two classes of common stock outstanding (1) as of December 31, 1994, or (2) as of December 31, 1999.

Second, we collected and analyzed stock price data regarding superior voting rights shares versus inferior voting rights shares. Because of this, we limited our study to corporations with classes of stock that differed only in voting rights. Other security features, such differences in dividend rights and liquidation preference, can also affect share price.

Third, to ensure that the price discount/price premium data were only related to voting rights, we excluded from our study all corporations with differing dividend, liquidation, and other security ownership rights.

We identified multiple stock class companies using the Standard & Poor's Compustat database. We identified all corporations listed in the Compustat database that had two classes of common stock outstanding as of either December 31, 1994, or December 31, 1999. From this list of multiple common stock class corporations, we eliminated all corporations with two classes of common stock with ownership differences other than voting rights.

From this reduced list, we next eliminated all multiple common stock class corporations (1) that were not domestic (i.e., United States) based companies, (2) that were inactively traded at any time during our observation period, and (3) that were penny stocks (defined herein as trading for less than $1 per share) at any time during the observation period.

The 1994 WMA DLVR/PVR Study

The first group of multiple stock class corporations used stock market data as of December 31, 1994 ("the 1994 Study"). We included 28 domestic corporations in the 1994 Study. For each corporation, both (1) the closing price as of December 30, 1994 (i.e., the December 30, 1994, closing price because

December 31, 1994, was a Saturday) and (2) the average closing price for the three-month period October to December 1994 were compared for each class of common stock.

This analysis also considered the following descriptive data: (1) the primary industry Standard Industrial Classification (SIC) code, as reported by Compustat, (2) the number of shares outstanding (in each class of stock) as of December 31, 1994, (3) the total market capitalization (including both (a) total common equity and (b) total equity), and (4) the composition (e.g. insider, institutional, block owners, etc.) of stock ownership.

The 28 companies analyzed in the 1994 Study, and their associated price, volume, and other descriptive data, are presented on Exhibit 1. The exhibits for this article are too large to fit in the small format of this book. Therefore, we have provided this chapter, along with all of the exhibits on our Web site in our section on Research. To view these exhibits, please go to www.willamette.com and select "Research."

For these 28 corporations, the mean PVR was 3.0 percent and the median PVR was 1.5 percent as of December 31, 1994. The mean PVR for the three-month period of October to December 1994 was 2.8 percent, and the median PVR for the same three-month period was 2.0 percent.

The mean DLVR was 2.9 percent and the median DLVR was 1.5 percent as of December 31, 1994. For the three-month period October to December 1994, the mean DLVR was 2.7 percent and the median DLVR was 2.0 percent.

For the 1994 Study, the analysis of the value of voting rights as a percent of total common equity value is presented in Exhibit 2.

For all 28 corporations included in the Exhibit 2 analysis, (1) the mean value of voting rights represented 0.8 percent of total common equity value and (2) the median value of voting rights represented 0.4 percent of the total common equity value. Both of these conclusions relate to pricing data as of December 31, 1994. These conclusions can be interpreted as follows: of the total value of all common equity ownership rights in the selected corporations, 0.8 percent (as the mean), and 0.4 percent (as the median) represented the single influence related to the value of voting rights only.

The 1994 Study also attempts to identify factors that affect the magnitude of the DLVR/PVR. We considered the following factors in the analysis: (1) the size of the subject company, (2) the stock exchange the stock is listed on, (3) the principal industry of the subject, (4) voting/nonvoting versus super voting/voting, and (5) the percent of stock owned by company founders/insiders.

The first factor we considered was the size of the subject company. We measured the size of the company using the total common equity value. As indicated in Exhibit 1, the Readers Digest Association, Inc., stock experienced a PVR "discount" of almost 9 percent. Readers Digest Association, Inc., was also one of the larger companies included in the 1994 Study, with a total common equity of near $5.4 billion.

The stock of the two largest companies in the 1994 Study, Tele Communications, Inc., and Viacom, Inc., experienced a PVR of 6.9 and 2.2 percent, respectively. Other companies with total common equity value over $1 billion experienced a PVR range of from 0 percent to over 5 percent. Accordingly, the large equity size does not predict/influence the size of the DLVR/PVR.

The smaller companies included in the 1994 Study did not indicate a pattern with regard to DLVR/PVR either. The two smallest companies (i.e., Federal Agriculture and Plymouth Rubber) both experienced a PVR of 0 percent. However, the next smallest company (i.e., Exx, Inc.) experienced a PVR of 1.6 percent. Therefore, we concluded that the size of the subject company is not a significant factor in predicting/influencing the size of the DLVR/PVR.

However, the 1994 Study indicates that as the size of the subject company increases, the value of voting rights tends to represent a smaller percentage of total common equity value outstanding. This is indicated in the four size categories presented at the bottom of Exhibit 2.

The second factor we considered was the stock exchange on which the subject company is listed. Common stocks listed on the Nasdaq experienced the highest mean and median PVR, 5.5 percent and 3.9 percent, respectively. For common stocks listed on the American Stock Exchange, the mean PVR was 2.5 percent and the median PVR was 1.6 percent.

The common stocks listed on the New York Stock Exchange experienced the lowest PVR, with a mean PVR "discount" of 2.4 percent and a median PVR "discount" of 1.2 percent. Due to the significant differences between the PVR indications, it appears the exchange on which a stock is traded does affect the magnitude of the PVR.

The third factor we considered was the principal industry of the subject company. The principal industry was determined using the SIC code. The multiple stock class corporations included companies in the following industries: (1) manufacturing, (2) transportation, communications, electric gas, and sanitary services, (3) retail trade, (4) finance, insurance, and real estate, and (5) services.

Companies operating primarily in the manufacturing industry experienced a mean PVR of 0.1 percent and a median PVR of 0.6 percent. Companies operating primarily in the transportation, communications, electric, gas, and sanitary services industry sector experienced a mean PVR of 1.8 percent and a median PVR of 1.4 percent.

Companies operating primarily in the retail trade industry experienced the highest mean and median PVR. The mean PVR was 7.3 percent and the median PVR was 6.3 percent. Companies operating primarily in the finance, insurance, and real estate industry sector experienced a mean PVR of 8.7 percent and a median PVR of 0 percent. There was one company that operated primarily in the services industry, and it had a PVR of 5.5 percent.

The lowest mean and median PVR was experienced by companies operating in the manufacturing industry. The highest mean PVR was experienced by companies operating in the finance, insurance, and real estate industry, and the highest median PVR was experienced by companies operating in the retail industry. However, the 1994 Study did indicate that as the size of the subject company increases, the value of voting rights tends to represent a smaller percentage of total common equity value outstanding. This is indicated in the four size categories presented at the bottom of Exhibit 2.

The fourth factor we considered was the relative voting rights relationship of the multiple classes of stock (i.e., whether the corporation had (1) voting/nonvoting classes of stock or (2) voting/supervoting classes of stock). The mean PVR for companies with both voting and nonvoting shares was 3.1 percent. The mean PVR for companies with both super voting and voting shares was lower, at 2.9 percent. However, the relationship of the median PVR was reversed. The median PVR for companies with both voting and nonvoting shares was 0.0 percent. The median PVR for companies with both super voting and voting shares was higher, at 2.7 percent. Accordingly, the relative voting rights classes of stock outstanding does not seem to predict/influence the size of the DLVR/PVR

The fifth factor we considered was the percentage of common shares outstanding that was controlled by company founders and/or insiders (e.g., management). There were only three companies in the 1994 Study where the largest single shareholder owned more than 50 percent of the outstanding shares. In one instance, the subject company actually experienced a "discount" related to the voting class of stock versus the nonvoting class of stock. In another such instance, there was no PVR related to the voting rights stock versus the nonvoting rights stock. And in the third instance, the indicated PVR was less than the mean PVR for all companies in the 1994 Study.

An analyst would expect that there would be a very small PVR if a single shareholder owned more than 50 percent of the outstanding shares. In such a case, the voting rights would not carry as much importance to the minority stockholders. This is because one majority shareholder could effectively control the vote.

For companies where corporate insiders owned a majority (or nearly a majority) of the voting shares outstanding, the PVR was generally negative. There was one instance where the PVR was 0 percent, and one instance where the PVR was 2.1 percent. In general, if a single individual or a handful of individual insiders owns the majority of the voting shares outstanding, then the PVR will be lower than would otherwise be, all other factors being equal.

The 1999 WMA DLVR/PVR Study

The second group of multiple stock class corporations were analyzed using stock market data as of December 31, 1999. The 1999 Study included 28 domestic corporations.

In the 1999 Study, we collected the same capital market data and the same descriptive company data in the 1994 Study. We calculated the DLVR/PVR was calculated using market closing stock price data as of December 31, 1999. As with the 1994 Study, we also considered the average daily closing stock prices for the three-month period October through December 1999.

The 28 companies analyzed in the 1999 Study, and their associated price, volume, and other data, are presented in Exhibit 3.

For the 1999 Study, the analysis of the value of voting rights as a percent of total common equity value is presented in Exhibit 4.

For the 1999 Study, the mean PVR was 12.7 percent for the entire sample of 28 corporations. This PVR conclusion is unexpectedly high given (1) the results of the 1994 Study and (2) the conclusions of previous published DLVR/PVR studies. It is noteworthy that one company, Acmat Corporation, experienced a PVR of 180 percent. As of December 31, 1999, the mean PVR excluding Acmat Corporation was 6.5 percent. The median PVR for all 28 companies as of December 31, 1999, was 2.8 percent.

The three-month price data indicated a mean PVR of 13.2 percent including Acmat Corporation and a 7.8 percent PVR excluding Acmat Corporation. The three-month median PVR was 0.6 percent.

As of December 31, 1999, the mean DLVR was 6.1 percent (excluding Acmat Corporation). As of December 31, 1999, the median DLVR was 2.7 percent. For the three months of October to December 1999, the mean DLVR was 7.2 percent (excluding Acmat Corporation). For the three months of October to December 1999, the median DLVR was 0.6 percent.

As indicated on Exhibit 4, the mean value of voting rights alone represented 2.8 percent of the total common stock value of the 28 corporations included in the 1999 Study. The mean value of voting rights alone represented 1.9 percent of the total common stock value of the 27 corporations included in the 1999 Study after excluding the outlier Acmat Corporation. The median value of voting rights alone represented 0.2 percent of the total common stock value of the 28 corporations included in the 1999 Study.

Even after removing outlier Acmat Corporation, the PVR results in 1999 were higher than the PVR results in 1994. To analyze what was affecting these results, we considered the same factors as for the 1994 Study results.

First, of the 9 companies with total common equity value over $1 billion, 6 companies experienced PVR "discounts." And, of the 9 companies that experienced PVR "discounts," 6 companies had a total common equity over $1 billion. One of the larger companies had a PVR of 0 percent, and the other two large companies had a PVR lower than the average.

All of the companies with total common equity value over $1 billion experienced a PVR lower than the average. The majority of companies with total common equity value under $100 million experienced a PVR greater than the average. Accordingly, there appears to be a stronger relationship between the size of the company and the PVR in the 1999 Study results than in the 1994 Study results.

The 1999 Study indicated that as the size of the subject company increases, the value of voting rights represents a smaller percentage of total common equity value outstanding. This is indicated in the four size categories presented at the bottom of Exhibit 4.

Second, unlike the 1994 data, the mean PVR for companies traded on the Nasdaq (excluding Acmat Corporation) in 1999 was the lowest of the three stock exchanges. The mean PVR of the Nasdaq companies was 4.0 percent and the median PVR of the Nasdaq companies was 1.2 percent.

The New York Stock Exchange and American Stock Exchange companies experienced a similar mean PVR, with 8.0 percent and 8.8 percent, respectively. The New York Stock Exchange companies experienced a median PVR of 2.8 percent and American Stock Exchange companies experienced a median PVR of 7.1 percent.

Third, the Study considered the principal industry of the subject company. We determined the principal industry using the SIC code. The multiple stock class corporations included companies in the following industries: (1) manufacturing, (2) transportation, communications, electric gas, and sanitary services, (3) retail trade, (4) finance, insurance, and real estate, and (5) services. Companies operating primarily in the manufacturing industry experienced a mean PVR of 5.7 percent and a median PVR of 3.0 percent. Companies operating primarily in the transportation, communications, electric, gas, and sanitary services industry sector experienced a mean PVR of 10.4 percent and a median PVR of 7.9 percent.

There was one company that operated primarily in the retail trade industry and it had a PVR of 11.8 percent. Companies operating primarily in the finance, insurance, and real estate industry sector experienced a mean PVR (excluding Acmat) of 3.8 percent and a median PVR of 10.9 percent. Companies operating primarily in the services industry experienced a mean PVR of 6.1 percent and a median PVR of 1.2 percent. The lowest mean and median PVR was experienced by companies operating in the finance, insurance, and real estate industry (excluding Acmat). The highest mean PVR was experienced by the one company operating in the retail industry, and the highest median PVR was experienced by companies operating in the finance, insurance, and real estate industries.

Fourth, the mean PVR was 5.6 percent for companies with voting and nonvoting shares. For companies with super voting and voting shares, the mean PVR was higher, at 7.2 percent (without Acmat). In 1994, the mean PVR for voting/nonvoting shares was higher than the overall mean PVR. And, the super voting/voting mean PVR was lower than the overall mean PVR.

The 1999 Study indicated the opposite relationship. The mean PVR for voting/nonvoting is lower than the overall mean PVR. And, the super voting/voting mean PVR is higher than the overall mean PVR. In the 1999 Study, the median PVR for companies with both voting and nonvoting shares was 1.4 percent and the median PVR for companies with both super voting and voting shares was 3.0 percent.

Fifth, there were only two companies where the largest shareholder owned more than 50 percent of the shares in the 1999 Study. One company experienced a PVR "discount" of 9.4 percent, while the other company experienced a PVR of 22.4 percent. Because the 22.4 percent PVR is unusual for a company where the majority of the shares are owned by a single shareholder, there is likely another factor responsible for producing that level of PVR.

There were five companies where insiders held a majority of the voting shares. The average PVR for these companies was significantly larger than the overall average PVR. This is the opposite result than the result concluded in the 1994 Study.

SUMMARY AND CONCLUSION

Estimating the appropriate valuation adjustment for voting rights is a common procedure in ESOP employer corporation stock valuations. Many valuation analysts have prepared studies to analyze the appropriate discounts/premiums related to voting rights. The DLVR/PVR study had the following research objectives:

1. to quantify the market-derived price discount related to the lack of voting rights (or inferior voting rights) of common shares,
2. to quantify the market-derived price premium related to the voting rights associated (or superior voting rights) of common shares, and
3. to quantify the value of voting rights alone as a percent of the total bundle of legal rights associated with common stock ownership.

It was also a research objective of the study to identify factors or attributes of a company that predict/influence the magnitude of the DLVR/PVR.

The WMA study concluded that the mean PVR was 3.0 percent and the median PVR was 1.5 percent, both as of December 31, 1994. The mean DLVR was 2.9 percent and the median DLVR was 1.5 percent, both as of December 31, 1994.

As of December 31, 1999, the mean PVR was 6.5 percent and the median PVR was 2.8 percent. As of December 31, 1999, the mean DLVR was 6.1 percent and the median DLVR was 2.7 percent. These results are consistent with previous DLVR/PVR studies of U.S. corporations on domestic stock exchanges. At least with regard to the corporate attributes considered in the WMA study, there was inconclusive evidence as to the factors that predict/influence the size of the DLVR/PVR.

As of December 31, 1994, the value of voting rights represents a mean 0.8 percent and a median 0.4 percent of the value of the total common equity of the selected multiple stock class corporations. As of December 31, 1999, the value of voting rights represented a mean 1.9 percent and a median 0.2 percent of the value of the total common equity of the selected multiple stock class corporations. And, for both time periods, the size of the voting rights as a percent of the total bundle of equity ownership rights was inversely related to the size of the equity value of the multiple stock class corporations.

In summary, the median PVR was 1.5 percent and the medium DLVR was 1.5% as of December 31, 1994. The median PVR was 2.8% and the median DLVR was 2.7% as of December 31, 1994. These conclusions are entirely consistent with previous published studies that indicated that the PVR and DLVR each range from about 1.5% to about 3.0% for domestic publicly traded corporations. It is not surprising that the 1999 results are at the upper end of the historical range. This is because stock indices reached historical highs at the end of the 1990s. As stock prices were generally higher in 1999 (compared to 1994), an analyst would expect all discounts and premiums calculated based on these stock prices to be larger in 1999 (compared to 1994).

The median value of voting rights as a percentage of total stockholder equity was 0.4 percent in 1994. The median value of voting rights as a percentage of total stockholder equity was 0.2% in 1999. While there are no previous studies to compare these results to, these conclusions indicate that voting rights typically represent a very small percentage (i.e., 0.2 percent to 0.4 percent) of the total stockholder equity of companies with multiple stock classes.

Table 1

Partial Listing of Recent DLVR/PVR Studies

DLVR/PVR Study Performed By	Years Covered in Study	Country/ Exchange	Number of Companies Analyzed	Concluded Premium for Voting Rights	Comments
Lease, McConnell, and Mikkelson	1940-1978	U.S.	30	5.44%	Mean, 30 companies
O'Shea and Siwicki	1989-1990	U.S.	43	3.80%	Mean
			33	2.40%	Mean, excluding 5 highest & 5 lowest companies
			43	1.30%	Median
			6	0.40%	Mean
			6	1.40%	Median
Houlihan Lokey Howard & Zukin	1994	U.S.	18	2.05%	Mean, 1 day
			18	1.46%	Median, 1 day
			18	1.52%	Mean, 60 day moving
			18	1.15%	Median, 60 day moving
			18	1.94%	Mean, 120 day moving
			18	1.29%	Median, 120 day moving
			18	2.53%	Mean, 180 day moving
			18	1.88%	Median, 180 day moving
			18	3.20%	Mean, 260 day moving
			18	2.73%	Median, 260 day moving
Smith and Amoako-Adu	1981-1986	Toronto	81	7.84%	Mean
			81	4.17%	Median
	1988-1992		81	19.31%	Mean (includes 2 companies with premiums > 100%)
			81	6.37%	Median
Zingales	1984-1990	U.S.	94	10.47%	Mean
			94	3.02%	Median
	1987-1990	Milan	84	81.50%	Mean
			84	73.70%	Median
Kunz and Angel	1990-1991	Switzerland	29	18.16%	Average, bearer stock
			29	6.47%	Average, registered stock

Table 1 (continued)

Partial Listing of Recent DLVR/PVR Studies

DLVR/PVR Study Performed By	Years Covered in Study	Country/ Exchange	Number of Companies Analyzed	Concluded Premium for Voting Rights	Comments
Rydqvist	1983-1990	Sweden	65	12.00%	Simple mean
			65	17.00%	Simple median
			65	4.00%	Adjusted mean
			65	4.00%	Adjusted median
Megginson	1995-1982	Britain	152	13.30%	Mean
Levy	1981	Israel	25	45.50%	Mean

References:

Lease, Ronald C., McConnell, John J., Mikkelson, Wayne H. "The Market Value of Control in Publicly Traded Corporations." *Journal of Financial Economics*, vol. 11, (1983), pp. 439-471.

O'Shea, Kevin C., Siwicki, Robert M. "Stock Price Premiums for Voting Rights Attributable to Minority Interests." *Business Valuation Review*, December 1991, pp. 165-171.

Much, Paul J., Fagan, Timothy J. "The Value of Voting Rights." Chapter 9B in *Financial Valuation* (New York: Warren Gorham & Lamont, 2000).

Smith, Brian F., Amoako-Adu, Ben. "Relative Prices of Dual Class Shares." *Journal of Financial and Quantitative Analysis*, vol. 30 (June 1995), pp. 223-239.

Zingales, Luigi. "What Determines the Value of Corporate Votes?" *Quarterly Journal of Economics*, November 1995, pp. 1047-1071.

______. "The Value of the Voting Right: A Study of the Milan Stock Exchange Experience." *The Review of Financial Studies*, vol. 7 (Spring 1994), pp. 125-148.

Kunz, Roger M., and James J. Angel. "Factors Affecting the Value of the Stock Voting Right: Evidence from the Swiss Equity Market." *Financial Management*, vol. 25 (Autumn 1996), pp. 7-20.

Rydqvist, Kristian. "Takeover Bids and the Relative Prices of Shares that Differ in their Voting Rights." *Journal of Financial Economics*, vol. 20 (1996), pp. 1407-1425.

Megginson, William I. "Restricted Voting Stock, Acquisition Premiums and the Market Value of Corporate Control." *The Financial Review*, May 1990, pp. 175-198.

Levy, Haim. "Economic Evaluation of Voting Power of Common Stock." *The Journal of Finance*, vol. 37, no. 1 (March 1982), pp. 79-93.

Chapter 14

ESOP Ownership Control Issues

INTRODUCTION

The economic benefits of ESOP ownership of employer corporation stock are numerous and significant. These economic benefits include: (1) providing employee benefits in a tax-advantaged manner, (2) improving employee morale and commitment, (3) providing for business continuity and widespread equity ownership, (4) providing a source of funding for corporate expansion and capital investments, and (5) serving as a take-over defense or as a means of perpetuating a distressed company.

The significance of these economic benefits of employer corporation stock ownership to the ESOP participants depends on numerous factors. These factors include the financial success of the sponsor company and the percentage of the sponsor company stock owned by the ESOP.

Similar to any other equity investor, an ESOP is often faced with the initial investment decision of whether to acquire a noncontrolling or a controlling ownership interest in the employer corporation equity. Unlike many other equity investors, however, the ESOP may initially purchase a noncontrolling ownership interest in the employer corporation based on a controlling or "enterprise," level of value.

This type of transaction may occur when the seller grants to the ESOP a "purchase right" that enables the ESOP to acquire sufficient additional stock within a reasonable time to bring the ESOP's ownership of voting stock to more than 50 percent. Further, the seller and the ESOP may enter into a "serial sale agreement." Such an agreement provides for the ESOP to acquire sufficient shares representing voting control based upon an agreed upon schedule.

Investors generally recognize that a controlling ownership position in a company has a significant value. This is because such an ownership position generally affords the shareholder the opportunity to effect change in the company. Accordingly, the following questions are important to an ESOP contemplating an ownership control transaction:

1. What is the economic value of the benefits that ownership control is expected to provide?
2. How much more would the ESOP be willing to pay to acquire these economic benefits?
3. How much more in additional remuneration would the ESOP expect to receive when it sells the ownership benefits?

In the 1988 proposed DOL Regulations, the DOL proposed that a plan may pay a "controlling interest value" only if a third party would pay such a premium value. The DOL proposed regulations also indicate that such a premium value is unwarranted unless the ESOP obtains both voting control and control in fact. While the DOL Regulations were never issued in final form, they still serve as professional guidance regarding the valuation of ESOP-owned stock on a controlling ownership interest basis.

The failure of an ESOP trustee to adhere to these guidelines and to adequately justify the purchase of employee stock at a controlling interest price can result in numerous sanctions pursuant to the Internal Revenue Code and ERISA. These sanctions may include the imposition of a substantial nondeductible excise tax on the stock seller, a possible undoing of the entire ESOP stock purchase transaction, the imposition of penalties by the DOL on the ESOP fiduciaries, the loss or diminution of related income tax benefits, and personal liability on the part of the ESOP fiduciaries—if they fail to recover the excess price paid in the transaction.

This discussion summarizes the following issues regarding the valuation of ESOP-owned employer stock on a controlling ownership interest basis—whether for stock purchase or sale purposes:

- factors valuation analysts should consider when applying an ownership control price premium,
- methods used to estimate the appropriate amount of any control price premium,
- how valuation methods affect the appropriateness and the magnitude of the control price premium,
- Department of Labor regulations,
- applying a control price premium when the ESOP purchases or sells a majority of the employer corporation voting stock,

- applying a control price premium when the ESOP purchases less than a majority of the employer corporation voting stock, and
- applying a control price premium in circumstances of "creeping" ESOP ownership.

FACTORS TO CONSIDER WHEN APPLYING AN OWNERSHIP CONTROL PRICE PREMIUM

Many business owners attach personal, or "psychic," value to the circumstance of being their own bosses. However, from an ESOP's perspective, any additional consideration paid to acquire ownership control (or received for relinquishing control) is typically attributable to the identifiable, quantifiable economic benefits of operational control. These economic benefits generally result from certain prerogatives, or rights, inherent within a controlling stock ownership position.

The common prerogatives of corporate ownership control include the right to:

1. appoint management;
2. establish management compensation and perquisites;
3. establish corporate policy and business focus;
4. acquire or liquidate assets;
5. establish and maintain (or terminate) business and contractual relationships;
6. acquire other companies, or liquidate, dissolve, sell out, or recapitalize the company;
7. sell or acquire treasury shares;
8. register the company's stock for a public offering;
9. declare and pay dividends;
10. change the corporate articles or bylaws;
11. enter into debt covenants and borrow funds; or
12. block any of the previous actions.

To estimate the value of a company on a business enterprise, or controlling ownership interest, basis, the analyst should consider, at the very least, each of the aforementioned factors. The analyst should consider the additional value of the rights inherent in a controlling ownership position—relative to the value of the rights that a noncontrolling stockholder position provides.

In essence, the additional value of ownership control represents the maximum additional economic benefits—typically represented by dividends, compensation, perquisites, contract rights, and other discretionary items—that a controlling ownership position would enable the controlling shareholder to enjoy (and that a noncontrolling stockholder could not expect).

MARKET EVIDENCE REGARDING OWNERSHIP CONTROL PRICE PREMIUMS

In general, a control value may be estimated (1) directly through the use of certain business valuation methods or (2) indirectly through the application of a control premium adjustment to the indicated value of the company stock estimate on a noncontrolling basis. To estimate the appropriate control premium adjustment, analysts generally consider data regarding prices paid in merger/acquisition control event transactions compared to the preacquisition noncontrolling interest transaction prices.

However, in analyzing the control price premium data, it is important to remember that the additional price paid in control event transactions over the noncontrolling value may reflect factors in addition to elements of ownership control. Such factors may include the post-merger synergistic benefits that are expected to accrue to a particular corporate buyer.

There are several sources of data that summarize the actual price premiums that were paid in control event transactions. One example of a source frequently used by analysts to estimate control premium adjustments is *Mergerstat Review*. This publication presents the price premium paid over the minority trading price reported five business days before the initial announcement of a control event merger or acquisition transaction. For example, for calendar 2003, *Mergerstat Review* reported an overall median acquisition price premium of 34.4 percent, based on an analysis of 326 total merger/acquisition transactions.

In instances where acquisition price premium data are available for several transactions involving companies that operate in the same industry as the subject company, this industry-specific transaction data may provide empirical evidence regarding the appropriate ownership control price premium.

HOW THE SELECTED BUSINESS VALUATION METHODS IMPACT THE APPROPRIATENESS AND MAGNITUDE OF A CONTROL PRICE PREMIUM

Within each of the generally accepted business valuation approaches—income, market, and asset-based—are methods that will provide a preliminary value indication that may reflect none, some portion, or substantially all of the economic benefits of ownership control. Additionally, the business valuation approaches and methods will result in value indications which represent either marketable or nonmarketable positions.

To form a relevant value opinion, the analyst should recognize the aforementioned levels of value that the selected valuation methods conclude related to the subject sponsor company and the subject ownership interest. When appraising employer corporation stock for the purpose of a control event transaction, the analyst could fail to recognize that a certain valuation approach or method produces a value indication that already reflects substantially all of the economic benefits of control. That failure could result in the ESOP paying more than adequate consideration for the controlling ownership interest. This overpayment situation could occur if the analyst inappropriately applies a control premium adjustment to a value indication that already concludes a control level of value.

Table 1 on the following page presents (1) a summary of generally accepted business valuation approaches and methods, (2) the implied levels of value typically reflected in a preliminary conclusion from each method, and (3) whether the application of an additional control premium adjustment is appropriate.

Table 1 presents a general summary regarding the appropriateness of applying a control premium adjustment to value indications resulting from the identified valuation method. As presented in Table 1, a key consideration regarding whether a control premium should be applied is represented by the degree to which the historical or expected economic earnings of the subject company have been adjusted to reflect the economic benefits of ownership control.

In addition, with regard to the market approach, the analyst should consider pricing conditions within the public markets as of the valuation date. That is, the analyst should consider whether implied control premiums reflected in the analysis of merged and acquired companies actually reflect acquisition (i.e., "synergistic") price premiums which the ESOP would not be expected to pay or receive.

Table 1

Generally Accepted Business Valuation Approaches and Methods Considerations of Typical Levels of Value

Valuation Approach	Valuation Method	Typical Level of Value Concluded	Typical Basis for the Level of Value Characteristics	Control Premium Adjustment Applicable?
Income	Discounted cash flow	Noncontrolling/ marketable	Use of unadjusted income measures	Yes
	Discounted cash flow	Controlling/ marketable	Use of adjusted income measures	No
	Direct capitalization	Noncontrolling/ marketable	Use of unadjusted income measures	Yes
	Direct capitalization	Controlling/ marketable	Use of adjusted income measures	No
Market	Guideline publicly traded company	Noncontrolling/ marketable	Use of stock market prices of noncontrolling blocks of stock	Yes
	Guideline merged and acquired company	Controlling/ marketable	Use of prices of controlling ownership interest transfers only	No
Asset-based	Asset accumulation	Controlling/ marketable	Assumes equityholder has ability to convert asset values into cash	No
	Adjusted net asset value	Noncontrolling/ marketable	Use of unadjusted income measures in capitalized excess earnings analysis	Yes
	Adjusted net asset value	Controlling/ marketable	Use of adjusted income measures in capitalized excess earnings analysis	No

DOL REGULATIONS

On May 17, 1988, the DOL issued the "Proposed Regulation Relating to the Definition of Adequate Consideration." According to the proposed regulation:

> The Department proposes that a plan purchasing control may pay a control premium, and a plan selling control should receive a control premium. Specifically, the Department proposes that a plan may pay such a premium only to the extent a third party would pay a control premium. In this regard, the Department's position is that the payment of a control premium is unwarranted unless the plan obtains both voting control and control in fact. The Department will therefore carefully scrutinize situations to ascertain whether the transaction involving payment of such a premium actually results in the passing of control to the plan. For example, it may be difficult to determine

> that a plan paying a control premium has received control in fact where it is reasonable to assume at the time of acquisition that distribution of shares to plan participants will cause the plan's control of the company to be dissipated within a short period of time subsequent to acquisition.* In the Department's view, however, a plan would not fail to receive control merely because individuals who were previously officers, directors or shareholders of the corporation continue as plan fiduciaries or corporate officials after the plan has acquired the securities. Nonetheless, the retention of management and the utilization of corporate officials as plan fiduciaries, when viewed in conjunction with other facts, may indicate that actual control has not passed to the plan within the meaning of paragraph (b)(4)(ii)(I) of the proposed regulation.
>
> *However, the DOL notes that the mere pass-through of voting rights to participants would not in itself affect a determination that a plan has received control in fact, notwithstanding the existence of participant voting rights, if the plan fiduciaries having control over plan assets ordinarily may resell the shares to a third party and command a control premium, without the need to secure the approval of the plan participants.

The DOL proposed regulation provides the only regulatory guidance regarding the appropriateness of an ESOP paying an ownership control premium for employer corporation stock.

APPLYING AN OWNERSHIP CONTROL PREMIUM WHEN THE ESOP PURCHASES OR SELLS A MAJORITY OF THE OUTSTANDING STOCK

When the ESOP purchases or sells a majority, or controlling, block of the outstanding voting stock of the employer corporation, the ESOP should expect to pay or receive some level of incremental consideration. This consideration is related to the additional value of the ownership control economic benefits received or transferred. As previously discussed, the level of incremental consideration may or may not be reflected in the value indication (1) resulting from the valuation approaches used and (2) as a result of the manner in which the income measures were developed.

When initially engaged to estimate the fair market value of a controlling ownership position for purchase or sale by an ESOP, analysts typically use those valuation methods which provide value indications on a business enterprise basis. Such valuation methods typically include: (1) the discounted cash flow method and the capitalization method (with income measures adjusted to reflect the economic benefits of ownership control), (2) the guideline merged and acquired company method, and (3) the asset accumulation method.

One of the primary benefits of using valuation methods that provide value indications on a business enterprise basis is that the analyst does not have to independently estimate the appropriate control premium adjustment. This is particularly important when merger and acquisition transaction activity within a certain industry is limited or nonexistent.

If the valuation methods used by the analyst initially provide value indications on a controlling ownership interest basis (such as the guideline publicly traded company method or income approach methods based on unadjusted income measures), the analyst should estimate the appropriate control premium adjustment. The typical methods used by analysts to estimate control premium adjustments were discussed above. And, these methods are generally based on an analysis of acquisition price premiums paid in the employer corporation's industry classification.

From the perspective of the analyst, and therefore from the perspective of the plan fiduciaries, it is important that the control premium adjustment included in the final value is supported by empirical market transactions and/or by expected economic benefits of control. The total control premium adjustment may reflect a combination of the impact of adjustment income measures and the application of some level of ownership control premium. The analysis should present valuation evidence that the ESOP is not (1) paying more than adequate consideration in an employer stock purchase or (2) receiving less than adequate consideration in an employer stock sale.

APPLYING CONTROL PREMIUM ADJUSTMENT WHEN THE ESOP PURCHASES LESS THAN A MAJORITY OF THE OUTSTANDING STOCK

In some circumstances, it is appropriate to apply a control premium adjustment even though the ESOP purchases less than a majority of the sponsor company's outstanding stock. According to the DOL proposed regulations:

> . . . if the plan purchases employer securities in small increments pursuant to an understanding with the employer that the employer will eventually sell a controlling portion of shares to the plan, a control premium would be warranted only to the extent that the understand-

ing with the employer was actually a binding agreement obligating the employer to pass control within a reasonable time.

In these circumstances, many analysts agree that an ESOP should be able to pay the amount that a hypothetical third-party buyer would pay for the subject employer stock. Important considerations in evaluating the appropriateness and magnitude of a control premium adjustment when the ESOP purchases less than a majority ownership interest include:

1. whether there is a binding agreement granting the ESOP the right to acquire enough voting stock to give the ESOP ownership control;
2. consideration as to whether the ESOP is able to exercise the right to acquire ownership control within a reasonable time after the subject stock purchase;
3. an analysis of ownership control, and consideration of any rights that the ESOP will not receive; and
4. evaluation of whether there is any ceiling or oversight rights regarding compensation and perquisites, especially to the selling stockholder(s), during the purchase option period.

APPLYING A CONTROL PREMIUM ADJUSTMENT IN CIRCUMSTANCES OF GRADUALLY INCREASING ESOP OWNERSHIP

Gradually increasing ESOP ownership is generally the result of (1) the purchase by the ESOP of additional shares of employer stock, (2) employer corporation stock contributions to the ESOP, or (3) the repurchase of non-ESOP shares by the sponsor company.

In situations where an ESOP moves over a period for time from a noncontrolling ownership position to a sizable block of stock with substantial influence, the analyst should consider applying some incremental value above that which would be accorded a noncontrolling ownership interest. This incremental value would reflect what a hypothetical willing buyer would be willing to pay for the economic advantages of control associated with the block of employer corporation stock owned by the ESOP.

SUMMARY AND CONCLUSION

This discussion identified many of the considerations that analysts make when estimating the fair market value of employer corporation stock on a business enterprise basis (controlling ownership interest basis). As the financial adviser to the ESOP, the analyst cannot provide sound economic advice to the ESOP trustee, whether for the purpose of an acquisition or a sale, if (1) the above-mentioned considerations are not appropriately addressed and (2) the related implications adequately reflected in the analyst's value conclusion.

The valuation analyst's failure to address these considerations can result in: (1) ESOP employer corporation stock purchase/sale transactions that are ultimately nullified, (2) significant taxes and penalties imposed on the non-ESOP stock seller, and (3) personal liability on the part of the ESOP plan fiduciaries.

Chapter 15

Valuation of S Corporation Stock

INTRODUCTION

Valuation analysts still debate the economic impact of income taxes on the fair market value of employer corporation securities when the employer has elected S corporation status. Until recently, this debate centered on whether it was more appropriate to use (1) an individual ordinary income tax rate or (2) a regular C corporation income tax rate to tax-affect the reported net income[1] of the S corporation. Regardless of which tax rate is used, there was a general consensus in the valuation profession that income taxes should be estimated and deducted from the S corporation net income. This "tax-affecting" procedure was performed when publicly traded C corporations were used as benchmarks or guideline companies in the S corporation valuation analysis.

Between 1999 and 2002, the U.S. Tax Court published three decisions that fundamentally challenged the way analysts value the stock of S corporations. In *Gross v. Commissioner*,[2] *Heck v. Commissioner*,[3] and *Adams v. Commissioner*,[4] the Tax Court held that estimated income tax should not be deducted from the projected S corporation net income when using the income valuation approach. Although these decisions focused on the income approach, the valuation theory used by the Tax Court conceptually extends to both the market approach and the asset-based approach. If analysts adopted the valuation theory used by the Tax Court, the economic implications would be significant. These implications extend beyond the federal gift and estate tax consequences of the three aforementioned judicial decisions. Now that an ESOP can own the stock of an S status employer corporation, the valuation of S corporations has become an important ESOP valuation issue.

This discussion summarizes (1) general economic characteristics of business valuation approaches, (2) certain differences in the income tax treatment of (a) S corporations and C corporations and (b) their respective stockholders, and (3) the differences in net economic benefit derived by S corporation and C corporation stockholders. A mathematical framework is provided that analysts may use to adjust the indicated value of S corporation equity securities when empirical studies/analyses of C corporations are used to estimate value.

As will be demonstrated, the analysis presented in this discussion is only relevant to the value of S status employer corporation securities that lack ownership control (i.e., that are valued on a noncontrolling ownership interest basis).

The valuation of ESOP-owned S corporation stock is still an evolving issues. Unlike most other topics in this Guide to ESOP Valuation, there is not a general consensus among valuation practitioners with regard to appropriate adjustments (if any) to make in the valuation of ESOP-owned S corporation stock. This discussion presents a de novo methodology with regard to S corporation valuation issues. This methodology appears to be reasonable with regard to the valuation of closely held S corporation stock for federal gift and estate tax purposes. This methodology is presented here for the purpose of instigating discussion among ESOP valuation practitioners. The S corporation valuation methodology presented in this discussion ultimately may—or may not—become the consensus among experienced ESOP valuation analysts.

BASIC PREMISES

There are two basic premises that affect this discussion. The first premise is that there are significant differences in the income tax treatment of (1) S corporation and C corporation employer companies and (2) their respective stockholders. These differences are briefly described below:

C corporations are subject to corporate income taxes at the entity level. Conversely, S corporation shareholders recognize a pro rata share of the reported net income of the S corporation on their personal income tax returns. In essence, the stockholders pay the corporate income tax of the S corporation on their personal income tax returns.

Under current tax law, dividends from C corporations are subject to dividend income tax rates at the shareholder level.[5] Conversely, dividends received by stockholders of S corporations are generally not subject to income taxes.

The undistributed income of an S corporation changes the tax basis of its equity securities. Conversely, the undistributed income of a C corporation does not change the tax basis of its equity securities.

The second premise is that capital markets are efficient, at least over the long term. Consequently, stock prices, investment rates of return, and price to earnings multiples of publicly traded C corporations inherently reflect the income tax treatment of C corporations and their respective stockholders.

Based on these two premises, there is a conceptual mismatch between (1) the economic characteristics of the empirical market data (i.e., investment rates of return, price to earnings pricing multiples, etc.) of publicly traded C corporations and (2) the economic benefits enjoyed by S corporation stockholders. These differences have the potential to distort the value of S corporation equity securities—when empirical studies of C corporations are used to estimate value.

It is difficult—if not impossible—to develop accurate and robust empirical studies of actual corporate security transactions that specifically isolate and quantify value differences solely attributable to the income tax characteristics of (1) S corporations and C corporations and (2) their respective shareholders. This is because of (1) the nearly infinite variety of corporate and individual security transaction structures and (2) the paucity of information available on transactions involving S corporations noncontrolling equity ownership interests.

Consequently, there is a need for a mathematical framework that conceptually addresses the relevant income-tax-related differences between S corporations and C corporations. There is also a need for a mathematical framework that permits the adjustment of estimated values of S corporation equity securities when publicly traded C corporations are used in the valuation analysis. In order to be useful, this mathematical framework should be applicable to the generally accepted business valuation approaches and methods.

BUSINESS VALUATION APPROACHES

There are three generally accepted business valuation approaches: (1) the income approach, (2) the market approach, and (3) the asset-based approach. The current S corporation valuation controversy has generally focused on the income valuation approach—and, notably, the discounted cash flow method. This is principally due to the fact that the *Gross*, *Heck*, and *Adams* decisions focused on whether it was appropriate to tax-affect S corporation projected net income within the income approach. The Tax Court found that it was not appropriate to tax-affect S corporation income when using a present value discount rate derived from empirical studies of guideline publicly traded S corporations.

Theoretically, the three business valuation approaches should arrive at similar value indications. However, eliminating the tax effect from the income approach has the potential of creating widely divergent value indications among the business valuation approaches. If S corporation equity securities have an inherent economic benefit vis-à-vis C corporation equity securities, then this economic benefit should be reflected in all business valuation approaches (and, not just in the income approach).

In order to assess whether the S corporation income tax status has an impact on the various business valuation approaches, it is necessary to understand (1) the general economic nature of corporate transactions and (2) how empirical studies of these transactions are reflected with the various business valuation approaches. In order to simplify the following explanations, this discussion groups into two categories: (1) income-based approaches and (2) asset-based approaches.

INCOME-BASED APPROACHES

For purposes of this discussion, the income approach and market approach are both classified as income-based approaches. The income approach uses projections of future income to estimate value. The market approach uses measurements of historical income to estimate value. The indicated value of equity provided by each of these approaches is based on (1) a measurement of income and (2) the application of a capitalization factor. For purposes of this discussion, a capitalization factor is defined as a percentage—or multiple—used to convert a measurement of income into a value indication. Capitalization factors used in the income approach may take the form of a single-period capitalization rate or a multi-period present value discount rate. Capitalization factors used in the market approach may take the form of a market-derived pricing multiple.

Income Approach

Within the income approach, there are a variety of valuation methods. The two most commonly used methods are (1) the discounted cash flow method and (2) the single-period direct capitalization method. These methods use a capitalization factor—typically derived from empirical studies of investment rates of return on publicly traded C corporations—to estimate the subject company value. Depending on the nature of the economic income being capitalized (i.e., net cash flow, net income, etc.), investment rates of return on guideline publicly traded companies are included in an analysis of the weighted average cost of capital (WACC) or other income capitalization rate models. Regardless of how they are used, public company investment rates of return provide the fundamental basis for calculating the capitalization factors used in the income approach.

A fundamental business valuation principle is that the economic characteristics of income and capitalization factors should be conceptually consistent in order to calculate the supportable estimates of value. In order to determine whether the economic characteristics of the income and capitalization factors are consistent with respect to S corporations, it is necessary to understand how investment rates of return are calculated.

Investors (including ESOP investors) in equity securities expect to receive an investment rate of return that is comprised of some combination of income (i.e., cash dividends) and capital gains or losses. The following formula presents the mathematical calculation of the investment rate of return for an equity security:

$$k_1 = \frac{(S_1 - S_0) + d_1}{S_0}$$

where:

k_1 = Investment rate of return during period 1

S_1 = Stock price at end of period 1

S_0 = Stock price at beginning of period 1

d_1 = Dividends paid during period 1

The above formula illustrates the fundamental principle that the investment rates of return on equity securities—and, therefore, the capitalization factors—are derived from a combination of the capital appreciation of the security ($S_1 - S_0$) and dividend payments (d_1).

Theoretically, capital appreciation and dividend payments are derived from the net income of the corporation. In other words, net income is either (1) paid to the stockholders in the form of dividends or (2) retained in the company (resulting in the capital appreciation).[6] Consequently, investment rates of return inherently reflect (1) corporate income taxes at the entity level, (2) capital gains taxes at the stockholder level, and (3) dividend income taxes at the stockholder level. To the extent that there are differences among the income, capital gains, and dividend income tax treatment of S corporations and C corporations and their respective stockholders, the value indications provided by the income approach are potentially distorted when investment rates of return of publicly traded C corporations are used to value S corporation equity securities.

Market Approach

Within the market approach, there are a variety of valuation methods. The two most commonly used methods are (1) the guideline publicly traded company method and (2) the guideline merged and acquired (M&A) company method.

The guideline publicly traded company method estimates the subject company value based on the application of a capitalization factor (i.e., market-derived pricing multiple) extracted from empirical studies of stock prices and financial fundamentals of comparative publicly traded C corporations. General investment theory tells us that these market-derived pricing multiples are based on the same fundamental principles as the investment rates of return used in the income approach. Essentially, a market-derived pricing multiple is an investment rate of return adjusted for future growth. Therefore, these pricing multiples inherently reflect the same economic attributes as publicly traded company investment rates of returns.

The guideline M&A company method estimates the subject company value based on the application of market-derived pricing multiples extracted from empirical studies of transaction prices and financial fundamentals of companies involved in merger or acquisition transactions. The guideline M&A company method typically provides a controlling ownership interest value indication of the subject company. When using this method to value an equity interest that lacks ownership control, a valuation discount for lack of control is typically applied.

This discount is often estimated using empirical studies of acquisition price premiums paid for publicly traded equity securities in control event merger or acquisition transactions. The inverse of this acquisition price premium is generally considered a reasonable proxy for the discount lack of control. When this discount for lack of control is appropriately estimated and applied, the analyst has essentially adjusted the M&A transaction pricing multiples to publicly traded company equivalent pricing multiples. As such, these adjusted M&A transaction pricing multiples—adjusted for lack of control—inherently reflect the same income tax characteristics as publicly traded company investment rates of return.

Therefore, to the extent that there are differences between the income tax treatments of (1) S corporations and C corporations and (2) their respective stockholders, the value indications provided by the market approach may be distorted. This potential distortion may result when (1) public company market-derived pricing multiples or (2) acquisition price premiums paid for publicly traded companies are used in the valuation analysis.

ASSET-BASED APPROACH

Within the asset-based approach, there are a variety of valuation methods. The two most common methods are (1) the asset accumulation method and (2) the adjusted net asset value (or excess earnings) method. The asset-based approach is not commonly used to value a noncontrolling equity ownership interest in an employer corporation. This is principally due to the fact that (1) profitable going-concern business enterprises typically have a variety of intangible assets that should be discretely valued in order to properly estimate total asset value and (2) the indication of value provided by the asset-based approach is typically on a controlling ownership interest basis. The combination of these two factors results in a business valuation approach that is difficult and expensive to implement when quantifying a noncontrolling equity ownership interest value.

Typically, the asset-based approach provides an equity value indication on an ownership control basis. As such, the indication of value should be adjusted with a discount for lack of control when valuing a noncontrolling equity interest. When this discount is quantified using price premiums paid for the merger or acquisition of publicly traded companies, the analyst has effectively adjusted the controlling interest value indication to a value that is conceptually consistent with the indication of value provided by the guideline publicly traded company method. As such, the value indication provided by the asset-based approach inherently reflects the same income tax characteristics as publicly traded company investment rates of return.

Therefore, to the extent that there are differences between the income tax treatment of (1) S corporations and C corporations and (2) their respective shareholders, the value indication provided by the asset-based approach may be distorted. This potential distortion may result when merger or acquisition price premiums paid for publicly traded companies are used in the valuation analysis.

In summary, the income approach, market approach, and asset-based approach can be used to estimate the C corporation publicly traded equivalent value of a noncontrolling equity ownership interest in a C corporation or an S corporation. Figure 1 on the following page illustrates this concept.

CONCEPTUAL MISMATCH BETWEEN S CORPORATIONS AND C CORPORATIONS

There are a variety of economic differences—both tax and nontax—between S corporations and C corporations. This discussion will not address the majority of these economic differences. Instead, the discussion summarizes

Figure 1

Business Valuation Approaches and Methods

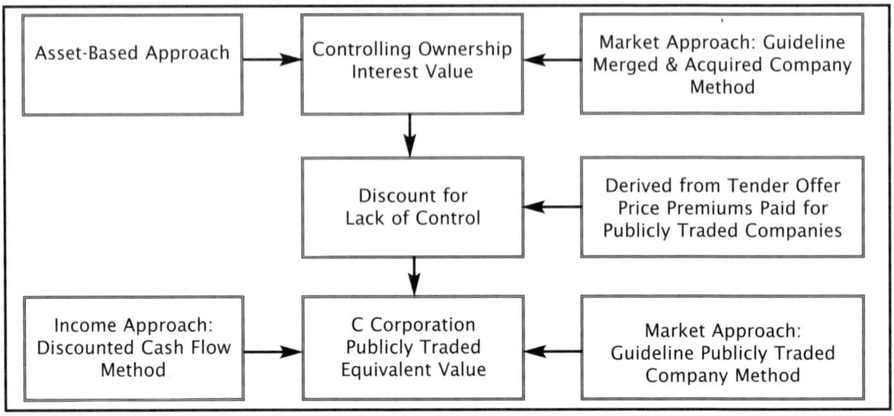

the valuation implications attributable to the income tax and capital gains tax differences between S corporations and C corporations at the stockholder level.[7] Exhibit 1, Net Economic Benefit to Stockholders, demonstrates these income-tax-related differences by calculating the net economic benefit derived by the stockholders of S corporations and C corporations. Exhibit 1 was created using the following assumptions:

- Distribution (i.e., dividend) payout ratio of 50 percent of net income.
- C corporation corporate income tax rate of 35 percent.
- Individual ordinary income tax rate of 35 percent.
- Dividend income tax rate of 15 percent.
- Capital gains income tax rate of 15 percent.
- Capital gains tax liability is economically recognized when incurred.
- Capital appreciation of equity is derived from increases in retained earnings on a dollar-for-dollar basis.

As demonstrated in Exhibit 1, the total net economic benefit derived by S corporation stockholders is different from the net economic benefit derived by C corporation stockholders. Historically, business valuation analysts have attempted to correct for these differences by estimating income taxes and subtracting this amount from the reported net income of the subject S corporation. Unfortunately, this adjustment does not properly resolve the economic mismatch.

Exhibit 1

Net Economic Benefit to Stockholders

	C Corp. ($)	S Corp. ($)
Income before Corporate Income Taxes	100,000	100,000
Corporate Income Taxes	(35,000)	NM
Net Income	65,000	100,000
Dividends		
Distributions to S Corporation Stockholders	NM	50,000
Income Tax Due by S Corporation Stockholders	NM	(35,000)
Net Cash Flow Benefit to S Corporation Stockholders	NM	**15,000**
Dividends to C Corporation Stockholders	32,500	NM
Dividend Tax Due by C Corporation Stockholders	(4,875)	NM
Net Cash Flow Benefit to C Corporation Stockholders	**27,625**	NM
Capital Appreciation		
Net Income	65,000	100,000
Dividends and Distributions	(32,500)	(50,000)
Retained Earnings (i.e., Net Capital Appreciation)	32,500	50,000
Effect of Increase in Income Tax Basis of Shares	NM	(50,000)
Taxable Capital Appreciation	32,500	0
Capital Gains Tax Liability	(4,875)	0
Net Capital Appreciation Benefit to Stockholders	**27,625**	**50,000**
Net Economic Benefit to Stockholders		
Net Cash Flow Benefit to Stockholders	**27,625**	**15,000**
Net Capital Appreciation Benefit to Stockholders	**27,625**	**50,000**
Total Net Economic Benefit to Stockholders	**55,250**	**65,000**

A review and analysis of Exhibit 1 leads to the following important conclusions:

- *The net economic benefit (the bottom line of Exhibit 1) to S corporation stockholders is greater than to C corporation shareholders regardless of the assumed dividend payout ratio.* This is due to the fact that S corporation stockholders have two distinct income tax advantages: (1) dividends are not taxable at the stockholder level and (2) undistributed (i.e., retained) earnings increase the tax basis of S corporation shares. C corporation shareholders do not enjoy either of these income tax benefits.
- *The net economic benefit to C corporation stockholders remains the same regardless of dividend payout ratio.* The dividend payout ratio alters the

proportion of the net economic benefit attributable to either dividends or capital appreciation. If dividends and capital appreciation are taxed at identical rates, the dividend payout ratio does not affect the total net economic benefit to the stockholder. However, if dividends and capital appreciation are taxed at different rates, changes in the dividend payout ratio will affect the total net economic benefit received by the stockholder. Under current federal income tax law, the tax rate on dividends and capital appreciation is equivalent. Therefore, the information provided on Exhibit 1 assumes that the income tax rates are identical for dividends and capital gains.

- *The net economic benefit to S corporation stockholders remains the same regardless of dividend payout ratio.* This is due to the fact that S corporation stockholders receive either cash—after the payment of income taxes on the reported net income of the S corporation—or tax-free capital appreciation in the value of the stock. The mix of economic benefit of either cash or tax-free capital appreciation changes as the dividend payout ratio changes. However, the net economic benefit to S corporation stockholders remains the same regardless of dividend payout ratio.

Exhibit 1 illustrates the differences in net economic benefit derived by S corporation and C corporation stockholders resulting from the disparate income tax treatment of each type of corporation and its respective shareholders. These differences result in an economic mismatch between (1) the information derived from empirical studies of transactions involving C corporation equity securities and (2) the net economic benefits enjoyed by S corporation stockholders.

Historically, analysts have attempted to correct for these differences by (1) estimating income taxes and (2) subtracting this amount from the reported net income of the subject S corporation. Unfortunately, this adjustment does not properly resolve the mismatch. Also, it is difficult—if not impossible—to formulate accurate empirical studies of equity security transactions that specifically isolate the economic differences solely attributable to the differing income tax treatments of C corporations and S corporations. Consequently, a mathematical framework that adjusts the indicated equity value of an S corporation to account for these differences would be beneficial. A suggested mathematical framework is provided in the following discussion. This model is referred to as the "S corporation economic adjustment."

THE S CORPORATION ECONOMIC ADJUSTMENT

The S corporation economic adjustment (SEA) provides a means to address the differences in net economic benefits between S corporation and C corporation stockholders.

The SEA contemplates the differing income tax treatments of S corporations, C corporations, and their respective stockholders. As such, the SEA is the first step in creating a mathematical framework that may be used to adjust the indicated value of noncontrolling equity ownership interests in S corporations. The SEA is based on equations that model the net economic benefits to (1) C corporation stockholders (NEB_C) and (2) S corporation stockholders (NEB_S).

The NEB_C equation is comprised of two principle components: (1) net cash received by stockholders from (a) dividends after the payment of income taxes at the entity level and (b) income taxes on dividends at the stockholder level and (2) net capital appreciation of the equity security after recognition of capital gains taxes at the stockholder level.

The equation for the first component of the NEB_C equation is provided below:

$$\text{Net Cash from Dividends} = I_p \times (1 - t_c) \times D_p \times (1 - t_d)$$

where:

I_p = Reported income prior to federal and state income tax ($I_p > 0$)

t_c = C corporation effective income tax rate

D_p = Dividend payout ratio

t_d = Income tax rate on dividends

The equation for the second component of the NEB_C equation is provided below:

$$\text{Net Capital Appreciation} = I_p \times (1 - t_c) \times (1 - D_p) \times (1 - t_{cg})$$

where:

I_p = Reported income prior to federal and state income tax ($I_p > 0$)

t_c = C corporation effective income tax rate

D_p = Dividend payout ratio

t_{cg} = Capital gains tax rate

Adding together the first and second components of the NEB_C equation results in an equation that models the total net economic benefit to the C corporation stockholder.

The NEB_C equation in its entirety is provided below:

$$NEB_C = [I_p \times (1 - t_c) \times D_p \times (1 - t_d)] + [I_p \times (1 - t_c) \times (1 - D_p) \times (1 - t_{cg})]$$

The NEB_S equation is less complex. The NEB_S equation simply multiplies S corporation reported net income by one minus the individual ordinary income tax rate $(1 - t_i)$. This is the only adjustment necessary due to the fact that the income tax paid at the stockholder level represents the only income tax-related economic drain to the reported net income of the S corporation. The remaining S corporation net income (i.e., after payment of income tax at the stockholder level) provides either tax-free dividends or tax-free capital appreciation[8] of the equity security. The NEB_S equation is provided below:

$$NEB_S = I_p \times (1 - t_i)$$

Obviously, there is a mathematical inequality between the NEB_C and NEB_S equations. This inequality represents the difference between the net economic benefit derived by S corporation stockholders and the net economic benefit derived by C corporation stockholders. This inequality is the SEA.

$$NEB_C = NEB_S - SEA$$

An algebraic manipulation of the above formula produces the SEA equation:

$$SEA = NEB_S - NEB_C$$

A detailed version of the SEA equation is provided below:

$$SEA = [I_p \times (1 - t_i)] - \{[I_p \times (1 - t_c) \times D_p \times (1 - t_d)] + [I_p \times (1 - t_c) \times (1 - D_p) \times (1 - t_{cg})]\}$$

The algebraically simplified version of the SEA equation is provided below:

$$\text{SEA} = I_p \times (t_c + t_{cg} - t_i - t_{ctcg} + D_{ptd} - D_{ptcg} - D_{ptctd} + D_{ptctcg})$$

The SEA equation quantifies the incremental net economic benefit of being an S corporation stockholder vis-à-vis a C corporation stockholder. As such, the SEA equation is useful in creating a factor that may be used to adjust the estimated equity value of a noncontrolling equity ownership interest in an S corporation. The calculation of this factor is provided in the following section.

S CORPORATION EQUITY ADJUSTMENT MULTIPLE (SEAM)

The SEA can be used to estimate the percentage economic benefit of being an S corporation stockholder vis-à-vis a C corporation stockholder by dividing the SEA by the NEB_C. This percentage is added to 1.0 to calculate a multiple that may then be used to adjust the indicated equity value of an S corporation when empirical studies/analyses of C corporations are used to estimate such value. This multiple is referred to as the S Corporation Equity Adjustment Multiple (SEAM).

The basic SEAM equation is provided below:

$$\text{SEAM} = 1 + \frac{\text{SEA}}{\text{NEB}_C}$$

A detailed version of the SEAM equation is provided below:

$$\text{SEAM} = 1 + \frac{[I_p \times (1 - t_i)] - \{[I_p \times (1 - t_c) \times D_p \times (1 - t_d)] + [I_p \times (1 - t_c) \times (1 - D_p) \times (1 - t_{cg})]\}}{[I_p \times (1 - t_c) \times D_p \times (1 - t_d)] + [I_p \times (1 - t_c) \times (1 - D_p) \times (1 - t_{cg})]}$$

The algebraically simplified version of the SEAM equation is provided below:

$$\text{SEAM} = 1 + \frac{(t_c + t_{cg} - t_i - t_c t_{cg} + D_p t_d - D_p t_{cg} - D_p t_c t_d + D_p t_c t_{cg})}{(1 - t_c - t_{cg} + t_c t_{cg} - D_p t_d + D_p t_{cg} + D_p t_c t_d - D_p t_c t_{cg})}$$

APPLICATION OF THE SEAM

Once the SEAM is calculated, the application of the SEAM in the valuation analysis is relatively simple. The analyst (1) estimates the C corporation publicly traded equivalent value of the subject S corporation equity and (2) multiplies this concluded value by the SEAM.

When estimating the C corporation publicly traded equivalent value of the equity of the S corporation, the following guidelines generally apply:

- When using the income approach, the analyst should estimate corporate level income taxes and deduct this amount from the projected net income of the S corporation.
- When using the market approach, the price to earnings multiples of the guideline publicly traded C corporations should be applied to the same earnings fundamentals of the subject S corporation as those used to calculate the same price to earnings multiples.
- When using any valuation approach that results in a controlling ownership interest indication of value, a discount for lack of control (DLOC) should be considered. If used, the DLOC should be estimated using empirical studies of acquisition price premiums paid for the equity securities of publicly traded companies in control event merger or acquisition transactions.

When the analyst multiplies the C corporation publicly traded equivalent value by the SEAM, the resulting value indication is an S corporation publicly traded equivalent value. In other words, the SEAM adjusted equity value indication is the hypothetical value of the subject S corporation equity as though an efficient capital market existed for S corporation equity securities. An illustration of this calculation is provided in Figure 2.

Figure 2

Application of the SEAM

C Corporation Publicly Traded Equivalent Value	X	S Corporation Equity Adjustment Multiple (SEAM)	=	S Corporation Publicly Traded Equivalent Value

The selection of the numerical components of the SEAM equation is properly left to the discretion of the analyst. However, the following is provided for consideration:

- C corporation effective income tax rate (t_c): The effective income tax rate of the publicly traded C corporations selected as comparative to the subject S corporation.
- Capital gains tax rate (t_{cg}): A composite of combined federal and state long-term capital gains tax rates.
- Individual ordinary income tax rate (t_i): A composite of combined federal and state individual income tax rates.
- Income tax rate on dividends (t_d): A composite of combined federal and state individual income tax rate on dividends.
- Dividend payout ratio (D_p): The dividend payout ratio of publicly traded C corporations selected as comparative to the subject S corporation.

The application of the SEAM is merely a step in the process of estimating the value of a noncontrolling equity ownership interest in an S corporation. Other factors—most notably the discount for lack of marketability (DLOM)—should be considered when estimating the value of a noncontrolling equity ownership interest in an S corporation. A discussion of the SEAM-specific factors to consider when estimating the appropriate DLOM is provided in the following section.

DISCOUNT FOR LACK OF MARKETABILITY

The DLOM is typically one of the most important and economically significant adjustments that a valuation analyst makes in the course of valuing a noncontrolling equity ownership interest in an employer corporation. The DLOM is intended to adjust the indicated value of the subject equity security from a publicly traded equivalent value (i.e., noncontrolling, marketable value) to an indication of value that represents the illiquid nature of the ESOP-owned security (i.e., noncontrolling, nonmarketable value). This valuation adjustment is relevant when valuing a noncontrolling equity ownership interest in (1) a closely held C corporation, as well as (2) a closely held S corporation.

When valuing an equity ownership interest in a closely held C corporation, the analyst adjusts the C corporation publicly traded equivalent value with a DLOM. The same holds true when the analyst has used the SEAM to estimate the S corporation publicly traded equivalent value. Figure 3 illustrates this procedure.

Figure 3

Application of the Discount for Lack of Marketability

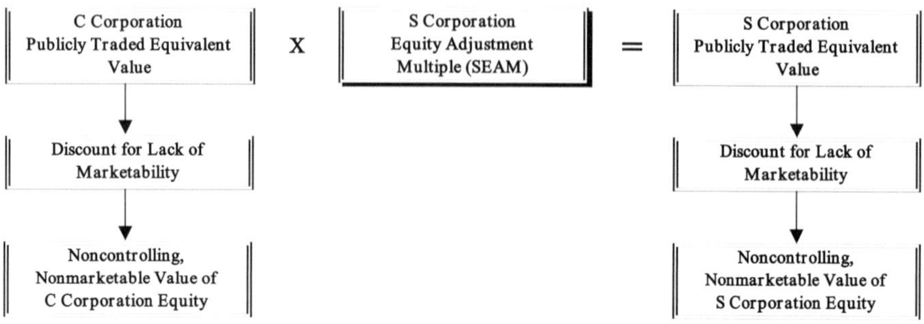

When using the SEAM in the valuation analysis, there are certain inherent assumptions that should be considered to properly estimate the DLOM. Also, it is important to consider the conceptual and theoretical characteristics of the empirical studies and/or quantitative methods used to estimate the DLOM. A discussion of the principal assumptions of the SEAM that may affect the selection of the DLOM is provided below.

PRINCIPAL ASSUMPTIONS OF THE SEAM AND THE DLOM

The SEAM is based on the following principal assumptions:

- The employer corporation will continue as an S corporation in perpetuity.
- Investors are indifferent between distributions and capital gains.
- There is a pool of qualified S corporation equity security buyers.
- Current income tax law regarding S corporations relevant to C corporations will continue in perpetuity.
- The subject S corporation will continue to be a profitable enterprise in perpetuity.

A brief discussion of each these principal assumptions—and potential analytical adjustments to the DLOM—is provided below.

S Corporation Perpetuity Assumption

Investors would not be willing to pay a price premium for an S corporation equity security if the S election would be revoked upon purchase. If the revocation of the S election of the employer corporation is a foreseeable near-term possibility, the SEAM should either (1) be adjusted to reflect the foreseeable revocation or (2) not be used.

Even if the S election is expected to continue in perpetuity, the SEAM does not specifically contemplate the risk of revocation. This is a unique risk to S corporations that is not contemplated by the DLOM used for C corporation equity security valuations. Consequently, when applying the SEAM, analysts should consider (1) whether the terms and conditions of shareholder agreements or corporate by-laws discourage stockholder behavior that may endanger the S election and (2) whether the subject S corporation is in danger of revocation of the S election. The presence of either of these conditions may require an adjustment to the DLOM or, in the case of an imminent S election revocation, the elimination of the SEAM from the analysis.

Distributions and Capital Gains

The SEAM adjusts the C corporation publicly traded equivalent value to an S corporation publicly traded equivalent value. As such, the SEAM inherently assumes that S corporation equity investors are indifferent between investment returns in the form of either cash distributions or capital appreciation. Given the closely held nature of S corporations, this is typically not the case.

The S corporation publicly traded equivalent value (as estimated by the SEAM) assumes that S corporation equity investors are indifferent between distributions and capital gains. This is because both elements of investment return are assumed to be equally liquid in an efficient capital market. Since S corporations are privately held, the capital gains investment return is rarely considered to be a liquid investment return. Consequently, the SEAM equation inherently assumes that the subject S corporation will distribute 100 percent of its net income, as this is the only way an S corporation investment return could be considered liquid. To the extent that the subject S corporation is expected to distribute less than 100 percent of its net income, the analyst should consider whether to make an adjustment to the DLOM. This type of analysis should be considered for both closely held S corporations and C corporations.

Under current U.S. tax law, capital gains taxes are not assessed until the asset is sold. However, both investment components of publicly traded equity securities (i.e., dividends and capital gains) are equally liquid and the investor can obtain the capital gains return by simply selling the security. Consequently, investors in publicly traded equity securities are assumed to recognize—and their investment behavior influenced by—the capital gains tax liability when incurred rather than when realized. Since the SEAM quantifies an S corporation publicly traded equivalent value, the inherent assumption is that S corporation equity investors recognize the economic impact of the capital gains tax treatment of S corporation equity securities when incurred rather than when realized. As discussed earlier, the SEAM assumes (1) capital gains are derived from retained earnings and (2) retained earnings increase the tax basis of the S corporation equity securities. Consequently, the capital gains investment returns to the S corporation equity security are assumed to be tax-free.

To the extent that the subject S corporation is retaining its income to fund future growth, the capital gains income tax benefit attributable to S corporation retained earnings may not be realized for some period of time. Consequently, the present value of this income tax benefit may be less than assumed in the SEAM adjusted indication of value. This factor should be considered in conjunction with the expected future distributions of the subject S corporation when estimating the DLOM.

When conducting a fair market value analysis (as is appropriate in ESOP valuation matters), the valuation analyst should be cautious when adjusting the DLOM for the assumed future capital gains tax benefit of S corporation equity securities. The fair market value standard inherently assumes the existence of (1) a willing buyer and a willing seller and (2) a liquidity event. Given these assumptions, the fair market value standard assumes the seller could liquidate his or her ownership interest at the price estimated by the business valuation analyst. Consequently, the investor could theoretically obtain the S corporation capital gains tax benefit associated with retained earnings at any time. This fact diminishes the argument that the S corporation capital gains tax benefit associated with retained earnings has minimal economic relevance.

Tax Status of Buyers and Sellers

The SEAM inherently assumes there is a pool of qualified S corporation equity security buyers that are willing to pay a price premium—over the C corporation publicly traded equivalent value—for the income tax attributes of an S corporation equity security. To the extent that there are no qualified S corporation buyers, the valuation analyst may wish to adjust the DLOM or consider whether it is appropriate to use the SEAM in the analysis.

Current Income Tax Law

The SEAM inherently assumes that current law related to the income tax treatment of S corporations vis-à-vis C corporations will continue in perpetuity. Given the uncertainty of future income tax law for both S corporations and C corporations, this is the most reasonable assumption. To the extent that disparate changes in income tax law for S corporations or C corporations are foreseeable, the analyst should assess the probability of these changes and adjust either (1) the DLOM or (2) the model components of the SEAM. The valuation analyst should be aware that most of the risk of change in income tax law is contemplated in the security prices of publicly traded equity securities.

Profitability Assumption

To the extent that the subject S corporation is not expected to be profitable for some or all of the foreseeable future, the analyst should consider the fact that the income tax attributes of an S corporation—as well as a C corporation—are dependent upon the ability of the subject employer corporation to generate a pretax profit. If the subject S corporation is not expected to be profitable, the analyst should consider whether the use of the SEAM is appropriate.

SUMMARY AND CONCLUSION

The SEAM may be used to adjust the value of a noncontrolling equity ownership interest in an S corporation from a C corporation publicly traded equivalent value to an S corporation publicly traded equivalent value. The SEAM contemplates the differences in net economic benefit attributable to stockholders resulting from the disparate income tax treatments of S corporations, C corporations, and their respective stockholders.

When using the SEAM to value a noncontrolling equity ownership interest in an S corporation, it is necessary to (1) conduct a careful and reasoned approached to the initial C corporation publicly traded equivalent value, (2) carefully consider the components and theoretical aspects of the SEAM, and (3) conduct a thorough analysis of the DLOM in order to conclude meaningful and appropriately supported indications of value. Analysts who value S status employer corporation securities for ESOP purposes should conduct the SEA analysis in this manner.

Notes:

1. Throughout this discussion, S corporation reported net income is defined as net income prior to the payment of federal and state income tax at the shareholder level.
2. *Gross v. Commissioner*, T.C. Memo 1999-254, *aff'd* 272 F.3d 333 (6th Cir. 2001).
3. *Heck v. Commissioner*, T.C. Memo 2002-34 (Feb. 5, 2002).
4. *Adams v. Commissioner*, T.C. Memo 202-80 (Mar. 28, 2002).
5. Throughout this discussion, the term "stockholder level" refers to a noncontrolling ownership interest in the equity of the subject business enterprise.
6. There are a multitude of economic factors that contribute to the capital appreciation (or depreciation) of equity besides retained earnings, including macroeconomic conditions, capital market conditions, general interest rates, transaction activity, etc. It is not feasible to mathematically model all of the components that either contribute to, or detract from the capital appreciation of an equity security. Therefore, this discussion is based on the assumption that capital appreciation is derived solely from retained earnings.
7. The general nature of these differences was summarized in the "Basic Premises" section of this discussion.
8. The capital appreciation of equity is derived from the undistributed earnings of the S corporation. Since undistributed earnings increase the income tax basis of the S corporation shares, the capital appreciation is thereby tax-free.

Chapter 16

Valuation Differences between Big and Small Companies

INTRODUCTION

The valuation of the employer corporation stock is an important consideration in virtually all ESOP formation and stock purchase/sale situations. And, the closely held businesses that become ESOP sponsor companies can range from very small family-owned businesses to billion dollar multinational corporations. Unfortunately, many valuation analysts apply the same set of approaches, methods, and procedures to the valuation of small businesses that they do to the valuation of multinational corporations. These analysts erroneously ignore many of the critical differences between big business and small business.

There are numerous differences between the valuation of big businesses and small businesses—particularly with regard to valuations performed for ESOP stock transaction purposes. Valuation analysts should carefully consider these differences in their selection of valuation methods, in their application of valuation procedures, in their search for and analyses of transactional data, and in their synthesis of value indications to reach the final value conclusion. In fact, the recognition of the employer corporation as either a big business or a small business is an important initial procedure in the ESOP stock valuation process.

There are three principal categories of differences between big businesses and small business that affect the stock valuation analysis. These three categories are: (1) structural differences—including operational, financial, and legal differences, (2) transactional differences—meaning the way that such businesses are actually bought and sold, and (3) market differences—in data, methodology, and analytical factors that are directly involved in the valuation process.

It is noteworthy that there are no specific valuation rules with regard to the differences between large and small businesses. In fact, there are no specific rules as to the definitions of—or the distinctions between—large and small businesses. Also, in terms of the three categories of differences mentioned above, not all big businesses are the same. Likewise, not all small businesses and professional practices are the same.

DEFINITIONS AND DISTINCTIONS

There is no specific definition of what size of employer corporation qualifies as a big business versus a small business. Likewise, there are no unambiguous distinctions between big businesses and small businesses.

The only fact that may be unambiguous when comparing big businesses and small businesses is that the distinctions are based on many more factors than just size alone. Exhibit 1 presents a list of several factors that distinguish big and small businesses, from a valuation perspective. It is noteworthy that this list is not intended to be comprehensive.

Structural Differences

The valuation analyst should consider the differences in the structure and operations of large businesses versus small businesses. Such differences do affect the availability of data for—and the analyses prepared during—the valuation. Exhibit 2 presents a nonexhaustive list of illustrative differences in the operations of big businesses versus small businesses.

Consideration of these structural differences is important because the valuation analyst needs to understand the workings (both financial and operational) of the employer corporation.

Transactional Differences

The valuation analyst should consider the differences in transactions involving large businesses versus small businesses. These transactional differences involve, simply, how the business would sell—if and when the business were put up for sale. Exhibit 3 presents a nonexhaustive list of illustrative differences in how big businesses are sold versus how small businesses are sold.

Consideration of these transactional differences is important because the ESOP valuation analyst attempts to model the actual market dynamics of buyers and sellers in the valuation process.

Market Differences

The valuation analyst should consider the differences in actual valuation variables and data elements with respect to big businesses versus small businesses. These factors directly affect the valuation methods selected, procedures performed, analyses made, and conclusions reached. Exhibit IV presents a nonexhaustive list of the market differences between big businesses and small businesses.

The analyst should consider these factors because they may directly affect the data used and the judgments made in the employer corporation valuation.

SUMMARY AND CONCLUSION

These differences between big businesses and small businesses may be second nature to experienced valuation analysts. However, these differences may not be intuitively obvious to less experienced ESOP valuation analysts (or to other ESOP practitioners). Nonetheless, these differences deserve serious consideration in the valuation of all businesses—but particularly for the valuation of an employer corporation.

These differences affect the availability of data, the applicability of valuation methods, the identification of valuation discounts and premiums, the quantification of capitalization rates and pricing multiples, the consideration of transactional comparability, the analysis of a transaction cash equivalency price, and—ultimately—the estimation of the value of the employer corporation securities.

For these reasons, the valuation of the small business employer corporation is often more professionally challenging than the valuation of the big business. This conclusion may seem counter-intuitive. This is because novice valuation analysts often start their professional careers assigned to the valuation of small businesses. Nonetheless, as the factors outlined in this discussion should indicate, the valuation of small business often requires more experience and more judgment than the valuation of big business employer corporations.

Exhibit 1

Typical Definitional Differences between Big Businesses and Small Businesses

Item	Factor	Big Businesses	Small Businesses
1	Size measured in revenue	generally over $50 million	generally less than $50 million
2	Ownership	some outside (non-employee or non-family) owners	all inside (employee or family) owners
3	Legal form	typically corporation	may be proprietorship, partnership, or corporation
4	Tax form	typically C corporation	typically S corporation (if a corporation), partnership, or sole proprietorship
5	Management	some professional managers (and few family member managers)	mostly all family member/ owner managers
6	Perceptions of business (separately consider perceptions of bankers, customers, suppliers, competitors, employees, and management)	company operates as a separate entity from the owners	company operations are inseparable from the owners
7	Ownership transition	company expected to survive the current owners	company may not survive the current owners
8	Institutional attributes	company operates as a business institution	company operates more as a convenient association of individuals/practitioners
9	Locations	numerous locations that may require separate management teams	one location with one management team
10	Management/organizational style	internal style/perception that "we are a professional organization"	internal style/perception that "we are a family-owned business"

Exhibit 2

Typical Structural and Operational Differences between Big Businesses and Small Businesses

Item	Factor	Big Businesses	Small Businesses
1	Debt financing availability	generally available—and independent of creditworthiness of owners	generally less available—alternate sources of financing often used—e.g. the owners contribute capital
2	Debt financing guarantees	typically personal guarantees not required	typically personal guarantees are required
3	Debt financing from owners	typically no loans from stockholders	often loans from stockholders
4	Organization	owners are often separate from management	owners are management
5	Compensation	employees paid wages for services; owners receive nonwage distributions; compensation for services and compensation for ownership are separate	employee/owners paid more or less than market wages; owners pay out all profits to themselves; compensation for services and return on ownership investment may be inseparable
6	Separate accounting	few transactions between company and owners	frequent transactions between company and owners (e.g. receivables, payables, personal expenses, extra bonuses)
7	Owner discretionary expenses	typically not paid by business	often paid by business
8	Management	may have outside board members and some outside senior management	all board members and all senior management are insiders
9	Separate transactions	company has separate transactions from owners	company transactions often not separable from owners
10	Investment diversification	owners have other investments	all owners' wealth tied up in the business
11	Operational transactions with owners	generally few transactions with owners	owners often own real estate and other assets and lease these to the company
12	Capital type	equity from outside (non-employee) owners; unsecured debt	equity from inside (employee) owners; secured debt
13	Capital mix	often more debt than equity	often more equity than debt
14	Capital cost	lower cost of debt lower cost of equity	higher cost of debt higher cost of equity

Exhibit 3

Typical Transactional Differences between Big Businesses and Small Businesses

Item	Factor	Big Businesses	Small Businesses
1	Buyer motivations	return on investment and/or return on equity—excluding salary considerations	buyer is often "buying a job"—so owner's salary is considered part of the total return on investment
2	Type of transaction broker	investment banker	small business/practice broker
3	Transaction costs	relatively lower—as a % of total business price	relatively higher—as a % of total business price
4	Transaction time	shorter time to close—compared to total price	longer time to close—compared to total price
5	Professional advisers	lawyers, accountants, investment/merchant bankers, financial advisers typically involved	few professional advisers typically involved
6	Reasons to buy/sell	typically business-related	typically personal
7	Acquisition financing	from buyer and from unrelated financing sources	from seller and from company's traditional financing source (e.g. commercial bank)
8	Stock versus asset sale	typically stock sale	frequently asset sale
9	Properties included in the sale	all business assets included in company stock	personal assets (e.g. owner-owned real estate) must be sold separately
10	Consideration paid for	sale of stock only	sale of business and non-compete and transitional employment agreements
11	Earn-out provision	less common	more common
12	Types/number of possible buyers	numerous	few
13	Sale of business conducted	nationally	locally
14	Type of buyer	could be passive/ financial investor	will be active owner/ manager (may be a current competitor or employee)

Exhibit 4

Typical Market Differences between Big Businesses and Small Businesses

Item	Factor	Big Businesses	Small Businesses
1	Guideline publicly traded company data	generally guideline companies available	often guideline companies not available
2	Guideline merged and acquired company data	generally guideline companies available	often guideline companies not available
3	Subject prospective financial information (e.g. budgets, projections, plans)	generally available	generally not available
4	Subject prospective operational information (e.g. budgets, forecasts, plans)	generally available	generally not available
5	Detailed listing of assets (tangible and intangible)	generally available	generally not available
6	Estimates of individual asset values (e.g. through property tax renditions, prior asset appraisals)	generally available	generally not available
7	Applicability of valuation discounts: key person, key customer, key supplier, lack of diversification-product, lack of diversification-location obsolescence-plant, obsolescence-technology, obsolescence-products	generally less applicable	generally more applicable
8	Owner exit plan	may be in place; at least exit is possible (e.g. an IPO)	likely not in place; exit may not be possible
9	Historical financial data quality	typically audited, GAAP	compiled or internally prepared, not GAAP
10	Historical financial data quantity	generally adequate	often not adequate
11	Historical operational data	generally adequate	may not be adequate
12	Confer with outside company advisers (e.g. accountants, lawyers)	generally available	generally not available
13	Availability of industry data	typically subject is a member of industry trade association	subject may not be a member of industry trade association
14	Availability of competitive position	typically management has data on competitive position	may not have accurate data on competitive position
15	Availability of competitive data	data available on public competitors	no data available on small, private competitors
16	Availability of economic data	national/regional economic data apply—and are readily available	local economic data apply—may not be readily available

Chapter 17

ESOPs and Government Contractors

INTRODUCTION

Ownership succession planning for government contractors, as for many other specialty businesses (construction contractors, franchises, professional associations, etc.), can be challenging for the business owner(s). This is because the practical ownership transition options for these companies are limited in relation to those of other business models.

First, few such companies have the option of implementing an initial public offering. A few large defense contractors have power to be the exception to this rule. Second, due to the inherently niche orientation of many of these businesses, there are few consolidation or strategic buyers. Third, these businesses generally do not exhibit rapid growth patterns. Therefore, they are typically not attractive acquisition targets for financial buyers.

As a result, many of these businesses attempt to structure an internal ownership succession plan. These ownership succession plans often include some form of either (1) management buyout or (2) a leveraged buyout using an employee stock ownership plan (ESOP). The leveraged buyout ownership succession plan using an ESOP structure is the topic of this discussion.

Implementing an ESOP for a closely held business can be a complicated process, regardless of the structure or industry underlying business. This complication increases when that business derives most, if not all, of its revenue from government contracting.

ESOPs provide tremendous economic opportunities to government contractors. However, when incorrectly implemented, ESOPs can also create significant pitfalls to government contractors. Without proper pre-planning, a government contractor could end up:

1. losing the opportunity to include the cost of the ESOP financing for reimbursement in its existing contracts for reimbursement,

2. accepting inferior financing terms, or even
3. losing a government contract.

This discussion is not designed to be an all-inclusive guide to ESOP planning. Rather, this discussion is intended to provide some insight into select areas where (1) pre-planning and (2) experience can enable government contractors (and the professionals serving them) to implement a successful ESOP transaction. This discussion focuses on the cost-plus type of privately held government contractors.

ESOP FEASIBILITY AND PRE-PLANNING

The process of deciding whether an ESOP stock purchase is a good strategy for a particular government contractor is, for the most part, very similar to any ESOP feasibility analysis. However, there are important differences in the ESOP feasibility analysis for a government contractor. Specifically, careful attention should be paid to

1. the nature of the government contracts,
2. the financial feasibility of the stock sale transaction, and
3. the retention of existing and future contracts.

Each of these three issues is discussed below.

Nature and Characteristics of the Government Contracts

The business model for cost-plus government contractors allows them to bid on government contracts in a manner that provides two cash flow sources from each contract. First, these contractors receive a predetermined fee for the work that has been performed. Second, in addition to the fee, these contractors have the ability to allocate certain internal costs to the government contracts.

These internal costs will be reimbursed above and beyond the compensation the contractor receives for its services. This business model is described by the term "cost-plus contracting."

For government contractors considering the implementation of an ESOP, the initial issue to analyze is whether or not the expense to retire the ESOP stock purchase debt can be allocated for reimbursement to the government contracts. In a best case scenario, all cash flow expense of the repayment of ESOP loan principal and interest would be reimbursable. In that case, the implementation of the business succession plan using an ESOP would have little effect on the cash flow of the employer corporation.

Unfortunately, it is not easy to achieve the obvious benefits of allocating all ESOP expenses to the company's government contracts. The first and foremost limitation is caused by the degree of competitiveness for the type of contracting the sponsor company is performing.

In a highly competitive industry sector, the government contractor may not be willing or able to add any additional expense to the contracts. In a less competitive industry sector, adding the ESOP-related expense the government contract may not be such an issue.

There is always some degree of sensitivity to increasing expenses that are allocated to governments contracts. The practical result is that most government contractors have the ability to absorb at least a portion of the ESOP-related expense into the existing structures. And, many contractors allocate all of the ESOP-related expense to their government contracts.

It is also important to understand the particular government department or agency from which the company derives its contracts. Believe it or not, some government agencies are more friendly toward ESOPs than others. Such agency-specific subjectivity may be troubling, but it is a reality of government contracting nonetheless.

In recent ESOP transactions with the Departments of Defense, Labor, and Education, each agency had a different attitude toward the proposed ESOP transaction. Surprisingly, the Department of Defense was the most amenable to the proposed ESOP transaction. The solution is for government contractors (1) to communicate with each of their contracting agencies and (2) to educate the agencies very early in the ESOP feasibility analysis process. Contracting agencies do not enjoy surprises.

Once the government contractor has decided that an ESOP is feasible, the first step is to contact the administrators that oversee the company's contracts. This may be one individual who handles all of the company's contracts. Or, it may be many different individuals in different departments. Regardless of the number, it is imperative for the subject contractor (1) to get the individual(s) involved early and (2) to get their preliminary approval for the allocation of additional cost to existing and future contracts with each department.

Government Contractor Financial Feasibility

Once the employer corporation receives some indication from the contract administrators that they are comfortable (at least to some degree) with the ESOP stock purchase transaction, it is important to produce financial models. These financial models should illustrate the post-ESOP projected financial statements. The projected financial statements should be prepared both with and without the ability to allocate the ESOP-related expense to contracts.

Obviously, the question of financial feasibility has an easy answer if the company can comfortably handle the additional ESOP-related expense. This is an important issue regardless of whether any portion of the ESOP-related expense is ultimately costed into its contracts.

More typically, the ESOP stock purchase transaction is going to be dependent on some portion of the ESOP-related expense being allocable to the government contracts. In that case, it is important for the corporation to work with its professionals to determine:

1. how much of the ESOP-related expense can be fit into the company's existing cost structure by a reallocation of other "pension" expenses and
2. how much of the ESOP-related expense will simply be additional allocable expense. Such additional allocable expense will typically be the major topic of discussion with the contract administrator.

In addition to the cash flow analysis outlined above, the employer corporation should start analyzing the company's borrowing capabilities. Government contractors are service companies. Therefore, government contractors typically have few, if any, tangible assets. Instead, the primary asset recorded on the typical government contractor balance sheet is accounts receivable.

The current ESOP stock acquisition lending environment is not particularly conducive to cash flow lending. Therefore, most government contractors will need to analyze the collateral available to potential lenders. The collateral may come in a number of forms. Some common examples of ESOP stock acquisition loan collateral include:

1. *Pledging a Portion of the Stock Sales Proceeds as Collateral.* Typically, the selling shareholder of a government contractor will pledge a portion of the sale proceeds as collateral for the ESOP stock purchase debt. The pledged assets are then held in a brokerage account in which the lender has a security interest.

A pledge account can be compared to owning a home. As the home loan is paid off and the value of the home increases, then the equity of the house increases and is usable by the owner. A pledge account is similar in that, as the loan is paid off and the value of the pledged account increases, then the principal is released from encumbrance.

Regardless of the mortgage, the homeowner has control of the use of the home. Similarly, the selling shareholder, within certain limits, has control over the management and investment of the pledged proceeds of the ESOP sale held in the pledge account.

2. *Company Assets or Selling Shareholder Real Estate.* The employer corporation may provide a portion of its accounts receivable as collateral for the transaction. However, this procedure creates unique issues that are discussed below.

   In addition, it is common for the selling stockholder to provide other personal assets, including real estate, as additional collateral. This is especially true where the building or real estate that the employer corporation occupies is owned by the selling stockholder in an individual capacity or through a separate entity.

3. *Seller Financing.* The stock sale can be structured to allow all or a portion of the debt to be seller financed. A benefit of seller financing is that it can provide attractive interest rates for the seller. In addition, experienced lenders may treat subordinated seller financing as equity for underwriting purposes.

Retention of Current and Future Government Contracts

Early in the process, the employer corporation management should analyze whether its existing contracts will be harmed by the implementation of the ESOP. An ESOP can affect contracts in two ways.

The first way occurs when a contract contains nonassignment or change in control provisions. The second way occurs when (1) the selling stockholder has all of the contracting relationships and (2) the stockholder's potential exit from the sponsor company (even if the plan is to transition over a number of years) may cause concern for the contract administrator.

In certain circumstances, the government contracts may contain nonassignment or change in control provisions that could be violated by the implementation and sale to the ESOP. This is especially true in construction government contracting. Therefore, it is important to review all contracts (1) to determine any potential pitfalls and (2) to obtain waivers from the contract administrator where applicable.

In this circumstance, it is better to be safe than sorry. If the language of the contract appears unclear, it is better to go ahead and get the waiver.

A less objective issue arises when the selling stockholder is the major "rainmaker" of the employer corporation and controls most, if not all, of the contracting relationships. All service companies depend upon relationships to drive revenue.

For government contractors, relationships are even more critical. In most government contract bidding situations, relationships are even more important than experience or bid comparisons.

Because the selling stockholder in many government contractor ESOPs has all the relationships, it is critical to communicate with those relationships and educate them ahead of time to create a comfort level with the transaction. In addition, the ESOP stock purchase transaction is, many times, the catalyst that forces the selling stockholder to implement a realistic plan for transitioning those relationships to successor management.

STOCK SALE TRANSACTION PROCESS

Once (1) all the parties have become comfortable with the initial plan and (2) several banks have been contacted to provide financing, there are still several unique issues that a government contractor should address prior to closing. These issues involve (1) an analysis of the current retirement plans of the employer corporation and (2) the careful negotiation of the credit facilities to fund the stock sale.

Analysis of the Company's Existing Retirement Plans

Under the Cost Accounting Standards (CAS) rules, certain items related to the retirement or pension plans of the company may be allocated and reimbursed under cost-plus government contracts. More specifically, such expenses are categorized and reimbursed under either CAS 412 or 415.

CAS 412 deals with expenses associated with providing employee benefits that would be classified as "pension" benefits. CAS 415 deals with expenses associated with providing employee benefits that would be classified as "deferred compensation" benefits. There has been a long debate over whether an ESOP fits within either CAS 412 or CAS 415. However, this issue is beyond the scope of this article.

It is important to note that the conservative approach is to structure the ESOP in such a manner that it clearly falls under CAS 412. This is because limitations and arguments more frequently arise in ESOPs that may be classified under CAS 415. Most ESOP practitioners agree that the easiest manner of assuring CAS 412 treatment is to provide within the ESOP plan document an optional form of benefit—in the form of a qualified joint and survivor annuity.

Many government contractors already have retirement plans in place prior to the adoption of the ESOP. These retirement plans are typically comprised of any or all of the following: (1) 401(k) plan which may include a profit-sharing provision, (2) a money purchase pension plan, and (3) a defined benefit pension plan.

As discussed above, the amount historically contributed to these retirement plans and reimbursed under the government contracts may be increased by the addition of an ESOP. Many times, some of these benefits may be eliminated to provide room for the ESOP, under both (1) the cost-plus contract limits and (2) applicable ERISA maximum contribution and annual addition rules.

The retirement plan analysis is essentially twofold: first, "what is the maximum contribution allowable under ERISA?" and, second, "what is the maximum expense that can be allocated to existing and future contracts?" The elimination of any existing employee benefit should be carefully analyzed to make certain that the actions taken are in compliance with ERISA.

More importantly, perhaps, the employer corporation management should determine that the substitution of the ESOP benefit in place of existing retirement plan benefits (1) will be acceptable to employees and (2) will not create a significant morale issue. Also, in the post-Enron environment, resources should be directed to analyze and maintain an acceptable degree of investment diversification for the employees.

Financing Issues

The biggest issues for a government contractor in financing a leveraged ESOP are to familiarize and to educate each individual lender. It is the responsibility of the government contractor—and its professional team—to ensure that each prospective lender appreciates the economics and structure of the proposed stock sale transaction.

The contractor's professional team will need to educate the potential lender on (1) the availability and types of collateral, (2) the cash flow effects of the stock sale transaction, and (3) the financing terms that are needed to make certain the needs of both the selling stockholder and employer corporation are satisfied.

Loan Collateral

As discussed above, government contractors often have limited sources of collateral. The one asset that is commonly used as loan collateral is the accounts receivable of the company.

An inexperienced lender (1) will often assume that it cannot obtain a valid security interest in the accounts receivable and (2) will disregard it for loan underwriting and credit proposal purposes. As accounts receivable may be a sizable asset, this could have a detrimental effect on the lender's ability to propose credit facilities.

To a lender unfamiliar with lending to government contractors, the procedures to creating a properly structured and perfected security interest in accounts receivable derived from government contracts are not overly difficult. But, these steps do take some education. Granting a security interest to the lender is not sufficient to provide it with a valid claim to the asset. Instead, the lender and contractor must follow the specific rules under the Assignment of Claims Act.

Generally the assignment of claims on the federal government are prohibited by either (1) the Anti-Claims Act or (2) the Anti-Assignment Act. Essentially, the Anti-Claims Act prohibits assignment of claims on completed projects, while the Anti-Assignment Act deals with assignment of work-in-process or executory contracts.

The Assignment of Claims Act amended these two Acts to provide an exemption for certain assignments to financial institutions. A financial institution (such as an ESOP lender) must follow a specific procedure in order to obtain an interest in such collateral.

The Assignment of Claims Act outlines the exemption requirements. However, the actual procedures for acquiring a valid interest in the collateral are outlined in the Federal Acquisition Regulations (FAR).

Under FAR 32.802, a contractor may assign monies due or to become due under a contract if all of the following conditions are met:

1. The contract specifies payments aggregating $1,000 or more.
2. The assignment is made to a bank, trust company, or other financing institution, including any federal lending agency.
3. The contract does not prohibit the assignment.
4. The assignee sends a written notice of assignment together with a true copy of the assignment to the:
   a. contracting officer or the agency head,
   b. surety on any bond applicable to the contract, and
   c. disbursing officer designated in the contract to make payment.

In addition to this basic procedural outline, there are FAR supplements that provide specific mechanics and procedures for different federal agencies, the Department of Defense being a good example.

The Assignment of Claims Act has no applicability to disputes between private parties. Therefore, compliance with the Act will not perfect a lender's security interest. To perfect its interest, the lender must also comply with the Uniform Commercial Code (UCC).

In summary, the lender must comply with both the Assignment of Claims Act and the UCC in order to create a properly perfected security interest in the assets.

Cash Flow Analysis

In addition to familiarizing the potential lender with the procedures required under the Assignment of Claims Act, it is also important to educate the potential lender on the economic realities of a leveraged ESOP sponsored by a government contractor.

As outlined above, the government contractor may have the ability to get reimbursed for up to 100 percent of the expense (both principal and interest) related to repayment of the ESOP loan. Even lenders that are familiar with ESOP lending may struggle with this concept. The goal is to educate the lender with regard to the practical cash flow effect that the ESOP will have on the employer corporation.

Because many of the costs associated with the ESOP will be reimbursed through the government contracts, the lender should gain a much higher degree of confidence in the stock sale transaction. And, the pricing and flexibility of the terms should reflect this confidence.

Coincidentally, ESOP practitioners will note that this is very similar to the education process involved in describing a 100 percent ESOP owned S corporation transaction. This is because the "tax shield" created by that transaction requires a similar lender analysis.

A careful lender will only provide credit for the reimbursement to the degree that the employer corporation can illustrate that the contract administrator has approved the transaction and the expense. Accordingly, preplanning and educating contract administrators become paramount.

Terms of the Credit Facility

Although all of the terms of the ESOP credit facility are important, the following terms need special attention in government contractor ESOPs: (1)

amortization period, (2) release methodology for pledged sale proceeds, (3) custody of pledged collateral, and (4) limitations placed upon investments in the pledged accounts.

The amortization period of the ESOP loan for a government contractor should be designed to correspond to the amount of expense that can be allocated and reimbursed from the government contracts on an annual basis. In many cases, this may involve negotiating a longer amortization schedule than in a comparable noncontractor ESOP stock sale transaction.

By matching up the amount of expense that can be reimbursed with the amortization of the loan, the government contractor minimizes negative cash flow effects on the employer corporation. This benefit will far outweigh any interest expense savings derived from a shorter amortization period, which incidentally should be reimbursable anyway.

As mentioned above, many government contractor transactions involve the pledge of sale proceeds to the lender as collateral for the loan. It is important to negotiate an objective release schedule in the commitment from the lender. It is not uncommon to have the pledged assets released on a dollar for dollar basis as (1) the ESOP stock purchase loan is repaid and (2) the assets held in the pledged account appreciate in value.

A worst case scenario is to leave it up to the lender to determine the release of pledged assets at their discretion. This will inevitably cause disagreement. And, it could strain the relationship of both the company and the selling stockholder with the ESOP lender.

In addition, it is also important to negotiate that dividend and interest income are released pursuant to the commitment in such a manner that the selling stockholder avoids the possibility of phantom income.

Many ESOP lenders desire that the pledged assets be held at the lender's brokerage arm. However, this is not a requirement under the UCC for a properly perfected security interest. Therefore, it is important to negotiate the flexibility for some, if not all, of the pledged proceeds to be held in a brokerage account of the selling stockholder's choosing.

The selling stockholder may certainly elect to use the lender to invest part or all of the proceeds. But, the selling stockholder should retain the flexibility to select his or her own investment advisers.

Finally, the flexibility to invest in a diversified portfolio can become a significant issue when using a pledgeback account as collateral. Some ESOP lenders will impose advance rates on the account. These advance rates effectively require the selling stockholder to keep the account invested in highly liquid investments (CDs, treasury bonds, etc.) for several years.

This type of provision should be unacceptable to the selling stockholder. With proper negotiation, many ESOP lenders will, instead, create a minimum acceptable grade of investment that must be maintained in the pledged account.

This standard requires the selling shareholder to invest in high quality investments. However, this standard does allow the selling stockholder to diversify the investments held in the pledged account.

SUMMARY AND CONCLUSION

A properly planned and structured government contractor ESOP stock sale transaction can be a powerful tool for business ownership succession planning. An ESOP structure can achieve the financial objectives of both (1) the selling stockholder and (2) the employer corporation.

In order to implement an ESOP successfully, a government contractor must be aware of (1) the special issues raised by the cost-plus business model, (2) the regulatory environment in which the contractor operates, and (3) the potential effects of an ESOP on the contractors government agency relationships and current government contracts.

This discussion was adapted from an article authored by Keith D. Butcher, Esq. Keith Butcher is a principal with Morgan Stanley ESOP Transaction Services Group, where he specializes in the financial analysis and structuring of complex ESOP leveraged buyout transactions. He can be reached at (202) 862-9030 or at keith.butcher@morganstanley.com.

Keith Butcher would like to thank Bill Whitehurst and Will Walker of Womble Carlyle Sandridge & Rice, PLLC, for their invaluable aid in producing this discussion.

The article on which this discussion is based was originally published in the Spring 2000 issue of Willamette Management Associates Insights. *This discussion was edited and updated by Daniel R. Van Vleet. Dan is a principal of Willamette Management Associates and the director of the firm's Chicago office.*

Chapter 18

Reasonableness of Retained Owner/Manager Compensation

INTRODUCTION

The reasonableness of executive compensation is an important issue in many ESOP stock purchase transactions. This conclusion is particularly true when (1) the ESOP acquires a noncontrolling interest in the stock of the sponsor company and (2) the selling stockholders are retained to manage the sponsor company.

Prior to the ESOP transaction, the privately held company owners/managers may pay themselves at whatever compensation levels they want. Frequently, private company owner/managers pay themselves total compensation equal to virtually all of the company profits. This owner/manager compensation is paid through some combination of base salary and periodic bonus payments.

After the ESOP stock purchase transaction, however, the retained private company owner/managers cannot continue to pay themselves all of the profits as compensation. This is because some of the sponsor company profits must be used to amortize the ESOP stock acquisition debt.

And, some of the sponsor company profits must be either (1) retained in the sponsor company or (2) paid out to all stockholders (including the ESOP stockholders). It is through both (1) capital appreciation (from retained earnings) and (2) current income (from dividend distributions) that the ESOP earns a fair rate of return on its equity investment.

ESOPS AND THE REASONABLENESS OF RETAINED OWNER/MANAGER COMPENSATION

Accordingly, ESOP financial advisers and ESOP trustees must ensure that the retained (non-ESOP) employer corporation owner/managers do not pay themselves more than a reasonable amount of executive compensation. The ESOP trustee is concerned that the retained owner/managers do not pay themselves unreasonable compensation amounts to the detriment of the ESOP stockholders. The ESOP lender is concerned that the retained owner/managers do not pay themselves unreasonable compensation amounts that jeopardize the sponsor company's ability to comfortably repay the ESOP stock acquisition debt.

This is why ESOP financial advisers, trustees, and lenders are all interested in determining what is a reasonable amount of executive compensation for the retained (non-ESOP) sponsor company owner/managers.

Determining the appropriate compensation structure for the retained owner/managers is often an important topic in the ESOP pricing, structuring, and financing negotiations. In addition, determining the appropriate process or protocol for the periodic setting/adjusting of the retained (non-ESOP) owner/manager compensation is an important negotiation topic in many ESOP formations.

This discussion summarizes the procedures commonly used by financial advisers in determining the reasonableness of employer corporation owner/manager executive compensation. These procedures are particularly relevant in situations where:

1. the ESOP acquires less than operational/ownership control of the employer corporation,
2. the selling stockholders retain operational/ownership control of the employer corporation, and
3. the selling stockholders are retained to manage the employer corporation on a going-forward basis.

REASONABLENESS OF RETAINED OWNER/MANAGER COMPENSATION FACTORS

When deciding the reasonableness of retained owner/manager compensation in an employer corporation, ESOP financial advisers often seek professional guidance from (1) Internal Revenue Service ("Service") publications and guidelines and (2) judicial precedent regarding the tax deductibility of close corporation owner/manager compensation payments.

There are several factors that the courts have considered to assess the reasonableness of employer corporation stockholder/ employee executive compensation. All of these factors effectively ask the question: if the closely held company was hiring a nonstockholder employee, how much compensation would be paid in an arm's-length employee negotiation?

Nine factors that courts often consider regarding the reasonableness of stockholder/employee compensation are delineated in a 50-plus-year-old judicial decision, *Mayson Manufacturing Company*, 178 F.2d 115 (6th Cir. 1949). The *Mayson Manufacturing Company* case is particularly relevant to ESOP financial advisers. This is because the reasonableness of compensation factors delineated in this case are almost identical to the factors specified by the Service in its audit manual (see Internal Revenue Manual Section 4.35.2.5.2.2 (3/1/02)).

The *Mayson Manufacturing Company* case outlined the following nine factors with regard to the reasonableness of stockholder/employee compensation:

1. the employee's particular qualifications for the job;
2. the nature, scope, and extent of the work actually performed by the employee;
3. the size and complexity of the particular business enterprise;
4. a comparison of salaries paid with the gross income and the net income;
5. the economic condition in and the background of the industry involved;
6. the particular company's dividend history;
7. comparable salaries in the industry;
8. the compensation paid to the company's other employees; and
9. the employee's prior years' compensation (especially for years in which the subject employee was clearly undercompensated).

According to *Henry Shotmeyer*, T.C. Memo 1980-238 (July 8, 1980), the reasonableness of compensation test is a cumulative one, focusing on all years in which the employee rendered services to the corporation. And, according to *Elliots, Inc.*, 716 F.2d 1241 (9th Cir. 1983), the above-mentioned Mayson factors should each be researched and analyzed, without giving undue weight to any one of the nine factors.

The following case review illustrates the application of the Mayson factors to a recent (2003) judicial decision. The issue in this particular case was the income tax deduction of stockholder/employee compensation in a regular C corporation. However, the court's application of the nine Mayson factors should be informative to ESOP financial advisers considering the reasonableness of retained owner/manager compensation after an ESOP stock acquisition.

RECENT APPLICATION OF THE MAYSON FACTORS IN THE HAFFNER'S SERVICE STATION CASE[1]

Haffner's Service Station ("Haffner's") was a closely held C corporation with three officers: (1) Haff, the president, (2) his father Emile, and (3) his mother Louise. During the years 1990 to 1992, Emile and Louise were paid 2.3 million dollars in bonuses by Haffner's. Upon audit, the Service claimed that (1) these bonuses represented unreasonably high executive compensation and, therefore, (2) these bonuses were not deductible to the C corporation.

At the trial court level, the Tax Court agreed with the Service regarding the disguised dividend nature of the parents' compensation. In this 2003 Appeals Court decision, the First Circuit affirmed the Tax Court's ruling.

In deciding whether stockholder/ employee compensation is unreasonable for income tax purposes, federal courts often use either (1) a single-factor independent investor test or (2) a multifactor test.

Using a single-factor independent investor test, the court asks whether an independent investor would be satisfied with the implied rate of return implicit on the hypothetical investor's investment in the subject corporation. This implied rate of return is calculated based on the company's taxable income—that is, a level of income after deducting the expense of the potentially excessive executive compensation.

The Appeals Court used a multifactor reasonableness of stockholder/employee compensation test in the *Haffner's Service Stations* case. The First Circuit enumerated the following ten factors that it considered to determine the reasonableness of the subject C corporation stockholder/ employee compensation:

1. The employee's qualifications—In the subject case, neither Emile nor Louise had extensive skills.
2. The nature, extent, and scope of the actual work—In the subject case, the Appeals Court concluded that the parents' work was nonessential.
3. The size and complexity of the subject business—In the subject case, the Appeals Court concluded that the Haffner's business was neither complex nor large.
4. Comparison of the executive compensation paid with the company's gross income (versus taxable income)—In the subject case, the percentage of Haffner's gross income represented by the subject executive compensation was very high.

5. The general economic conditions—In the subject case, there were no unusually adverse economic conditions to overcome during the 1990 to 1993 period; therefore, the Appeals Court concluded that Emile and Louise did not cause the company's financial success.
6. Comparison of salaries paid (a) to stockholder distributions and (b) to retained earnings—There were no dividends paid to the stockholders in the Haffner's case. And, the Appeals Court did not determine if the stockholders had received a reasonable rate of return on their investment in the Haffner's stock.
7. Prevailing rates of compensation for comparable positions in comparable companies—There was no information presented to the Appeals Court by either litigant to determine this factor in the Haffner's case.
8. The company's salary policy for other (nonshareholder) employees—No other nonstockholder employee was paid a six-figure level of compensation at Haffner's.
9. Whether the compensation paid to stockholder/employees in prior years was deficient—In the years at question, Emile and Louise needed money to finance a family lawsuit; the Appeals Court concluded that they had not been undercompensated in any prior years (i.e., the 1990 to 1992 payments did not represent "catch-up" compensation for prior year deficiencies).
10. Absence of a pension/profit sharing plan—There was no documented pension or profit sharing plan for any of the employees at Haffner's.

ILLUSTRATIVE REASONABLENESS OF EMPLOYER CORPORATION SHAREHOLDER/EMPLOYEE COMPENSATION ANALYSIS

Acme Widget Employer Corporation ("Acme") is considering an ESOP formation. The two company founders/stockholders, Harry Smith and Ben Jones, are considering the sale of 30 percent of the Acme common stock to an ESOP. Smith and Jones will continue to own the remainder of the outstanding Acme common stock.

Smith and Jones will be retained as owner/managers of Acme. The ESOP financial adviser is concerned with the reasonableness of Smith's executive compensation on a post-ESOP, going-forward basis.

This Acme "mini case study" illustrates the quantitative components of a typical reasonableness of executive compensation study. In a comprehensive reasonableness of compensation analysis, both the quantitative and the qualitative Mayson factors would be considered. This example—and the associated analyses—are deliberately simplified and are presented for illustrative purposes only.

Acme manufactures and distributes widgets. Acme is a regular C corporation for federal income tax purposes. Harry Smith serves as both (1) the president/chief executive officer and (2) the chief marketing officer of the corporation.

Smith is (and will continue to be) a principal stockholder of Acme. Pre-ESOP, Smith and Jones own 80 percent and 20 percent of the Acme common stock, respectively. Post-ESOP, Smith and Jones will own 56 percent and 14 percent of the Acme common stock, respectively. Post-ESOP, the ESOP will own the remaining 30 percent of the Acme common stock.

For the 2005 year (i.e., after the sale of stock to the ESOP), Acme is projected to generate revenue of $10 million. Also, for the 2005 year, the average assets of Acme are projected to be $2 million. For the 2005 year, Acme will pay Smith $1.2 million in executive compensation.

Both pre-ESOP and post-ESOP, Smith is the controlling shareholder. Smith sets Jones' compensation, presumably on an arm's-length basis. Therefore, the ESOP financial adviser is not particularly concerned with the issue of Jones' compensation. However, Smith also sets his own compensation. Accordingly, the ESOP financial adviser (and the trustee) are interested in assessing: is this level of owner/manager compensation reasonable for Smith?

Exhibit 1 summarizes a simplified salary survey analysis. Such an analysis looks to published executive compensation survey data. Such data are typically presented (1) by size of company and (2) by industry.

In this particular example, the financial adviser considered four different executive salary surveys:

1. the Economic Research Institute (ERI) Executive Compensation Assessor as of July 1, 2004;
2. the Watson Wyatt Data Services 2004/2005 Top Management Comp Calculator;
3. *Compensation in Manufacturing*, 24th edition, 2004, by Abbott, Langer & Associates, Inc.; and
4. *Widget Weekly 2004 Salary Survey*, published by the American Widget Association.

Exhibit 1 presents a range of the maximum reasonable compensation levels for executives performing comparable duties to Smith at comparable companies. Based on the various published salary survey analyses summarized in Exhibit 1, the indicated range of maximum reasonable executive compensation for Smith is $850,000 to $1,292,000.

Exhibit 2 summarizes a simplified financial ratio analysis. Exhibit 2 presents the total reasonable executive compensation levels for all of the corporate officers (as a group) of Acme Widget Employer Corporation.

Exhibit 2 reports illustrative industry financial ratio data from two commonly referenced annual publications: the *Almanac of Business and Financial Ratios* and the *RMA Annual Statement Studies*. Exhibit 2 presents data from the 2004 editions of these publications—that is, the most recent empirical data available at the time of the ESOP financial adviser's analysis.

The particular financial ratio analysis presented on Exhibit 2 considers the executive compensation levels for all company officers as a group. Therefore, it is noteworthy that Acme has two corporate officers: (1) Harry Smith (who will be paid $1.2 million in 2005) and (2) Ben Jones, vice president, chief financial officer, and secretary (who will be paid $800,000 in 2005). Therefore, in 2005, total officer compensation for Acme will be $2.0 million.

After subtracting Ben Jones's $800,000 compensation, the Exhibit 2 financial ratio analysis presents a residual range of the maximum reasonable executive compensation for Harry Smith. Based on the various financial ratio analyses summarized in Exhibit 2, the indicated range of maximum reasonable executive compensation for Smith is $1,070,000 to $2,500,000.

Exhibit 3 summarizes a simplified independent investor test with regard to the reasonableness of Smith's executive compensation. The independent investor test is a single factor test that has been widely accepted by the courts in recent years.

The independent investor test is based on a fair rate of return on capital (typically, total equity capital) analysis. Exhibit 3 presents (1) an estimated value for the Acme total owners' equity during 2005 (presumably, that estimated value should be equal to the ESOP stock purchase transaction valuation) and (2) a hypothetical independent investor's expected fair rate of return on the owners' equity capital.

Subtracting (1) the independent investor's expected fair return on owners' equity capital from (2) the company's pretax net income indicates (3) a reasonable level of executive compensation available for the subject company total officer group.

After subtracting Ben Jones's $800,000 compensation, the Exhibit 3 independent investor test analysis presents a residual range of the maximum reasonable executive compensation for Harry Smith. Based on the independent investor test summarized in Exhibit 3, the indicated maximum reasonable executive compensation for Smith is $1,220,000.

Exhibit 4 summarizes the conclusions from the three reasonableness of executive compensation analyses presented in this Acme Widget Employer Corporation mini case study.

Based on the reasonableness of executive compensation analyses illustrated in Exhibits 1, 2, and 3, and summarized in Exhibit 4, the projected $1.2 million executive compensation for Harry Smith for 2005, is not unreasonable.

Of course, this example—and the corresponding analyses—are deliberately simplified. And, only the quantitative reasonableness of compensation analyses are illustrated in this example.

In an actual reasonableness of compensation analysis, both qualitative and quantitative analyses would be considered. Nonetheless, the ESOP financial adviser (and the ESOP trustee) may conclude that it is not unreasonable to use Smith's projected $1.2 million compensation expense (1) in the ESOP stock valuation and (2) in the ESOP pricing/structuring negotiations.

SUMMARY AND CONCLUSION

The reasonableness of retained owner/manager executive compensation is an important issue in ESOP stock purchase negotiations and pricing decisions. This is particularly true when the (non-ESOP) selling stockholders (1) will retain ownership/operational control of the sponsor company and (2) will be retained to manage the sponsor company.

In such cases, the ESOP financial adviser (and the ESOP trustee) should assess the reasonableness of the retained owner/managers' compensation with regard to both (1) stock valuation/pricing and (2) stock purchase/investment decisions.

This discussion reviewed the factors that the courts and the Service routinely consider in assessing the reasonableness of stockholder/employee executive compensation for federal income tax purposes. These factors should provide professional guidance to financial advisers in assessing the reasonableness of retained owner/manager compensation for ESOP formation and ESOP-owned stock valuation purposes.

Notes:

1. *Spicer Accounting, Inc. v. Commissioner*, 918 F.2d 90 (9th Cir. 1990).

Exhibit 1

Acme Widget Employer Corporation
Reasonableness of Retained Owner/ Manager Executive Compensation
Salary Survey Analysis

ERI Executive Compensation Assessor [a]

	Median	75th Percentile	90th Percentile
	$	$	$
1	229,000	281,000	460,000
2	205,000	280,000	390,000
	434,000	561,000	850,000

Watson Wyatt Comp Calculator [b]

	Median	75th Percentile	90th Percentile
	$	$	$
1	307,600	469,100	820,000
2	215,600	255,800	472,000
	523,200	724,900	1,292,000

Abbott Langer *Compensation in Manufacturing* [c]

	Median	90th Percentile
	$	$
1	300,000	607,000
2	200,500	413,700
	500,500	1,020,700

Widget Weekly Salary Survey [d]

	Median	75th Percentile
	$	$
1	330,000	520,000
2	244,000	330,000
	574,000	850,000

Indicated Range of Maximum Reasonable Executive Compensation Levels: $850,000 to $1,292,000

Notes:

[a] Line 1: Widget manufacturing, revenue between $10 and $15 million, chief executive officer position.
Line 2: Widget manufacturing, revenue between $10 and $15 million, chief marketing officer position.

[b] Line 1: Widget manufacturing, sales of $10 million, chief executive officer position.
Line 2: Widget manufacturing, sales of $10 million, chief marketing officer position.

[c] Line 1: Widget manufacturing, revenue between $10 and $15 million, chief executive officer position.
Line 2: Widget manufacturing, revenue between $10 and $15 million, chief marketing officer position.

[d] Line 1: Widget manufacturing, revenue of $10 million, chief executive officer position.
Line 2: Widget manufacturing, revenue of $10 million, chief marketing officer position.

Exhibit 2

Acme Widget Employer Corporation Reasonableness of Retained Owner/ Manager Executive Compensation Financial Ratio Analyses

Total Officers' Compensation as a % of Revenue

Almanac of Business & Industrial Ratios [a]		*RMA Annual Statement Studies* [a]		
Industry Code	Mean Percent	Industry Code	Median Percent	75th Percentile
123456	18.7%	123456	25.7%	31.0%

Range of Reasonable Executive Compensation Levels
For All Officers as a Group

	Industry Financial Ratio Observations		
Total Officers' Compensation— as a % of Revenue	18.7%	25.7%	31.0%
Multiplied by: Acme Widget Employer Corporation Annual Revenue	$10,000,000	$10,000,000	$10,000,000
Equals: Reasonable Total Officers' Compensation Levels	$1,870,000	$2,570,000	$3,100,000
Indicated Range of Maximum Reasonable Executive Compensation Levels [b]	$1,870,000	to	$3,100,000
Less: Officer Compensation Paid to Ben Jones	800,000		800,000
Equals: Residual Indicated Range of Maximum Reasonable Executive Compensation for Harry Smith	$1,070,000	to	$2,500,000

Notes:

[a] Widget manufacturing companies, asset size from $1 to $5 million.
[b] For all (i.e., both) corporate officers of Acme Widget Corporation.

Exhibit 3

Acme Widget Employer Corporation
Reasonableness of Retained Owner/ Manager Executive Compensation
The Independent Investor Test
Fair Return on Equity Capital Analysis

	Actual 2001 $	Actual 2002 $	Actual 2003 $	Actual 2004 $	Projected 2005 $
Total Revenue	8,000,000	8,600,000	9,000,000	9,500,000	10,000,000
Total Expenses [a]	4,200,000	5,000,000	5,050,000	5,000,000	7,100,000
Pretax Net Income	4,500,000	4,500,000	4,450,000	4,500,000	2,900,000
Fair Return on Equity Capital Analysis:					
Estimated Value of Total Owners' Equity Capital	9,000,000	9,500,000	10,000,000	10,500,000	11,000,000
Multiplied by: Pretax Expected Fair Rate of Return on Owners' Equity Capital [b]					8%
Equals: Fair Return on Value of Owners' Equity Capital					880,000

Residual Reasonableness of Executive Compensation Analysis:	
Projected 2005 Pretax Net Income (Including all Projected ESOP Expense)	2,900,000
Maximum Reasonable Total Officers' Executive Compensation [c]	2,020,000
Less: Officer Compensation Paid to Ben Jones	800,000
Equals: Residual Maximum Reasonable Executive Compensation for Harry Smith	1,220,000

Notes:

[a] Including operating expense, interest expense, all ESOP-related expense for 2005, but before officers' compensation expense.

[b] The total expected rate of return on owners' equity capital includes two components: (1) current income (or dividend yield) rate of return and (2) long-term capital appreciation (or capital gain yield) rate of return. The indicated 8% expected rate of return in this simplified example represents only the current income component of the total expected rate of return on owners' capital.

[c] Pretax net income for 2005 ($2,900,000) less fair return on the value of owners' equity capital ($880,000) equals $2,020,000.

Exhibit 4

Acme Widget Employer Corporation
Reasonableness of Retained Owner/ Manager Executive Compensation
Post-ESOP Stock Purchase Transaction
Summary and Conclusion

Exhibit Reference	Retained Owner/Manager Executive Compensation Analysis	Indicated Range of Maximum Reasonable Compensation
1	Salary Survey Analysis	$850,000 to $1,292,000
2	Financial Ratio Analysis	$1,070,000 to $2,500,000
3	Independent Investor Test	$1,220,000
Harry Smith Projected Post-ESOP 2005 Executive Compensation		$1,200,000
Is Harry Smith's Projected Post-ESOP 2005 Executive Compensation Reasonable?		Yes

Chapter 19

ESOP-Related Valuation Expert Testimony

INTRODUCTION

ESOP valuation analysts and financial advisers are often called on to perform litigation support services, including expert testimony. The various ESOP-related areas of litigation support analysis and expert testimony include: ESOP formation and structuring valuations, periodic compliance ESOP valuations, the purchase or sale of employer corporation securities, and other events requiring an independent valuation and/or transactional fairness opinion.

In such controversies, ESOP participants or government regulators (such as the U.S. Department of Labor and the Internal Revenue Service) may bring litigation claims against various ESOP parties. These parties may include: the employer corporation, the ESOP legal counsel, the ESOP trustee, the ESOP administrator, and the financial adviser/valuation analyst. In these controversies, the ESOP participants may claim economic damages related to fraudulent or negligent valuation or financial advisory services. Furthermore, the government regulators may assess income taxes, fines, and other penalties related to allegedly inaccurate valuation or negligent financial advisory services.

ESOP valuation experts–and ERISA attorneys–should be aware of several recent court cases that have applied and interpreted the *Daubert* guidelines with regard to expert testimony. For purposes of this discussion, the *Daubert* guidelines refer to the factors articulated by the U.S. Supreme Court in *Daubert v. Merrell Dow Pharmaceuticals, Inc.* (113 S.Ct. 2786, 125 L.Ed. 2d 469 (1993)). These factors are applied by federal trial courts in the performance of their "gatekeeping" function. The trial court's gatekeeping function is the process of including or excluding expert testimony under Federal Rules of Evidence (FRE) Rule 702.

The *Daubert* guidelines specifically apply in federal courts to expert testimony offered under FRE Rule 702. Litigation actions brought under

ERISA and/or the Internal Revenue Code are generally a matter for federal jurisdiction. However, ESOP valuation analysts should realize that these federal guidelines may also influence the gatekeeping activities of state and local trial courts.

It is the objective of the *Daubert* gatekeeping requirement to ensure the reliability and relevancy of expert testimony. The *Daubert* factors are used by the trial court to consider whether an expert witness, when basing testimony on professional studies or on personal experience, employs in the courtroom the same level of intellectual rigor that characterizes the practice of an expert in the relevant field. As will be discussed below, the *Daubert* case originally applied to scientific expert testimony. And, the *Daubert* factors were originally used to help clarify what type of analysis is considered science and what is considered "junk science."

Several recent published decisions (at both the Court of Appeals and the Supreme Court levels) have concluded that the trial courts gatekeeping inquiry into both relevance and reliability applies not only to scientific testimony but to all expert testimony. Accordingly, ESOP valuation analysts and financial advisers should be aware of—and should attempt to comply with—these expert testimony guidelines. This category of ESOP valuation practitioners includes appraisers, economists, accountants, financial advisers, and industry experts who offer expert testimony regarding the fair market value of ESOP-owned securities within the context of Federal Rules of Evidence Rule 702.

THE *DAUBERT* FACTORS

Under Rule 702, trial judges have historically been the "gatekeepers" regarding the admission of expert evidence in federal cases. Traditionally, though, trial judges would rarely disqualify expert witnesses or exclude expert witness testimony. Rather, they would limit the areas in which the expert was allowed to offer testimony. Trial judges would typically allow witnesses to testify and then afford that testimony its "due weight" in their final deliberations. However, in *Daubert*, the Supreme Court articulated specific factors that trial judges should consider with regard to the admission or exclusion of expert testimony.

In the *Daubert* case, a medical doctor testified before the trial court and presented a radical medical opinion. That opinion was unsupported by either the relevant professional literature, the medical research scientific standards, any recognized professional organizations, or any concurring medical research colleagues. With regard to the admission of this testimony, the questions that trial court faced were twofold: (1) whether the doctor was truly a scientific expert or merely a "hired gun" and (2) whether the expert testimony was based on medical expertise or was merely "junk science." With regard to the admissibility of expert testimony, the *Daubert* court wrestled with the following three issues:

1. Whether the expert will be testifying as to scientific knowledge.
2. Whether the testimony based on scientific knowledge will assist the trier of fact in determining the ultimate issue.
3. Whether the proposed scientific method has demonstrated validity or reliability.

The *Daubert* court applied the following four factors to determine the reliability of the particular expert's scientific theory or technique:

1. *Testing*—can the theory or technique be tested, or has it been tested?
2. *Peer reviews*—has the theory been subjected to peer review or publication, which aids in determining flaws in the method?
3. *Error rates*—are there established standards to control the use of the technique?
4. *Acceptability*—is the technique generally accepted in the relevant technical community?

In its published decision, the Supreme Court noted (1) that the *Daubert* factors should be applied flexibly, (2) that the four factors were merely illustrative, and (3) that other factors could argue in favor of testimony admissibility.

SONS OF *DAUBERT*

During the last several years, many trial courts have applied the *Daubert* factors. In addition, several appellate court decisions have sustained, expanded, and interpreted the factors. First, this discussion references a few illustrative *Daubert* applications. Second, this discussion summarizes two recent decisions that make it clear that the *Daubert* factors apply as much to valuation and economic analysis testimony as they do to scientific testimony.

In *General Electric Co. v. Joiner*, 118 S.Ct.512, 139 L.Ed. 2d 508 (1997), the Supreme Court concluded that federal courts of appeals must apply an abuse-of-discretion standard when they review a trial court's decision to admit or exclude expert testimony. That judicial standard applies as much to the trial court's decisions about how to determine reliability as to its ultimate conclusion, the Supreme Court ruled. The Supreme Court also concluded that whether the specific *Daubert* factors are appropriate measures of reliability in a particular case is a matter the law grants the trial judge broad latitude to determine. The Supreme Court noted that this is the same broad latitude that the trial judge enjoys with respect to his or her ultimate reliability determination.

Several courts (and several appellate courts) have applied the *Daubert* factors to exclude valuation-related expert testimony. For example, in *Andrew J. Whelan, et al. v. Tyler Abell, et al.* (Civil Action nos. 87-442 and 87-1763, U.S. District Court (D.C. Sept. 25, 1996)), the judge excluded the financial valuation expert testimony of a PricewaterhouseCoopers partner, Hugh Penny, CPA. The damages issue in the case involved the fair market value of the plaintiffs' shares of a closely held corporation (Animated Playhouse Corporation). The plaintiffs' expert used only one valuation method (a discounted cash flow method) that relied upon speculative financial projections. Applying the four *Daubert* factors to test the admission of the expert testimony under Rule 702, the District Court judge concluded: "The undue prejudice that would be caused to Defendants by allowing the highly speculative testimony of Mr. Penny is clear. Accordingly, the Court has excluded his testimony."

In *Frymire-Brinati v. KPMG Peat Marwick*, 3 F.3d 183 (7th Cir. 1993), the Court of Appeals excluded the testimony of another CPA valuation expert. The damages issue in this case involved the fair market value of plaintiff's partnership interests in a real estate development company. Again, the plaintiff's expert used only one valuation method (again, a discounted cash flow method) to value the subject partnership interests. Explaining its exclusion of the valuation-related expert testimony, the Court of Appeals specifically noted that the CPA valuation expert "conceded that he did not employ the methodology that experts in valuation find essential."

Kumho Tire Company

In *Kumho Tire Company, Ltd., et al. v. Patrick Carmichael, et al.*, 119 S. Ct. 1167 (1999), the Supreme Court clearly ruled that the *Daubert* factors, and the trial court's gatekeeping function regarding the admission of expert testimony, do not apply only to "scientific" experts. Rather, the *Daubert* factors also apply to all "technical" or "other specialized" experts.

The *Kumho Tire* case involved personal injury damages and manufacturer's liability. When the tire on the vehicle driven by Patrick Carmichael blew out and the vehicle overturned, one passenger died and other passengers were injured. The plaintiffs claimed that the blown-out tire was defective. The claim was based upon the deposition testimony of tire failure analyst Dennis Carlson Jr. Carlson intended to testify at the trial that, in his expert opinion, a defect in the tire's manufacture or design caused the blow-out. This expert opinion was based on a visual and tactile inspection of the tire.

The defendants moved to exclude Carlson's testimony at trial. This motion was made on the ground that his methodology failed to satisfy Rule 702 of the Federal Rules of evidence. Applying the four *Daubert* factors, the District Court judge excluded Carlson's expert testimony. The plaintiffs appealed.

The Eleventh Circuit reversed the District Court's decision. The Court of Appeals held that the District Court had erred as a matter of law in its application of the four *Daubert* factors. The Court of Appeals ruled (1) that the *Daubert* decision was limited only to a scientific context and (2) that the *Daubert* factors could not be applied to Carlson's testimony because that testimony is characterized as "skill-or-experience-based." The defendants appealed.

Writing for the Supreme Court in the *Kumho Tire* opinion, Justice Beyer stated unambiguously:

> The Daubert "gatekeeping" obligation applies not only to "scientific" testimony, but to all expert testimony. Rule 702 does not distinguish between "scientific" knowledge and "technical" and "other specialized" knowledge, but makes it clear that any such knowledge might be the subject of expert testimony. It is the Rule's word "knowledge," not the words (like "scientific") that modify that word, that establishes a standards of evidentiary reliability.

Explaining the Supreme Court's agreement with the trial court's decision, Justice Beyer concluded:

> In Daubert, this Court held that Federal Rule of Evidence 702 imposes a special obligation upon a trial judge to "ensure that any and all scientific testimony . . . is not only relevant, but reliable." The initial question before us is whether this basic gatekeeping obligation applies only to "scientific" testimony or to all expert testimony. We, like the parties, believe that it applies to all expert testimony.

Accordingly, in *Kumho Tire*, the Supreme Court concurred with the trial court and excluded the tire expert's testimony based on an application of the four *Daubert* factors.

Target Market Publishing

In *Target Market Publishing, Inc. v. ADVO, Inc.*, 136 F.3d 1139 (7th Cir. 1998), the Seventh Circuit decided the appeal of another case involving the exclusion of testimony by a CPA valuation expert witness. In this case, the Court of Appeals decisively concluded that the *Daubert* factors apply to financial valuation and economic damages testimony.

In 1993, Target Market Publishing, Inc. ("Target") entered into a one-year contract with ADVO, Inc. ("ADVO") to prepare and distribute a direct-mail advertising publication called Select Auto. The project involved selling automobile dealers exclusive advertising rights at a flat rate in the monthly publication. The two companies were to share equally any profits earned from the Select Auto enterprise.

In April 1994, Target brought suit against ADVO, claiming breach of contract and breach of fiduciary duty. After the close of discovery, ADVO filed a motion for summary judgment maintaining Target could not prove its claim that it had sustained damages of at least $75,000 as a result of the failed Select Auto project.

In its response to the motion for summary judgment, Target relied on an expert report prepared by Bruce W. Burton, an accountant and business appraiser from the accounting firm Deloitte & Touche. The ADVO lawyers replied that "the Burton report is pure speculation, based on utterly implausible assumptions and unreliable methodology." In this statement, the District Court agreed with ADVO. The District Court disregarded the business valuation expert's report and granted summary judgment for ADVO. Target appealed.

The Seventh Circuit had to decide whether the District Court had properly excluded the report of the plaintiff's expert under the *Daubert* factors as part of the trial court's "gatekeeping" function. In concluding that the trial court had properly applied the *Daubert* standards, the Seventh Circuit made an interesting analogy:

> If, for instance, an expert who was well qualified as an astronomer offered to testify based on lengthy and careful observation that the sun revolves around the earth, a court would not be obliged to submit the testimony to the jury. The Supreme Court recently upheld a district court's decision to exclude expert testimony on the ground that it "did not rise above 'subjective belief or unsupported speculation.'" (See *General Electric Co. v. Joiner*)

Further explaining its agreement with the trial court's decision, the Seventh Circuit decision stated the following:

> We note first that the Supreme Court has recently resolved any ambiguities concerning the standard of review that the courts of appeals are to apply in reviewing a district court's evidentiary rulings under Daubert. The standard of review is the same one applied to other evidentiary rulings—that is, abuse of discretion. Applying the abuse of discretion standard, the Supreme Court affirmed, stating that "nothing in either Daubert or the Federal Rules of Evidence requires a district court to admit opinion evidence which is connected to existing data only by the ipse dixit of the expert. A court may conclude that there is simply too great an analytical gap between the data and the opinion proffered." (See *General Electric Co. v. Joiner*)

The Seventh Circuit concluded that the District Court did not abuse its discretion in applying the four *Daubert* factors to exclude the expert report of the CPA valuation expert.

THE VALUATION ANALYST AND THE *DAUBERT* STANDARD

There are no specific rules that a valuation analyst must comply with in order to ensure acceptance under the *Daubert* expert testimony standard. Rather, there is a general litmus test. As described in the Supreme Court's original decision in *Daubert*, the general litmus test is "What is the standard practice of an expert in the relevant field?" The question remains pretty much the same for ESOP-related valuation and economic damages expert testimony: What is the standard practice of an expert in this particular analytical discipline?

Based on a synthesis of the various court's decisions in the various sons of *Daubert* cases, ESOP practitioners should consider the following guidelines when presenting valuation and economic damages expert testimony. These guidelines are only suggestions. Compliance with these guidelines cannot assure a trial court's acceptance of the valuation analyst's testimony. These guidelines are presented as a practical "top 10 list" of considerations (1) to help improve the valuation analyst's work product and (2) to help the valuation analyst comply with the standard practice of an expert in the ESOP valuation and economic damages field.

Guideline 1: *Know the relevant professional standards.* The valuation analyst should be aware of and be familiar with the promulgated professional standards that are applicable to the analysis. These standards may be promulgated by government or regulatory agencies (e.g., the Department of Labor or the Internal Revenue Service). Or, the standards may be issued by professional organizations or societies (e.g., the ESOP Association or the National Center for Employee Ownership). In order to comply with the professional standards appropriate in the particular field, the valuation analyst first has to be knowledgeable of the relevant professional standards.

Guideline 2: *Apply the relevant professional standards.* Whenever possible, the analyst should apply the appropriate recognized and promulgated professional standards (1) to the analytical work product and (2) to the proffered expert testimony. There may be extraordinary circumstances in which the relevant standards may not apply or, practically, cannot be applied. For example, there may be data availability limitations. When the valuation analyst cannot comply with professional standards (due to data limitations or some other reason) that fact normally should be disclosed in the analysis work product and expert testimony. Similarly, when the valuation analyst does comply with all relevant professional standards, that fact should be attested to in the analysis work product and expert testimony.

Guideline 3: *Know the relevant professional literature.* Professionals in any discipline generally know what the authoritative textbooks are in their field. They also know what the most authoritative journals (whether peer-reviewed or not) are in their field. Along these lines, ESOP valuation and economic damages experts are not expected to agree with all of the leading textbooks or periodicals. However, they would be expected to recognize the leading textbooks and periodicals. This is because the leading publications will generally discuss the recognized theories, procedures, and standards within a particular discipline or profession.

Guideline 4: *Know the relevant professional organizations.* Professionals in any discipline generally know what the recognized organizations, societies, and associations are in their profession. Within a given profession, it is not expected that a practitioner join every single institute or society. That may be duplicative and cost-prohibitive. However, ESOP practitioners should be familiar with the names of the leading professional organizations in the ESOP discipline. This is particularly true with regard to organizations or associations that grant professional designations, promulgate professional standards, or publish authoritative journals.

Guideline 5: *Use generally accepted analytical methods.* There is usually a reason why some analytical methods and procedures become generally accepted over time—and others do not. The valuation analyst should be able to distinguish between what are and are not the generally accepted methods within the discipline. Normally, the valuation analyst should use the profession's recognized methods and procedures. In such cases, the analyst should assert such compliance with generally accepted methodology. Occasionally, an analyst may not be able to use the profession's recognized methods and procedures. This may occur with regard to a unique set of facts and circumstances. When the valuation analyst has to develop a de novo methodology, that departure from generally accepted practices should be disclosed. And, the reasons for the departure should be explained in the analytical work product and in the expert testimony.

Guideline 6: *Use multiple analytical methods.* Whenever possible, the valuation analyst should use multiple approaches, methods, and procedures in an ESOP valuation or economic damages engagement. The use of multiple methods allows for mutually supportive evidence upon which to derive an analytical conclusion. The use of multiple analytical methods helps to identify an aberrational outlier conclusion. And the use of multiple analytical methods mitigates the perception that the valuation analyst has selected the one particular procedure that would result in a biased analytical conclusion. Of course, the analytical methods that are used should be the methods generally used by experts in that particular discipline.

Guideline 7: *Synthesize the conclusions of the multiple analytical methods.* In virtually any type of quantitative or qualitative analysis, the use of multiple methods also allows for a reconciliation and synthesis of alternative indications in the process of deriving a final analytical conclusion. As indicated in Internal Revenue Service Revenue Ruling 59-60, this synthesis should involve an assessment of the relative strengths and weaknesses of the alternative methods used. This synthesis should involve some form of weighting or reconciliation (whether implicit or explicit) of the results of the alternative methods used. And, this synthesis should involve some explanation (or justification) for (1) why certain analytical methods were selected and (2) why certain analytical methods were rejected.

Guideline 8: *Disclose all significant analytical assumptions and variables.* In virtually all analyses (especially valuation and economic damages analyses), there are both implicit and explicit assumptions, variables, and conditions. Some of these assumptions may be relatively insignificant or insensitive (i.e., a material change in the assumption will not materially affect the analytical conclusion). Some of these assumptions may be significant and sensitive. Generally, the valuation analyst should (1) identify, (2) quantify (if possible), and (3) justify the most important analytical assumptions and variables. While this disclosure may not always occur in the analytical work product (e.g., where the client has requested conclusionary opinions only), this disclosure is usually helpful to the trier of fact during expert testimony.

Guideline 9: *Subject the analysis to peer review.* Most ESOP practitioners agree that the process of peer review (usually performed by a professional colleague within the analyst's firm) is extremely beneficial. The peer review (some firms call this a professional standards review) often identifies analytical weaknesses, internal inconsistencies, mathematical errors, logic flaws, or disclosure inadequacies. Obviously, this peer review should occur after the analysis is completed but before the expert testimony is presented. Such a peer review should give the analyst confidence to assure the trier of fact that there are no logical, methodological, or mathematical flaws in the analysis.

Guideline 10: *Test the valuation analysis and the conclusion for reasonableness.* Before offering ESOP-related expert testimony, the valuation analyst should assess the overall acceptability of the analysis and of the analytical conclusion. The analyst should consider the relevance of the methods selected and the data used. The valuation analyst should consider the overall reasonableness of all assumptions and projections in comparison to the actual history (if any) of the particular employer corporation fact set. And by any logical or empirical standards, the analyst should assess the overall reasonableness of the indicated analytical results. If the valuation analyst is not convinced of the reasonableness of the analysis, it is likely that the trier of fact will not be convinced of the reasonableness of the expert testimony.

These top 10 guidelines are suggestions for ESOP valuation and economic damages analysts to consider with regard to compliance with the *Daubert* expert testimony factors. If a de novo theory or methodology is being used in the particular case, the ESOP practitioner should (1) disclose that, (2) explain the departure from the traditional theories or methods, and (3) justify the departure decision. Otherwise, the fundamental lesson of *Daubert* is that ESOP expert witnesses should (1) use generally accepted methods and procedures and (2) comply with the relevant professional standards that are generally recognized within their analytical discipline.

SUMMARY AND CONCLUSION

It is clear that trial courts and courts of appeal are broadly applying—and broadly interpreting—the general *Daubert* expert testimony principles. It also is clear that trial courts have concluded that the *Daubert* principles apply to all expert matters that fall within FRE Rule 702. FRE Rule 702, with respect to all expert matters, "establishes a standard of evidentiary reliability."

Accordingly, ESOP valuation and economic damages analysts who provide expert testimony should be aware of, and should comply with, the four *Daubert* factors. The federal courts broadly apply the *Daubert* factors (with appropriate modifications) to decide the acceptance or rejection of ESOP-related valuation and economic damages expert witness testimony.

Valuation and economic damages analysts who practice in the ESOP discipline should also be aware that state and local trial courts are also influenced by the *Daubert* factors. Accordingly, ESOP practitioners should carefully consider the four *Daubert* factors when presenting valuation and/or economic damages testimony before all triers of facts.

Section IV

ESOP Financial Adviser Issues

Chapter 20

ESOP Transaction Fairness Opinions

INTRODUCTION

The current volume and pricing of merger and acquisition (M&A) activity may motivate ESOP fiduciaries to analyze potential transactions more carefully than in the past. For purposes of this discussion, an ESOP fiduciary could be an independent trustee, the former controlling stockholder, or an administrative committee.

In a potential M&A transaction involving the stock of the employer corporation, an ESOP fiduciary has an obligation to consider the investment opportunity as it compares to other available investments. Other available investments are those investments that are considered reasonable alternatives to the proposed M&A transaction.

If proper due diligence procedures are not followed, an ESOP fiduciary could be held personally liable for approving an unsound transaction. Therefore, a written fairness opinion from the ESOP's independent financial adviser is an integral component of most ESOP acquisition transactions. The objective of such a fairness opinion issued by an independent financial adviser is to ensure that the ESOP stock purchase transaction can withstand the scrutiny of (1) the U.S. Department of Labor, (2) the Internal Revenue Service, and (3) the ESOP beneficiaries.

Typically in an ESOP stock purchase transaction, the independent financial adviser is retained by the fiduciary who is responsible for representing the ESOP's interests related to the proposed transaction. As part of the due diligence related to the proposed M&A transaction, the ESOP's independent financial adviser is asked to provide a written opinion, known as a fairness opinion, stating that the proposed transaction is fair to the ESOP.

OVERVIEW OF AN ESOP FAIRNESS OPINION

A fairness opinion is a letter prepared by the ESOP's independent financial adviser that states whether or not a transaction is fair. Fairness is assessed (1) from a financial point of view, (2) as of a specific date, and (3) based on certain assumptions, limitations, and procedures.

An ESOP transaction fairness opinion has two purposes:

1. to provide the ESOP fiduciary with essential information and
2. to act as an element of proof that the ESOP fiduciary used reasonable business judgment in making an investment decision on behalf of the ESOP.

Although fairness opinions are not legally required, it is prudent for an ESOP fiduciary to obtain such an opinion. The fairness opinion may support a finding that the ESOP fiduciary made an informed business judgment in the event of litigation.

It is important to note that a fairness opinion does not recommend an ESOP transaction nor does it provide a legal opinion on an ESOP transaction. It is the responsibility of the ESOP fiduciary to determine if the transaction is appropriate. The financial adviser's role is to provide an opinion of the transaction "from a financial point of view."

In order to clarify the meaning of "from a financial point of view," an ESOP participant should understand what a nonfinancial point of view is. In any complex corporate control M&A transaction, an ESOP participant may ask questions such as:

1. Is now a good time to sell?
2. I bought my stock for higher than the deal price. How can this be fair?

Although these questions are valid concerns, these queries involve different questions of fairness which do not necessarily have anything to do with financial fairness.

RECENT CASE LAW

A recent court case, *Leonard Minzer, et al. v. Gerald C. Keegan, et al.* [218 F.3d 144 (2nd Cir. 2000)], highlights the importance of understanding the meaning of fair "from a financial point of view." The fairness opinion in this case did not purport to suggest that the merger was the highest potential price, but only that the "consideration . . . [was] fair, from a financial point of view."

In the *Leonard Minzer* case, the transaction fairness opinion specifically noted, in bold, capitalized letters: "the . . . opinion . . . does not address the underlying business decision . . . to engage in the merger and does not constitute a recommendation. . . ."

In its decision, the Appeals Court stated that the appellants must allege with particularity, "provable facts," undercutting the statement that the merger was "fair from a financial point of view." Such a fact may be that the merger price did not adequately reflect the present value of expected future net cash flow to the shareholders. No such allegation was made in this case.

In the *Minzer* case, the appellants did allege that the transaction was priced lower than the average bank industry merger in terms of a book value pricing multiple. However, such an allegation indicated nothing about the transaction's financial fairness—absent an allegation of facts suggesting that this pricing multiple differential did not reflect appropriately priced risk variations.

Nonetheless, the proxy statement clearly suggested that the company's lower book value price premium was explained by the above-average risk of the transaction.

This Second Circuit Appeals Court decision provides an example of how case law helps define the meaning of fair "from a financial point of view."

WHEN TO OBTAIN AN ESOP FAIRNESS OPINION

Because fairness opinions subject the independent financial adviser to great exposure, often a substantial professional fee is required for this service. The ESOP fiduciary needs to weigh the cost against the benefit when obtaining a fairness opinion.

Typically, the size and complexity of the employer corporation purchase/sale transaction is the primary factor that determines whether a fairness opinion is needed for ESOP purposes.

The following list illustrates the many situations (1) where a transaction involving an ESOP-owned company is subject to challenge and (2) where an independent financial adviser's fairness opinion is appropriate:

1. the creation of an ESOP,
2. the termination of an ESOP,

3. a significant purchase of employer corporation stock by an ESOP,
4. whenever there is a transaction with a controlling stockholder or a member of a control group,
5. transactions outside of the ESOP that significantly affect the capital structure of the sponsor company and, thereby, affect the value of the ESOP-owned shares.

In the first three of these situations, a fairness opinion from a qualified independent financial adviser is appropriate, obviously. Less obvious examples of situations where a change in the capital structure of the sponsor company could impact the value of the ESOP-owned shares—and for which the opinion of the ESOP's financial adviser may be helpful—include the following:

1. New shares of sponsor company common stock are issued—This could result in dilution in the value of the ESOP's shares.
2. A preferred security is created and distributed—This may give another equity holder a superior right to dividends and may result in a decline in the value of the ESOP-owned stock.
3. The sponsor company takes on a large amount of long-term debt—The ESOP-owned stock value could be reduced because another stakeholder has a superior claim in the case of corporate liquidation.

WHO IS QUALIFIED TO ISSUE ESOP FAIRNESS OPINIONS?

Some of the factors for ESOP fiduciaries to consider when evaluating an independent financial adviser for purposes of requesting a transaction fairness opinion include:

1. avoid financial advisers with a conflict of interest and avoid entering into contingent fee arrangements, both of which could impair the independence of the financial adviser, and
2. evaluate the financial adviser's general valuation expertise and specific experience regarding the business valuation of similar businesses in similar industries.

SUMMARY AND CONCLUSION

ESOP fiduciaries are responsible for showing that, during the course of analyzing a potential M&A transaction, proper due diligence was conducted and the transaction price was the highest price reasonably available. This responsibility for ESOP fiduciaries has been defined by several recent court cases.

Therefore, the written advice of the ESOP's independent financial adviser is an important procedure in the analysis of a potential employer corporation transaction purchase/sale. This statement is especially true if the ESOP fiduciary's investment decision may be challenged in the future.

Chapter 21

Procedures to Avoid Overpaying in ESOP Acquisitions

INTRODUCTION

ESOP trustees and ESOP financial advisers are concerned that an ESOP does not pay more than fair market value in an employer corporation stock purchase transaction. This concern is based on the ERISA "adequate consideration" test for employer stock purchase transactions.

Likewise, ESOP employee participants and ESOP acquisition debt lenders are also concerned that an ESOP does not pay more than fair market value, particularly with regard to the leveraged acquisition of a controlling interest in the employer corporation. In fact, all parties to the ESOP transaction have an interest in seeing that the ESOP does not "pay too much" in an employer corporation stock agreement.

For purposes of this discussion, "paying too much" is defined as any one of the following conditions:

1. The ESOP pays a total consideration in excess of the employer corporation stock fair market value.
2. The ESOP pays a total consideration in excess of the employer corporation stock's intrinsic value (i.e., the present value of the expected post-acquisition economic benefits to the ESOP acquirer).
3. The ESOP pays a total consideration that will result in a transaction internal rate of return (IRR) that is less than the ESOP's cost of capital.

By the end of 2004, the national stock market indices (including NYSE, Nasdaq, DJIA, and S&P) recovered from a four-year downturn in investor returns. At the same time, the M&A markets were rebounding—in terms of both deal volume/number of transactions and deal size/valuation pricing multiples. This rebound occurred across both industry segments and deal sizes.

Accordingly, this is an opportune time for ESOP trustees and financial advisers to (1) reflect on the overvaluation pricing mistakes of the last bull market and (2) consider developing/implementing systematic procedures to minimize the potential of overpaying for an ESOP to overpay in a current employer corporation stock purchase transaction.

There are many reasons why an ESOP may pay too much in an employer corporation acquisition. Some of these reasons are industry-specific or organization-specific. Some of the reasons are institutional. For example, investment bankers and sell-side financial advisers are often compensated for closing the deal at the highest negotiated price, and not for closing the deal at fair market value. Some of the reasons are structural. For example, sell-side financial analysts may price the deal according to a predetermined investment hurdle rate that may or may not equal the ESOP's cost of capital.

There are human behavior explanations for why ESOPs pay too much. Sometimes employees become overly enthusiastic about the expected economic and psychological benefits of employee ownership.

After the M&A market bubble burst in the late 1990s, explanations for why acquirers overpaid were presented in both business and academic journals. In contrast to analyzing why corporate acquirers historically paid too much, this discussion will focus on procedures that can help an ESOP to avoid overpaying in an employer corporation acquisition.

In other words, instead of examining the corporate M&A sins of the past, this discussion focuses on due diligence and pricing procedures that will result in economically sound ESOP stock acquisitions. These procedures relate to investigating, pricing, negotiating, and structuring the employer corporation stock purchase transaction. These procedures are intended to result in a stock purchase transaction price and structure consistent with the ESOP's strategic and corporate finance objectives, or, alternatively, to allow the ESOP to recognize and reject an overpriced transaction.

The following discussion presents a "top 10 list" of ESOP stock acquisition due diligence and transaction analysis procedures. These procedures can assist an ESOP trustee and financial adviser to avoid overpriced stock purchase transactions. Certainly, this is not a comprehensive list of all transaction pricing and structuring procedures. Rather, this listing is intended to present procedures that are fundamental and yet frequently overlooked—

even by experienced ESOP trustees and financial advisers. This top 10 list is not presented in any particular order of importance or priority.

TRANSACTION VALUATION PROCEDURES

Procedures 1 through 5 apply principally to the ESOP stock purchase transaction valuations. Procedures 6 through 10 relate principally to structuring the ESOP stock acquisition transaction. All procedures are intended to assist all parties to the ESOP to avoid overpaying for the employer corporation stock purchase transaction.

Procedure 1—Consider Multiple Valuation Approaches and Methods

Many ESOP financial advisers are most comfortable using the income approach and, specifically, the discounted cash flow (DCF) method to value the employer corporation acquisition target. The DCF method is conceptually sound and allows for a great deal of analytical rigor. This method is particularly well suited to analysis of (1) changing financial projections and (2) alternative valuation variables. For example, the DCF method allows for the estimation of both equity and enterprise (i.e., invested capital) value based on alternative debt service, capital structure, and rate of return assumptions.

Nonetheless, the DCF method is only one of several income approach valuation methods. And, the income approach is only one of several business valuation approaches. The ESOP financial adviser should consider the application of several different direct capitalization and yield capitalization methods as part of an income approach valuation analysis. Likewise, the ESOP financial adviser should consider the application of alternative methods within the market approach and asset-based approach to employer corporation stock valuation.

Applying several different valuation approaches and methods allows the ESOP financial adviser to: (1) develop a multi-faceted perspective of the employer corporation value, (2) triangulate a pricing conclusion within a range of values, (3) consider factors and variables that are not emphasized in the DCF method, (4) identify aberrational value indications from within a normal range of prices, and (5) quantify the sensitivity of price indications to small changes in valuation model inputs.

Procedure 2—Consider the Application of Asset-Based Approach Valuation Methods

Many ESOP financial advisers are not particularly experienced with asset-based approach business valuation methods. In the asset-based approach, the employer corporation value is the sum of the current values of (1) financial assets (e.g., receivables, inventory, investments), (2) tangible assets (e.g., real estate and personal property), (3) discrete intangible assets (e.g., patents, copyrights, trademarks, workforce), and (4) goodwill less the current values of (5) short-term liabilities (to estimate enterprise value) and (6) long-term liabilities (to estimate equity value). Typically, the most difficult aspects of asset-based approach methods are the identification and valuation of the employer corporation off-balance-sheet, discrete intangible assets.

The asset-based approach methods may require more analytical time and effort than income approach or market approach valuation methods. These methods also may require a more rigorous acquisition due diligence investigation of the employer corporation than other valuation methods. However, the additional due diligence effort invested in performing an asset-based approach valuation analysis not only provides an additional value indication in the final pricing synthesis and conclusion. The additional due diligence effort also increases the reliability and documentation of all other valuation pricing analyses.

Because the asset-based approach requires the ESOP financial adviser to value all of the employer corporation tangible and intangible assets, the valuation effectively creates a preliminary transaction purchase price allocation. This purchase price allocation can be used (1) to consider the pro forma effect of the transaction on the employer corporation financial statements and (2) to model the income tax implications of alternative transaction prices/structures. The discrete asset valuations can be used for purposes of (1) analyzing proposed transaction financing terms and (2) identifying sale/leaseback and other creative financial structures. Asset-based approach procedures help the ESOP financial adviser identify/quantify contingent liabilities (e.g., taxation, litigation, regulatory, environmental, etc.) that are not explicitly considered in other business valuation approaches.

Procedure 3—Quantify Both the Stand-Alone Fair Market Value and the Buyer-Specific Acquisition Value of the Target

Fair market value is generally defined as the price a typically motivated willing buyer would pay and a typically motivated willing seller would accept for the subject business enterprise. This definition of value generally considers only the economic benefits that would be available to the typical willing buyer of the employer corporation. In other words, unique buyer-specific synergies and post-merger economic benefits should be excluded from a fair market value analysis. This definition of value generally considers only the assets that the employer corporation has available to sell on a stand-alone basis. In other words, intangible assets created (or enhanced) only as a result of specific buyer actions/attributes should be excluded from a fair market value analysis.

Acquisition value (also called investment value) is generally defined as the highest price a specific buyer would be willing to pay to a specific seller for the subject business enterprise, given a buyer-specific set of investment criteria. This definition of value generally considers the total expected economic benefits of the combined acquirer/employer corporation entity. In other words, buyer-specific synergies and post-merger economic benefits could be included in an acquisition value analysis.

Similarly, employer corporation intangible assets that are created or enhanced by the acquirer's financial/operational attributes would be included in the acquisition value analysis. In addition, the valuation analyses would be based on buyer-specific investment criteria—for example, discount rate, direct capitalization rate, payback period, and so on. This is true even if these buyer-specific investment criteria are not consistent with market-derived valuation pricing variables.

Typically, the specific buyer's acquisition value is greater than the employer corporation stand-alone fair market value. Of course, this outcome is not a forgone conclusion. The employer corporation acquisition value for a particular buyer (with an unusually high cost of capital, for example) may be lower than the employer corporation fair market value. Of course, in a competitive bidding situation, that buyer would never be the successful acquirer of the employer corporation. In a competitive market, that buyer could be easily outbid by the "typical" willing buyer. Accordingly, it is unlikely that an employer corporation would ever sell for less than its stand-alone fair market value.

There are two reasons why ESOP financial advisers should quantify both the fair market value and the acquisition value of the employer corporation. First, such an analysis requires the ESOP financial adviser to (1) identify and (2) quantify the expected merger-specific economic benefits. Second, such an analysis should help the ESOP financial adviser in negotiating the pricing for the transaction.

There are several reasons why an ESOP financial adviser would want to identify/quantify specific post-merger benefits. First, this procedure gives the ESOP financial adviser the opportunity to assess whether the expected post-acquisition benefits will also be available to the ESOP as the acquirer of all of (or a controlling interest in) the employer corporation. Second, quantifying the expected post-acquisition benefits allows the ESOP financial adviser to estimate what a third-party acquirer may offer as a competing bid to purchase the employer corporation.

There are also several ways in which an ESOP financial adviser would use the expected post-merger benefits in the deal price and structure negotiations. It should be reiterated that the ESOP can never pay more than fair market value for the employer corporation stock. However, an ESOP stock sale transaction can offer some very attractive economic benefits to the selling stockholders—such as the Section 1042 deferral of the capital gains tax on the stock sale. The ESOP financial adviser may be able to quantify these ESOP transaction benefits. Then the ESOP financial adviser can demonstrate to the selling stockholder that the economic benefits of the sale to the ESOP are greater than the price increment associated with a specific buyers investment value.

Procedure 4—Perform a Sensitivity Analysis of the Important Valuation Variables

Among the sensitivity analysis scenarios, the ESOP financial adviser may consider: (1) a valuation with the most likely post-acquisition financial projections and (2) a valuation of the post-deal "worst case scenario" for the employer corporation. There are several reasons why sensitivity analysis may be useful in the transaction pricing and structuring negotiations. These reasons are described below.

First, the sensitivity analysis can identify a range of possible values for the employer corporation. This would indicate that the ESOP financial adviser should not negotiate a transaction price outside of this range of possible values. Depending on the procedures performed, the sensitivity analysis may also identify probabilities associated with the possible value outcomes. This would allow the ESOP financial adviser to negotiate a price within the most likely range of possible values.

Second, the sensitivity analysis can identify the most sensitive valuation variables—that is, variables where a small change in the variable input causes a large change in the value indication. It is important to identify the most sensitive variables so that the ESOP financial adviser can subject those variables to a particularly robust due diligence investigation. It is also important to identify the most sensitive variables so that employer corporation management can focus on those variables after the ESOP acquisition is closed.

Third, the sensitivity analysis can help quantify the risk of overpaying for the employer corporation. This is particularly true when the sensitivity analysis quantifies the values associated with (1) the worst case target company scenario and (2) other pessimistic target company scenarios. The sensitivity analysis should help the ESOP financial adviser to develop a clear understanding of the value implications of unfavorable employer corporation operating results.

Procedure 5—Carefully Consider the Value Implications of Business Cycles with Respect to the Employer Corporation, the Employer Corporation Industry, and the General Economy

Considerations of the relevant business cycles may be grouped into two categories: (1) the length and shape of the typical business cycle and (2) where the employer corporation is situated in the current business cycle as of the valuation date. Business cycle considerations may affect the ESOP stock purchase valuation in several ways.

First, most employer corporation financial projections indicate continuous increases in operating performance after the valuation date. The ESOP financial adviser should consider if such a projection is inconsistent with the historically cyclical nature of the employer corporation business. The ESOP financial adviser should consider the current operating results compared to where the employer corporation is in its current business cycle.

If the employer corporation is currently at the nadir of its business cycle and approaching an expansionary phase, then continuously increasing projections may not be unrealistic. However, if the employer corporation is currently at the zenith of its business cycle and approaching a contractionary phase, then more conservative projections may be more reasonable. The ESOP financial adviser should consider the current stage of the employer corporation business cycle when assessing the reasonableness of any employer corporation financial projections.

Second, an analysis of where the employer corporation industry currently sits on its industry business cycle can help identify the expected level of competition to the employer corporation. The current stage of the industry business cycle could affect: (1) expected product pricing, (2) expected product innovation/new product introductions, (3) the number of companies expected to enter/leave the industry in the short term, and (4) the general level of supply and demand for products in the employer corporation industry.

Third, an analysis of where the regional/national economy sits in the general economic cycle can help identify expected changes in the macroeconomic factors that influence the employer corporation stock valuation. The current phase of the general economic cycle could affect: (1) expected interest rates, (2) the availability of capital for employer corporation expansion plans, (3) the expected price inflation and cost inflation in the employer corporation industry, (4) the availability/price of labor in the employer corporation industry, and (5) the relative pricing (due to exchange rates) of foreign demand/competition for the employer corporation products.

Procedure 6—Structure the ESOP Acquisition Transaction so That the Seller Has a Continued Interest in the Success of the Employer Corporation

This procedure involves structuring the employer corporation stock purchase. This procedure includes deal structure provisions such as: the use of seller contractual earn-out provisions, step-purchase transactions, and seller retention of some class of equity security. The objective of these contractual provisions is to have the employer corporation seller and/or target key employees continue to have an economic interest in the success of the employer corporation.

There are two reasons to use such provisions. First, the seller (as an individual or corporate entity) and key employees should have an economic incentive to make the ESOP acquisition successful. It should be in their economic self-interests to work hard to achieve the greatest subsequent payments in the earn-out/step-purchase/retained equity redemption phase of the transaction. Second, such provisions reduce the downside risk to the ESOP. That is, if the financial performance goals or other contract provisions are not met, subsequent payments are not made. That means that the total consideration ultimately paid by the ESOP to the seller is less than it would have been if the acquisition was more successful.

There are two drawbacks associated with the use of contract provisions that continue the involvement of the seller and/or key employees in the employer corporation. First, the use of such contract provisions adds a degree of complexity to the transaction. Obviously (and intentionally), the seller is not completely removed from the employer corporation at the time of the closing. Therefore, the ESOP may not (1) obtain absolute control of the employer corporation or (2) be rid of all obligations to the seller until the conclusion of the earn-out or other contract provisions. Second, in the case of a successful acquisition, the ESOP may have to make substantial post-closing payments to the seller. This may increase the total consideration paid for the employer corporation, when compared to an all-cash-at-closing price. Nonetheless, the larger total consideration does not mean that the ESOP paid too much to the seller. This is because the subsequent payments are not made unless the employer corporation exceeds financial projections or other stated benchmarks.

Procedure 7—Incentivize Employer Corporation Management with Contracts Containing Performance Incentives, Stock Options, or Direct Equity Investments

The objective of this incentive compensation is to motivate employer corporation management to (1) remain with the employer corporation after the ESOP acquisition and (2) implement the ESOP's goals. The attitude of target company management is often one of the most important elements in the success of the ESOP acquisition. Employer corporation management personnel who are committed to finding new jobs at new companies will not be dedicated to ensuring that the ESOP achieve the maximum return on its investment. Alternatively, employer corporation management personnel who are appropriately motivated and compensated will work assiduously to make the ESOP acquisition a financial/operational success.

There are numerous compensation methods that are available to (1) encourage employer corporation management to stay and (2) motivate employer corporation management to internalize the ESOP's financial goals. These methods include stock and/or cash bonus plans, incentive stock option plans, plans that allow management to retain/obtain direct ownership of equity securities, plans that compensate management with indirect ownership of synthetic equity securities, and others.

All of these compensation plans have a common attribute: the employer corporation management income and/or wealth increases if (1) the employer corporation achieves predetermined post-acquisition benchmarks or (2) the acquisition is deemed successful by reference to some other predetermined goals or benchmarks. In short, the greater return the ESOP earns on the acquisition, the greater return employer corporation management earns on the acquisition.

As with any procedure, there are drawbacks to such special acquisition-related compensation plans. If the acquisition is successful, employer corporation company executives may earn much more in the short term than market-level compensation amounts. However, these drawbacks can be mitigated by (1) managed expectations and (2) effective communication. It is true that employer corporation managers may be highly compensated in the first few years following the transaction. However, they must earn that compensation by achieving predetermined goals. And, if the acquisition is successful, that will increase the long-term value to the ESOP.

Procedure 8—Make Your Final Offer *the Final* Offer

There is typically a great deal of negotiation that occurs during the ESOP stock acquisition process. This includes negotiation over both the price and the structure of the deal. And, that's just the beginning. After the price and structure are agreed to in principal, considerable negotiation occurs with regard to each of the terms and conditions of the ESOP stock purchase agreement. However, this recommended procedure relates to the deal pricing negotiation.

After (1) the ESOP financial buyer has performed the valuation analyses and (2) the ESOP trustee and selling stockholder have participated in several iterations of price negotiations, the ESOP should submit one best and final offer for the employer corporation stock. The seller should understand that this is the final offer. The price negotiation process has completed. If the seller accepts the buyer's final offer, the transaction will be consummated. If the seller rejects the ESOP's final offer, then the stock purchase transaction will be terminated. No additional negotiations will take place.

The ESOP should offer the highest fair market value price it is willing to pay in this best and final offer. If the offer is accepted, the ESOP will not pay too much. However, the ESOP should be disciplined to ensure that it does not exceed its "final" offer in a succeeding round of negotiations.

Procedure 9—Be Prepared to Walk away from the Transaction if the Seller Does Not Accept the Final Offer

Of course, this procedure relates to recommended procedure 8. If the seller does not accept the best and final offer, the ESOP should be prepared to withdraw from the negotiations. The employees may be disappointed in that outcome, because a great deal of time and effort was expended on the negotiations. However, continued negotiation after the rejection of a final offer (1) causes the ESOP trustee to lose credibility as a negotiator and (2) almost ensures that the ESOP will ultimately pay too much for the employer corporation.

If the final offer is not accepted, the ESOP trustee should discontinue negotiations. The continued pursuit of the current transaction will likely result in an imprudent investment decision. After the negotiations are terminated, the ESOP trustee should still accept communications from the seller. After all, the seller may ultimately accept the ESOP's final offer, after a period of reconsideration.

Procedure 10—Obtain an Independent Assessment of the Deal Price/Structure before Committing to the Transaction

This procedure involves retaining (and listening to) the professional advice of an independent financial adviser. This independent assessment should result in a formal fairness opinion. However, in addition to a formal fairness opinion, the financial adviser can provide informed, objective advice to the ESOP trustee regarding the transaction price parameters.

Of course, the financial adviser trusted with this important task should be independent of the transaction. In other words, this financial adviser is not one of the investment bankers who brought the deal to the seller or to the ESOP. Those financial intermediaries will likely be compensated based on a percentage of the ultimate transaction price. Accordingly, they are motivated to have a transaction close at any price—so that they will earn their performance fees. Rather, what the ESOP needs at this point in the negotiation process is totally unbiased, objective, independent advice. This financial adviser should not have any economic disincentive to tell the ESOP trustee "the price is getting too high; you should call the deal off."

SUMMARY AND CONCLUSION

It is fairly easy to identify situations where buyers overpaid for acquisitions after the fact. It is also fairly easy to specify the criteria that determine when a corporate acquirer paid too much in an M&A transaction. These criteria have been adequately discussed in the literature. However, what is important to ESOP trustees and financial advisers is to establish procedures that minimize the probability of paying too much for the next ESOP stock purchase transaction.

This discussion has presented 10 relatively simple procedures to assist ESOP financial advisers to avoid overpricing ESOP stock purchase transactions. This list of procedures is not comprehensive. There are certainly other procedures that ESOP trustees may consider to avoid overpaying in employer corporation acquisition situations. And, even these procedures will not ensure that a particular ESOP will not overpay for a particular employer stock acquisition. However, these procedures will generally assist ESOP financial advisers from getting caught in the ESOP stock acquisition overpricing trap.

Chapter 22

Valuation and Financial Adviser Due Diligence Procedures

INTRODUCTION

ERISA requires an ESOP to pay no more than adequate consideration when investing in employer corporation securities. These employer corporation securities include both common stock and convertible preferred stock.

The ERISA adequate consideration requirement has two general components:

1. a fair market value determination and
2. a good faith process.

This means that the ESOP trustees and fiduciaries must determine—in good faith—the fair market value of the employer corporation securities that are bought or sold by the ESOP. This determination must be made in compliance with certain regulations issued by the Internal Revenue Service and by the DOL.

This discussion presents a checklist that may be considered by ESOP valuation analysts in their conduct of an ESOP securities valuation and/or in the performance of an independent financial adviser's due diligence. Such a financial adviser's due diligence would be performed prior to the issuance of a fairness opinion related to an ESOP purchase or sale of employer corporation stock.

This checklist may also be used by ESOP trustees and fiduciaries in their good faith assessment of (1) an ESOP employer corporation stock valuation or (2) an independent financial adviser's opinion related to an ESOP purchase/sale transaction. This checklist may also be used by ESOP administrators and by other ESOP advisers (e.g., attorneys, accountants, etc.) who rely on ESOP stock valuations.

There are numerous caveats associated with this checklist, as will be discussed below. These caveats should be carefully considered before this checklist is applied in an actual ESOP stock valuation or financial adviser's due diligence analysis.

TRANSACTIONS INVOLVING AN OPINION OF ADEQUATE CONSIDERATION

The following types of transactions involving an ESOP and employer corporation stock typically require the assessment of adequate consideration:

- a contribution of employer corporation stock to the ESOP;
- a contribution of cash to the ESOP, where the cash is then used to buy employer corporation stock (either directly from the corporation or from other shareholders);
- the purchase of employer corporation stock from the ESOP trustee;
- the distribution of cash to the ESOP participants in place of the distribution of employer corporation stock; and
- the purchase of employer corporation stock from ESOP participants by the ESOP trustee.

In each of these types of transactions, the ESOP trustee or fiduciary must address the adequate consideration of the transaction. The checklist presented in this discussion is intended to be useful in that assessment of adequate consideration.

VALUATION OPINIONS AND FAIRNESS OPINIONS

As part of the adequate consideration assessment, the fair market value of the employer corporation stock must be estimated. This estimation is typically documented and reported in a valuation opinion report.

Some transactions involving ESOP-owned securities also involve an assessment of the fairness—from a financial perspective—of the proposed employer stock purchase transaction. This is particularly true in the case of multi-investor ESOP stock purchase transactions. In these cases, an independent financial adviser typically will perform a financial advisory due diligence—and issue a fairness opinion. The checklist presented in this discussion is also intended to be useful in the assessment of transactional fairness.

CAVEATS REGARDING THE CHECKLIST

It is important for the reader to consider several caveats regarding the use of any standardized stock valuation or independent financial adviser due diligence checklist.

First, the checklist should not substitute for the financial adviser's (or for the trustee's) independent professional judgment.

Second, the following checklist is not intended to be comprehensive and all-inclusive. For example, it does not discuss every available ESOP employer stock valuation method—but only the more common ESOP stock valuation methods.

Third, the terminology used in the checklist may have several interpretations. For example, the checklist refers generally to "premiums and discounts." The reader should understand that this term includes consideration of all related valuation adjustments, such as the discount for lack of marketability, the effects of the repurchase liability, the discount for lack of ownership control/premium for ownership control, and the effects of abnormal levels of leverage.

Fourth, this checklist does not include a complete consideration of all of the aspects of a leveraged ESOP stock purchase transaction or of a leveraged ESOP employer stock valuation. For example, the checklist does not describe due diligence procedures related to (1) a review of the terms and conditions of the debt indenture agreement or (2) an analysis of the employer corporation's ability to meet its debt service obligations.

Fifth, this checklist assumes that the valuation subject is the stock of an employer corporation for which there is no generally recognized secondary market. In other words, this checklist relates to the valuation of a closely held employer corporation.

Finally, this checklist relates to the due diligence process—and not to the content of a valuation opinion report or of a financial adviser's opinion. Therefore, this checklist does not include a "table of contents" for an ESOP valuation report. However, since this is an important issue to parties relying on ESOP employer stock valuations, valuation analysts agree that any written ESOP valuation report should include an assessment of the following factors:

1. the nature of the subject business and the history of the business enterprise;
2. the economic outlook and the condition and outlook of the specific industry;
3. the book value of the subject securities and the financial condition of the subject business;
4. the earnings capacity of the employer corporation;
5. the dividend-paying capacity of the employer corporation;
6. whether or not the subject business enterprise has goodwill or other intangible value;
7. the market price of securities of corporations engaged in the same or a similar line of business that are actively traded in a free and open market;
8. the marketability, or lack thereof, of the subject securities; and
9. whether or not the seller would be able to obtain an ownership control price premium with regard to the subject employer corporation stock.

CHECKLIST NOT A SCORE CARD

This checklist should not be used to derive a quantitative score used to evaluate an ESOP stock valuation opinion or financial adviser's fairness opinion. That is, the fact that an individual analysis did not receive a "score" of 100 does not indicate that the analysis is not in compliance with promulgated regulations and professional practices. Regardless of the checklist score, such an analysis may still be professional and competent. And, such an analysis may conclude the appropriate basis on which to assess adequate consideration in an ESOP stock sale/purchase transaction.

Likewise, the fact that an individual analysis received a very high "score" does not necessarily indicate that the analysis was prepared in compliance with all promulgated regulations and professional practices. Regardless of the checklist score, such an analysis may still be lacking in professional competence. And, such an analysis may be an inadequate basis on which to assess adequate consideration in an ESOP stock purchase/sale transaction.

The checklist is just that—a convenient checklist that valuation analysts and ESOP fiduciaries can use as a procedural reminder in the conduct of—and the assessment of—ESOP stock valuations and financial advisory opinions. The checklist may be used to document whether the requisite procedures were (or were not) performed. But this checklist will not evaluate the analytical quality and the professional judgment involved in the performance of the actual procedures.

SUMMARY AND CONCLUSION

The following checklist lists the most common procedures that are performed during an analytical process. That process is either an ESOP stock valuation or a financial adviser's due diligence leading to a fairness opinion in an ESOP stock purchase/sale transaction.

The checklist is presented as a useful reminder to ESOP valuation analysts, to ESOP fiduciaries, and to other ESOP advisers. It may be useful in the conduct of an ESOP valuation or a financial advisory analysis. It may also be helpful in the review and assessment of an ESOP valuation report or of a financial adviser's analysis and opinion.

However, the checklist should not be used as a substitute for the experience and judgment of the professional valuation analyst or of the independent financial adviser. And, the checklist should not substitute for the good faith due diligence, prudence, and professional care of the ESOP trustee or ESOP fiduciary.

Checklist of Common ESOP Stock Valuation and Financial Adviser Due Diligence Procedures

Y N N/A

I. Engagement letter and/or engagement work product

☐ ☐ ☐ A. State the purpose and objective of the engagement
1. Identify the analysis purpose (fairness opinion, annual stock valuation, etc.)
2. Identify the analysis objective (estimate fair market value of the ESOP ownership interest, etc.)

☐ ☐ ☐ B. Define the assignment
1. Identify the retaining party
2. Identify the entity being appraised
3. Identify the current form of the subject organization (C corporation, S corporation, limited partnership, etc.)
   a. Indicate state of incorporation
   b. Indicate date incorporated
4. Identify the specific ownership interest being appraised
5. Identify the valuation date ("as of" date of the analysis)

☐ ☐ ☐ C. Document the standard of value and premise of value

Y N N/A

1. Identify and define the appropriate standard of value (fair market value, fair value, etc.)
2. Identify and define the appropriate premise of value—based on highest and best use considerations (value in use as a going concern, value in exchange on an orderly disposition basis, etc.)

☐ ☐ ☐ D. Document the appropriate level of value
1. Identify the level of marketability of the subject securities
2. Identify the level of ownership control of the subject securities

II. Due diligence/collection of data

☐ ☐ ☐ A. Collect and review company documents and information
1. Request financial information (typically last five years and latest interim financial statements)
   a. Income statements
   b. Balance sheets
   c. Statements of changes in financial position
   d. Capital statements
   e. Explanatory footnotes and supplemental disclosures to the financial statements
2. Request a list of subsidiaries and/or financial ownership interests in other companies (including relevant historical financial information)
3. Request other financial information
   a. All current operating budgets, financial projections, or business forecasts
   b. Other financial schedules (depreciation, inventory, receivables, payables, open purchase/customer orders, production backlog, etc.)
   c. Existing contracts/leases (employment agreements, noncompete agreements, labor agreements, customer contracts, real estate leases, etc.)
   d. Amounts and description of insurance in force (key person, property/casualty, etc.)
   e. Compensation schedule for senior management and all employee/stockholders (salary, options, etc.)
   f. Prior valuation reports (prepared for any purpose)
   g. Schedule of dividends paid
4. Request company legal documents
   a. Articles of incorporation, bylaws, amendments, etc.
   b. Any existing buy-sell agreements, options, rights of first refusal, etc.
   c. Minutes from recent board of directors meetings
   d. Minutes from recent stockholder meetings
   e. List of all stockholders
      1) number of shares owned by each, and/or

Y N N/A

2) number of shares owned by senior management

f. Descriptions of all recent prior transactions of the subject stock and any recent bona fide offers to purchase the company and/or the subject securities

g. ESOP transaction documents
   1) ESOP-related loan agreements
   2) Stock purchase agreements
   3) ESOP plan and trust documents
   4) Other documents that may impact the rights of the securities

5. Request other relevant operational information
   a. History and description of the business
   b. Copies of marketing, advertising, promotional materials
   c. Copies of products/services brochures and current price lists
   d. Locations in which the company operates
   e. Major customers by annual dollar volume
   f. Major suppliers by annual dollar volume
   g. Major competitors (and size and/or market share, if available)
   h. Breakdown of personnel (by department or function) and resumes of senior management
   i. Descriptions of all patents, trademarks, copyrights, and other owned/licensed intellectual properties
   j. Description of any contingent and/or off-balance-sheet assets and liabilities
   k. List of industry or trade associations, industry or trade publications, and corporate memberships of the subject business
   l. Description and current appraisals (if available) of all nonoperating assets of the subject business
   m. Operational (i.e., production, sales, backlog) budgets, projections, or forecasts
   n. Strategic, competitive, or business plans

☐ ☐ ☐ B. Conduct management interviews

1. Interview senior management in all relevant functional areas, regarding:
   a. Historical operations and results
   b. Prospective operations and results
   c. Responsibility for functional areas
   d. Strategic/competitive strengths, weaknesses, opportunities, and threats (SWOT)

2. Discuss with senior management and/or outside legal counsel any pending or potential litigation or claims
   a. Commercial litigation
   b. Employment disputes
   c. Occupational and safety issues
   d. Environmental issues

Y N N/A

- e. Income/property tax disputes
- f. Other controversy matters

☐ ☐ ☐ C. Conduct plant/site inspections
1. Inspect representative plants and sites; consider:
   a. Adequacy of the current capacity of existing plants, facilities, and equipment
   b. Functional and technological adequacy of existing plants, facilities, and equipment
2. Discuss condition/capacity of plants and sites with management representatives; consider:
   a. Future expansion and capital investment plans
   b. Competitive effects of planned plant and facility changes

III. Economic environment (as of valuation date)

☐ ☐ ☐ A. Consider (research and analyze) the national/internal economic environment

☐ ☐ ☐ B. Consider (research and analyze) the regional/local economic environment

☐ ☐ ☐ C. Consider the economic relationships to the performance of the company—quantify significant relationships of economic performance with the performance of the company

IV. Industry environment

☐ ☐ ☐ A. Consider (research and analyze) the industry in which the company operates

☐ ☐ ☐ B. Consider (research and analyze) the nature and history of the industry

☐ ☐ ☐ C. Consider (research and analyze) the current outlook for the industry

☐ ☐ ☐ D. Consider (research and analyze) the current outlook for any compelling/complimentary industries

☐ ☐ ☐ E. Consider (research and analyze) the current outlook for any compelling/complimentary companies

V. Fundamental position of the company

☐ ☐ ☐ A. Consider the subject company capitalization and ownership
1. Analyze all classes of stock, including rights, seniority, voting, etc. of each class
2. Analyze total outstanding shares and distribution of ownership of each class

☐ ☐ ☐ B. Consider the subject company history and operations
1. Review company history
2. Analyze total outstanding shares and distribution of ownership of each class
   a. Locations and markets served
   b. Products, service lines, and customer base
   c. Competition
      1) Current and projected market size
      2) Position of the subject company within the industry

Y N N/A

3) Subject company competitive strengths and weaknesses
d. Strategic position within industry
e. Management and workforce
f. Overall positive and negative aspects of the subject operations

☐ ☐ ☐ C. Consider the outlook for the company—review strategic plans, projections, and current business outlook

VI. Financial statement adjustments and analysis

☐ ☐ ☐ A. Make appropriate financial statement adjustments
1. Adjust inventory, as appropriate
a. LIFO vs. FIFO
b. Inventory write-offs and/or write-downs
2. Adjust for excessive/insufficient management or employee/shareholder compensation, as appropriate
3. adjust for nonrecurring items, as appropriate (e.g., unusual gains/losses, insurance proceeds, nonrecurring revenues, and/or expenses, etc.)

☐ ☐ ☐ B. Perform historical financial statement analysis
1. Calculate and analyze common-size financial statements
2. Compute and analyze financial and operating ratios, including:
a. Size
b. Growth
c. Liquidity
d. Profitability
e. Turnover/activity
f. Leverage
3. Identify and explain any significant financial trends

☐ ☐ ☐ C. Perform prospective financial statement analysis
1. Identify key financial variables (e.g., capacity constraints, cost/volume/profit relationships, etc.) for:
a. Same or a similar line of business
b. Size
c. Trading activity/pricing evidence
d. Financial condition
2. Adjust financial statements of the selected guideline companies (e.g., adjust the guideline companies to make them more comparative to the subject company, i.e., "apples to apples")
3. Identify appropriate earnings and operating fundamentals
4. Calculate market-derived pricing multiples for the guideline companies
5. Analyze range of market-derived pricing multiples
a. Statistical analysis of range of pricing multiples
b. Correlation with performance factors (e.g., growth, returns, etc.)
6. Compute and analyze financial and operating ratios for the guideline companies, including:
a. Size

Y N N/A

b. Growth
c. Liquidity
d. Profitability
e. Turnover/activity
f. Leverage

7. Compare the subject company to the guideline companies
8. Select the appropriate transaction pricing multiples for the subject company
9. Apply the selected multiples to the appropriate subject company earnings and operating fundamentals
10. Synthesize an estimate of value—subtract the market value of subject company debt in invested capital valuation analyses
11. Identify any appropriate valuation premiums/ discounts (for the specific level of the subject business interest)
12. Quantify any appropriate valuation premiums/ discounts (for the specific level of the subject business interest)
13. Apply any appropriate valuation premiums/discounts (for the specific level of the subject business interest) capitalization) method (if appropriate)

☐ ☐ ☐ D. Develop projected results of operations for valuation analysis:

1. Review and analyze projections related to prospective results of company operations
2. Develop the appropriate economic income fundamentals for analysis—e.g., net cash flow, which considers:
   a. Earnings
   b. Noncash expenses (depreciation, amortization, etc.)
   c. Capital expenditures
   d. Working capital requirements
3. Develop the appropriate yield capitalization present value discount rate, with consideration to:
   a. Capital market environment
   b. Risk-free rates of return
   c. Equity rates of return (and/or equity risk premiums)
   d. Company-specific risks/required rates of return, with consideration to:
      1) Expected attainability of company projections
      2) Degree of financial/operating leverage
      3) Degree of diversification of the business base
      4) Capital structure of the subject company
      5) Typical capital structure in the subject industry

Y N N/A

4. Develop an estimate of the terminal/residual value, with consideration to:
   a. Terminal/residual year financial fundamentals (e.g., net cash flow projection)
   b. Terminal/residual year direct capitalization rates (e.g., as derived from the Gordon growth model)
5. Apply the derived present value discount rate to the estimated economic income projection (e.g., net cash flow), including:
   a. The discrete projection period of periodic economic income
   b. The terminal/residual value estimate
6. Calculate an estimate of value—subtract the market value of subject company debt from the invested capital valuation estimate
7. Identify any appropriate valuation premiums/ discounts (for the specific level of the subject business interest)
8. Quantify all appropriate valuation premiums/ discounts (for the specific level of the subject business interest)
9. Apply any appropriate valuation premiums/discounts (for the specific level of the subject business interest)

☐ ☐ ☐ E. Perform an asset-based approach—asset accumulation method (if appropriate)

1. Adjust all on-balance-sheet assets to market value (e.g., current assets, tangible personal property, real estate, etc.)
2. Identify all off-balance sheet intangible assets
3. Estimate the value of all off-balance-sheet intangible assets
4. Estimate the value of the total on-balance-sheet and off-balance-sheet tangible and intangible assets
5. Adjust all liabilities to market value (including consideration of off-balance-sheet and contingent liabilities)
6. Calculate an estimate of the overall subject company equity value (as the total market value of all assets less the total market value of all liabilities
7. Identify any appropriate valuation premiums/ discounts (for the specific level of the subject business interest)
8. Quantify any appropriate valuation premiums/ discounts (for the specific level of the subject business interest)
9. Apply any appropriate valuation premiums/discounts (for the specific level of the subject business interest)

☐ ☐ ☐ F. Consider other relevant valuation methods

1. Consider the application of any alternative valuation methods

Y N N/A

2. Perform the appropriate alternative valuation methods or document that such alternative methods are not applicable

☐ ☐ ☐ G. Prepare a reconciliation and synthesis of value
1. Determine the relevance of the respective valuation approaches used in the analysis
2. Weight the alternative estimates of value
3. Identify any appropriate valuation premiums/discounts (for the subject securities)
4. Quantify any appropriate valuation premiums/discounts (for the subject securities)
5. Apply any appropriate valuation premiums/discounts (for the subject securities)
6. Synthesize an estimate of value for the subject company and/or subject securities

☐ ☐ ☐ H. Reach a value conclusion—conclude the appropriate fair market value estimate for the appraisal subject

VIII. Documenting and reporting the results of the financial adviser's due diligence

☐ ☐ ☐ A. Prepare engagement workpapers—prepare and maintain workpapers and files that document the financial advisory due diligence

☐ ☐ ☐ B. Prepare a fairness opinion, as requested
1. Describe the proposed securities purchase transaction
2. Analyze the proposed securities purchase transaction in order to conclude whether the ESOP is paying no more for the subject securities than any other typical willing buyer would pay
3. Opine on the fairness of the proposed securities purchase transaction from a financial point of view, with consideration of the concluded fair market value for the subject securities

IX. Documenting and reporting the results of the valuation analysis

☐ ☐ ☐ A. Prepare engagement workpapers—prepare and maintain workpapers and files that document the valuation analysis

☐ ☐ ☐ B. Prepare a valuation opinion and valuation report
1. Opine on the adequate consideration with regard to the subject employer corporation securities
2. Opine on the fair market value of the subject employer corporation securities
3. Prepare a valuation report containing the following information:
    a. A summary of the qualifications of the principal valuation analyst(s)
    b. A statement of the subject security value, a statement of the methods used in estimating that value, and the reasons for the valuation in light of those methods
    c. A full description of the subject employer corporation securities

Y N N/A

d. The factors taken into account in making the valuation, including any restrictions, understandings, agreements or obligations limiting the use or disposition of the subject employer corporation securities
e. The purpose for which the valuation was made
f. The relevance or significance accorded to the valuation methods taken into account
g. The effective date of the valuation
h. In cases where a valuation report has been prepared, the signature of the person making the valuation and the date that the valuation report was signed

Section V

ESOP Trustee Issues

Chapter 23

ESOP Trustee Fiduciary Duties

INTRODUCTION

The following discussion examines the duties of the trustee of an employee stock ownership plan ("ESOP trustee"). This discussion considers (1) the governing principles of the Employee Retirement Income Security Act of 1974, as amended ("ERISA"), (2) the application of those ERISA duties to general administration, and (3) the on-going administrative responsibilities of the ESOP trustee.

This discussion also summarizes (1) the legal actions that may be take against the ESOP trustee for breach of its fiduciary duties and (2) the legal remedies available to the ESOP plan.

GUIDING PRINCIPLES

Overriding ERISA Fiduciary Standards

General fiduciary standards, as outlined in ERISA, are the core fiduciary duties that apply to all trustee actions. These standards supersede the specific duties presented in the second half of this discussion. As provided under ERISA, general fiduciary law requires a fiduciary to manage and administer the trust:

- solely in the interests of ESOP plan participants and beneficiaries;
- for the exclusive purpose of (1) providing benefits to ESOP plan participants and their beneficiaries and (2) defraying reasonable expenses of administering the trust;
- with the care, skill, prudence, and diligence, which, under the circumstances then prevailing, a prudent man acting in like capacity and familiar with such matters would use in the conduct of an enterprise of a like character and with like aims;

- in accordance with the ESOP plan and trust agreement insofar as the plan and trust agreement are consistent with ERISA; in the event of a conflict, ERISA would require the ESOP trustee to act in a manner that is consistent with the ERISA fiduciary standards listed below (the "Overriding ERISA Fiduciary Standards"); also the ESOP trustee would not be required to follow the plan or trust agreement, but must act in accordance with the Overriding ERISA Fiduciary Standards; and
- in accordance with applicable requirements of law.

Additionally, the ESOP trustee must not cause the plan to engage in a transaction if the ESOP trustee knows or should know that the transaction would be prohibited (1) under ERISA Section 406 or (2) under Internal Revenue Code Section 4975(c). For example, it would be a prohibited transaction for the ESOP trustee to pay a price in excess of fair market value for employer corporation stock.

Continuing Responsibilities

A number of fundamental continuing responsibilities have evolved from the general Overriding ERISA Fiduciary Standards described above. The primary continuing general responsibility is to assure that the plan's investment in the employer corporation common stock ("employer stock") continues to satisfy the Overriding ERISA Fiduciary standards by being a prudent investment, solely in the interests of participants and beneficiaries, for the exclusive purpose of providing them benefits (and defraying reasonable administrative expenses).

One way for the ESOP trustee to discharge this continuing duty is (1) by monitoring the sponsor company and the value of employer corporation stock and (2) by making inquiry and taking action as appropriate. In general, an ESOP trustee should follow the company's investment activities as an investor would (not as a manager would). However, in a given instance, the ESOP trustee may desire very detailed information about a given transaction or circumstance.

The ESOP trustee should also be kept advised of potential problems and should seek advice of counsel when unusual events occur. To properly discharge this responsibility, the ESOP trustee should:

- Review the operations and financial condition of the company to determine whether the plan's investment in employer stock continues to satisfy the Overriding ERISA Fiduciary Standards. In addition, a permanent record file of reports and statements reviewed should be maintained.

- As part of the review, the ESOP trustee should obtain copies of all documents to which the ESOP trustee is entitled.
- The items described above should be reviewed carefully. The purpose of the review is to ensure that there are no material circumstances requiring further action. If further action is indicated, the ESOP trustee is required to commence appropriate measures to address the issue or issues.
- The ESOP trustee should consult with financial and legal counsel to consider the annual valuation and any special valuations of the employer corporation stock.

General ESOP Trustee Duties

Trust assets are to be invested in employer stock and are not diversified, subject to the obligation to keep short-term liquid investments invested in prudent investments. Cash contributions, cash dividends, and funds held pending investment in employer stock should also generally be held in prudent investments.

The ESOP trustee's powers, duties, and responsibilities should be set forth in the ESOP trust document although they may also be duplicated in the plan document.

GENERAL ADMINISTRATION AND INITIAL SET-UP

The ESOP trustee negotiates in its sole discretion any and all terms of any purchase of employer corporation stock, including borrowing funds for that purpose. The ESOP trustee will then enter into the series of transactions resulting in the trust owning all or a portion of the outstanding common stock of the employer corporation. These negotiations are subject to the Overriding ERISA Fiduciary Standards.

The following is a list of some of the specific duties that the ESOP trustee must perform in connection with any purchase of employer corporation stock:

- The ESOP trustee must engage in a diligent, independent investigation of the company that issues the security.
- The ESOP trustee must visit the sponsor company premises, review relevant corporate governance documents, and interview management.

- The ESOP trustee must engage his or her own advisers and not merely accept the hand-picked advisers of the seller
- The ESOP trustee must actively participate in the negotiation of the price and terms of the investment and cannot rely passively on advisers to do so.
- The ESOP trustee must have the experience and knowledge that enables him or her to understand the nature of the investment.
- The ESOP trustee must undertake an independent review of the terms of the ESOP stock purchase loan and other financing terms.
- The ESOP trustee must question his or her advisers about (1) their conclusions, (2) the basis of their conclusions, and (3) the underlying analysis (that is, the ESOP trustee must scrutinize the work of the advisers).
- The ESOP trustee must furnish to the advisers any relevant data or information he or she may have that is otherwise not publicly available.
- When purchasing an equity security, the ESOP trustee must investigate the solvency of the employer corporation post-transaction.
- When an ESOP trustee accepts a successor trustee appointment, the ESOP trustee must (1) review the predecessor's records and actions and (2) make an assessment of the effectiveness thereof.

ESOP TRUSTEE INDEMNIFICATION

The ESOP trustee may be indemnified by the employer corporation (except for willful misconduct or gross negligence of the ESOP trustee) to the extent lawfully allowable. The employer corporation may maintain liability insurance for the ESOP trustee, unless the ESOP trustee and the corporation reasonably agree it is unavailable or too expensive.

REGULAR RESPONSIBILITIES (ON-GOING OR RECURRING)

An ESOP trustee has a general custodial duty to hold and keep safe all trust assets and to keep records of their receipt, disbursements, and value. The ESOP trustee must hold, invest, and distribute the trust fund in accordance with the terms of the trust and ERISA. However, the ESOP trustee is not normally responsible for administrative or participant account record keeping. Additionally, subject to Overriding ERISA Fiduciary Standards, trust assets must be acquired at fair market value.

Contributions/Distributions

In addition to being responsible for (1) receiving contributions from the sponsor company and (2) applying them to repay any loans in accordance with the ESOP loan agreements, the ESOP trustee is responsible for making distributions to participants. The ESOP participants may elect to take a distribution in either cash or stock.

Generally, the plan administrator will provide the ESOP trustee with information regarding (1) the distribution to be made to the participants, (2) the timing of such distributions, and (3) the amount of each distribution.

The ESOP trustee must notify the company if any amount directed to be distributed remains unclaimed. "Unclaimed" in this context means that the check representing a distribution is returned because the addressee cannot be located. The ESOP trustee must then withhold appropriate taxes from cash amounts distributed and make appropriate deposits with IRS Form 941-E. Participants are entitled to put any stock distributed to them back to the sponsor company (or in some cases to the trust) as described in the plan.

Generally, the trust obtains cash for distribution and expenses from the sponsor company (1) by putting employer stock to the company in exchange for cash, (2) by obtaining an interest-free advance from the sponsor company at a time when the stock is not permitted to be put to the company, or (3) by receiving an advance cash contribution (of an amount that cannot exceed the total annual contribution limit).

Normally, stock may only be put to the sponsor company on a valuation date. The valuation date generally occurs once per year. It is the ESOP trustee's responsibility to notify the sponsor company of the plan's need for cash and to determine the amount of employer corporation stock, if any, to be put to the sponsor company.

In obtaining cash from the company, the ESOP trustee must be extremely cautious to avoid causing the plan to enter into a prohibited transaction. For example, the ESOP trustee may sell stock to the sponsor company only if it receives in return at least the fair market value of that stock on the date of transfer. Because ESOPs maintained by privately held companies generally value their stock only once a year, such sales are difficult to accomplish properly.

Employment of Agents and Advisers

The ESOP trustee, in his or her sole discretion, may employ attorneys, accountants, investment bankers and other advisers, and agents that the trustee believes to be reasonably necessary. The fees and expenses of such consultants may be paid either with trust assets or by the sponsor company.

Voting of Company Stock

Stock allocated to plan participants' accounts will be voted at the ESOP trustee's discretion. This is true unless the plan provides otherwise. The ESOP trustee will also vote the stock allocated to participant's accounts in the case of a merger, consolidation, asset sale, or liquidation of the sponsor company, in accordance with the directions of participants. Such directions will be communicated to the ESOP trustee by the plan participants.

Where the ESOP trustee has not received instruction from plan participants on an issue, the ESOP trustee will have discretion to vote the shares unless the trust document states otherwise. Because participant voting instructions must be kept confidential, the ESOP trustee should consider retaining an independent third party (1) to tally individual instructions and (2) to communicate aggregate voting instructions to the ESOP trustee.

The voting of allocated and unallocated shares is subject to the Overriding ERISA Fiduciary Standard. Securities not yet allocated to participants' accounts are voted by the ESOP trustee in his or her discretion unless the trust document provides otherwise. When responding to a tender offer, the ESOP trustee will tender or withhold from tender at the trustee's discretion, again, unless the trust document provides otherwise.

The ESOP trustee's responsibilities regarding voting and exercise of other shareholder rights may not be delegated.

The foregoing rules regarding voting and other shareholder rights only apply to the extent not inconsistent with applicable law. Therefore, it is necessary to review applicable law each time a vote or other exercise of shareholder rights occurs.

Annual Employer Stock Valuation

As of the last day of the plan year (or other valuation dates specified by the ESOP plan and trust), the trust assets, including employer stock, must be valued. In addition, a valuation date must be declared to determine if a material change in the value of company securities has occurred. A valuation date automatically occurs on the date of an ESOP termination.

Communications

The ESOP trustee must also keep accurate and detailed records of all transactions for review by the sponsor company. Generally, this requires that the ESOP trustee maintain a balance sheet and keep a record of receipts and disbursements.

In addition, the ESOP trustee must submit an annual (or more frequent) report to the sponsor company (as of each valuation date). The report should list holdings and transactions and contain additional information regarding the trust fund's assets and transactions requested by the sponsor company in order to enable the company to comply with its reporting requirements (primarily IRS Form 5500).

The ESOP trustee should also prepare and submit to the company for filing with the ESOP's annual return/report Form 5500, a Schedule P (Annual Return of Fiduciary of Employee Benefit Trust). The Schedule P is filed in order to trigger the beginning of the three-year statute of limitations on taxes which may be imposed on the trust.

Qualified Domestic Relations Orders and Claims

If served with a court order regarding payment of a participant's benefits, the ESOP trustee should refer it to the sponsor company to determine whether it is a "qualified domestic relations order." The ESOP trustee must promptly advise the company of any asserted claim that may trigger the sponsor company's indemnification obligation.

Resignation or Removal

An ESOP trustee may resign or be removed on advance written notice to (in the case of resignation) or from (in the case of removal) the company. Upon resignation or removal, an ESOP trustee must submit a final report and execute any documents to vest title in a successor trustee as appointed by the sponsor company.

The Overriding ERISA Fiduciary Standards may preclude a resignation or the acceptance of a removal if an issue involving fiduciary concerns arises. For example, there may be an obligation to take legal action prior to resigning or being removed. In such a situation, the ESOP trustee should consult counsel.

Termination of Plan and/or Trust

The board of directors of the company may terminate the plan and trust. Upon termination, the ESOP trustee will continue to hold and administer assets in accordance with the written plan and trust termination provisions until all assets are distributed.

Company Remedies in Event of Default under the ESOP Loan Agreement

If the ESOP defaults under the ESOP loan agreement, the employer corporation may exercise any rights available to it under ERISA and the Code and regulations thereunder. However, assets (i.e., company stock) in the trust may be transferred only upon and to the extent of a failure to meet the payment schedule on the loans. Certain other restrictions also apply.

No Restrictions on Employer Stock

Other than the put rights and the limited right of first refusal described herein, the employer corporation stock may not be made subject to any other put, call, or other option or buy-sell or similar arrangement.

FIDUCIARY LIABILITY

Various actions can be taken against an ESOP trustee, as a fiduciary, for breach of its duties. Remedies include restoration of the actual economic loss to a plan which may be caused by a breach of fiduciary duty. ERISA provides the basis for a suit against an ESOP trustee for a breach of fiduciary duty.

Any person who is a fiduciary with respect to a plan who breaches any of the responsibilities, obligations, or duties imposed upon fiduciaries:

1. shall be personally liable:
    a. to make good to such plan any losses to the plan resulting from each such breach and
    b. to restore to such plan any profits of such fiduciary that have been made through the use of assets of the plan by the fiduciary, and
2. shall be subject to such other equitable or remedial relief as the court may deem appropriate including removal of such fiduciary.

The computation of a loss under ERISA for a breach of fiduciary duty requires a comparison of actual investment returns on the ESOP trustee's improper investments with that which the plan would have earned had the funds been available for other plan purposes. ERISA Section 409 allows for the return of profits of the fiduciaries through the use of plan assets even where no losses have been incurred by the plan.

Whether the plan has suffered losses or the action is for disgorgement of fiduciary profits, there must be a causal connection between (1) the breach of fiduciary duty and (2) the losses or profits. In other words, ERISA does not impose liability for all losses to the plan or forbid all profits of the fiduciaries.

Although ERISA provides for "other equitable or remedial relief as the court may deem appropriate," a participant may not obtain punitive damages from the ESOP trustee under that section. It may provide for such damages in an action brought on behalf of the plan, however. Also, punitive damages may be available to a plan participant under another section of ERISA.

In addition, an ESOP trustee may be assessed a civil penalty by the U.S. Department of Labor in an amount equal to 20 percent of the amount recovered by the plan from The ESOP trustee.

This discussion was adapted from an article authored by Marilyn H. Marchetti, John Banasek, and Danielle Montesano. Marilyn Marchetti and John Banasek are senior vice presidents and Danielle Montesano is a vice president of GreatBanc Trust Company in Oak Brook, Illinois. They may be reached at (630) 572-5121.

The article from which this discussion was adapted was originally published in the Spring 2000 issue of Willamette Management Associates Insights.

This discussion was reviewed and updated by James O'Sullivan, Esq. Jim is a senior manager in the Willamette Management Associates New York City office.

Chapter 24

Trustee Considerations Regarding an ESOP Transaction

INTRODUCTION

When an acquisition, sale, tender offer, or plan termination of an ESOP has been proposed, the employer or corporation management and board of directors, as well as the ESOP trustee, are faced with many complex issues and choices. The acquisition or sale of an ESOP-owned company and subsequent termination or amendment of the plan can be the "end game" for an employee ownership strategy.

Whether the sale results from the long-term success of the sponsor company or from financial distress, it is always a challenging time for the managers of the sponsor company, the board, and the ESOP trustee. The acquisition or sale is a time for the ESOP trustee to bring together a team of attorneys and valuation professionals to assure that the interests of the ESOP participants and their beneficiaries are protected.

FIDUCIARY DECISIONS

The fiduciary decisions related to the sale or other disposition of an ESOP are fundamentally the same as for the formation of an ESOP. The ESOP trustee must assure himself or herself (1) that the ESOP is receiving no less than adequate consideration for the employer corporation securities it is selling and (2) that the sale transaction is fair to the ESOP from a financial point of view.

Additional rules and concerns come into play when (1) the ESOP is still leveraged and (2) the trust is expected to pay off the remaining ESOP stock purchase debt before making any distributions. Paying off the ESOP stock purchase debt and the allocation of proceeds in the sale transaction are issues that the ESOP trustee and trustee's advisers must evaluate.

The ESOP trustee should keep in mind that any decision by the company to terminate the ESOP is a settlor function and not a fiduciary decision. The determinations by the ESOP trustee (1) that the consideration received is adequate and (2) that the transaction is fair are fiduciary decisions. The decision by the employer corporation management to terminate the plan is not a fiduciary decision.

What if an Unsolicited Offer Is Made for the Sponsor Company?

The Role of the Board

Usually, an unsolicited offer to purchase the sponsor company will be made to the board of directors. Rarely is an offer made directly to the ESOP trust, even if the trust is the 100 percent owner of the sponsor company. If an offer is made directly to the trust, except in rare circumstances, the offer should be referred to the employer corporation board of directors for their analysis and decision.

The employer corporation board of directors has a fiduciary responsibility to maximize shareholder value for all shareholders, including the ESOP trust. The employer corporation board will have the primary responsibility for negotiating the terms and conditions of any offer for the benefit of the shareholders. The board is required to evaluate every bona fide offer and decide whether to recommend it to stockholders. To help in its evaluation, the employer corporation board (1) will often use the services of a financial advisory firm separate from the ESOP's adviser and (2) will typically receive a fairness opinion from that firm.

In rare cases, the financial advisory firm that provides the fairness opinion to the employer corporation board will allow the ESOP trustee to rely on that opinion. However, in all transactions, the ESOP trustee will require an adequate consideration and fairness opinion from its financial adviser, while the board may not always require an opinion.

The Role of Sponsor Company Management

The employer corporation management has a duty to the sponsor company and its board of directors. In a sale situation, employer corporation management will be interviewed extensively and will be called upon to provide due diligence support and information. Management will usually need to provide volumes of information and spend hours in interviews.

Management may need to summarize data and prepare long-range forecasts. In addition, employer corporation management may have conflicts of interest where their own self-interests are involved in negotiating any "golden parachutes," employment contracts, stock option packages, or termination agreements.

The Role of the ESOP Trustee

The ESOP trustee has a fiduciary responsibility to the ESOP plan participants and their beneficiaries. Once the employer corporation board of directors recommends an offer to the stockholders, the ESOP trustee must evaluate the offer to determine (1) that adequate consideration will be received by the trust and (2) that the offer is fair to the ESOP from a financial point of view. The ESOP trustee must also determine whether it is prudent for the ESOP to enter into the transaction.

One of the challenges of receiving an unsolicited offer is that competitive offers often don't exist for comparison purposes. When available, an analysis of multiple offers from the marketplace greatly assists in the determination of adequate consideration and fairness, especially for a distressed company.

Often, the ESOP trustee is afforded an opportunity to negotiate the terms of the offer along with the board in order to assure that the terms will meet the adequate consideration and fairness tests when evaluated by the trustee's financial adviser. The early involvement of the ESOP trustee and its financial adviser reduces unnecessary costs and delays by putting together an offer that can be accepted by the trustee.

The structure of the transaction may be such that the ESOP trustee is required to accept voting direction from the ESOP participants with respect to their allocated shares. In this case, the ESOP trustee will want to assure that the company makes full disclosure to the participants of all the appropriate information concerning the offer. The ESOP trustee will also want to arrange for the confidential tallying of the plan participant directions.

Prior to selling the ESOP-owned shares, the ESOP trustee will want to receive the input from its counsel that the transaction (1) doesn't violate sponsor company charter documents or any of the terms of ERISA and (2) is structured in an appropriate and legal way. The ESOP trustee will also want to receive an opinion from its financial adviser (1) that the transaction value is not less than adequate consideration and (2) that the transaction is fair to the ESOP from a financial point of view.

Finally, the ESOP trustee will have to determine that the proposed transaction is prudent. In doing so, the ESOP must determine that a prudent man would sell the company under the proposed terms. Usually this means comparing the terms of the proposed transaction with other available options and determining that this is the preferred course of action.

What if the Board Decides to Solicit Offers?

The Role of the Employer Corporation Board

Sometimes the employer corporation board of directors may decide to hire an investment-banking firm to solicit offers for the sponsor company. In many cases, this occurs when the sponsor company is either doing much better than anyone expected or much worse than anyone expected. In the case of an ESOP that owns a noncontrolling ownership interest, this may occur as a result of the timing of the liquidity needs and desires of the controlling shareholder(s). In addition, the sponsor company may pursue a sale of the company due to industry consolidation or other strategic pressures. The employer corporation board (1) should inform the ESOP trustee that it has decided to pursue this strategy and (2) should keep the ESOP trustee informed of the progress.

The Role of Employer Corporation Management

As a reminder, the employer corporation management has a duty to the sponsor company and the board of directors. In a situation where the board has decided to solicit offers, it will be in much the same situation as with an unsolicited offer. Furthermore, management's jobs may be threatened in the case of a synergistic sale, further increasing the pressure on management. However, sponsor company management is critical to the successful negotiation of any transaction. And, as a result, the board and the ESOP trustee should ensure that management are key contributors to the process.

In some cases, however, the sponsor company management may decide to make an offer (a management buy-out, or MBO)—independently or in competition with other offers. This can give rise to significant conflict of interest possibilities. Management would like to win the sponsor company for the least consideration while their fiduciary responsibility to the board requires them to maximize the consideration received. Sometimes employer corporation management must resign or be placed on leave during negotiations.

The Role of the ESOP Trustee

The ESOP trustee has a fiduciary responsibility to the ESOP participants and their beneficiaries. Once the employer corporation board of directors has decided to solicit offers, the trustee should remain informed of the progress. The ESOP trustee and its financial adviser should be knowledgeable regarding all competing offers in order to assess (1) the adequate consideration and (2) the fairness of the final transaction.

As with an unsolicited offer, the ESOP trustee will usually be afforded an opportunity to negotiate the terms of the offer along with the board in order to assure that the terms will meet the tests of adequate consideration and fairness in the final analysis.

As with an unsolicited offer, the structure of the transaction may be such that the ESOP trustee is required to accept voting direction from the participants with respect to their allocated shares. In this case, the ESOP trustee will want to assure that the sponsor company makes full disclosure to the participants of all the relevant information concerning the offer. The ESOP trustee will also want to arrange for the confidential tallying of the participant directions.

The ESOP trustee will need to receive the input from its counsel that (1) the sale/purchase transaction doesn't violate any of the terms of ERISA and (2) the sale/purchase transaction is structured in an appropriate and legal way prior to selling shares. The ESOP trustee should also receive an opinion from its financial adviser that the transaction value (1) is not less than adequate consideration and (2) is fair to the ESOP from a financial point of view.

The ESOP trustee will work with all of the parties involved in the transaction to determine that the proposed transaction is prudent for the ESOP trust.

What Is the Role of the Independent Financial Adviser to the ESOP?

The proposed regulations from the DOL require the ESOP trustee to have an independent financial adviser assess the company. The financial adviser can help evaluate the complex terms of each offer and effectively compare multiple offers. The financial adviser usually issues an opinion to the ESOP trustee (1) that the ESOP trust is receiving no less than adequate consideration and (2) that the transaction is fair to the ESOP from a financial point of view.

It is important throughout any negotiations that the independent financial adviser remain solely responsible to the ESOP trustee and independent of any other party to the transaction. The role of the independent financial adviser is as an adviser and not as a fiduciary. Thus, the independent financial adviser provides financial advice to the ESOP trustee, and the ESOP trustee makes the final fiduciary decisions.

The independent financial adviser must consider at least the following items in its analysis of transaction-related analyses:

1. The fair market value of the employer corporation stock bought or sold by the ESOP. In the case of a transaction where the ESOP and other shareholders are receiving stock from the acquirer as the form of consideration, the financial adviser must also evaluate the fair market value of the equity proceeds. These proceeds should include any liquidity discount if it is not a publicly traded security or is otherwise restricted.
2. The allocation of transaction proceeds among the ESOP trust and all other shareholders.
3. The effect of the remaining ESOP stock purchase debt, if any.
4. The effect of complex capital structures on the ESOP's ownership position.
5. An analysis of any management employment or incentive contracts, or termination payments.
6. The financial provisions and implications of all transaction-related documents.
7. The financial effects of any required escrows or indemnities.
8. Any other aspects of the transaction that affect the consideration or terms.

Communication between the independent financial adviser and the ESOP trustee is essential throughout the transaction process. Any significant issues should be addressed as early as possible in order to be sure the ESOP trust participates effectively in negotiations. The independent financial adviser should prepare a report for the ESOP trustee that includes all aspects of the transaction description and analyses. A formal presentation of the report and its conclusions should be made to the ESOP trustee before the transaction's anticipated closing.

How Can the Trustee Ensure a Fair Deal for the ESOP?

Prudence

Prudence in an ESOP transaction, whether buying or selling shares, is a matter of judgment, taking all facts into consideration. The trustee in an ESOP transaction has the responsibility to make sure that the transaction is fair to the trust, its participants, and its beneficiaries. The negotiations during the transaction must be at arm's length.

After the fact, the ESOP trustee may be called upon to convince the Department of Labor (1) that the transaction was prudent, (2) that the consideration received was adequate, and (3) that the transaction was fair. In light of potential conflicts, having an independent trustee evaluate the transaction is highly recommended but not required.

Due Diligence

The ESOP trustee must be familiar with the employer corporation. The trustee must understand the company management, the competition, and the industry well enough to assess whether or not an offer is adequate. The trustee must know that the employer corporation by-laws and board of director minutes are current and present no conflicts with the terms of the offer. The ESOP trustee must be knowledgeable of any environmental issues with respect to any properties owned by the company. Finally, the ESOP trustee must be aware of any outstanding or threatened litigation or other contingent liabilities.

In general, the ESOP trustee can only be an effective negotiator if he or she is fully knowledgeable about the sponsor company and its operations.

If the offer is for an exchange of stock or includes both cash and stock, then the ESOP trustee and its advisers must also perform due diligence on the acquiring company. The trustee must be comfortable with the adequacy of consideration received in whatever form.

Escrow

Often, the acquiring company will want some cash or other form of the proceeds held in escrow for a period of time. The ESOP trustee must be familiar enough with the acquiring company and its operations to negotiate the amount and terms of the escrow.

Usually, the ESOP trustee and its advisers will deduct the escrow amount from any proceeds when deciding the question of adequate consideration. In determining whether or not adequate consideration is being received, the ESOP trustee must assume nothing will be received from the escrow account.

Legal Advice

Legal counsel who is independent of the sponsor company and knowledgeable about ESOPs and financial transactions should represent the trustee. Legal counsel should become familiar with the employer corporation, the ESOP plan, and any existing loan agreements and notes. Counsel should assist in negotiations to assure (1) that adequate due diligence is performed and (2) that all legal requirements are met. The ESOP's legal counsel is also instrumental (1) in reviewing and interpreting the transaction documents and (2) negotiating the legal terms of the transaction based on the ESOP trustee's requests.

Dealing with Debt

Often the ESOP is still leveraged when a sale transaction takes place. Deciding who pays off any remaining ESOP debt can be a question of both adequate consideration and fairness in evaluating the terms of the offer. This issue is rarely clear-cut. It must be negotiated by the ESOP trustee, and it is an important reason to have an independent trustee.

The ESOP debt may be between the company and the ESOP trust, or the ESOP debt may be between outside lenders and the ESOP trust, or some combination of the two. If the ESOP debt is with the sponsor company, then the sponsor company may have the choice of forgiving the debt or demanding payment.

If the ESOP debt (or related company debt) is with outside lenders, then it must be paid off during the transaction. In one alternative, the sponsor company can pay the debt from the transaction proceeds, thereby spreading the cost among all stockholders. In another alternative, the ESOP can be required to pay the debt solely from its portion of the transaction proceeds, thereby placing the burden on the ESOP participants. In many cases, a solution that represents a compromise between the first two alternatives results from negotiations between the ESOP trustee and the non-ESOP stockholders.

If there are unallocated shares that are held in trust pledged against the ESOP debt, or if there is a due-on-sale provision or other contractual arrangement in the original ESOP documents, the ESOP trustee may have to accept the liability for the remaining ESOP debt in a sale transaction. If the plan is going to be terminated, the ESOP debt must be repaid.

If the sponsor company is obligated to make annual contributions adequate to service the ESOP debt, the trustee may effectively negotiate a sharing of the remaining ESOP debt obligation among all stockholders, in recognition of their obligation for these contributions. The independent financial adviser will assist the ESOP trustee in negotiating to receive its fair share of the proceeds plus the present value of the future company contribution requirement that will be foregone because of the plan termination.

These questions all play into the negotiations and the ESOP trustee may have to be in a position to demonstrate to the Department of Labor that it negotiated aggressively on the issue of paying off ESOP debt.

Equity Allocation

In a multiple-party transaction or when there are stockholders other than the ESOP involved in the sale, the allocation of equity proceeds among all stockholders is often a contentious issue. This issue can be compounded when there is ESOP debt remaining to be paid off.

The independent financial adviser working exclusively for the ESOP trustee can help to evaluate the economic returns to the various parties to the transaction. It is not mandatory that the economic returns be equal. It is mandatory, however, that the returns reflect relative risks so that the financial adviser can opine that the transaction is fair to the ESOP trust.

What Are Some Alternative Outcomes for the ESOP Plan and Its Participants?

Terminate the Plan

Terminating an ESOP first requires that the plan document be brought up to date with all Internal Revenue Code and ERISA requirements. It then requires that a Form 5310 be filed with the Service requesting a favorable determination on the termination.

Once the favorable determination has been received, the plan can be terminated and the plan assets can be distributed. When a plan is terminated, all participants become immediately vested. Plan participants then have the opportunity to take their distributions individually or roll them over to another qualified plan or to an IRA. If the participants elect to receive their distribution directly, the trust will withhold and remit to the Internal Revenue Service the 20 percent federal withholding. And, if they have not yet reached 59½ years old, the usual 10 percent early withdrawal penalty will apply.

The benefit for either the existing company or the acquiring company of terminating the plan is that any requirements for annual contributions cease along with the administration costs. The potential cost is that termination requires full vesting of all the ESOP participants, which potentially gives them access to all of their assets. For some employees, this may encourage them to terminate their employment prematurely, leaving the company shorthanded.

Convert the Plan to a 401(k) or Profit Sharing Plan

Another option is to amend the ESOP plan document and convert it into a 401(k) or profit sharing style savings plan. This option has the advantage of keeping the ESOP participants on the plan's vesting schedule and encouraging their continued employment. If the amended plan meets the conditions of Code Section 404(c), then it also reduces the fiduciary risk on the company and the ESOP trustee by shifting the investment decisions to the plan participant.

The amended plan must abide by Code Section 411(d)(6) which protects certain benefits within the plan. The amended plan must be submitted to the Service with a Form 5300 in order to receive a favorable determination.

Merge the Plan with Another ESOP

If another ESOP-owned company is acquiring the sponsor company, a merger of the two plans is often the best answer. This can be very helpful in merging two ESOP-owned company cultures. The shares held in the plan at the new company must be "qualified employer securities." Therefore, the design of the sale transaction must be such that the ESOP trust receives shares of the new company during the transaction.

When the two plans are merged, the surviving plan must protect the benefits of the most liberal plan. If amendments to the plan document are required, they must be submitted to the Service with a Form 5300 for a favorable determination letter.

Maintain the Plan as an ESOP at the Acquiring Company

The shares held in the plan at the new company must be "qualified employer securities." The design of the transaction must be such that the ESOP trust receives shares of the new company during the transaction. All vesting and other provisions of the plan remain in force.

SUMMARY AND CONCLUSION

The acquisition, sale, or other termination of an ESOP plan is usually a complex transaction involving many parties. The ESOP trustee has the same three basic fiduciary standards as when the ESOP was created: (1) the trust must receive adequate consideration, (2) the transaction must be fair to the ESOP from a financial point of view, and (3) the course of action must be prudent.

The acquisition, sale, or other termination of an ESOP plan is a time to bring the ESOP trustee's team together, including independent counsel and the independent financial adviser, to carefully analyze all aspects of the pending transaction.

This discussion is adapted from an article authored by E. Vaughn Gordy. Vaughn Gordy is a senior vice president and trust officer of LaSalle Bank N.A. He can be reached at (312) 904-2476 or at vaughn.gordy@abnamro.com.

This article from which this discussion was adapted was originally published in the Spring 2001 issue of Willamette Management Associates Insights.

This discussion was edited and updated by Charles Wilhoite. Charles is a principal of Willamette Management Associates, and he is resident in the firm's Portland, Oregon, office.

Chapter 25

Trustee Duty to Monitor Transactions

INTRODUCTION

A corporation that sponsors an ESOP will often enter into a transaction, or take a corporate action, that does not (1) directly involve the ESOP, (2) require the vote of the ESOP trustee, or (3) require a pass-through vote of the ESOP participants. These types of corporate transactions may include the following:

1. the acquisition by the sponsor company of the stock or assets of another company,
2. the issuance of options or other synthetic equity by the sponsor company, and
3. the redemption of large quantities of shares from non-ESOP stockholders.

An ESOP trustee's fiduciary obligations require that the trustee review and monitor these types of transactions, if they are material. This is true (1) even if the ESOP trustee is not a party to these transactions and (2) even though state corporate law does not require stockholder approval for these transactions to be valid.

Often, this duty can present a business relationship dilemma for the ESOP trustee. This is because the employer corporation management does not want the trustee to be involved in reviewing the transaction. Unfortunately, there is not much case law regarding the ESOP trustee's duty to monitor material transactions. Consequently, there is little judicial precedent that a trustee can stand behind when attempting to convince employer corporation management that it is the duty of the ESOP trustee to monitor a material transaction.

THE TRUSTEE'S DUTY—U.S. DEPARTMENT OF LABOR GUIDANCE

One clear source of guidance for ESOP trustees is Department of Labor Bulletin 94-2.[1] This Bulletin states: ". . . an investment policy that contemplates activities intended to monitor or influence the management of corporations in which the plan owns stock is consistent with a fiduciary's obligations under ERISA where the reasonable fiduciary concludes that such monitoring or communication with management, by the plan alone or together with other shareholders, is likely to enhance the value of the plan's investment in the corporation, after taking into account the costs involved."

The Department of Labor Bulletin goes on to state that there is a reasonable expectation that monitoring or influencing corporate management will likely enhance the value of the ESOP-owned stock where the stock is privately held and not publicly traded.

The Department of Labor added that mergers and acquisitions, debt financing, capitalization, executive compensation, financial and nonfinancial measures of corporate performance, business plans, and other workforce practices are examples of matters where monitoring would be considered appropriate. The Department of Labor concluded that ESOP trustee oversight may be carried out by meetings with employer corporation management—as well as by exercising any other legal rights that a shareholder may have.

THE TRUSTEE'S DUTY—GUIDANCE FROM *ARMSTRONG V. AMSTED INDUSTRIES*

The recent case *Juan Armstrong, et al., v. Amsted Industries, Inc., et al.*[2] created confusion related to the ESOP trustee's obligations to monitor corporate transactions. Amsted Industries, a large manufacturer of industrial products, was wholly owned by its ESOP.

The plaintiff ESOP participants sued (1) both members of the Amsted Industries management and (2) the independent ESOP trustee, related to various ERISA violations. One of the plaintiffs' claims centered around the trustee's failure to sufficiently consider the Amsted Industries acquisition of Varlen Corporation for approximately $800 million.

In the Varlen acquisition transaction, the total purchase price was financed through debt issued by a third-party lender. Specifically, the plaintiffs argued that the ESOP trustee did not properly conduct an investigation into:

1. the proposed acquisition transaction or
2. the resulting risk that the sponsor company would not be able to meet its growing repurchase liability because of the debt incurred to finance the corporate acquisition.

The ESOP trustee defended its actions by claiming (1) that the Amsted Industries acquisition of Varlen was not a fiduciary act to which ERISA applies and (2) that, even if it were, the trustee did in fact take the appropriate steps to monitor the transaction. The court ultimately granted the ESOP trustee's motion for summary judgment.

In the *Armstrong v. Amsted Industries* decision, the court held that the Varlen acquisition was a business decision and not a fiduciary decision. The court reached this conclusion because the Varlen acquisition did not directly involve the ESOP plan assets. The court concluded that the ESOP trustee could not be held liable for failing to override an employer's business decision. The court also stated that the parties' factual disputes regarding the ESOP trustee's involvement in the Varlen transaction are "inconsequential." This conclusion was reached because the ESOP trustee had no fiduciary duty to independently review the acquisition transaction.

Notwithstanding the court's language, the attorneys that litigated this matter have stated (1) that the court's decision did not dispense with the ESOP trustee's duty to monitor and (2) that, in fact, the ESOP trustee's duty to monitor corporate transactions is as important as ever. These attorneys also said that the trustee's ability to present evidence that showed it did monitor the transaction was a material factor in the court's decision to grant summary judgment.

The *Armstrong v. Amsted Industries* record is replete with evidence of the steps the ESOP trustee took to monitor the Varlen acquisition. For example, the trustee consulted with its financial advisers and legal advisers on a regular basis. And, the ESOP trustee met with Amsted's general counsel to discuss the transaction. The trustee also attended employer corporation board meetings during which the transaction was discussed. Furthermore, the ESOP trustee made sure that it was provided with regular updates on the transaction throughout the process.

In *Armstrong v. Amsted Industries,* the court also considered it important that the ESOP trustee was independent. The court held that decisions of independent and experienced fiduciaries are entitled to great deference. However, decisions of fiduciaries with a conflict of interest (i.e., management trustees) do not receive nearly the same deference from the court.

Therefore, if the ESOP trustee is a member of company management and the sponsor company undertakes a material transaction that requires trustee review, then the trustee should consider hiring an independent trustee for purposes of monitoring that particular transaction.

THE TRUSTEE'S DUTY TO MONITOR CORPORATE TRANSACTIONS

In assessing its duty to monitor a corporate transaction, an ESOP trustee should ask itself the following simple question: If a bankruptcy or liquidation or other financial calamity befell the sponsor company following the transaction, would the trustee be comfortable on the witness stand under examination from a plaintiff's lawyer, knowing that it had not reviewed, analyzed, or monitored the transaction? If the answer to this question is "no," then the ESOP trustee should probably monitor the transaction.

Once the ESOP trustee has established that the action proposed by the sponsor company requires monitoring, the trustee must answer the corollary question of whether or not the transaction is material. If the transaction is not material, it may not warrant monitoring. Unfortunately, again there is no rule of thumb or longstanding precedent as to what constitutes a "material" transaction.

One test for materiality is to consider the amount of consideration being paid in the transaction. An ESOP trustee may consider a transaction material where the consideration being paid by the sponsor company is equal to or greater than 10 percent of the current fair market value of the sponsor company's stock. However, facts and circumstances surrounding the proposed transaction, and not only the amount of consideration being paid, need to be considered.

For example, suppose that ABC Corp., with an equity value of $50 million, purchased XYZ Inc. for only $500,000. Suppose further that XYZ Inc. was located on the site of a former landfill. In this case, the transaction certainly could be considered material because of the potential environmental exposure. This conclusion is true even though the transaction consideration is less than 10 percent of the ABC Corp. equity value. The ESOP trustee should interview management of the sponsor company in order to learn additional facts and circumstances that could have a financial impact on the sponsor company and, consequently, negatively affect the employer corporation stock value.

THE PROCESS OF MONITORING CORPORATE TRANSACTIONS

In carrying out its monitoring duties, the ESOP trustee needs to ensure that its process is sound and well documented. The trustee should be kept informed of:

1. the progression of the transaction and
2. the material deal points.

The ESOP trustee can do this by communicating regularly with sponsor company attorneys and the financial adviser.

Prior to the closing of the transaction, the ESOP trustee should require its financial adviser and attorneys to make a presentation to the trustee, or the governing committee of an institutional trustee. The presentation made by the trustee's advisers should summarize the transaction and the material deal points. The ESOP trustee should also consider whether it should require the financial adviser to render an adequate consideration opinion or a fairness opinion to the trustee.

The ESOP trustee can insert itself further into the process if it is informed that certain material deal points—for example, price, indemnities, liabilities being assumed—create too much risk for the ESOP participants or are otherwise egregious.

In the unlikely event that this occurs, the ESOP trustee could then request a meeting with employer corporation management to further discuss the issues. If the meeting is denied, the ESOP trustee could consider writing a letter to employer corporation management and the board of directors that addresses its concerns. This helps to prove the soundness of the ESOP trustee's process.

DOCUMENTATION LESSONS FROM *CHAMPLAIN ENTERPRISES*

The recent case of *Joseph Henry and Michael Malinky v. Champlain Enterprises, et al.*,[3] highlights the importance of maintaining thorough records of the ESOP trustee's process of monitoring the transaction. The issue in this case was whether the purchase by the ESOP of convertible preferred stock from members of management was a prohibited transaction. The prohibited transaction issue was raised because the stock purchase price exceeded "adequate consideration."

Although this case does not involve the ESOP trustee's duty to monitor, it provides useful insight related to a trustee's responsibility to document the performance of its duties. The ESOP trustee in this case lost and was held liable for $7.75 million in damages. This was because the court did not believe the ESOP trustee had produced sufficient records at trial showing that it had questioned, tested, or analyzed its financial adviser's conclusions. The court reached its decision even though the ESOP trustee probably had performed each of these duties.

FINAL CONSIDERATIONS

It is clear that the ESOP trustee should not consider its duty to monitor as an opportunity:

1. to second guess employer corporation management or
2. to replace employer corporation management decisions with its own.

The ESOP trustee's duty is to stay informed and to understand the transaction's impact on the employer corporation stock value owned by the ESOP.

As discussed above, the ESOP trustee's duty is to take further action only when warranted. The trustee should also make sure that its lawyers and financial advisers do not unduly interfere with the sponsor company's lawyers and financial advisers.

Finally, an ESOP trustee can avoid frustrating clients by explaining to company management at the time the trustee is engaged that it is required to monitor certain transactions. The ESOP trustee should also provide evidence as to the execution of this monitoring duty. The trustee will find sponsor company management more comfortable with the idea of the trustee's involvement by explaining that:

1. it does not intend to prevent employer corporation management's objective to consummate transactions and
2. it does not intend to replace employer corporation management's qualified business judgments with its own.

SUMMARY AND CONCLUSION

The ESOP trustee's fiduciary duties require that it take an active role in monitoring the sponsor company's material transactions. This monitoring procedure not only complies with the trustee's fiduciary duties, but it also protects the corporate transaction against future legal challenges (as illustrated in the *Armstrong v. Amsted Industries* case).

Notes:

1. 29 CFR 2509.94-2.
2. No. 01 C 2963, 2004 U.S. Dist. LEXIS 14776 (N.D. Ill. July 29, 2004).
3. No. 01-CV-1681, 2004 U.S. Dist. LEXIS 21734 (N.D.N.Y. Oct. 29, 2004).

This discussion is adapted from an article authored by Marilyn Marchetti and James E. Staruck. Marilyn Marchetti is a senior vice president at GreatBanc Trust Company in Oak Brook, Illinois. Marilyn can be reached at (630) 572-5131 or mmarchetti@greatbanctrust.com. James Staruck is a vice president at GreatBanc Trust Company in Oak Brook, Illinois. Jim can be reached at (630) 572-5137 or jstaruck@greatbanctrust.com.

The article from which this discussion was adapted originally appeared in the Winter 2005 issue of Willamette Management Associates Insights.

This discussion was edited and updated by Timothy Meinhart. Tim is a senior manager of the firm, and is resident in our Chicago office.

Chapter 26

Corporate Governance Procedures in ESOP-Owned Companies

INTRODUCTION

Corporate governance, with an emphasis on developing a financial plan to address a sponsor company's repurchase obligation, is not a new concept to ESOP employer corporations. However, the attendant implications of corporate governance have recently taken on greater importance than ever before. In the last five years, prominent corporate failures (including companies sponsoring qualified retirement plans holding company stock such as United Airlines) have made front-page news.

In general, there are two types of corporate failures:

1. failures due to general economic, competitive, and operational problems, and
2. failures due to deliberate wrongdoing, such as corporate fraud, that result in a substantial loss of stockholder value.

Recent examples of corporate fraud and the large-scale collapses of certain public companies have resulted in increased emphasis on corporate governance. These events have also prompted some of the most sweeping corporate governance reforms since the 1930s. In addition to executives from Enron and WorldCom, some well-respected corporate ESOP trustees have also been subject to litigation. These ESOP trustees have been held liable for failing to:

1. properly perform due diligence,
2. properly monitor the activities of sponsor company management (i.e., in conflict of interest situations where a sponsor company director is also the trustee),

3. properly assess the value of the employer corporation stock purchased by the ESOP, or
4. properly assess the impact of the sponsor company's repurchase liability of the ESOP.

As a result, ESOP trustees, boards of directors, auditors, valuation firms, lenders, and sponsor company advisers are focusing attention on the increased responsibilities of the board of directors, management, and the ESOP trustee. In addition, employer corporation management—as well as ESOP trustees and ESOP lenders—are focused on the task of transforming these evolving philosophies and principles into best practice for sponsor companies.

POTENTIAL DIVIDE BETWEEN EMPLOYER CORPORATION MANAGEMENT AND THE ESOP TRUSTEE

The potential divide between employer corporation management (and the employer corporation board of directors) and the ESOP trustee has been subject to debate for several years. And, this debate has yet to be definitively resolved. The primary issue in this debate is the necessary separation between stock ownership and operational control.

An ESOP trustee, the buyer of the sponsor company equity, is a shareholder that owns all or part of the sponsor company. And, by law, the ESOP trustee cannot pay more than fair market value for the purchase of the employer corporation stock. Employer corporation management is primarily responsible for:

1. managing the sponsor company's operations and
2. preparing financial projections (projections that become an integral part of most employer corporation stock valuations).

In an ESOP ownership situation (as well as in a public corporation situation), operational control should be ceded to a centralized management team in order to create stockholder wealth. As a result, sponsor company management typically has expectations to share in (1) any profits the company generates and (2) any assets the company accumulates. The ESOP trustee will typically encourage such management prerequisites as an incentive for management to grow the employer corporation for the benefit of all stockholders—including the ESOP.

Accordingly, the interests of employer corporation management should be consistent with the interests of the ESOP trustee. This is because both parties want (1) the business to succeed and (2) the value of the employer corporation stock to increase. However, in the ownership/control dynamic, the interests of the ESOP trustee and the interests of employer corporation management sometimes differ.

From a management team perspective, sponsor company management has a desire to:

1. receive more equity and compensation than may be permitted under the terms of the ESOP,
2. own property, such as real estate and equipment, that is leased to the sponsor company (in order to increase management's personal income), and
3. operate the sponsor company so as to increase the amount of cash to be available for distribution in salaries and bonuses.

In fact, employer corporation management may be more interested in increasing cash flow available for compensation/bonuses (i.e., the cash model) than in increasing the equity value of the sponsor company stock (i.e., the equity model). As a result, company management is often averse to having a corporate institutional trustee serve as the ESOP fiduciary.

However, many boards of directors, as well as many ESOP advisers, believe that it is good corporate governance to have an independent, qualified corporate ESOP trustee serve the interests of the ESOP. The practical benefits of good governance and transparency, emanating from a concern for corporate integrity and image, have registered with many management teams, boards of directors, lenders, and corporate ESOP trustees.

EMPLOYER CORPORATION AND FIDUCIARY OBLIGATIONS IN AN INITIAL ESOP STOCK PURCHASE TRANSACTION

As part of establishing an ESOP, lenders, companies, and ESOP trustees typically focus on the following obligations, among other things:

1. the importance of the employer corporation establishing and maintaining proper corporate governance, including (a) consideration of the proper size and makeup of the board of directors, (b) the establishment

of a compensation committee, (c) the establishment of a corporate governance committee, (d) the establishment of an audit committee, and (e) the establishment of an ESOP committee;

2. the importance of the employer corporation board of directors (or of a committee of the board of directors) establishing and maintaining a financial policy that (a) forecasts the ESOP repurchase liability and (b) establishes a financial plan to address the funding of other sponsor company financial obligations; and
3. the importance of properly structuring the ESOP legal documentation from the following perspectives: (a) corporate governance, (b) repurchase liability, (c) corporate growth, and (d) employee benefits.

The employer corporation board of directors and the ESOP trustee should be involved in ensuring (1) that proper due diligence is completed on the sponsor company and (2) that the ESOP plan documents (as well as other corporate governance documents) are drafted with consideration for the objectives of (a) the employer corporation and (b) its management.

All ESOP plan documents contain diversification and distribution provisions which satisfy the minimum ESOP qualification requirements of the Internal Revenue Code. Compared to other qualified plans, an ESOP plan document contains special distribution provisions unique to ESOPs. These provisions include:

1. the right to demand that the distributions be paid in the form of company stock if the sponsor company is a C corporation or
2. a payment in cash if the sponsor company is an S corporation.

There are also ESOP distribution timing requirements (i.e., one (1) year following separation for death, retirement, and disability and by the end of the fifth (5th) year following a normal separation). Since distribution provisions impact the decisions of the employer corporation board of directors and since the board of directors is responsible for addressing the sponsor company's repurchase liability, sponsor companies focus on the economic impact created by the ESOP document.

Many boards of directors, as well as ESOP lenders and ESOP trustees, have a repurchase liability forecast performed as part of structuring an ESOP stock purchase transaction. This repurchase liability study is performed in order to determine the size and timing of the future financial obligation.

In addition, many employer corporation boards of directors work with company management to use such information in developing a financial plan. This financial plan incorporates various funding vehicles available to the employer corporation. Such a financial plan allows the employer corporation to address the future financial obligation of the repurchase liability. The financial plan provides the board of directors, and the ESOP trustee, with meaningful repurchase information to both forecast and fund the repurchase obligation on an annual basis.

EMPLOYER CORPORATION AND FIDUCIARY OBLIGATIONS FOR A MATURE ESOP-OWNED COMPANY

As ESOP-owned companies mature, boards of directors are confronted with new issues related to the ongoing operations of the sponsor company. These issues include:

1. retaining and motivating management to increase stockholder value and
2. continuing to plan for the ESOP repurchase liability obligation.

As the financial plan is updated, the board of directors should consider the importance of maintaining the integrity and trust (1) of the management team and (2) of the ESOP trustee. This is accomplished by following corporate governance best practices—by ensuring (1) that the board of directors addresses issues confronted by the employer corporation and (2) that the appropriate committees satisfy their responsibilities to the board of directors).

In addition, the employer corporation board of directors should consider evaluating the following factors on an annual basis:

1. corporate objectives relating to ESOP ownership (i.e. retaining a high quality management team, and implementation of a management succession plan);
2. corporate financial objectives and business plan (including a close examination of the current year audit report and management letters);
3. management expectations and ESOP expectations (i.e., compensation of management);
4. ownership interests of non-ESOP stockholders (i.e., the management team);

5. current repurchase liability forecast;
6. corporate objectives and approach to funding its ESOP repurchase liability obligations;
7. prior distributions from the ESOP;
8. ESOP restrictions created by the ESOP loan and contribution deduction limitations;
9. long-term objectives of management and the employer corporation (i.e., electing or maintaining S corporation status for federal income tax purposes);
10. actual and projected cash flow of the sponsor company; and
11. structure of the ESOP distribution provision and distribution policy.

By establishing and updating the sponsor company financial plan, the board of directors satisfies its fiduciary responsibility to the stockholders. And, the board of directors is better prepared to address a variety of issues confronted by the ESOP-owned company. With regard to the sponsor company's repurchase obligation, the board of directors will be in a better position to use a combination of the following funding vehicles:

1. existing cash in the ESOP,
2. cash flow of the employer corporation by either making new company contributions or paying dividends for the purpose of purchasing the company stock from the participants,
3. borrowing money from the employer corporation senior lender or from life insurance policies purchased by the sponsor company,
4. using money from a sinking fund established by the board of directors for such purposes, or
5. offering management or private equity the opportunity to purchase capital stock from the employer corporation (i.e., with proceeds used to fund the sponsor company's repurchase liability obligation).

In a recent court case, the ESOP trustee successfully argued that the board of directors is ultimately responsible for monitoring and addressing the ESOP-owned company's repurchase liability. However, ESOP trustees still need to be diligent in their efforts. At a minimum, the ESOP trustee should meet with the board of directors at least annually (and be in contact with the management team and the ESOP committee on a more frequent basis). The ESOP trustee should also encourage the board of directors:

1. to follow and implement corporate governance best practices and
2. to have some dialogue with respect to the repurchase liability of the sponsor company.

In addition to meeting with employer corporation management during the annual valuation process, the ESOP trustee should monitor its investment in sponsor company stock by having frequent contact with the (1) employer corporation management team and (2) the board of directors.

SUMMARY AND CONCLUSION

Financial scandals around the world and recent court cases against some highly regarded ESOP trustees have emphasized the importance of certain basic functions. In particular, these recent events emphasize the importance of: (1) strong corporate governance, (2) independence both from an ESOP trustee and board of directors perspective, and (3) the board of directors focusing on the current and future financial plan of the employer corporation.

The standards and guidelines implemented by public companies as a result of recent legislation are familiar to many experienced ESOP professionals. The counsel provided by a team of experienced ESOP advisers leads to the implementation of best practices for ESOP-owned companies.

For those ESOP-owned companies that have not yet implemented best practices, the financial scandals and the resulting changes in the law should be a wake-up call (1) to implement best practices and (2) to make a positive impact on the employer corporation.

This discussion is adapted from an article authored by John A. Kober, Esq. John Kober is a partner at the law firm of Morgan, Lewis & Bockius LLP in Dallas, Texas. John can be reached at (214) 438-1550 or jkober@morganlewis.com.

The article on which this discussion is based originally appeared in the Winter 2005 issue of Willamette Management Associates Insights.

This discussion was edited and updated by Gregg Gaffen. Gregg is a senior manager of Willamette Management Associates and is resident in the firm's Chicago office.

Chapter 27

Corporate Governance Issues in ESOP-Owned Companies

INTRODUCTION

One of the essential components of an effective capital market is trust. Investors will avoid markets, corporations, and managements that they don't trust. This observation applies equally to publicly traded, privately held, and employee-owned companies. Stockholders place their trust in the corporation's board of directors to protect their financial interests. And, the corporation board of directors places its trust in company management to effectively manage the assets of the company.

Stockholders benefit from the trust engendered by effective regulations that are both (1) widely recognized and (2) strictly enforced. For public traded companies, there are numerous regulatory agencies (1) that establish rules and (2) that oversee the adherence to those rules. These regulatory agencies have enforcement authority if the rules are broken. Stockholders of publicly traded corporations, including public corporations with ESOPs, enjoy an increased level of trust in the capital market as a result of this regulation.

Both stockholders and employees should have confidence in the effectiveness of corporate governance for the companies in which they place their trust. The recent experience of Enron, WorldCom, Adelphia and other corporations indicate that no investor, including an ESOP trustee, can rely solely on the regulatory agencies for adequate disclosure of all corporate activities. Effective corporate governance is also important for engendering investor and employee trust.

Privately held corporations have significantly less oversight from regulatory agencies. In fact, some business owners prefer to keep their companies private for that very reason. Often, a single (or a small number of stockholders) owns all of the shares of a closely held company. Often, all the shares of the private company are held by family members. If there is more than one stockholder, the rights of the stockholders are often defined by a stockholder agreement.

An ESOP investment in a privately held employer corporation (often in the form of a noncontrolling ownership position) is a challenging situation from a corporate governance perspective. The principal business owner may be willing to share stock ownership with the employees. However, the principal business owners may not be willing to (1) share ownership or operational control, (2) share detailed financial information, or (3) retain independent directors.

An ESOP formation provides one of the few opportunities for a private company owner to sell a portion, rather than the whole, of an ownership interest in a corporation. Once the ESOP purchases the closely held corporation stock, however, the ESOP becomes a nonfamily stockholder. And, the corporation has fiduciary duties to the plan participants. This situation often brings about changes in corporate governance for the closely held employer corporation. Dealing with the ownership control and corporate governance issues of an employer corporation is one of the responsibilities of the ESOP trustee.

HISTORY OF BREACHES OF TRUST

When a stockholder is not also a manager of the closely held company, an implicit bargain between the owners and managers becomes the heart of the corporate model. The management promises to operate the company in the owners' best interest. And, the stockholders promise to allow the management to make the operating decisions necessary to run the company.

In *The Wealth of Nations*, Adam Smith stated: "The directors of such companies . . . being the managers rather of other peoples' money than their own, it cannot be well expected that they should watch over it with the same anxious vigilance with which the partners in a private company frequently watch over their own. . . . Negligence and profusion, therefore, must always prevail more or less, in the management of the affairs of such a company." In other words, the very existence of nonmanagement stockholders contributes to an environment of corporate neglect.

After the stock market crash of 1929, congressional investigators uncovered widespread insider trading, stock price manipulation, and the diversion of corporate funds to management's personal use. The Securities Act of 1933 was enacted to require disclosure of corporate information. And, the Securities and Exchange Commission ("the SEC") was established in 1934 to enforce the provisions of the '33 Act. These changes were implemented to protect the interests of nonmanagement stockholders.

There is no getting around the "principal-agent problem." If you own a house and hire a contractor, you are the principal and he/she is the agent. How can you ensure that the contractor will do his work as if he owned the house? These are "agency costs."

An evolving understanding of agency costs gave rise to the concept of "shareholder value." The principal premise of this concept is that managers as agents should be rewarded for increasing stock value, an accomplishment that benefits the owners. In the 1980s, investors such as T. Boone Pickens and Carl Icahn created shareholder value by using the leveraged buy-out (LBO). In an LBO transaction, private investors and company management would take a company private, minimize operating costs, and then re-IPO it at a much higher value. Senior executives who got on the shareholder value bandwagon prospered. And, senior executives who continued to work for employees, community, and customers often lost their jobs.

When the junk-debt market crashed in the late 1980s (as evidenced by the demise of such companies as Macy's and Revco), the LBO structure fell out of favor as a means to align the interests of managers and owners. In its place, executive stock options became popular as a tool to increase shareholder value. However, the use of this tool to align shareholders and management has been fraught with inconsistencies.

As an example, the Accounting Principles Board decided that the cost of stock options was not to be expensed on a company's income statement. In 1994, the Financial Accounting Standards Board tried to change this accounting principle and require that executive stock options be expensed. Several congressman including Joe Lieberman (D-CT) and Diane Feinstein (D-CA) threatened to dismantle the FASB if it changed the rule regarding the accounting for stock options. This Congressional position allowed the use of executive stock option programs to continue.

The fact that the expense of executive stock options was not recognized when the option was granted, resulted in higher earnings per share (EPS). And, the popularity of executive stock option grants caused widespread short term thinking on the part of corporate managers. Executive stock options were often granted just before positive earnings announcements. Companies engaged in share buy-back programs. These share buy-back programs were financed through considerable leverage (1) to buy back shares and (2) to increase the per share value. However, these actions did little to preserve or increase long-term shareholder value.

GOOD GOVERNANCE MATTERS

In 2002, *Business Week* reported, "For three years after the list ["Ranking of Best and Worst Boards," 1996] appeared, the stocks of companies with the Best Boards outperformed those with the worst by 2 to 1. But as the economy slowed starting in 2000, the Best Boards companies retained much more of their value, returning 51.7 percent versus –12.9 percent for the Worst Boards companies ... Ralph V. Whitworth, the director who nurtured Waste Management Inc. through its accounting crisis and engineered governance turnarounds there and at Apria Healthcare, says investors in well-governed companies are buying a form of insurance."[1] The cost of this insurance is far outweighed by the enhanced returns to shareholders evidenced by good corporate governance.

The pundits can draw many conclusions from a review of the corporate scandals that came to light in recent years:

1. The scandals appear to have resulted from systematic problems in management compensation, regulation, reporting and governance, that failed to keep in check executives who lacked integrity.
2. Regulations failed to keep pace with market economics and market trends.
3. The old view of corporate governance—which allowed companies and individuals to wink at conflicts of interest—is not acceptable or in the shareholders' best interests.
4. Effective boards of directors matter. Stockholders have the right to expect corporate boards of directors to hold company CEOs accountable.

CORPORATE GOVERNANCE STANDARDS

In corporate law, board of directors members are generally charged with a few very broad standards of performance. Corporate directors have broad latitude and freedom to conduct business within those standards.

In legal terms, board members are primarily charged with (1) a duty of care and (2) a duty of loyalty. Generally, corporate director decisions are guided by the " business judgment rule."

Duty of Care

Boards of directors have a fiduciary responsibility (1) to the company and (2) to the company shareholders. The shareholders entrust the directors with their capital to invest in the assets of the company. It is the board of directors' fiduciary duty to see that those assets are managed for the benefit of the corporate stockholders.

The general standard is that a director must discharge his or her duties: (1) in good faith, (2) with the care an ordinarily prudent person in a like position would exercise under similar circumstances, and (3) in a manner that he or she reasonably believes to be in the best interest of the corporation. A director can demonstrate fulfillment of the duty of care by:

1. regularly attending corporate meetings,
2. carefully reviewing company information,
3. relying on the reports of others,
4. establishing and adhering to agendas, and
5. making regular inquiries of management and other board members.

The responsibility of the board of directors changes if the company becomes insolvent and approaches bankruptcy. In this case, the lenders and debtholders begin to assume the role of debtors-in-possession, and the debtholders become the owners. The job of the board of directors becomes one of preserving the company and its assets—in order to maximize value to the debtholders.

If the board of directors becomes aware of an offer to purchase the company, the duty of care gives it the responsibility to assure that the offer is in the interest of shareholders. The board must take steps to see that the offer price is the highest price it can reasonably obtain.

The board must investigate to see that the acquirer is financially able to complete the transaction. The board must determine (1) that the transaction is in the long-term best interest of the shareholders and (2) that the plans and goals currently in place for the company would not exceed the value of the offer.

Duty of Loyalty

The general standard for the duty of loyalty relates to conflicts of interest, opportunity, and confidentiality. In its *Corporate Directors Handbook,* the American Bar Association indicated the following: "The duty of loyalty requires directors to exercise their powers in the interests of the corporation and not in the directors' own interest or in the interest of another person (including a family member) or organization.... It is the manner in which an interested director and the board deal with a conflict that determines the propriety of the transaction and of the director's conduct. The duty of loyalty has a number of specific applications:

1. Conflicts of Interest. An interested director should seek approval by disinterested directors of interested transactions or conduct and should disclose that interest and describe to the board members all material facts concerning the matter know to the director. The board members should then act on the matter with complete candor, accuracy, and inclusiveness before the action is taken. An interested director should abstain from voting on the matter and, in most situations leave the meeting while the disinterested directors discuss and vote."[2]
2. Corporate Opportunity. In some circumstances the duty of loyalty requires that a director make a business opportunity available to the corporation before the director may pursue the opportunity (1) for the director's own or (2) for another's account. "If a director believes that a contemplated transaction might be found to be a corporate opportunity, the director should make full disclosure to the board and seek its authorization to pursue the opportunity."[3]
3. Loyalty also means keeping confidential the information the director receives through the activities of the board. Not only can the director not use the information for personal gain, he or she may not disclose the information in any manner that could cause harm to the corporation.

Business Judgment Rule

"The duty of care is qualified by the business judgment rule. This business judgment rule is well established in case law. This rule protects a disinterested director from personal liability to the corporation and its shareholders. This is true even though a corporate decision the director has approved turns out to be unwise or unsuccessful.

In reviewing a disinterested director's conduct, a court will not substitute its judgment (particularly in hindsight) for that of the director, provided that the director:

- acted in good faith,
- was reasonably informed, and
- rationally believed the action taken was in the best interests of the corporation."[4]

The business judgment rule exists to protect and promote full and free exercise of managerial power granted to directors of corporations. The meaning of the business judgment rule has been clarified through many court decisions.

The determination of whether a business judgment is an informed one turns on whether the directors have informed themselves "prior to making a business decision, of all material information reasonably available to them" (*Aronson v. Lewis*, 473 A.2d 805 (Del. 1984)).

Other courts have held that there can be no protection for directors who have made unintelligent or unadvised decisions (*Mitchell v. Highland-Western Glass*, 167 A. 831 (Del.Ch. 1933)). However, there is a presumption that a board's business judgment was an informed one, a presumption which must be rebutted by the attacking party (*Aronson*, supra at 812).

Each director has a fiduciary duty to become informed in preparation for the decisions to be made. Fulfillment of the fiduciary function requires more than the mere absence of bad faith or fraud. Courts have held that, in representing the financial interests of others, the director must satisfy an affirmative duty to protect those interests. The director must proceed with a critical eye in assessing all relevant information.

Smith v. Van Gorkom (488 A.2d 858 (Del. 1985)) is a class action suit brought by shareholders against the defendants, Trans Union Corporation ("Trans Union" or the "Company") and its directors. In this case, the plaintiffs sought the rescission of a cash-out merger (and alternative relief in the form of damages) of the Company into defendant New T Company. After trial, the Court of Chancery granted judgment for the directors.

The stockholders appealed the *Smith v. Van Gorkom* trial court's decision. The Supreme Court of Delaware reversed the trial court's decision, holding that:

1. the board's decision to approve the proposed merger was not illustrative of informed business judgment;
2. the board was grossly negligent in approving amendments to the original merger proposal; and
3. the board failed to fully disclose all relevant and material facts to the shareholders prior to soliciting their approval of the merger.

As a result of this case, under Delaware law director liability under the business judgment rule is predicated on gross negligence concepts.

ESOP TRUSTEE FIDUCIARY STANDARDS

ESOP trustees have a fiduciary duty to the participants of the plan. The assets of an ESOP must be held and managed for the exclusive purpose of:

1. providing benefits to participants and their beneficiaries and
2. defraying reasonable expenses of administering the plan.

Individuals acting as trustee for an ESOP are considered to have unlimited personal liability for any breaches of fiduciary duty. For this reason, many companies elect to hire an outside trustee, typically a financial institution such as a bank.

The Department of Labor has taken the position that the exclusive purpose rule requires the ESOP trustee to consider the interests of plan participants solely in their capacities as participants in a plan providing for retirement benefits. Under this view, the ESOP trustee must not take into consideration whether a given decision will preserve employment for plan participants. Rather, the trustee is to consider exclusively the financial interest of the participants in their future retirement income.

However, one federal court has held that fiduciaries acted properly when using a discount for lack of control for the valuation of stock distributed to plan participants, despite the fact that the plan owned a controlling ownership interest in the sponsor company's stock. This conclusion was because the fiduciary's decision was in furtherance of the plan's goal of maintaining continued employee ownership (*Foltz v. U.S. News & World Report*, 865 F.2d 364 (D.C. Cir. 1989)).

In addition to the exclusive purpose principle, ERISA Section 404(a) states that a fiduciary must discharge its duties "solely in the interest of the participants and beneficiaries." This principle of "solely in the interest" is not dissimilar to the concept of duty of loyalty for corporate boards of directors regarding conflicts of interest, opportunity, and confidentiality.

For the ESOP trustee, some conflicts of interest are not prohibited (see ERISA Section 408(c)(3)). For this reason, officers and employees of an employer corporation may serve as trustees of an employee benefit plan sponsored by the employer corporation. However, ESOP trustees must subordinate their personal interests to the interests of the ESOP participants.

POTENTIAL FOR CONFLICT BETWEEN THE BOARD AND THE ESOP TRUSTEE

It has been the policy of LaSalle Bank NA to decline offers to take positions on the boards of directors of client companies. This is true even when the

ESOP trust owns 100 percent of the client company. It is the bank's view that there are potential conflicts of interest that could complicate a vote on some issues. The directors are chartered to act in the interest of the company and its stockholders.

While the ESOP trust is a stockholder (sometimes the only stockholder), the ESOP trustee's duty of loyalty is to the participants and beneficiaries. The board makes compensation, investment, and financial structure decisions—while the ESOP trustee's sole duty is to protect and enhance the benefits available to the ESOP plan participants.

In an ESOP-owned company, the percentage of the employer corporation that the ESOP owns can have a dramatic effect on how much influence the ESOP trustee has (1) over the board of directors and (2) over corporate governance in general. If the ESOP trustee (1) is in a majority control position and (2) can vote to replace one or more board members, then the ESOP trustee can be influential. If the trust owns a noncontrolling ownership position and can't control the membership of the board, then the ESOP trustee must seek other methods to be influential.

RESEARCH ON DIRECTORS

Recently, the National Association of Corporate Directors (NACD) surveyed directors of privately held companies.[5] The results are tabulated from 108 independent responses, although not every question was answered on every form returned. This survey included data from privately held companies. There was no indication of the percentage of employee ownership in the respondent companies. The data, however, are informative about the governance of privately held companies.

The results of this NACD survey are presented in Figure 1 on the following page. In the survey, half of the respondents indicated that they only served on the board of their own company. And another 27 percent of respondents indicated that they only served on one other board. This may be a positive fact—in that directors appear to be solely or primarily focused on the company for which they serve.

Figure 1

National Association of Corporate Directors Survey
Outside Board Service by Survey Respondents

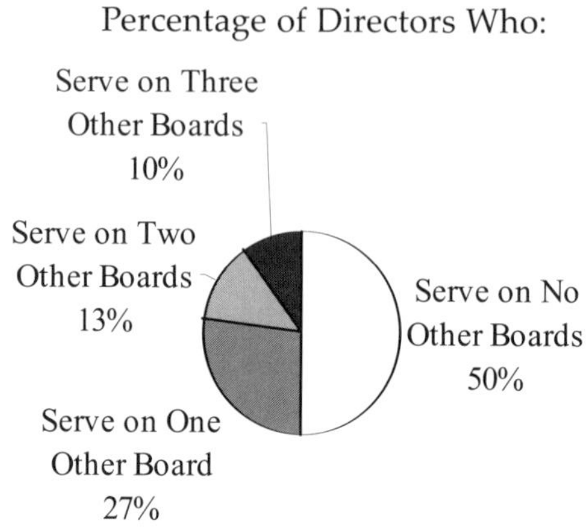

"Half of the respondents (50%) surveyed serve on boards ranging in size from seven to nine members."[6] The distributions of board of director size is presented in Figure 2:

Figure 2

National Association of Corporate Directors Survey
Board Size

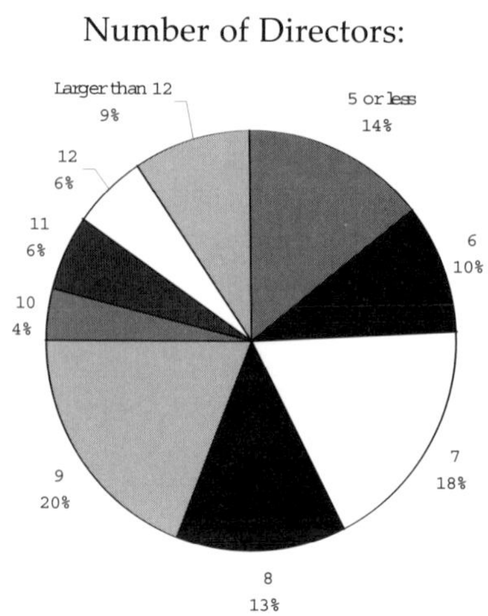

In the NACD survey, most respondents said "they believe the optimal size for a private company board is also from seven to nine members."[7] In addition, most survey respondents (82 percent) also believe that a majority of directors should be independent: "49% believe that more than half the directors on a board should be independent and 33 percent take independence a step further and say that all directors except the CEO should be independent."[8]

As shown in Table 1 below, "many boards (78%) have a standing audit committee and most (84%) have a standing compensation committee. Over half (58%) of the respondent companies have a nominating committee, and more than six in 10 (64%) have an executive committee."[9]

Table 1

National Association of Corporate Directors Survey
Composition of Board Committees

Standing Committee	% of Respondent Companies	Average Number of Meetings Per Year
Audit	78%	3+
Compensation	84%	2 - 3
Nominating	58%	1 - 2
Executive	64%	3
Finance	34%	—

Overall, the NACD survey provides guidance as to corporate governance common practices among privately held companies.

REGULATION

Regulations can provide a means for ESOP trustees to influence directors even in private companies where the regulations don't directly apply. Directors know that they can be held legally accountable. And, directors get some degree of protection if they adhere to regulations in effect for public companies. The Securities and Exchange Commission (SEC), the New York Stock Exchange (NYSE), Nasdaq, and Congress have all been moved to impose new corporate governance regulations.

The SEC has actively reviewed changes to its policies. For example, "on January 22, 2003, the SEC voted to charge board audit committees with screening tax-shelter schemes, rather than laying down an absolute ban on accountants selling such shelters to audit clients."[10] The SEC has the final authority over publicly traded companies.

However, each individual stock exchange may also impose corporate governance standards. For public companies, the standards have been raised as a result of the 2002-era corporate scandals. For example, "the NYSE and NASDAQ proposed new listing standards that will require stricter definitions of independence for outside directors, more muscular nominating and compensation committees, and adoptions of governance codes."[11] Public companies must adhere to the standards of these exchanges or risk de-listing.

In July of 2002, Congress passed the Sarbanes-Oxley Act. The Sarbanes-Oxley Act places considerable attention on the audit function, both on the external auditors and on the audit committee of the board. The Sarbanes-Oxley Act included the following specifications for public companies:

1. A ban on company loans to executives.
2. A requirement that the audit committee be comprised of independent directors.
3. Limits on auditors providing nonaudit services.
4. A requirement that CEOs and CFOs sign off on company financial statements.

The Conference Board Commission also developed recommendations to improve corporate governance and to protect stockholders' interests. The Commission's recommendations include the following:

1. Compensation committee members should have no relationship to the company.
2. Substantial majority of directors should be independent.
3. Boards should seriously consider shareholder proposals.
4. Compensation shouldn't be benchmarked to industry medians.

Clearly, the corporate scandals of the past few years have resulted in increased concern over the security of shareholders' investments. As a result, many of the governing bodies have sought to modify and to improve the standards by which they hold public companies accountable. These actions are an effort to restore investors' faith and trust in the public capital markets.

STRUCTURAL CHANGES ARE NOT THE ONLY SOLUTION

Too often regulations fall short of being completely effective. The regulations place a heavy administrative burden on all companies. And, sometimes, regulations fail to detect the few companies that seek to intentionally deceive the system. This is where trust comes into play. Once this trust is violated, it is difficult, if not impossible, to re-establish.

It is important that boards of directors get good, reliable, informed advice on which to base their decisions. In addition, the composition of the board is an important element in successful decision-making.

In selecting members of a corporate board of directors, having a group of individuals with diverse backgrounds is important. First, it is important that some of the directors be intimate with the industry. This often comes from insiders to the company. While an independent director could have industry knowledge gleaned from his work with a competitor, it would be difficult to manage confidentiality and potential conflicts with that director.

However, CEOs need more than industry knowledge from the board. They also need strategic advice, human resource advice, legal advice, technology advice, and tactical negotiating advice. They need financial and accounting advice, financial engineering advice, legislative advice, and real estate advice.

It is important that all of this advice be trustworthy. This advice must come from individuals who the CEO knows are intelligent, informed, and respectful.

As an example, let's look at the governance at CSX Corporation. Without a doubt, CSX Corporation is proud of its board of directors. And, without a doubt, the CSX board of directors acts solely in the interest of its shareholders. CSX spokesman Adam Hollinsworth says, "CSX has long sought the best governance practices."[12]

However, a closer scrutiny of CSX is informative:

1. The company lent money to its executives for purchases of CSX stock. When the shares' value fell below what the executives owed, the shares were returned and millions in executive loans forgiven.
2. Two former compensation committee chairmen bought luxury vacation properties from CSX, one of which was not publicly offered for sale.

3. The company regularly rejects shareholder proposals.
4. The company aims to put its executives among the 35 percent best-paid executives at similar-sized companies.
5. The compensation of CSX Chairman John Snow doubled between 1995 and 2001, while CSX profit decreased and the CSX share price severely under performed the overall market.
6. Since 1993, CSX has experienced a decline in the quality of it's compensation practices "almost exactly coincident with the decline in the company's fortunes," according to a report to be issued soon by the Corporate Library, a non partisan research firm.

Yet, even with these practices in place, Institutional Shareholder Services ranked CSX's corporate governance in the top 27 percent of all blue-chip firms.

Recently, President George W. Bush appointed John Snow to the position of Secretary of the Treasury. While chairman of CSX, Mr. Snow was hailed for his leadership position in a Blue-Ribbon panel pushing for sweeping changes in corporate practices.[13]

All of this puts ESOP trustees of privately held companies in a more difficult position to impose these standards, which may or may not be effective, on private companies.

REMOVING A DIRECTOR

Removing a director who is not performing up to the required level can be challenging. This is true whether the director is an outsider, an insider, or even the chief executive.

To effect any governance changes at the employer corporation, the ESOP trustee must work within the role of a company stockholder. Often the rights and responsibilities of stockholders are described in a stockholder agreement. The strength of the ESOP trustee's position will be dictated (1) by the percentage ownership of the trust and (2) by the terms of any stockholder agreement to which the trustee is a party.

Sometimes, the ESOP trustee can use the annual stockholder vote to effect a change on the board. However, it is the board—not the ESOP trustee—that must make any decisions about employment changes for the management team. If the board member is also an employee of the company, then terminating the employee relationship is exclusively a board decision. The ESOP trustee must work closely with the board to effect any changes in employer corporation management.

In considering whether to remove a director, the ESOP trustee must work closely with the outside directors (assuming it is not the outsider to be removed). Usually, the outside board members will retain counsel to guide them through the process. A decision must be made whether the termination is for cause. Any employment contracts should be reviewed, and estimates should be made on the financial impact of the decision on the sponsor company.

It is the board of directors that terminates an individual's employment. However, it is the stockholder who terminates a board position. It is often preferable to attempt a negotiated settlement in such circumstances.

SUMMARY AND CONCLUSION

Corporate governance for ESOP-owned companies (and for all companies) has received substantially more visibility as a result of the recent "headline" corporate governance failures. It could be argued that directors and management of ESOP-owned companies have to meet even higher corporate governance standards than directors and management of other companies.

The employees are the beneficial owners of the employer corporation through the ESOP trust. The ESOP trust gives them a greater voice in the strategies and management of the employer corporation than they may otherwise have.

The ESOP trustee is required to listen to the voice of the employees. However, the ESOP trustee is not required to take every—or any—action requested by employees.

The ESOP trustee has a fiduciary duty to manage the investment in the employer corporation shares held in the ESOP trust for the retirement benefit (1) of the participants and (2) of their beneficiaries. This duty will be best accomplished by assuring that the board of directors is adhering to good, effective, ethical governance standards—standards that will foster trust among all constituencies of the employer corporation.

Notes:

1. Louis Lavelle, "The Best & Worst Boards," *Business Week*, Oct. 7, 2002, p. 108.
2. *Corporate Directors Handbook*, 2nd ed. (Chicago: American Bar Association, 1994), p. 12.
3. Ibid.
4. Ibid., p. 13.
5. "2001–2002 Private Company Governance Survey," The National Association of Corporate Directors, April 2002.

6. Ibid., p. 4.
7. Ibid.
8. Ibid.
9. Ibid.
10. "Reform: Business Gets Religion," *Business Week*, Feb. 3, 2003, p. 41.
11. Ibid.
12. Tom Hamburger and Greg Ip, "Snow Faces Text on DSC Director Deals," *The Wall Street Journal*, Jan. 20, 2003, p. A4.
13. Ibid.

This discussion is adapted from an article authored by E. Vaughn Gordy. Vaughn Gordy is a senior vice president and trust officer at LaSalle Bank, N.A., in Chicago, Illinois. Vaughn can be reached at (312) 904-2476 or at vaughn.gordy@abnamro.com.

The article from which this discussion was adapted was published in the Spring 2003 issue of Willamette Management Associates Insights.

This discussion was edited and updated by Curtis Kimball. Curt is a principal of Willamette Management Associates and the director of the firm's Atlanta, Georgia, office.

Chapter 28

Corporate Governance Issues and ESOP Transaction Financing

INTRODUCTION

This discussion presents the ESOP acquisition lender's perspective on the corporate governance issues related to ESOP-owned companies. Prior to the collapse of Enron Corporation, ESOP-owned companies, ESOP acquisition lenders, ESOP trustees, and most ESOP financial advisers did not pay particular attention to corporate governance issues. However, corporate governance has become one of the most important aspects (if not the most important aspect) of an ESOP stock acquisition transaction.

After an ESOP stock acquisition transaction has been completed, it is often very difficult to make changes to the instruments that affect employer company corporate governance. The post-Enron lending environment is affected by both the current economic conditions and corporate governance. Accordingly, at the time of the ESOP stock acquisition, it is important to establish a framework on how the ESOP lending group will affect corporate governance. It is reasonable to expect the ESOP lender to be concerned about sponsor company corporate governance from both an operational and a legal compliance standpoint.

THE ESOP LENDING ENVIRONMENT AFFECTS CORPORATE GOVERNANCE

The economic, accounting, and lending environments have all significantly changed over the last few years. Accordingly, ESOP acquisition lenders are much more active in all aspects of an ESOP stock purchase transaction. In today's environment, ESOP lenders require certain changes that affect the operations of the sponsor company from a corporate governance standpoint. And, such changes may involve the very corporate structure of the sponsor company.

ESOP lenders may require certain changes to the structure of the ESOP acquisition transaction. This is because various financing sources are typically used to fund an ESOP stock acquisition transaction.

In general, the economy has influenced ESOP financing sources from a lending perspective, as follows:

1. The senior lending markets have contracted and the lending standards have tightened, as indicated in Table 1.

Table 1

Typical Senior Debt Lending Standards Regarding ESOP Stock Acquisition Financing

Year	Senior Debt to EBITDA Ratio
1998	6.0 times EBITDA[1]
1999	4.0 times EBITDA
2000	3.5 times EBITDA
2001	2.5 times EBITDA
2002	2.5 times EBITDA
2003	2.0 times EBITDA
2004	2.0 times EBITDA

2. Senior lenders have generally shifted from offering cash-flow-based acquisition loans to asset-based acquisition loans.
3. Senior lenders have generally limited the type of mezzanine debt they find acceptable in ESOP stock acquisition transactions.

As a result of these lending trends, the typical senior loan amount in 2004 was a much lower percentage of the total ESOP acquisition financing than it was three or four years ago. If the ESOP acquisition transaction is structured as an S corporation ESOP, some lending groups will give the employer corporation credit for the ESOP-related income tax savings. This accommodation typically increases the senior debt to EBITDA ratio from 2.0 times to 3.0 times.

To complete an ESOP stock acquisition transaction in today's lending environment, a combination of financing sources is typically used by employer corporations. These financing sources include:

- senior debt financing,
- mezzanine debt financing,
- subordinated note financing from the selling stockholder,
- employees being permitted to use some of their profit sharing money to acquire employer corporation stock,
- private equity investment,
- employees being permitted to use some of their 401(k) employee deferrals to acquire employer corporation stock, and
- retained management direct equity investment.

In light of this current economic and lending environment, an employer corporation may structure the ESOP stock acquisition transaction in the following manner:

1. A C corporation Section 1042 transaction (in order for the selling stockholders to be eligible to postpone recognition of the capital gains tax on the sale of employer corporation stock to the ESOP).
2. A combination of senior debt, mezzanine debt, selling shareholder subordinated debt, and profit sharing/401(k) plan funds are used as the acquisition financing sources.
3. The employer corporation, as a condition of the ESOP lending group, must elect S corporation status for federal income tax purposes ("S corporation status") as soon as is legally possible to do so.[2]

One effect of using multiple financing sources in an ESOP stock acquisition is that the lenders view themselves as investors in the employer corporation. Accordingly, the lenders may have competing interests, and they may require:

1. the implication of certain sponsor company corporate governance and financial controls, such as: requiring the appointment of outside directors, placing limitations on the payment of executive compensation and expenses over a predetermined amount, and placing limitations on acquisitions and capital expenditures;
2. the full disclosure of information on all parties involved in the ESOP stock acquisition transaction, including the corporation's professional advisers and their respective experience levels; and
3. the full disclosure of pro forma financial information completed on a post-transaction basis (taking into account the future ESOP repurchase

liability of the employer corporation), with an explanation for any deviation from generally accepted accounting principles (GAAP).

ESOP LOAN STRUCTURE MAY AFFECT CORPORATE GOVERNANCE

The most common way to structure an ESOP acquisition loan is for the lender to make a loan directly to the employer corporation (the "outside loan"), to be followed by a second "inside" loan from the employer corporation to the ESOP (the "ESOP loan"). The outside loan is typically secured by the assets of the employer corporation (or the stock of its operating subsidiaries). The stock purchased by the ESOP is typically pledged back to the employer corporation to secure the ESOP loan.

The employer corporation's security interest in the shares purchased by the ESOP may be assigned to the lenders as additional security for the outside loan. However, any security in the shares of corporation stock held by the ESOP assigned to the lenders must be annually released by the lenders as the ESOP acquisition loan is paid off.

If a mezzanine lender and/or selling shareholder subordinated note holder (collectively, "junior lenders") are part of the ESOP acquisition financing, then the loan structure will typically include (1) warrants or (2) cash appreciation rights. Since the interests of the junior lenders are subordinated to those of the senior lender, the junior lenders will typically require the following contractual conditions:

1. the right to select an independent director, and
2. the right to select a person to serve on an independent audit committee of the employer corporation board of directors.

If the employer corporation is an S corporation, the senior lender will require that the warrants and cash appreciation rights be structured in such a way that those warrants and cash appreciation rights do not constitute a second class of stock. And, the senior lender will typically require other S corporation corporate governance protections.[3]

It is very important to the ESOP lenders that the employer corporation:

1. retain its S corporation income tax status; or, if the corporation is a C corporation, that the terms of the ESOP loan mirror the terms of the outside loan (so that there is no cash flow leakage);

2. retain all of the cash from operations either (a) to repay the acquisition debt or (b) to expand the subject business (i.e., so that there is no cash flow leakage to the remaining stockholders or to the selling stockholders); and
3. retain both (a) current management and (b) management oversight through the retention of experienced directors.

In addition, the ESOP lenders may require all or any of the following conditions that will influence the employer corporation corporate governance.

Corporate Structure

To ensure that the ESOP lenders have control over their collateral, the lenders may require the employer corporation to set up a holding corporation with operating subsidiary companies. The holding corporation would:

1. sponsor the ESOP and
2. pledge the assets and stock of its subsidiaries as collateral for the ESOP acquisition loan.

As a result, the ESOP lenders will have the ability to accelerate their rights to the loan collateral without having to deal directly with the ESOP. This is an example of how the ESOP lenders may superimpose corporate governance concerns over the current sponsor company corporate structure.

Retention of the Board of Directors and Retention of Management

The strength of the employer corporation's board of directors and management team is an important consideration for the lenders in any ESOP acquisition transaction. This consideration is especially important where the ESOP is implemented as an exit strategy for selling stockholders who were previously active in the management of the borrowing corporation.

First, the ESOP lenders (1) must be satisfied with the experience and qualifications of the current management team and (2) conclude that current management is capable of operating the employer corporation's business in a profitable manner. Second, the ESOP lenders may also require additional conditions related to the employer corporation management and board of directors. These management/board of directors conditions typically include:

1. one or two of the members of the board of directors should be qualified outside individuals,
2. the management team members should have employment contracts with appropriate retention incentives and noncompete covenants, and
3. the selling stockholders should be limited as to the amount of compensation and other forms of income they can earn from the ESOP corporation.

If the selling stockholders are planning to continue their involvement in the affairs of the employer corporation's business, the ESOP lenders may require them to enter into written employment agreements. These employment agreements typically set forth (1) the terms of compensation and (2) the terms of employment.

Audit Committee and Financial Covenants

The ESOP lenders may also require the employer corporation:

1. to have annual audits performed by an independent accounting firm and
2. to establish an audit committee of the board of directors, consisting of qualified outside individuals.

In addition, (1) the ESOP lenders' assessment of the employer corporation's industry (in both absolute and trend line terms) and (2) the employer corporation's competitive position within the industry will be dealt with through financial and nonfinancial covenants. Accordingly, the employer corporation may be restricted in what it can do until its acquisition indebtedness is reduced to certain pre-established levels.

Financial Reporting

In underwriting any proposed extension of credit, the ESOP lender will require employer corporation management to forecast the amount of corporation cash flow that will be available for debt service. As a result, the ESOP lenders will typically:

1. require more timely periodic financial reporting and
2. place limitations on the uses of the employer corporation cash flow (such as discretionary payments that affect the corporation's cash flow).

Among other things, such cash flow use restrictions may include limitations on (1) capital expenditures, (2) plant/line of business expansion expenditures, and (3) payments to stockholders.

S Corporation ESOP Requirement

The financing of the ESOP acquisition transaction is sometimes predicated on the employer corporation electing S corporation status as soon as it is legally possible. In such a case, the employer corporation must meet certain requirements to be treated as an S corporation for federal income tax purposes.[4]

The expansion of the S corporation stockholder eligibility provisions to include ESOPs has opened up possibilities for significant cash flow availability through the income tax savings.[5] Accordingly, ESOP lenders recognize the cash flow benefits obtained by a properly structured ESOP S corporation election. The employer corporation itself will not be subject to income tax under the general S corporation rules.[6] And, although the income will be passed through to its sole stockholder (i.e., to the ESOP), no shareholder-level tax (or unrelated business income tax) will be imposed. This is because the ESOP trust is a tax-exempt entity.[7]

The ESOP lenders may require covenants and amendments to the sponsor company's corporate charter documents to ensure:

1. the S corporation tax status is not inadvertently terminated (e.g., by limitations on who can be a shareholder) and
2. compliance with the S corporation anti-abuse ESOP rules (e.g., limitations imposed on the use of ESOPs by S corporations where only a small number of employees will receive significant benefits under the ESOP).[8]

The S corporation anti-abuse ESOP rules prohibit allocations under an ESOP to "disqualified persons" if those persons own or are deemed to own more than 50 percent of the corporation's outstanding shares. In general, disqualified persons are individuals (1) who own or (2) who are deemed to own 10 percent or more of the shares held by an S corporation ESOP.

The lenders contemplating an ESOP loan to a corporation that has (or will be electing) S corporation status will require assurance—through a covenant and default provisions—that the ESOP employer corporation will be operated in compliance with these special S corporation anti-abuse ESOP rules.[9]

ESOP Plan Design

The lenders typically will have input on the design of the ESOP plan in order to ensure:

1. there is no unexpected cash leakage and
2. there is no unexpected liability placed on the employer corporation.

In addition, the ESOP lenders, as discussed above, (1) will require the employer corporation to do certain things and (2) will confirm that the transaction is structured in such a way as to assure that:

1. the loan will qualify as an exempt loan and
2. the corporation will quality as an S corporation (or the C corporation is eligible to deduct principal and interest of the outside loan).

Among other things, the ESOP lender typically will require:

1. that the ESOP be maintained as a tax-qualified plan,
2. that the terms of the ESOP loan satisfy all of the requirements for qualification as an exempt loan, and
3. that certain provisions in the ESOP slow down the repurchase liability obligation of the employer corporation.

Debt-Paying Capacity Covenant Limitations

Since the employer corporation typically becomes highly leveraged after completing an ESOP acquisition transaction, the lender typically:

1. will treat the ESOP loan as an investment in the employer corporation and
2. will require or prohibit the corporation from doing certain things.

If (1) the level of debt needed to achieve the corporation's objectives is beyond the comfort level of the ESOP lenders, and if (2) reducing the size of the acquisition transaction or arranging for the transaction to be completed in stages is not acceptable to the corporation, then (3) the ESOP lenders may require certain credit-enhancement procedures.

There are several possible procedures to the credit enhancement of ESOP acquisition transactions (assuming the employer corporation has sufficient cash flow).[10] Several of these credit enhancement procedures are described below:

1. *Pledge of Qualified Replacement Properties.*

   If the ESOP acquisition loan is designed to fund a C corporation Section 1042 transaction, the lender may require that the qualified replacement properties purchased by the selling stockholders be pledged as an additional source of collateral. As a result, the selling stockholders may also require certain contractual promises that affect the sponsor company corporate governance.

2. *Seller Notes.*

   The selling stockholders could provide partial financing for an ESOP stock purchase by accepting payment of a portion of the purchase price for their shares in the form of subordinated notes from the ESOP. These seller notes would be subordinated to the interests of the senior lenders. These seller notes:

   a. could bear attractive interest rates to the selling stockholders and

   b. serve as an alternative to (or be in addition to) bringing mezzanine lenders or outside equity investors into the transaction.

   As a result, the selling stockholders may require certain contractual promises that affect sponsor company corporate governance. In addition, the senior lender will require certain contractual promises (to protect its interest) that influence corporate governance.

3. *Management Investment.*

   Another procedure for overcoming a collateral shortfall in connection with a proposed ESOP acquisition loan is to arrange for retained management to directly invest in the transaction. This is a very attractive means of credit enhancement from the ESOP lender's perspective. This is because this credit enhancement procedure serves to tie the current management team into the subject business.

   In most cases, however, the management team members may not have sufficient net worth to provide a meaningful equity investment in the employer corporation. As a result, the employer corporation may need to be restructured in a manner that includes a limited liability corporation to permit management investment. The exploration of this topic is beyond the scope of this discussion.

4. *Use of Funds from Other Benefit Plans.*

   A corporation adopting an ESOP typically will have a pension, profit-sharing, or 401(k) plan in place. It may be possible to access some of the funds in these plans to provide supplemental financing for an ESOP acquisition transaction.

   The use of funds from other employee benefit plans to finance an ESOP stock purchase requires compliance with (1) ERISA and (2) federal and state securities laws. In addition, the ESOP trustee will typically require certain contractual promises that affect the sponsor company corporate governance.

5. *Mezzanine Debt and Private Equity Investment.*

   If a mezzanine lender (or a private equity group) is used to complete the ESOP acquisition transaction, the senior lender will want to make sure:

   a. its loan is fully collateralized and

   b. there is no cash flow leakage.

   Using mezzanine debt or private equity is another way by which the employer corporation could address a collateral shortfall. Mezzanine debt and private equity investment typically will:

   a. underwrite a loan on the basis of a corporation's cash flow and

   b. provide debt in excess of the collateral value of the employer corporation's assets.

   As a result, the mezzanine debt and private equity financing will typically require certain contractual promises that affect corporate governance. And, private equity financing typically will require contractual control.

Repurchase Obligations

ESOP lenders will take into account the impact of the sponsor company repurchase liability on the corporation's cash flow. This is because participants in an ESOP:

1. generally have the right to demand payment of their benefits in the form of shares of the employer corporation and
2. can require the employer corporation to repurchase such shares upon distribution which could influence corporate governance).[11]

As a result, ESOP lenders will typically require certain limitations to be placed on the employer corporation.

Trustees

ESOP lenders will assess their investment loan risk by analyzing the liability exposure to the employer corporation associated with who is serving as trustee of the ESOP—that is, an insider or a professional outside trustee. Most ESOP acquisition lenders will require an outside (i.e., independent) professional trustee:

1. to reduce the liability exposure and
2. to avoid any possible problems that could arise where the trustee was also the selling stockholder or an employee.

Even though this situation is not prohibited by ERISA, ESOP lenders are sensitive to making acquisition loans where there is an inside trustee. And, some ESOP lenders feel that an inside trustee may affect the employer corporation's ability to liquidate the debt. This is because of the increased liability exposure to the employer corporation.

Inside trustees are often presented with difficult conflicts of interest. For example, inside ESOP trustees may be subject to pressure from the selling stockholders (to whom they may be beholden for their jobs):

1. to accept a stock price that is higher than appropriate or
2. to take on more acquisition debt than it is prudent for the employer corporation to bear.

At a minimum, inside trustees are put in a difficult position to negotiate with their superiors regarding these matters. If, as a result, (1) the price paid by the ESOP for the employer corporation stock exceeds fair market value or (2) the transaction otherwise is imprudent, the transaction will violate applicable laws. And, that violation will result in the imposition of large penalties on the employer corporation.

ESOP lenders will not want to incur the risk of the employer corporation's projected cash flow being jeopardized by liabilities or penalties arising out of violations of the ESOP regulations. And, more generally, ESOP lenders will not fund a prohibited transaction. In addition, most ESOP lenders feel it is simply a better practice to appoint an independent, professional trustee.[12]

Service Providers

ESOP lenders will typically assess the experience and reputation of the service providers involved with (1) the employer corporation and (2) the acquisition transaction. Even though ESOP lenders may not require the employer corporation to make changes to their service provider group, the lenders will assess the service provider's experience as part of their investment loan risk as they decide to participate in the transaction.

SUMMARY AND CONCLUSION

After considering the current lending environment and the current focus on a corporate governance state of affairs, it is important for corporate owners/management to carefully consider corporate governance issues prior to the implementation of an ESOP.[13] In particular, it is important for corporate stockholders/management to be aware of the corporate governance issues that ESOP lenders will focus on as the corporation negotiates with the lenders in structuring the ESOP acquisition financing.

Notes:

1. A common benchmark used by lenders to make this determination is EBITDA, which means "earnings before interest, taxes, depreciation, and amortization."
2. In order for a transaction to take advantage of the benefits of the S corporation ESOP structure, there are many requirements that must be satisfied by the corporation in light of its S corporation status.
3. It should be noted that warrants and cash appreciation rights are considered synthetic equity for purposes of the anti-abuse S corporation ESOP law. Internal Revenue Code Section 409(p).
4. Internal Revenue Code Section 1361(c)(6).
5. For a thorough discussion of the rules relating to S corporation ESOPs and of the tax-savings and other planning opportunities with S corporation ESOPs, see, David Ackerman, "ESOPs and S Corporations" (Chapter 8), *Selling to an ESOP*, 7th ed. (Oakland, CA: National Center for Employee Ownership, 2002).
6. Internal Revenue Code Section 1363(a).
7. Internal Revenue Code Sections 401(a), 501(a), and 512(e)(3).
8. Internal Revenue Code Sections 409(p). For detailed descriptions of the anti-abuse rules for S corporation ESOPs, see, John Kober "The New S Corporation

ESOP," 30 Tax Mgmt. Comp. Plan. J. 36 (2002); and David Ackerman, "New Anti-Abuse Rules for S Corporation ESOPs," *ESOP Report* (July 2001).

9. Internal Revenue Code Section 409(p).
10. See Josephs, "Senior Credit Underwriting for ESOP Transactions," *Journal of Employee Ownership Law & Finance* (Fall 2000).
11. If the stock is not publicly traded, the participants have the right to require that the employer corporation repurchase any shares distributed to them; and even if distributions by the ESOP to terminated participants will be made in cash, the source of the funds will be the corporation sponsor.

    In effect, the employer corporation will be required to repurchase the shares allocated to a terminated participant's account in order to provide the ESOP with the funds necessary to make a benefits distribution.
12. For a thorough discussion of the fiduciary responsibilities of ESOP trustees, see Kober, "Enron: Impact on ESOPs and Being a Fiduciary of an ESOP," 30 Tax Mgmt. Comp Plan J. 159 (2002); and Ackerman, "Questions and Answers Regarding the Duties of ESOP Fiduciaries," *Journal of Employee Ownership Law and Finance* (Fall 2001).
13. See Gordy, "Corporate Governance in ESOP Companies," Willamette Management Associates *Insights*, Spring 2003.

This discussion is adapted from an article originally authored by John A. Kober, Esq. and David Ackerman, Esq. John A. Kober and David Ackerman are partners with Morgan Lewis & Bockius,LLP. Mr. Kober can be reached at (214) 438-1550 or at jkober@morganlewis.com. Mr. Ackerman can be reached at (312) 324-1170 or at dackerman@morganlewis.com.

The article from which this discussion was adapted originally appeared in the Autumn 2003 issue of Willamette Management Associates Insights.

This article was edited and updated by Jeffrey Tarbell. Jeff is a principal of Willamette Management Associates and is resident in the firm's Portland, Oregon, office.

Section VI

ESOP Stock Valuation Case Study

Chapter 29

Employer, Inc., Fair Market Value As of December 31, 2004

NOTE: This ESOP employer corporation stock valuation report is presented for illustrative purposes only. It is presented to illustrate the typical contents and format of a stock valuation report with regard to a small employer corporation. The company information, industry data, economic data, stock price/volume data, and guideline company financial data are all hypothetical. These data are not intended to represent actual industry, economic, stock market, or company data as of the indicated dates.

March 15, 2005

Mr. Institution L. Trustee
Trustee of the Employer, Inc.
Employee Stock Ownership Plan
1000 N.E. Fifth Avenue
Portland, Oregon 97000

Dear Mr. Trustee:

At your request as Trustee of the Employer, Inc. Employee Stock Ownership Plan (the "ESOP"), we conducted a valuation of the Employer, Inc. ("Employer" or the "Company"), common stock. This opinion summarizes our valuation analysis and value conclusion.

The objective of our analysis is to estimate the fair market value of 3,127 shares of Employer common stock ("the Subject Stock"), as of December 31, 2004 (the "Valuation Date").

The purpose of our analysis is to provide an independent valuation opinion to assist you with the ESOP administration and regulatory compliance. Our analysis was conducted for the stated purpose only. No other purpose is intended or should be inferred.

Employer is a footwear manufacturing company that produces high-end sandals and boots. The Company sells its footwear to specialty outdoor stores throughout the United States and in many foreign countries. Company revenue in the most recent fiscal year was approximately $11.8 million.

The standard of value used in this analysis is fair market value. For purposes of this analysis, we define fair market value as "the amount at which property would change hands between a willing seller and a willing buyer when neither is acting under compulsion and when both have reasonable knowledge of the relevant facts."

Our analysis takes into consideration Internal Revenue Service Revenue Ruling 59–60, which outlines the general approaches, methods, and factors to consider in the valuation of the common stock of closely held companies and thinly traded public corporations.

Our analysis was conducted under the valuation premise of value in continued use, as a going concern. This premise of value assumes that Employer will continue to operate as an income-producing business enterprise. In our opinion, and based on our analysis, the premise represents the highest and best use of the Subject Stock.

This valuation included our review of certain financial data related to Employer's historical and projected results of operations. These data included, but were not limited to, reviewed financial statements for the fiscal years ended December 31, 2003 and 2004, compiled financial statements for 2001 and 2002, internally-prepared financial statements for 2000, and management-prepared projected balance sheets and income statements for the fiscal years ending December 31, 2005 through 2007. We relied on these data as fairly presenting the Employer results of operations and financial position. We have not audited these data as part of our analysis. Therefore, we express no opinion or other form of assurance regarding these data.

In addition, our analysis included discussions with management regarding the history, current position, and prospects of Employer. In connection with this analysis, Aaron Analyst and Peter Principal visited the Employer corporate headquarters and distribution facility in Portland, Oregon, and Eugene, Oregon, respectively.

We understand that the ESOP holds a "put" option. That put option allows Company employees receiving distributions—upon termination, retirement, death, or disability—to sell their shares either to the ESOP or to the Company at the then fair market value. The economic effect of this put option is considered in our valuation.

In our analysis, we considered all generally accepted business valuation approaches and methods, including the income approach, the market approach, and the asset-based approach. Based on the quantity and quality of available data, we relied on: (1) the market approach—guideline publicly traded company method, (2) the market approach—guideline merged and acquired company method, and (3) the income approach—discounted cash flow method.

Based on our analysis, as more fully described in the attached valuation report, it is our opinion that the fair market value of the Employer common stock, as of December 31, 2004, is $11,552,000, or $11.55 per share.

This per share value is based on 1,000,000 shares of common stock issued and outstanding.

Based on the fact the ESOP owns 3,127 shares of Employer common stock, the fair market value of the Subject Stock, as of December 31, 2004, is $36,117.

We are independent of Employer, and we have no current or future financial interest in the Employer common stock. Our fee for this analysis is in no way contingent upon the value conclusions reached.

The accompanying statement of contingent and limiting conditions, certification, and professional qualifications of the principal analyst are integral parts of this valuation opinion.

Very truly yours,

WILLAMETTE MANAGEMENT ASSOCIATES

Peter Principal, CPA/ABV, CBA

Attachments

Fair Market Value of Employer, Inc. Common Stock as of December 31, 2004

Table of Contents

I. COMPANY OVERVIEW

History and Background

Approximately 14 years ago, Employer sandals were created in the home of the Company's founder, Frederick D. Founder. Mr. Founder, previously a custom shoemaker and river guide, created the Employer Deschutes sandals to overcome the drawbacks of the then available sandals. The original sandals were designed for the most demanding consumer. They featured Vibram outsoles, sturdy polyurethane footbeds, an innovative strap design, and an unconditional warranty.

In 1991, when larger footwear manufacturing companies started to offer sport sandals, the size of the market increased dramatically. Employer continued to focus on the technical, high-end of the market, and Mr. Founder maintained a no advertising strategy. Employer sales and marketing efforts focused on information by providing retailers with expert knowledge of the product's design. The Employer unit volume growth was moderate but steady as Employer managers gained experience in business development and manufacturing processes. As the Company size increased, its original corporate values were maintained. These corporate values included an unwavering focus on function and quality.

Employer, Inc., is an S corporation for federal income tax purposes. Employer, Inc. is an independent footwear manufacturing company based in Denver, Colorado. Over 90 percent of the Company's 2004 revenue consisted of the Employer Deschutes sandals, the Company's flagship product.

Current Operations

To meet the increasing demand for its products, Employer grew from Mr. Founder's home (where sandals were made one pair at a time), to a company of 100 employees capable of producing in excess of 1,200 pairs of sandals a day. Headquartered in Portland, Oregon, the company operates out of a 20,000 square foot sandal manufacturing facility. In addition to Portland, the Company's products are also manufactured in both Singapore and Germany.

Employer currently ships to more than 900 storefronts in the United States, and it also exports to many foreign countries. The Deschutes sandals are typically sold through high-end backpacking/camping shops, with additional representation in higher-end and comfort/casual shoe stores. Some of the larger retailers that stock Employer products include REI, Hudson Trail Outfitters, Adventure 16, and Whole Earth Provision

Company. The Employer Deschutes sandals retail price is between $90 and $105 a pair.

Employer has a market share of approximately 25 percent (measured by dollars) in the nylon sandals/specialty stores market. The Company has less than a 2 percent market share in the leather sandals and boots market. The Company's primary competitor is Teva Sport Sandals, Inc., a division of Decker's Outdoor Corp.

Employer Outlook

Employer recently developed the following two products in addition to its performance sandals: (1) leather hiking boots and (2) slip-on sandals.

The Employer leather hiking boots were developed to more comfortably fit consumers. And, the Employer leather hiking boots feature less padding and fewer synthetic fillers than the competitive products. By offering a specialized fit, Employer sets itself apart from other boot manufacturers. Other features of the boots include exceptional breathability, a simple elegant appearance, and a lightweight design. The Employer boots have a retail price of between $180 and $230.

The Employer slip on sandals combine easy, slip-on convenience with the same supportive contours and quality materials as their predecessors. The Company has three styles of the slip-on sandal, which range from a simple flip flop to a fully adjustable sandal. The slip on sandals have a retail price of between $50 and $75.

Additional product lines that are currently under development include: leather sandals, leather shoes, and a contoured footbed shoe insert. These products are complimentary to the Company's current line of products. However, these products represent a shift in the Company's target market from the specialty outdoor market to the larger footwear market.

Currently, over 90 percent of the Company's revenue is in the specialty outdoor market. In five years, Employer management projects that the specialty outdoor market segment will account for only 35 percent of Company revenue.

The ESOP Transaction

In 2003, the Company implemented an ESOP program. In 2004, the Company sold 3,127 shares of its common stock to the ESOP. Employer management indicated that it intends to make annual contributions to the ESOP to allow for the purchase of Company stock. However, Company management reserves the right to suspend such contribution in any year where profit performance does not warrant such contribution. There is no debt associated with the Employer ESOP.

Ownership and Capitalization

The Company is capitalized with one class of voting common stock, with no par value. As of December 31, 2004, there were a total of 1,000,000 shares outstanding.

The ownership of the Company's common stock as of December 31, 2004, is presented in Table 1.

Table 1

Employer Inc.
Common Stock Ownership
As of December 31, 2004

Shareholder	Number of Shares	Percent Ownership
Frederick Founder	974,999	97.50%
Margaret Mead	7,374	0.74%
Doug James	4,000	0.40%
Ed Smith	3,500	0.35%
The ESOP	3,127	0.31%
Jerry Black	2,250	0.23%
Ed White	2,000	0.20%
Al Green	1,500	0.15%
Dave Brown	1,000	0.10%
Rob Love	250	0.03%
Total (Rounded)	1,000,000	100.00%

Prior Transactions in the Company Common Stock

At the end of 2003, the only Company stockholder was Frederick Founder. During 2004, the Company sold 3,127 shares of stock to the ESOP at a price of $8.90 per share. The $8.90 price was the estimated fair market value of the Employer stock, based on an independent appraisal.

Subsequently, in June 2004, a stock option plan was implemented that granted Employer certain directors, key managers, and sales representatives the opportunity to purchase shares of the Company. As part of this plan, several individuals purchased Company stock at $8.90 per share.

Financial Statement Analysis

An important procedure in the common stock valuation is an analysis of the subject company operating performance over time. Past revenue and earnings growth can provide an indication of future growth and can put the subject Company's earnings in an historical context. Other things being equal, a company with increasing revenue and earnings is worth more than a company with little or no revenue or earnings growth.

The following discussion summarizes the key trends in the Employer financial statements during the latest five-year period.

Balance Sheets

The Employer balance sheets as of December 31, 2000, through 2004, are presented in Exhibit 1.

- Current assets represented 75.4 percent of total assets at December 31, 2004. This percentage is similar to historical levels. The largest component of current assets was inventory, which accounted for $3.1 of the $3.6 million current assets. In 2004, the inventory balance was significantly greater than prior periods. This is due to (1) the rollout of the slip-on sandal product line and (2) approximately $700,000 in slow-moving inventory. This slow-moving inventory related to two unsuccessful product launches by the Company in 2004. Inventory balances are generally largest around the month of December in preparation for the upcoming shoe season. Approximately 80 percent of the Company's sales occur between January and June.
- Accounts receivable represented 8.5 percent of total assets at December 31, 2004, and ranged between 6.8 percent (2000) and 14.0 percent (2003) over the five years, as presented in Exhibit 1.
- Net fixed assets increased by approximately $356,000 in 2003 and by approximately $314,000 in 2004. The increases in 2003 and 2004 related principally to (1) an investment in a new comprehensive ERP system and (2) an investment in molds, lasts, and tooling related to new products. The Company typically incurs between $400,000 and $450,000 of capital expenditures per year.
- Total assets equaled $4.7 million at December 31, 2004. Total assets have increased at a compound annual growth rate of 39.9 percent since 2000.

- Historically, the Company's line of credit is largest at year-end. Similar to the inventory balance, the amount borrowed against the line of credit is a result of seasonal factors. The Company typically borrows from its line in the fourth quarter of the year to fund the build-up of inventory in preparation for the upcoming shoe season. By the middle of the year, the line of credit is generally paid off.
- Other interest-bearing debt equaled approximately $540,000 in 2003, and approximately $900,000 in 2004.
- Total stockholders' equity was $1.45 million as of December 31, 2004, or 30.5 percent of total liabilities and stockholders' equity. Total stockholders' equity increased at a compound annual growth rate of 19.1 percent since 2000.

Income Statements

The Employer income statements for the fiscal years ended December 31, 2000, through 2004, are presented in Exhibit 2.

- Between 2000 and 2004, revenue increased from $3.4 million to $11.8 million, at a compound annual growth rate of 36.3 percent. The annual revenue growth rate has slowed in each year since 2000. The revenue growth rate in 2004 was 11.6 percent, the lowest growth rate reported since 2000. According to Employer management, the lower growth rate was caused by (1) the nationwide economic slowdown and (2) two unsuccessful product launches by the Company.
- The Company's gross profit margin was 47.7 percent in 2004, down from 51.0 percent in calendar 2002 and 50.2 percent in calendar 2003.
- Total operating expenses of $4.2 million in 2004 represented 35.8 percent of revenue. Total operating expenses as a percent of revenue ranged from 35.4 percent to 35.8 percent in the past three years.
- Pretax income increased from $806,777 in 2000 to $1.3 million in 2004, a compound annual growth rate of 13.4 percent. Over the last five years, the Employer pretax margins ranged from a low of 11.3 percent to a high of 23.7 percent. For calendar 2004, the pretax margin was 11.3 percent, at the low end of the range of pretax margins since 2000. As an S corporation, the Company did not pay federal income taxes in 2001 through 2004.

Statements of Cash Flows

The Employer statements of cash flows for the fiscal years ended December 31, 2000, through 2004, are presented in Exhibit 3.

- Employer had positive operating cash flow in each of the last five years. Operating cash flow equaled $575,780 in 2004, lower than the operating cash flow in 2003. This decrease was due to the build-up in inventory.
- Over the periods presented, capital expenditures ranged from a low of $230,300 (in 2001) to a high of $665,000 (in 2004).
- Historically, stockholder distributions have been made in an amount equal to the personal income tax liability of the Company's controlling stockholder. This personal income tax liability is associated with the total income reported by the Company.

Financial Statement Normalization Adjustments

Exhibit 4 presents certain normalization adjustments made to the Employer income statements. We made normalization adjustments in order to eliminate nonrecurring and/or nonoperating items, as well as the calculation of various financial fundamentals used in our analysis.

We made one normalization adjustment to the Employer earnings. As presented in Exhibit 4, we added (subtracted) the loss (gain) from the sale of Company assets.

Financial and Operating Ratios

Exhibit 5 presents a summary of selected financial and operating ratios for Employer for the fiscal years ending December 31, 2000, through 2004.

- The current and quick ratios provide rough indications of the Employer ability to service its current obligations. The current ratio was near a five-year low at 1.4 in the most recent year, a decrease from 1.7 at the end of fiscal 2003.
- Working capital is a measure of the margin of protection for current creditors. The Employer working capital was greater than $1 million in each of the past three years.
- Activity ratios indicate how efficiently a company is utilizing its assets. Days in inventory was at a five-year high in 2004, and asset turnover was at a five-year low.
- The Company's debt coverage ratios measure the amount by which earnings could decline without impairing its ability to meet its fixed interest payments. Employer had adequate levels of interest coverage over the last five years.

- In addition to indicating profits and returns over a period, profitability ratios assist analysts in evaluating Company management performance. The Employer profitability measures (which have been adjusted as described above) were the lowest of the five-year period in 2004. However, compared to industry standards, Employer has impressive profitability ratios. The Company's pretax profit margin was 11.7 percent in 2004, and pretax return on average equity was 96.2 percent in 2004.

II. UNITED STATES ECONOMY ANALYSIS

Economic expansion continued in the fourth quarter of 2004, although at a slower pace than in the third quarter of the year. The growth rate in the fourth quarter of 2004 was less than half the third quarter growth rate.

The nation's trade deficit decreased in November 2004. The national trade deficit was the smallest deficit in 13 months. Exports were ahead moderately, while imports decreased slightly.

The Federal Reserve Bank decreased short-term interest rates for the first time in 2004 at its June 25, 2004, meeting. The federal funds rate was decreased to a 45-year low. The discount rate also was decreased. The Federal Reserve Bank short-term interest rates were unchanged from June at the end of December 2004. Large U.S. banks responded to the Federal Reserve Bank's interest rate cut in June 2004 by decreasing their prime lending rate moderately. That rate remained in effect at the end of December 2004.

The U.S. dollar decreased significantly against major foreign currencies since early 2003. But the decrease didn't trigger unwelcome side effects such as increasing inflation.

The consumer price index (CPI) increased modestly in December 2004. Core consumer prices, which exclude food and energy, increased slightly in December 2004.

The personal consumption expenditure (PCE) price index increased at a modest annual rate in the fourth quarter of 2004. Federal Reserve officials watch the PCE closely. Currently, the price indices are below their preferred minimum rate.

Nonagricultural total employment increased in December 2004 by a small amount. Employment decreased in manufacturing for the 41st consecutive month. Employment in the retail sector decreased and job losses also were recorded in finance and state governments. Temporary employment agencies, however, added jobs. Other service sector areas that added jobs were education and health care. Construction companies also added jobs.

The unemployment rate in December 2004 decreased to a 14-month low. Unemployment decreased because many potential workers gave up looking for jobs.

The U.S. Labor Department reported the Employment Cost Index (ECI) increased modestly in the final quarter of 2004. Benefit costs were ahead moderately in the fourth quarter of 2004 and wages increased by a small amount.

Personal income increased slightly in December 2004. The personal savings rate decreased in December 2004 to the lowest rate since December 2003.

Consumers took a break in the fourth quarter of 2004, helping to subdue economic growth. A decrease in spending for automobiles was an important factor in the lower rate of growth in the 2004 last quarter. In December 2004, consumer spending increased. Retail sales increased slightly in December 2004. Excluding automobile purchases, retail sales increased only slightly.

Consumer debt has more than doubled in the past 10 years. That debt includes credit cards and automobile loans, but not mortgages. Consumers increased their borrowing by a moderate amount in December 2004, but total consumer debt reached a new record amount.

The Conference Board's Consumer Confidence Index decreased in December 2004. However, December 2004 figures still suggests slow growth.

Total construction spending was at its highest level ever in December 2004. Residential private construction increased modestly, while nonresidential private construction decreased by a moderate amount. Public construction spending increased slightly in December. Housing starts in December 2004 increased significantly. It was the fastest pace since February 1984. Home building permits, an indicator of future construction, increased in December 2004.

New home sales decreased in December 2004. The inventory of unsold homes on the market increased in December 2004 to the highest level since June 1989. Existing home sales increased in December 2004. Inventories of existing homes for sale decreased in December 2004. Freddie Mac reported the interest rate on a 30-year, fixed mortgage was at the same as at the end of December 2003.

The Dow Jones Industrial Average (DJIA) increased significantly in 2004. For 2004, the S&P 400 Industrials and the S&P 500 Composite both increased sharply. The Nasdaq Composite increased in 2004 and the Nasdaq Industrials increased at a rapid pace.

Output at the nation's factories, mines, and utilities increased slightly in December 2004. Mining output was flat, manufacturing output increased modestly, and utility production decreased in December 2004. Capacity utilization at factories, mines, and utilities held steady in December 2004. There appears to be a glut of manufacturing capacity around the world.

Factory orders in the United States increased moderately in December 2004. Orders for durable goods increased slightly, and nondurable goods orders increased a moderate amount. Orders for nondefense capital goods, a proxy for future business investment, increased modestly in December 2004.

The Institute of Supply Management (ISM) reported its manufacturing index increased in December 2004. It was the sixth consecutive month of growth in the manufacturing sector. The prices paid index of the ISM report showed manufacturers continued to pay higher prices for the 22nd consecutive month.

The ISM indicated that activity in the service sector decreased in December 2004. The report indicated the sector isn't growing as fast as it had in previous months. The prices index for the nonmanufacturing sector continued to report higher prices.

The producer price index (PPI) of wholesale prices increased in December 2004. Most of the gain was due to increased energy prices.

In the fourth quarter of 2004, businesses increased spending on equipment and software at a brisk pace. This was the second consecutive quarter of double-digit growth in this sector.

It is estimated that U.S. households will receive $30.0 billion more in income tax refunds in 2005 than in 2004. With other tax cuts factored in, such as lower dividend and capital gains taxes and business breaks, the total economic stimulus in the coming months will be close to $100 billion, according to the chief economist at Wrightson ICAP, a research firm.

The manufacturing sector won't be a drag on the economy in 2005. However, the manufacturing sector won't be a growth engine either. Manufacturing now represents less than 17 percent of GDP and 12 percent of the workforce, but it spills over into other sectors of the economy. The National Association of Manufacturers expects manufacturing production to increase 6.1 percent in 2005.

Sales of existing homes are expected to decrease to about 5.8 million in 2005. New home sales and residential home construction are both expected to decline by about 3 percent. Home price increases are anticipated to decrease from 8.0 percent in 2004 to around 4.6 percent in 2005.

The economic expansion should continue at a healthy and sustainable pace in 2004 according to *Value Line Investment Survey* analysts. Strength will spread across most of the consumer and industrial markets. Corporate earnings are expected to increase further, helped by improving demand and more cost cutting. However, inflation needs to be monitored because of the increase in energy prices in 2004 and the potential for higher raw material costs due to an increase in demand.

The sources for this section include: *The Wall Street Journal*; *Barron's*; *The Oregonian*; *Worth*; Associated Press; Institute of Supply Management; *Value Line Investment Survey*; Dow Jones Business News; Realtor.org; Bureau of Labor Statistics; U.S. Census Bureau; and Reuters Limited.

III. INDUSTRY ANALYSIS AND OUTLOOK

Footwear Industry Overview

Our analysis considers the state of the footwear industry as of the Valuation Date. Employer sells high performance sandals and boots. Employer is also developing leather sandals and leather shoes.

The U.S. footwear industry consists of about 100 manufacturers, 1,500 wholesalers, and 30,000 retail outlets, as well as shoe departments in a large number of department, discount, and clothing stores.

The typical U.S. shoe manufacturer is small, with annual revenue of $10 million and fewer than 100 employees. U.S-made products are mostly private-label men's shoes. Materials, mainly leather, account for approximately 50 percent of a footwear company's costs.

Brand names are the most valuable assets of a shoe manufacturing company. Shoe manufacturers design new styles on an ongoing basis, keeping track of European and American trends and tastes. Models are marketed to retailers using an in-house sales' force and independent sales representatives. Retailers usually place orders with shoe manufacturers three to four months ahead of expected delivery time, on a purchase order basis that allows for cancellations.

Footwear styles include athletic, casual, dress, sandal, and sport/hiking. However, any given shoe design may combine categories. Footwear can be made out of leather, canvas, or other materials that are either natural or manmade. A footwear manufacturer will typically determine what is most important to its customers: fashion or function. Producers of athletic and sport/hiking footwear also develop technology to improve comfort and performance.

The footwear industry (often discussed in terms of 'footwear and apparel') is mature, diverse, characterized by intense competition, and comprised of price-conscious consumers. In 2004, consumers spent $40.56 billion on footwear (latest available), a decrease of 5.0 percent from $42.58 billion in 2002, according to the U.S. Department of Commerce. In 2004, the average price of footwear continued to decline as consumers sought price bargains and lower-priced casual shoes grabbed a greater share of the mix. The U.S. Department of Labor consumer price index for footwear decreased to 119.6 in 2004, from 121.4 in 2003. In 2002 and 2001, the index was at 123.0 and 123.8, respectively.

According to SGMA International, a strong second half resulted in a 4.9 percent increase in unit sales of athletic footwear and a 4.5 percent rise in spending in 2004. In 2004, retro/classic styled shoes, which had been the dominant fashion from the previous several years, appeared to decrease in popularity.

Competition

Despite years of consolidation activity, the apparel and footwear industries are extremely competitive and highly fragmented. This is most likely due to low barriers of entry: all a manufacturer needs are good designs that attract department store and/or specialty buyers. If a designer gets orders, he or she can contract the production for the item to a low-cost, independent manufacturer, usually outside the United States.

Consumers also wield considerable power over footwear manufacturers, as they can readily switch from one product or brand to another. To dissuade them from doing so, manufacturers attempt to increase brand awareness and build brand loyalty among consumers. A strong brand image typically gives a manufacturer more pricing flexibility by creating perceived switching costs for the consumer.

Competition from oversees has also put pressure on the industry. Shoe prices reached a peak in 1998 and have since declined. The intensely competitive nature of a business with a mature market and low-cost overseas' production facilities has kept prices at the same levels they were 10 years ago. Shoe imports, which increased 10 percent from 2000 to 2003, were predominately from China, Italy, Brazil, and Indonesia, with China accounting for two-thirds in 2003.

Demographics

According to Standard & Poor's, understanding target markets is a key to success in the apparel and footwear business. Among the important demographic trends in the United States, baby boomers are outgrowing their focus on fashion, while the younger generations are an emerging, though elusive, source of demand.

Members of the baby boom generation (individuals born between 1946 and 1964), constitute 77 million Americans. Although this demographic has increasing disposable income, their enthusiasm towards spending on apparel and footwear has dampened.

Generation Y (individuals born between 1977 and 1994) comprises 75 million individuals, and is an increasingly prosperous market for apparel and footwear companies. According to a 2003 study conducted by Harris Interactive, teenage girls spent 75 percent of their earnings on clothing and related accessories, while boys spent 52 percent of theirs. The Generation Y demographic is considered fickle, trendy, and difficult to market.

Industry Trends

The following trends have an effect on the footwear manufacturing industry as of the Valuation Date:

Internationalization

The footwear industry is global in nature, with large manufacturers selling products in different countries over several continents. A multinational strategy allows manufacturers facing a slow economy in one country to keep expanding revenues by focusing on selling in another country's faster growing economy.

Shorter Cycles

In the past, retail stores often carried apparel and footwear months in advance of the season in which they would be worn. Today, consumers tend to buy closer to need. To meet this demand, manufacturers have had to shorten design, development, production, and distribution cycles. In response, footwear companies are emphasizing market research in order to track consumer needs and trends.

Price Deflation

Average selling prices for most footwear has seen a long-term downtrend. Contributing factors include the continued influx of imports, retail promotions, and market share gains by discounters. The pressure on prices has threatened margins at many footwear companies.

Although overall apparel and footwear sales have increased (in total dollars) since 1999, average selling prices have declined, as indicated by the apparel consumer price index (CPI) published by the Bureau of Labor Statistics. In 2004, the footwear CPI decreased 1.8 percent to 118.5 (1982-84=100) compared to 2003. Recent consolidation in the industry is expected to support the firming of retail prices. However, Standard & Poor's projects that excess retail capacity will ultimately lead to decreasing prices.

Diversification

To expand and survive, many footwear companies are diversifying their product offerings by offering either an extension of a current line, or developing a new line. Companies are diversifying through internal research and development efforts or through acquisition.

Retailer Consolidation

Shoe chains have increased in recent years, while single-brand shoe stores have faded. Consolidation has been driven partly by efficiencies of scale. Chains can more easily maintain and manage a large inventory than can independent stores, routing individual products to stores where they are selling best and running a lower risk of inventory obsolescence. Chains can also negotiate lower prices for high volume orders.

Consumer Confidence

One of the most important statistics for the apparel and footwear industry is consumer confidence. Consumer confidence, a precursor to consumer spending has been notably unstable in the last several quarters. In the fourth quarter of 2003, the index began declining and in the March 2004, was at a nine-year low of 61.4 (1985=100).

Industry Outlook

With the economic recovery gaining traction, footwear sales should benefit from resurgent consumer spending. However, consumers remain focused on bargains, and deflationary pricing pressure is likely to continue. Accordingly, Standard & Poor's expects branded apparel companies offering fashion-right products at attractive prices to outperform the overall industry.

The footwear industry faces a highly competitive but improving environment. Standard & Poor's anticipates that footwear sales should show modest gains in 2005, building on momentum gained in the second half of 2004. Economic growth, and improving job market, and a higher level of consumer confidence during the year could spur consumers to revamp their footwear collection.

Gross domestic product (GDP) and consumer confidence are both of great importance to the footwear industry. GDP increased 3.1 percent in 2004, and is projected by Standard & Poor's to increase 4.5 percent in 2005. Consumer confidence is also projected to perform better in 2005 than 2004. For 2005, Standard & Poor's projects that personal consumption expenditures will increase 3.4 percent, from 3.1 percent in 2004.

IV. BUSINESS VALUATION APPROACHES AND METHODS

Business Valuation Approaches

Several approaches are available for the valuation of privately owned business interests. The generally accepted valuation approaches are typically grouped into three categories. While the individual names of these three generally accepted business valuation approaches vary, the generic names are the asset-based approach, the income approach, and the market approach.

Asset-Based Approach

This valuation approach considers the fair market value of the Company assets (both tangible and intangible) and the current value of the Company liabilities (both contingent and recorded). The asset-based approach typically involves a valuation (either discrete or collective) of the following assets: current assets (such as cash and marketable securities, accounts receivable, and inventory); tangible personal property (such as machinery and equipment); real estate (land and buildings, including leasehold improvements and land held for resale); and intangible assets (such as patents, copyrights, customer lists, contracts, trademarks, a trained and assembled workforce, and goodwill). This approach typicall involves a valuation (either discrete or collective) of the following liabilities: current liabilities (such as trade accounts payable and accrued liabilities); notes payable; and contingent liabilities (such as environmental contamination and other regulatory actions, income tax audit exposure, and legal exposures).

Income Approach

The common methods in the income approach include the discounted cash flow method and the direct capitalization method.

The discounted cash flow method involves a projection of the company results of operations for a discrete, multi-year period. The discrete cash flow projection is then converted to a present value. The discount cash flow method also involves a terminal value analysis, at the conclusion of the discrete projection period. The terminal value is converted to a present value. The sum of (1) the present value of the discrete cash flow projection and (2) the present value of the terminal value indicates the value of the subject company.

The direct capitalization method involves dividing a market-derived direct capitalization rate into a normalized estimate of future income. The conclusion of the division procedure indicates the value of the subject company.

Market Approach

The prices of securities of companies in the same or similar lines of business provide valuable information to the rational common investor. The common methods of the market approach use a selected sample of guideline security/company prices with selected financial/operating fundamentals of the guideline companies/transactions. This comparison results in market-derived valuation pricing multiples. These market-derived pricing multiples are analyzed so as to extract pricing multiples to apply to the subject company. The sources of guideline companies include both publicly traded corporations and merger and acquisition transactions.

Approaches Used in the Valuation of Employer, Inc.

In our valuation, we used the guideline publicly traded company method (a market approach method), the discounted cash flow method (an income approach method), and the guideline merged and acquired company method (a market approach method).

Guideline Publicly Traded Company Method Analysis

It has been stated that values are best tested in the marketplace. One of the methods of estimating the value of closely held company stock is to look to the public markets for evidence of the prices investors are willing to pay for the stock of companies in the same (or similar) lines of business.

The principal procedures in the guideline publicly traded company method are:

- the identification and selection of guideline publicly traded companies;
- the calculation of market-derived pricing multiples based on a comparison of (1) the guideline companies' quoted trading prices and (2) the guideline companies' financial fundamentals;
- the selection of the appropriate market-derived pricing multiples to apply to the subject company's financial fundamentals;
- the calculation of one or more value indications for the subject company based on the application of the selected market-derived pricing multiples;
- the selection of the relative emphasis (or weight) to be placed on each of the resulting value indications; and
- the estimation of an overall value indication from this method.

Selection of the Guideline Publicly Traded Companies

To begin our search for guideline publicly traded companies, we determined the most appropriate Standard Industrial Classification (SIC) codes for Employer. Employer most closely resembles companies in the SIC code 3021—Rubber and Plastics Footwear, and 3100—Leather and Leather Products. In conducting our search for guideline publicly traded companies, we used the Disclosure, Inc., and the Standard & Poor's Corporations databases.

The Compact D/SEC database published by Disclosure, Inc., contains detailed financial and textual information on approximately 12,000 publicly traded companies. The information is derived from documents filed with the Securities and Exchange Commission (SEC) and is updated on a weekly basis.

S&P Corporate Descriptions database contains strategic and financial information on approximately 12,000 corporations with securities publicly traded on the New York, American, and regional stock exchanges; the Nasdaq system; and various stock exchanges in Canada and abroad.

The following is a summary description of each of the guideline publicly traded companies we selected for our analysis of Employer.

Deckers Outdoor Corp. (Deckers) designs and markets innovative, functional, and fashion-oriented footwear. This footware developed for both high performance outdoor activities and everyday casual lifestyle use. Currently, the company offers three primary product lines under the following brand names: (1) Teva—high performance sports sandals and rugged outdoor and casual footwear; (2) Simple—innovative shoes that combine the comfort elements of athletic footwear with casual styling; and (3) Ugg—authentic sheepskin boots and other footwear. Sales of Teva products represented 65.4 percent of the Deckers fiscal 2003 revenue.

K-Swiss, Inc. (K-Swiss) designs, develops and markets an array of athletic footwear for high-performance sports use, fitness activities and casual wear under the K-Swiss brand. The company also designs and manufactures footwear under the Royal Elastics brand. The company's strategy is to combine classic styling with high quality components and technical features designed to meet performance requirements of specific sports. Casual footwear accounted for approximately two-thirds of K-Swiss revenue in its fiscal 2004.

Lacrosse Footwear, Inc. (Lacrosse) is a leader in the design, development, marketing, and manufacturing of premium quality protective footwear and clothing. These products are distributed to the sporting and outdoor, farm and agriculture, general utility and occupational markets. The company markets its products primarily under the Lacrosse, Rainfair, and Danner brands through selected distributors and independent representatives. The Lacrosse products are characterized by innovative, functional design; durability; performance features; and quality materials.

Maxwell Shoe Company, Inc. (Maxwell) designs, develops and markets casual and dress footwear for women and children under multiple brand names. Each of the Maxwell brand names is targeted to a distinct segment of the footwear market. The company's brands include Mootsies Tootsies, Sam & Libby, Dockers, J.G. Hook, and AK Anne Klein. The company's strategy is: (1) to leverage its existing competitive strengths, including its strong manufacturing relationships and focused brand management, and (2) to increase profitability in its share of the women's and children's footwear markets. Company management plans to achieve these strategies by (1) further strengthening its existing footwear brands and its private label business and (2) expanding its brand portfolio through a combination of acquisition, licensing, and development of additional brands in the future.

Rocky Shoes & Boots, Inc. (Rocky) sells rugged outdoor, occupational, military, and casual footwear, and Rocky branded outdoor gear. Rocky brand products emphasize quality, patented materials, such as Gore-Tex waterproof breathable fabric, Cordura nylon fabric, Cambrelle cushioned lining and Thinsulate thermal insulation. The outdoor footwear line is the company's largest product line, representing 46.7 percent of fiscal 2003 revenue.

Saucony, Inc. (Saucony) designs, develops, and markets performance-oriented athletic footwear, athletic apparel and casual leather footwear. The principal Saucony products are: (1) technical running, walking and outdoor train shoes, and athletic apparel, (2) technical running shoe models from the early 1980s, the company's classic footwear line, (3) athletic apparel, and (4) shoes for coaches and officials and casual leather walking and workplace footwear. The company's products are sold in the United States at more than 5,500 retail locations and at the company's 12 factory outlet stores. The Saucony brand is recognized for its technical innovation and performance.

Vans, Inc. (Vans) is a leading global sports and lifestyle company that merchandises, designs, sources, and distributes Vans-branded active/casual and performance footwear, apparel, and accessories for core sports. Over the past seven years, the Vans focus has been proprietary branding with the goal of creating a leadership position for the company's brand and strong emotional connections with its customers. The Vans brand targets 10- to 24-year-old participants, enthusiasts, and emulators of the core sports culture. Vans distributes its products through over 2,000 U.S. domestic wholesale accounts.

Weyco Group, Inc. (Weyco) is engaged in one line of business: the manufacture, purchase, and distribution of men's footwear. The company does not sell women's or children's shoes. The principal brands of shoes sold by the company are Florsheim, Nunn Bush, Nunn Bush NXXT, Brass Boot, Stacy Adams, and SAO by Stacy Adams. The Weyco products consist of both (1) mid-priced quality leather dress shoes and (2) quality casual footwear of man-made materials or leather.

Invested Capital Valuation Procedures

Invested capital valuation procedures are commonly used in the valuation of closely held companies. These procedures are used in order to minimize capital structure differences between the subject company—Employer—

and the selected guideline companies. The greater the differences between the capital structure of the subject company and the guideline companies, the more appropriate it is to use invested capital valuation procedures.

For purposes of this analysis, we refer to total invested capital as the MVIC (market value of invested capital). For purposes of this analysis, MVIC is defined as follows:

Market value of short-term interest-bearing debt
\+ Market value of long-term interest-bearing debt (including capitalized leases)
\+ Market value of preferred stock outstanding
\+ <u>Market value of common stock outstanding</u>
= Market value of invested capital

As the above formula implies, the market value of common stock can be calculated by subtracting (1) the market value of interest-bearing debt and (2) the market value of preferred stock outstanding from (3) the MVIC.

Since 80 percent of the Employer revenue is earned in the first half of the year, and since the Employer inventory must be built up in the fourth quarter of the preceding year, the Company's line of credit varies significantly from month to month. The largest line of credit balances occur in the November and December months, and the smallest line of credit balances occur in the July and August months. In 2004, the line of credit balance ranged from a low of $0 to a high of $1.8 million. The Employer average monthly line of credit balance outstanding in 2004 was $912,301.

To calculate the Company's interest-bearing debt as presented in Exhibit 4, given the seasonal fluctuation of the line of credit, we relied on the average monthly line of credit balance of $912,301.

Therefore, as presented in Exhibit 4, the total interest-bearing debt is $1.807 million. This total interest-bearing debt balance is comprised of (1) long-term debt (including the current portion) of $894,297 and (2) the average line of credit balance of $912,301.

We considered the following invested capital valuation pricing multiples for projected fiscal 2005 (when available) and the latest 12 months (LTM) periods:

1. MVIC/Earnings before interest and taxes (EBIT)
2. MVIC/Earnings before interest, taxes, depreciation and amortization (EBITDA)

3. Market value of equity (MVE)/Net income
4. MVIC/Revenue

As presented in Exhibit 6, the guideline publicly traded company method indicates the value of the Employer common stock, as of December 31, 2004, is $12,455,000 (rounded) before consideration of any applicable valuation adjustments.

Discounted Cash Flow Method Analysis

The discounted cash flow (DCF) method is a common business valuation method. This is because it reflects the trade-off between investment risk and expected return that is integral to the common stock investment process. Expectations of investment return are normally based on an assumption that the entity generating the return is a going concern. Generally, common stocks are purchased with the expectation of stock price appreciation. Expected stock price appreciation is strongly influenced by expectations about a company's cash flow capacity.

A DCF analysis estimates value on the basis of future economic income over an investment time horizon. Using empirical market data, macroeconomic and industry evidence, and the underlying fundamental trends for the subject company, the DCF analysis applies a present value discount rate to expected future cash flow. This present value procedure results in a estimation of the net present value of the cash flow projection.

We conducted our DCF analysis on an invested capital basis. We used net cash flow on an invested capital basis as the appropriate measure of economic income.

The Employer weighted average cost of capital (WACC) is the appropriate discount rate to apply to invested capital net cash flow.

The value estimated by this DCF analysis is the Employer market value of invested capital. We then subtracted the Employer interest-bearing debt (as calculated in Exhibit 4) to estimate the market value of the Employer common stock.

Derivation of Cash Flow

Discrete Cash Flow Projection. Exhibit 12 and Exhibit 13 present management's projected balance sheets and income statements, respectively, for fiscal 2005 through 2007. Based on (1) information presented in

Exhibits 12 and 13, (2) our analysis of the Company historical results of operation, and (3) the outlook for Employer, we calculated invested capital net cash flow (NCF) for 2005 through 2007. For purposes of this analysis, we define NCF as:

  Net income
\+ Interest x (1 - Tax rate)
\+ Depreciation and amortization expense
– Capital expenditures
– Increases (or + decreases) in Working capital
= Invested capital net cash flow

We used the mid-year discounting convention to discount the Employer NCF. This discounting convention assumes that Employer cash flow is received evenly throughout the year.

Terminal Cash Flow and Terminal Value. Although the discrete cash flow projection runs through the year 2007, Employer has value beyond that date. This is because Employer is expected to generate cash flow indefinitely into the future. The value of the Company in the last year of the discrete projection period is defined as the terminal value. The terminal value cash flow is based on the year 2007 projected cash flow increased by the expected long-term growth rate of 4.0 percent. The direct capitalization rate assigned to the terminal period cash flow is the WACC (as described below) less the 4.0 percent expected long-term growth rate.

Present Value Discount Rate

We estimated the required rate of return on Employer invested capital by analyzing the weighted average cost of capital (on both debt and equity) for the Company. Exhibit 14 presents the calculation of the Employer WACC at 17.4 percent.

The WACC incorporates market-derived evidence of the cost of debt and equity as of the Valuation Date. These expected rates of return are weighted based on the relationship of the Company's market value of debt to its estimated market value of equity.

Cost of Equity. In a rational investment environment, an investor has various alternative investments for funds. The investor will require a rate of return on these investments that is a function of: (1) the expected rate of inflation, (2) the rate of return currently offered above inflation on a riskless investment, and (3) a return to compensate for the relative uncertainty (additional risk) of the projected future cash flow. The required return on an investment is a function of the investment risk inherent in the expected return flow.

The required rate of return for Employer common stock incorporates the perceived risks, as they were known on the Valuation Date, relative to the empirical evidence of guideline investments. In developing this rate of return, we used the modified capital asset pricing model (CAPM). For purposes of this analysis, we define the modified CAPM as follows:

Risk-free rate
\+ (Long-term equity risk premium x Beta)
\+ Small stock equity risk premium
\+ <u>Company-specific equity risk premium</u>
= Cost of equity capital

First, we estimated the appropriate risk-free rate of return. The risk-free rate of return incorporates investors' expectations for the real rate of return on a riskless investment and the impact of expected inflation on the investors' purchasing power. We selected the risk-free rate based on the 20-year Treasury bond rate. The 20-year bond rate was 5.1 percent as of the Valuation Date.

Second, in order to estimate the long-term equity risk premium, we researched historical equity returns above the risk-free rate over a long-term investment horizon. According to the Ibbotson Associates *Stocks, Bonds, Bills and Inflation: 2004 Yearbook* (SBBI '04), the arithmetic equity risk premium on the Standard & Poor's 500 Composite Common Stock Index above the risk-free rate (as measured by 20-year Treasury bonds) was 7.0 percent over the 1926–2003 period of the study.

Third, risk denotes the prospect of volatility of expected returns. A statistic that measures such volatility relative to the S&P 500 Composite is called *beta*. For beta, we relied on the median of the betas of our selected guideline publicly traded companies. This market-derived median beta was 0.90.

Fourth, we added a small stock equity risk premium. The beta calculations are based on comparison of returns of individual securities versus the return of the entire market. Beta, however, does not include all of the size risk present in companies that are smaller than those used to calculate the market beta. Thus, return on equity for companies with a capitalization below the market average must be increased to account for the size difference.

According to the data provided in Ibbotson Associates SBBI '04, the appropriate size decile for Employer is the smallest size decile—that is, size decile 10. The largest company in decile 10 has a capitalization of $141.5 million, which is nearly 10 times the estimated Employer capitalization. Companies in decile 10 should have an additional 5.67 percent added to their cost of equity to account for their smaller size. Therefore, we added an additional 5.67 percent based on the 10 size equity risk premium data to the cost of equity capital.

An additional unsystematic (i.e., company-specific) risk premium is often appropriate to reflect risks specific to an investment in a particular closely held company. Based on: (1) the smaller size of the Company relative to the companies used by Ibbotson Associates to calculate the small stock premium, (2) the Company dependence on Frederick Founder, (3) the lack of diversification of the Company's product line, (4) the risk associated with meeting the management-prepared income projections, and (5) other qualitative factors, we included a 3.0 percent company-specific equity risk premium in our estimation of the appropriate cost of equity.

As presented in Exhibit 14, the combination of these factors results in a cost of equity capital of 20.1 percent for the Company.

Cost of Debt. We derived the Employer cost of debt capital by reviewing the current interest rate costs of the Company's debt structure as of the latest reporting period prior to the Valuation Date. The actual Employer pretax cost of debt is 4.25 percent.

Because debt is tax deductible, we adjusted the rate for an estimated income tax rate of 43 percent. This 43 percent income tax rate is based on the Company's tax rate implicit in management's projections. This after-tax adjustment is appropriate since the interim cash flows and terminal values were estimated on an after-tax basis.

As presented in Exhibit 14, the after-tax cost of Employer debt is 2.4 percent. We used this 2.4 percent as the Company's cost of debt.

Weighted Average Cost of Capital. We relied on the Employer capital structure in estimating the Company weighted average cost of capital. We estimated that the appropriate debt to total capital for Employer was approximately 15.0 percent.

Based on this weighting, the Employer WACC (based on a 2.4 percent cost of debt and a 20.1 percent cost of equity), is 17.4 percent.

Discounted Cash Flow Method Value Indication

The total of the discrete cash flow value and the terminal value is $14,492,000, as presented in Exhibit 11. This amount represents the indicated Employer market value of invested capital.

Subtracting the Employer interest-bearing debt of $1,807,000, indicates the value of the Employer common stock, as of December 31, 2004, is $12,690,000, before consideration of any applicable valuation adjustments.

Guideline Merged and Acquired Company Method Analysis

The principal procedures in the guideline merged and acquired company method are described as follows:

- the identification and selection of guideline merged and acquired companies;
- the determination of the actual cash equivalent transaction price for each selected merger or acquisition transaction;
- the selection of appropriate market derived pricing multiples to be applied to the subject company financial fundamentals;
- the calculation of one or more value indications for the subject company based on the selected transaction-based pricing multiples;
- the selection of the relative emphasis (weight) to place on each of the resulting value indications; and
- the estimation of an overall value indication from this method.

Selection of the Guideline Merged and Acquired Companies

To begin our search for guideline merged and acquired companies, we determined the appropriate Standard Industrial Classification (SIC) codes for Employer. As previously discussed, Employer most closely resembles companies in the SIC code 3021—Rubber and Plastics Footwear, and SIC code 3100—Leather and Leather Products.

The following is the description of the single guideline merged and acquired company we selected:

Teva Sport Sandals, Inc.

(Teva) sells footwear and apparel through a catalog and an on-line website. On November 25, 2002, Deckers acquired (1) the worldwide Teva patents, trademarks, and other assets from Mark Thatcher and (2) certain assets and liabilities of Teva. The price paid for Teva's assets was $62.3 million. Teva is Employer's primary competitor in its core market. Prior to the acquisition, Deckers was selling the Teva line of sport sandals under license agreements with Mr. Thatcher.

As discussed above, sales of Teva footwear accounts for approximately two-thirds of Deckers' total sales. At the time of the acquisition, Deckers expected that its fiscal 2004 EBITDA would increase approximately $6 million. This expected increase is due primarily to the elimination of approximately $5 million of minimum annual royalty payments.

Invested Capital Valuation Procedures

As previously discussed, invested capital valuation procedures are commonly used in the valuation of closely held companies. These procedures are used in order to minimize capital structure differences between the subject company—Employer—and the selected guideline merged and acquired companies. The greater the differences between the capital structure of the subject company and the guideline merged and acquired companies, the more important it is to use invested capital valuation procedures.

We considered the following invested capital valuation pricing multiples in our analysis:

1. MVIC/LTM EBIT
2. MVIC/Projected EBITDA
3. MVIC/LTM EBITDA
4. MVE/Net income

As presented in Exhibit 15, the guideline merged and acquired company method indicates that the value of the Employer common stock, as of December 31, 2004, is $15,722,000, before consideration of any applicable valuation adjustments.

Discount for Lack of Control

The value indicated by the guideline merged and acquired company method represents a marketable, controlling ownership interest level of value. This is because the valuation pricing multiples are derived from control event ownership transition transaction.

Since our subject is a noncontrolling ownership interest in Employer, we adjusted the guideline merged and acquired company method value indication to reflect the value of a noncontrolling ownership interest. We selected the appropriate discount for lack of control adjustment by analyzing control price premium empirical evidence.

The empirical support for a discount for lack of ownership control is substantial. The holder of a noncontrolling ownership interest in Employer cannot unilaterally (1) compel payment of special dividends, (2) force the liquidation of the Company, or (3) sell any of the Company assets. In short, the holder of the a noncontrolling ownership interest in Employer common stock does not have any control over Company affairs.

A willing buyer contemplating a purchase from a willing seller of the noncontrolling ownership interest in Employer would experience these same elements of lack of control. Therefore, regardless of the Employer controlling ownership interest value, a willing buyer will not purchase a noncontrolling ownership interest except at a price discount from the proportionate share of the Company total common stock value.

The most appropriate procedure to quantify a discount for lack of control is to examine tender offer data. Fellows and Painter articulated the conceptual basis for such an analysis by pointing out that:

> In fact, there are only differing degrees of control; when control is entirely absent, there is only its absence. . . . A minority discount, then, is a corollary of a majority premium and depends on the latter for its validity. A discount for lack of control is only appropriate if the amount discounted already includes a majority premium.

The common evidence of the appropriate discount for lack of control is the study of cash tender offers. By looking at price premiums offered during an acquisition tender offer for control of a publicly traded company, analysts approximate the value difference between controlling and noncontrolling ownership interests.

In studies performed by Willamette Management Associates and others, controlling ownership interest price premiums vary widely, with the median price premium of approximately 45 percent to 50 percent over the average public market price in the months just prior to the tender announcement. The high end of the range is usually a price premium of over 100 percent and the low end of the range is usually a discount of about 10 percent, both extremes clearly indicating special factors involved. A price premium for ownership control of 45 percent to 50 percent is mathematically equivalent to a discount for lack of control of about 30 percent to 35 percent.

According to *Mergerstat Review*, the average acquisition price premium paid over the pre-tender offer market price in publicly traded company acquisitions was approximately 60 percent in 2003.[1]

Table 2 presents a 10-year summary of acquisition price premiums, and the implied discounts for lack of control, as calculated by *Mergerstat Review:*

Table 2

Employer, Inc.
Acquisition Price Premium Data
and Implied Discounts for Lack of Control

Historical Price Premium Data

Year	Acquisition Price Premium	Implied Discount for Lack of Control	Number of Acquisition Transactions
1994	41.9%	29.5%	260
1995	44.7%	30.9%	324
1996	36.6%	26.8%	381
1997	35.7%	26.3%	487
1998	40.7%	28.9%	512
1999	43.3%	30.2%	723
2000	49.2%	33.0%	574
2001	57.2%	36.4%	439
2002	59.7%	37.4%	326
2003	62.3%	38.4%	371

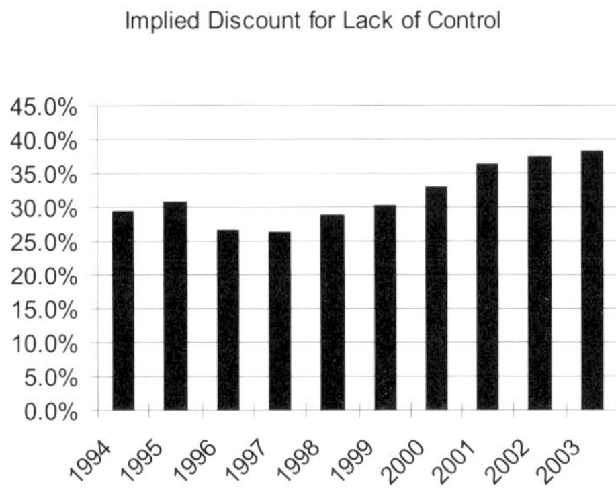

Source: *Mergerstat Review 2004* (Santa Monica, CA: FactSet Mergerstat, LLC, 2004).

The 2003 mean acquisition price premium of 62.3 percent equates to a discount for lack of control of approximately 38.4 percent. The discount for lack of control is calculated as (1 - 1 ÷ (1 + acquisition price premium). The 10-year median acquisition price premium from 1994 to 2003 is 44.0 percent. This average equates to a median discount for lack of control of 30.6 percent.

To estimate the appropriate Employer ownership control price premium, we considered that the Company is significantly more profitable than the median of the guideline publicly traded companies, as presented in Exhibit 7. It is unlikely that a different controlling shareholder would be able to run the Company as efficiently as Employer is currently being managed, given this level of profitability. This factor would indicate a discount for lack of control that is lower than what the above-listed empirical evidence suggests.

In addition, the ownership control price premium data presented above indicate price premiums paid for expected synergistic benefits in addition to stand-alone ownership control benefits. The inclusion of acquisition-specific expected synergistic benefits inflates the ownership control premium (and the discount for lack of control) data. Since the standard of value for this valuation is fair market value, and that standard assumes a hypothetical willing buyer, the synergistic portion of the ownership control premium data should not be included when calculating a discount for lack of control. This factor would also indicate a discount for lack of control lower than that indicated by the above-listed empirical data.

In summary, in our opinion, a discount for lack of control of 15 percent (i.e., a discount below the average discount implied by the published ownership control price premium studies), is appropriate for Employer.

Guideline Merged and Acquired Company Method Value Conclusion

Applying a 15 percent discount for lack of control to the marketable, controlling ownership interest value of $15,722,000 (derived from the guideline merged and acquired company method) indicates that the marketable, noncontrolling ownership interest value of the Employer common stock, as of December 31, 2004, is $13,360,000 (rounded).

This valuation analysis is summarized in Exhibit 15.

Valuation Synthesis

As presented on Schedule A, the value indications for the Employer common stock, as of December 31, 2004, range from $12,455,000 to $13,360,000.

In our opinion, each of the three valuation methods used in this analysis provides relevant information regarding the fair market value of Employer common stock. Therefore, we assigned equal weight to each of the three valuation methods as presented in Schedule A. This assignment of equal weight is based on our assessment of the quality and quantity of data underlying each valuation method.

Based on the factors described above, and in our opinion, the fair market value of the Employer common stock, as of the Valuation Date (on a marketable, noncontrolling ownership interest basis), is $12,835,000.

However, there is no active market for the exchange of the Employer common stock. Therefore, we need to consider a discount for lack of marketability with regard to the Subject Stock.

In analyzing the fair market value of privately held company stock for ESOP purposes, a discount for lack of marketability should be considered

This is because the privately held company stock does not have the same liquidity as does publicly traded company stock.

Discounts for lack of marketability are generally based on either (1) restricted stock studies or (2) pre-initial public offering studies. These published empirical studies are consistent in indicating an average discount for lack of marketability ranging from 35 percent to 45 percent.

The factor that distinguishes ESOP-owned shares from non-ESOP-owned shares in a closely held corporation is the "put" option associated with the ESOP-owned shares. A put option requires the employer corporation to repurchase the distributed employer securities. The practical effect of the ESOP put option is to enhance the marketability and liquidity of the plan participant's ownership interest. The economic effect of the ESOP put option is to reduce, or eliminate, the appropriate discount for lack of marketability.

We considered the Employer ESOP put option in selecting the appropriate discount for lack of marketability for the Subject Stock.

In our opinion, given the terms of the ESOP put option and the financial strength of the Company, the appropriate discount for lack of marketability is 10 percent.

Value Conclusion

Based on (1) an indicated marketable, noncontrolling ownership interest value for Employer common stock of $12,835,000 and (2) a discount for lack of marketability of 10 percent, the fair market value of Employer common stock, as of December 31, 2004 (on a nonmarketable noncontrolling ownership interest basis), is $11,552,000, or $11.55 per share.

As of the Valuation Date, the ESOP held 3,127 shares of Employer common stock.

Therefore, the total fair market value of the Employer common stock held by the Employer ESOP, as of December 31, 2004, is $36,117, as presented in Schedule A.

Schedule A

Employer, Inc.
Fair Market Value of Common Stock
Valuation Synthesis and Conclusion
As of December 31, 2004

Valuation Analysis	Exhibit Reference	Value Indication $000	Value Indication Weight	Weighted Value $000
Market Approach--Guideline Publicly Traded Company Method	6	12,455	33.3%	4,152
Income Approach--Discounted Cash Flow Method	11	12,690	33.3%	4,230
Market Approach--Guideline Merged and Acquired Company Method	15	13,360	33.3%	4,453
			100.0%	
Indicated Value of Common Stock (on a marketable, noncontrolling ownership interest basis)				12,835
Less: Discount for Lack of Marketability at 10%				(1,284)
Fair Market Value of Common Stock (on a nonmakretable, noncontrolling ownershpi interest basis)				11,552
Number of Shares Outstanding (000)				1,000
Fair Market Value Per Share (Rounded)				$ 11.55
Number of Common Shares Owned by the ESOP (000)				3.127
Fair Market Value of Common Shares Owned by the ESOP ($)				$ 36,117

Sources: As indicated above, and Willamette Management Associates calculations and estimates.

APPENDIX A
STATEMENT OF CONTINGENT AND LIMITING CONDITIONS

This valuation is subject to the following general contingent and limiting conditions:

1. We assume no responsibility for the legal description or matters including legal or title considerations. Title to the subject stock is assumed to be good and marketable unless otherwise stated.
2. The subject stock is appraised free and clear of any or all liens or encumbrances unless otherwise stated.
3. We assume responsible ownership and competent management with respect to the subject stock.
4. The information furnished by others is believed to be reliable. However, we issue no warranty or other form of assurance regarding its accuracy.
5. We assume no hidden or unapparent conditions regarding the subject stock.
6. We assume that there is full compliance with all applicable federal, state, and local regulations and laws unless the lack of compliance is stated, defined, and considered in the report.
7. We assume that all required licenses, certificates of occupancy, consents, or legislative or administrative authority from any local, state, or national government, or private entity or organization have been or can be obtained or reviewed for any use on which the opinion contained in this report is based.
8. Unless otherwise stated in this report, we did not observe, and we have no knowledge of, the existence of hazardous materials with regard to the subject stock. However, we are not qualified to detect such substances. We assume no responsibility for such conditions or for any expertise required to discover them.
9. Possession of this report does not carry with it the right of publication. It may not be used for any purpose by any person other than the client to whom it is addressed without our written consent, and, in any event, only with proper written qualifications and only in its entirety.
10. We, by reason of this opinion, are not required to give testimony or to be in attendance in court with reference to the subject stock unless arrangements have been previously made.

11. Neither all nor any part of the contents of this report shall be disseminated to the public through advertising, public relations, news, sales, or other media without our prior written consent and approval.
12. The analyses, opinions, and conclusions presented in this report apply to this engagement only and may not be used out of the context presented herein. This report is valid only for the effective date specified herein and only for the purpose specified herein.

APPENDIX B CERTIFICATION

We hereby certify the following statements regarding this valuation analysis:

1. We have not personally inspected the subject stock.
2. We have no present or prospective future interest in the subject stock.
3. We have no personal interest or bias with respect to the subject matter of this report or the parties involved.
4. Our compensation for this analysis is in no way contingent upon the value reported or upon any predetermined value.
5. To the best of our knowledge and belief, the statements of facts contained in this report, upon which the analyses, conclusions, and opinions expressed herein are based, are true and correct.
6. Aaron Analyst provided significant professional assistance regarding the analyses, opinions, and conclusions set forth in this report.
7. The reported analyses, opinions, and conclusions are limited only by the reported contingent and limiting conditions, and they represent our unbiased professional analyses, opinions, and conclusions.
8. The reported analyses, opinions, and conclusions were developed, and this report has been prepared, in conformity with the requirements of the professional organizations of which we are members.
9. Disclosure of the contents of this valuation report is subject to the requirements of the professional organizations of which we are members related to review by their duly authorized representatives.

APPENDIX C

PROFESSIONAL QUALIFICATIONS OF THE PRINCIPAL ANALYST—PETER PRINCIPAL, CPA/ABV, CBA

Peter Principal is a principal of Willamette Management Associates. His practice includes valuation consulting, economic analysis, and financial advisory services.

Peter has performed the following types of valuation assignments: gift tax appraisals, estate tax valuations, ESOP feasibility studies and appraisals, business and stock valuations, divestiture and spin-off valuations, litigation support appraisals, merger and acquisition valuations, fairness opinions, solvency analyses, post-acquisition purchase price allocation appraisals, ad valorem assessment appeal appraisals, intangible asset appraisals, marital dissolution valuations, economic damage calculations, and appraisal review. He has also provided expert witness testimony at deposition and in court.

Peter has valued the following types of business entities and securities: closely held corporations—entity value, closely held corporations—noncontrolling ownership interests, public corporations—restricted stock, complex capital structures (various classes of common/preferred stock, options, warrants), general and limited partnership interests, joint ventures, proprietorships, professional services corporations, professional practices, LLPs and LLCs, license agreements, and franchises.

Peter has performed business and stock appraisals in the following industries: accounting, advertising, agriculture, apparel, automobile dealerships, aviation, banking, broadcasting, brokerage, cable television, cellular telephone, cement, chemical, communications, computer services, construction and contracting, distribution, education, entertainment, equipment leasing, fast food, food service, forest products, retail grocery stores, health care, high-tech, hotel and hospitality, insurance, leasing, manufacturing, medical and dental practice, mining, money management, newspaper, pharmaceuticals, plastics, printing, publishing, railroads, ranching, real estate holding companies, recreational services, restaurant, retailing, shipping, telecommunications, television broadcasting, textiles, transportation and trucking, and wholesaling.

In addition, Peter has managed engagements requiring the quantification of the value and/or remaining useful life for the following types of intangible assets: certificates of need, computer software, customer relationships, employment contracts, favorable leases, franchise agreements, going-concern value, goodwill, in-process research and development, medical charts and records, noncompete covenants, patent applications, royalty agreements, trained and assembled workforce, trademarks, and trade names.

Previous Experience

Before joining Willamette Management Associates, Peter was a senior consultant in the financial consulting group for Ernst & Young, an international accounting firm. During his employment with Ernst & Young, Peter completed several business and stock valuations and litigation support appraisals.

Prior to that, Peter was a securities analyst with Edward D. Jones & Co., a national brokerage firm. During his employment with Edward D. Jones & Co., Peter valued publicly traded securities and made purchase and sale recommendations to stockbrokers.

Education

Master of Business Administration, Finance, Washington University Graduate School of Business

Bachelor of Science, Business Administration, Finance, University of Missouri at Columbia

Professional Affiliations

Peter is a certified public accountant and is accredited in business valuation (CPA/ABV) by the American Institute of Certified Public Accountants. Peter is also a certified business appraiser (CBA).

Notes:

1. *Mergerstat Review 2004* (Santa Monica, CA: FactSet Mergerstat, LLC, 2004).

Exhibit 1a

Employer, Inc.
Balance Sheets

	As of December 31,					As of December 31,				
	2004	2003	2002	2001	2000	2004	2003	2002	2001	2000
	$	$	$	$	$	%	%	%	%	%
ASSETS										
Current Assets:										
Cash	18,334	93,004	47,817	-	240,717	0.4	2.8	1.9	-	19.4
Accounts Receivable	406,665	470,203	335,922	155,453	84,720	8.5	14.0	13.2	11.2	6.8
Inventories	3,101,425	1,972,259	1,705,130	922,066	681,094	65.1	58.9	66.9	66.6	54.9
Prepaid Expenses	62,244	-	-	-	779	1.3	-	-	-	0.1
Total Current Assets	3,588,668	2,535,466	2,088,869	1,077,519	1,007,310	75.4	75.7	82.0	77.8	81.1
Fixed Assets, Cost:										
Machinery and Equipment	493,019	374,406	NA	NA	NA	10.4	11.2	NA	NA	NA
Furniture and Office Equipment	959,918	603,350	NA	NA	NA	20.2	18.0	NA	NA	NA
Leasehold Improvements	102,209	79,250	NA	NA	NA	2.1	2.4	NA	NA	NA
Sandal Molds	432,820	321,884	NA	NA	NA	9.1	9.6	NA	NA	NA
Total Fixed Assets	1,987,966	1,378,890	NA	NA	NA	41.7	41.2	NA	NA	NA
Accumulated Depreciation	(859,005)	(564,195)	NA	NA	NA	(18.0)	(16.8)	NA	NA	NA
Net Fixed Assets	1,128,961	814,695	459,035	306,137	234,110	23.7	24.3	18.0	22.1	18.9
Other Assets:										
Unamortized Loan Fees	-	-	292	632	-	-	-	0.0	0.0	-
Deposits	44,487	-	-	-	-	0.9	-	-	-	-
Total Other Assets	44,487	-	292	632	-	0.9	-	0.0	0.0	-
TOTAL ASSETS	4,762,116	3,350,161	2,548,196	1,384,288	1,241,420	100.0	100.0	100.0	100.0	100.0

Exhibit 1b

Employer, Inc.
Balance Sheets

	As of December 31,					As of December 31,				
	2004	2003	2002	2001	2000	2004	2003	2002	2001	2000
	$	$	$	$	$	%	%	%	%	%
LIABILITIES & EQUITY										
Liabilities:										
Current Liabilities:										
Checks in Excess of Bank Balance	-	-	-	40,155	-	-	-	-	2.9	-
Accounts Payable	432,998	366,905	343,624	123,528	138,850	9.1	11.0	13.5	8.9	11.2
Taxes Payable	38,769	26,122	26,426	180,566	263,650	0.8	0.8	1.0	13.0	21.2
Accrued Wages	188,420	204,274	109,322	31,493	16,268	4.0	6.1	4.3	2.3	1.3
Accrued Interest	2,358	1,721	575	2,974	2,114	0.0	0.1	0.0	0.2	0.2
Line of Credit	1,754,745	800,000	493,156	407,734	2,282	36.8	23.9	19.4	29.5	0.2
Current Portion of Long-Term Debt	100,000	86,994	33,520	23,708	-	2.1	2.6	1.3	1.7	-
Total Current Liabilities	2,517,290	1,486,016	1,006,623	810,158	423,164	52.9	44.4	39.5	58.5	34.1
Long-Term Debt	794,297	453,840	67,287	32,647	97,265	16.7	13.5	2.6	2.4	7.8
Total Liabilities	3,311,587	1,939,856	1,073,910	842,805	520,428	69.5	57.9	42.1	60.9	41.9
Equity:										
Common Stock	3,286	3,286	3,286	3,286	3,286	0.1	0.1	0.1	0.2	0.3
Retained Earnings	1,447,243	1,407,019	1,471,000	538,197	717,706	30.4	42.0	57.7	38.9	57.8
Total Equity	1,450,529	1,410,305	1,474,286	541,483	720,992	30.5	42.1	57.9	39.1	58.1
TOTAL LIABILITIES & EQUITY	4,762,116	3,350,161	2,548,196	1,384,288	1,241,420	100.0	100.0	100.0	100.0	100.0

Sources: Reviewed financial statements for the years ended December 31, 2003 and 2004, compiled financial statements for 2001 and 2002, internally prepared financial statements for 2000, and Willamette Management Associates calculations.

Exhibit 2a

Employer, Inc.
Income Statements

	Fiscal Years Ended December 31,					Fiscal Years Ended December 31,				
	2004	2003	2002	2001	2000	2004	2003	2002	2001	2000
	$	$	$	$	$	%	%	%	%	%
Revenue	11,771,106	10,552,035	7,858,516	4,941,333	3,408,262	100.0	100.0	100.0	100.0	100.0
Growth Rate	*11.6%*	*34.3%*	*59.0%*	*45.0%*	*108.6%*					
Cost of Goods Sold:										
Beginning Inventories	1,972,259	1,705,130	922,066	681,094	NA	16.8	16.2	11.7	13.8	NA
Purchases	4,179,589	3,196,744	2,743,939	1,502,143	NA	35.5	30.3	34.9	30.4	NA
Direct Labor	1,138,542	1,593,180	1,330,106	805,551	NA	9.7	15.1	16.9	16.3	NA
Manufacturing Overhead	1,654,082	814,548	591,503	410,911	NA	14.1	7.7	7.5	8.3	NA
Unabsorbed Manufacturing Exp.	312,935	-	-	-	NA	2.7	-	-	-	NA
Ending Inventories	(3,101,425)	(2,059,326)	(1,738,933)	(922,066)	NA	(26.3)	(19.5)	(22.1)	(18.7)	NA
Total Cost of Goods Sold	6,155,982	5,250,276	3,848,681	2,477,633	1,250,677	52.3	49.8	49.0	50.1	36.7
Gross Profit	5,615,124	5,301,759	4,009,835	2,463,700	2,157,585	47.7	50.2	51.0	49.9	63.3
Operating Expenses:										
Selling and Shipping Expenses:										
Commissions	951,676	861,575	661,079	397,530	NA	8.1	8.2	8.4	8.0	NA
Sales Wages	581,378	208,689	195,464	113,025	NA	4.9	2.0	2.5	2.3	NA
Advertising and Promotion	453,247	318,235	173,764	120,023	NA	3.9	3.0	2.2	2.4	NA
Depreciation/Amortization	-	36,250	26,613	22,549	NA	-	0.3	0.3	0.5	NA
Other Selling and Shipping	480,065	267,164	189,992	248,625	NA	4.1	2.5	2.4	5.0	NA
Total Selling and Shipping	2,466,366	1,691,913	1,246,912	901,752	NA	21.0	16.0	15.9	18.2	NA

Exhibit 2b

Employer, Inc.
Income Statements

	Fiscal Years Ended December 31,					Fiscal Years Ended December 31,				
	2004	2003	2002	2001	2000	2004	2003	2002	2001	2000
	$	$	$	$	$	%	%	%	%	%
Administrative and General:										
Salaries & Wages	500,670	1,081,858	828,748	481,846	NA	4.3	10.3	10.5	9.8	NA
Employee Benefits	72,082	218,747	70,193	56,977	NA	0.6	2.1	0.9	1.2	NA
ESOP Contribution	23,761	27,831	-	-	NA	0.2	0.3	-	-	NA
ESOP Administration	22,332	12,000	-	-	NA	0.2	0.1	-	-	NA
Depreciation/Amortization	106,518	36,542	27,454	28,503	NA	0.9	0.3	0.3	0.6	NA
Other Administrative and General	511,075	665,476	604,966	345,858	NA	4.3	6.3	7.7	7.0	NA
Total Administrative and General	1,236,438	2,042,454	1,531,361	913,184	NA	10.5	19.4	19.5	18.5	NA
Product Development	507,960	-	-	-	NA	4.3	-	-	-	NA
Total Operating Expenses	4,210,764	3,734,367	2,778,273	1,814,936	1,334,865	35.8	35.4	35.4	36.7	39.2
Operating Income	1,404,360	1,567,392	1,231,562	648,764	822,720	11.9	14.9	15.7	13.1	24.1
Growth Rate	*-10.4%*	*27.3%*	*89.8%*	*-21.1%*	*197.2%*					

Exhibit 2c

Employer, Inc.
Income Statements

	Fiscal Years Ended December 31,					Fiscal Years Ended December 31,				
	2004	2003	2002	2001	2000	2004	2003	2002	2001	2000
	$	$	$	$	$	%	%	%	%	%
Other Recurring Income (Expense):										
Interest Expense	(76,299)	(44,507)	(62,156)	(31,042)	(23,642)	(0.6)	(0.4)	(0.8)	(0.6)	(0.7)
Gain on Disposition of Assets	-	4,736	2,000	-	NA	-	0.0	0.0	-	NA
Gain on Items Destroyed in Fire	-	-	2,628	-	NA	-	-	0.0	-	NA
Currency Translation	27,475	-	-	-	NA	0.2	-	-	-	NA
Loss on Obsolete Molds	(43,144)	-	-	-	NA	(0.4)	-	-	-	NA
Interest Income	-	2,574	-	2,258	NA	-	0.0	-	0.0	NA
Other	21,223	-	-	-	7,699	0.2	-	-	-	0.2
Total Other Recurring	(70,745)	(37,197)	(57,528)	(28,784)	(15,943)	(0.6)	(0.4)	(0.7)	(0.6)	(0.5)
Pretax Income	1,333,615	1,530,195	1,174,034	619,980	806,777	11.3	14.5	14.9	12.5	23.7
Growth Rate	*-12.8%*	*30.3%*	*89.4%*	*-23.2%*	*208.3%*					
Income Taxes	-	-	-	-	(290,440)	-	-	-	-	(8.5)
Net Income	1,333,615	1,530,195	1,174,034	619,980	516,337	11.3	14.5	14.9	12.5	15.1

Sources: Reviewed financial statements for the years ended December 31, 2003 and 2004, compiled financial statements for 2001 and 2002, internally prepared financial statements for 2000, and Willamette Management Associates calculations.

Exhibit 3a

Employer, Inc.
Statements of Cash Flows

	Fiscal Years Ended December 31,			
	2004	2003	2002	2001
	$	$	$	$
OPERATING ACTIVITIES:				
Net Income	1,333,615	1,530,195	1,174,034	619,980
Adjustments to reconcile net income to net cash provided by operating activities:				
Depreciation and Amortization	307,857	163,788	121,812	108,451
Loss on Disposition of Assets	43,144	(4,736)	(4,628)	-
Net change in operating assets and liabilities:				
Accounts Receivable	63538	(134,281)	(180,469)	(70,733)
Inventory	(1,129,166)	(267,129)	(783,064)	(240,972)
Prepaid Expenses and Deposits	(106,731)	-	-	-
Accounts Payable	66,093	23,281	220,099	(37,542)
Taxes Payable	12,647	(304)	(154,140)	139,682
Accrued Expenses	(15,217)	96,098	75,430	17,912
Net cash provided by operating activities	575,780	1,406,912	469,074	536,778
INVESTING ACTIVITIES:				
Proceeds from Sale of Capital Assets	-	-	2,000	-
Insurance Proceeds from Items Destroyed in Fire	-	12,873	61,703	-
Expenditures to Replace Items Destroyed in Fire	-	(8,137)	(65,384)	-
Capital Expenditures	(665,267)	(519,156)	(268,064)	(230,312)
Net cash used in investing activities	(665,267)	(514,420)	(269,745)	(230,312)

Exhibit 3b

Employer, Inc.
Statements of Cash Flows

	2004 $	2003 $	2002 $	2001 $
FINANCING ACTIVITIES:				
Decrease of Checks In Excess of Bank Balance	-	-	(40,155)	40,155
Proceeds of Short-Term Borrowing	4,826,803	4,125,910	592,916	407,734
Repayments of Short-Term Borrowings	(3,872,058)	(3,819,066)	(507,495)	-
Proceeds of Long-Term Borrowing	500,000	593,158	79,713	
Repayments of Long-Term Borrowings	(146,537)	(153,131)	(35,260)	(20,414)
Shareholder Distributions	(1,293,391)	(1,594,176)	(241,231)	(1,002,637)
Net cash used in financing activities	14,817	(847,305)	(151,512)	(575,162)
NET INCREASE (DECREASE) IN CASH	(74,670)	45,187	47,817	(268,696)
CASH, BEGINNING OF YEAR	93,004	47,817	-	268,696
CASH, END OF YEAR	18,334	93,004	47,817	-
INTEREST PAID	75,662	43,362	64,554	28,354

NOTE: Statement of cash flows not available for 2000.

Sources: Reviewed financial statements for the years ended December 31, 2003 and 2004, compiled financial statements for 2001 and 2002, and Willamette Management Associates calculations.

Exhibit 4a

Employer, Inc.
Adjustments to Income and
Market Value of Invested Capital Financial Fundamentals

	Fiscal Years Ended December 31,				
	2004	2003	2002	2001	2000
	$	$	$	$	$
Revenue [a]	11,771,106	10,552,035	7,858,516	4,941,333	3,408,262
Reported Pretax Income [a]	1,333,615	1,530,195	1,174,034	619,980	806,777
Adjustments to Net Income:					
Loss (Gain) on Disposition of Assets	43,144	(4,736)	(4,628)	-	-
Total Adjustments	43,144	(4,736)	(4,628)	-	-
Adjusted Pretax Income	1,376,759	1,525,459	1,169,406	619,980	806,777
(1 - income tax rate) [b]	0.57	0.57	0.57	0.57	0.57
Adjusted Net Income	784,753	869,512	666,561	353,389	459,863
Market Value of Invested Capital Financial Fundamentals:					
Adjusted Pretax Income	1,376,759	1,525,459	1,169,406	619,980	806,777
Plus Interest Expense [a]	76,299	44,507	62,156	31,042	23,642
Equals Earnings before Interest and Taxes (EBIT)	1,453,058	1,569,966	1,231,562	651,022	830,419
Plus Depreciation/Amortization [a]	307,857	163,788	121,812	108,451	50,142
Equals Earnings before Interest, Taxes, Depr. & Amort. (EBITDA)	1,760,915	1,733,754	1,353,374	759,473	880,562

Exhibit 4b

Employer, Inc.
Adjustments to Income and
Market Value of Invested Capital Financial Fundamentals

	Fiscal Years Ended December 31,					
	2004		2003	2002	2001	2000
	$		$	$	$	$
Balance Sheet Financial Fundamentals December 31, 2004:						
Book Value of Equity ($)		Interest-Bearing Debt ($)				
Book Value of Common Equity	1,450,529	Line of Credit [c]				912,301
Book Value of Preferred Equity	-	Long-Term Debt				894,297
Total Book Value of Equity	1,450,529	Total Interest-Bearing Debt				1,306,598
Tangible Book Value of Equity	1,450,529					
Ending Number of Shares Outstanding	1,000,000					
Tangible Book Value Common Equity Per Share	1.45					

[a] As presented on Exhibit 2.
[b] Based on Company management projections.
[c] Average line of credit balance for the months January 2004 through December 2004.

Sources: Exhibits 1, 2, 3, and Willamette Management Associates calculations.

Exhibit 5

Employer, Inc.
Financial and Operating Ratio Analysis

	Fiscal Years Ended December 31,				
Financial and Operating Ratios	2004	2003	2002	2001	2000
LIQUIDITY RATIOS					
Current Ratio	1.4	1.7	2.1	1.3	2.4
Quick Ratio	0.2	0.4	0.4	0.2	0.8
Working Capital ($)	1,071,378	1,049,450	1,082,246	267,361	584,146
Invested Capital ($)	2,244,826	1,864,145	1,541,573	574,130	818,256
ACTIVITY RATIOS					
Sales/Average Receivables	26.8	26.2	32.0	41.1	39.2
Days in Receivables	14	14	11	9	9
Cost of Sales/Inventory	2.4	2.9	2.9	3.1	2.3
Days in Inventory	150.4	127.8	124.6	118.1	161.8
Working Capital Turnover	11.1	9.9	11.6	11.6	11.7
Fixed Asset Turnover	12.1	16.6	20.5	18.3	22.6
Asset Turnover	2.9	3.6	4.0	3.8	3.1
COVERAGE/LEVERAGE RATIOS					
Interest Expense Coverage [a]:					
EBIT	19.0	35.3	19.8	21.0	35.1
EBITDA	23.1	39.0	21.8	24.5	37.2
Cash Flow/Cur. Mat. LTD [a]	0.6	1.2	1.5	1.1	223.5
Fixed Assets/Equity	0.8	0.6	0.3	0.6	0.3
Equity/Invested Capital (%)	64.6	75.7	95.6	94.3	88.1
PROFITABILITY RATIOS (%) [a]					
Pretax Income/Average Equity	96.2	105.8	116.0	98.2	154.3
Pretax Income/Average Assets	33.9	51.7	59.5	47.2	73.8
Pretax Income/Sales	11.7	14.5	14.9	12.5	23.7
Net Income/Average Equity	54.9	60.3	66.1	56.0	87.9
Net Income/Average Assets	19.3	29.5	33.9	26.9	42.1
Net Income/Sales	6.7	8.2	8.5	7.2	13.5
Cash Flow/Average Equity	76.4	71.6	78.2	73.2	97.5
Cash Flow/Average Assets	26.9	35.0	40.1	35.2	46.6
Cash Flow/Sales	9.3	9.8	10.0	9.3	15.0
EBIT/Avg Invested Capital	70.7	92.2	116.4	93.5	101.5
EBITDA/Avg Invested Capital	85.7	101.8	127.9	109.1	107.6

LTD = Long-term debt
EBIT = Earnings before interest and taxes
EBITDA = Earnings before interest, taxes, depreciation & amortization
Cash flow = Net income plus Depreciation expense
Invested capital = Equity plus Interest-bearing debt
NA = Not available
[a] Coverage and profitability ratios are based on pretax and after-tax income adjusted per Exhibit 4.

Sources: Exhibits 1, 2, 4, and Willamette Management Associates calculations.

Exhibit 6a

Employer, Inc.
Guideline Publicly Traded Company Method
Value Summary

Financial Fundamental	Employer, Inc. $000	Market-Derived Pricing Multiples High	Low	Median	Selected Pricing Multiple [a]
Earnings before Interest and Taxes					
Projected	2,209	13.9	4.7	12.9	9.7
Latest 12 Months	1,453	15.3	9.7	10.4	7.8
Earnings before Interest, Taxes, Depreciation, and Amortization					
Projected	2,648	13.9	4.6	10.0	7.5
Latest 12 Months	1,761	13.8	8.4	9.5	7.1
Net Income					
Projected	1,297	21.6	7.7	14.5	10.9
Latest 12 Months	785	24.6	11.8	15.9	11.9
Revenue	11,771	2.15	0.72	1.09	1.12

Exhibit 6b

Employer, Inc.
Guideline Publicly Traded Company Method
Value Summary

Financial Fundamental	Market Value of Invested Capital $000	Less: Interest-Bearing Debt $000	Market Value of Equity $000	Value Indication Weight	Weighted Value Indication $000
Earnings before Interest and Taxes					
Projected	21,381	(1,807)	19,575	0.10	1,957
Latest 12 Months	11,361	(1,807)	9,554	0.15	1,433
Earnings before Interest, Taxes, Depreciation, and Amortization					
Projected	19,788	(1,807)	17,982	0.10	1,798
Latest 12 Months	12,537	(1,807)	10,730	0.15	1,610
Net Income					
Projected			14,143	0.10	1,414
Latest 12 Months			9,345	0.15	1,402
Revenue	13,171	(1,807)	11,364	0.25	2,841
				1.00	
Indicated Value of Common Stock (on a marketable, noncontrolling ownership interest basis)					12,455

[a] The earnings multiples selected are equal to 75% of the median due to the Employer smaller size, lack of product diversification, dependence on key management, and other qualitative factors. The revenue multiple selected is based on comparison of Employer profitability and the profitability of the selected guideline publicly traded companies.

Sources: Exhibit 10 and Willamette Management Associates calculations.

Exhibit 7a

Employer, Inc.
Guideline Publicly Traded Company Method
Common-Size Financial Statements

Financial Fundamentals	Deckers Outdoor Co. 12/31/03 %	K-Swiss 12/31/04 %	Lacrosse Footwear 10/31/03 %	Maxwell Shoe Co. 10/31/04 %	Rocky Shoes &Boots 12/31/03 %
BALANCE SHEET					
ASSETS					
Cash & Equivalents	3.2	34.7	-	56.1	6.3
Accounts Receivable	17.0	21.7	25.1	24.5	24.1
Inventory	13.9	31.4	38.6	8.2	33.9
Other Current Assets	2.2	3.3	7.2	1.3	2.7
Total Current Assets	36.4	91.2	70.9	90.1	66.9
Fixed Assets (at Cost)	7.9	7.4	35.9	8.1	66.1
Acc. Depreciation	(4.8)	(3.7)	(27.7)	(5.9)	(38.3)
Net Fixed Assets	3.2	3.7	8.2	2.3	27.8
Intangible Assets	57.8	3.1	17.7	8.4	2.4
Other Assets	2.6	2.1	3.2	(0.8)	2.9
TOTAL ASSETS	100.0	100.0	100.0	100.0	100.0
LIABILITIES & EQUITY					
Accounts Payable	10.6	8.3	7.7	0.8	2.4
Accrued Expenses	2.7	7.3	4.8	5.5	2.8
Current Portion LTD	3.2	-	2.6	-	0.7
Other Interest-Bearing Debt	-	-	13.8	-	-
Other Current Liabilities	1.6	-	-	0.7	(0.0)
Total Current Liabilities	18.1	15.6	28.9	7.1	5.9
Long-Term Debt	28.7	-	4.6	-	15.3
Deferred Income Tax	-	1.4	1.1	1.4	-
Other Liabilities	-	6.5	7.7	-	2.2
Total Liabilities	46.7	23.5	42.3	8.5	23.4
Stockholder's Equity	53.3	76.5	57.7	91.5	76.6
TOTAL LIABILITIES & EQUITY	100.0	100.0	100.0	100.0	100.0
SIZE					
Assets ($Mill)	122.4	234.6	60.8	173.0	68.4
Revenues ($Mill)	99.1	429.2	97.8	225.0	89.0
MVIC ($Mill)	238.4	854.1	67.9	251.6	135.6
INCOME STATEMENTS					
Revenue	100.0	100.0	100.0	100.0	100.0
Operating Expenses	55.5	54.9	71.2	73.2	69.1
Gross Margin	44.5	45.1	28.8	26.8	30.9
General & Administrative Expenses	35.4	24.1	27.5	15.8	21.0
Depreciation Expense	2.6	0.4	3.2	0.8	4.5
Operating Profit	6.5	20.6	(1.8)	10.2	5.4
Interest Expense	0.3	0.1	1.8	-	1.6
Other Income (Expenses), Net	(0.1)	-	0.2	0.6	0.5
Pretax Income	6.1	20.5	(3.5)	10.7	4.3
Income Taxes	2.6	8.0	(1.2)	4.1	1.1
NET INCOME	3.5	12.5	(2.2)	6.7	3.2

LTD = Long-term debt

Sources: Forms 10-K and Exhibits 1, 2, 4, and Willamette Management Associates calculations.

Exhibit 7b

Employer, Inc.
Guideline Publicly Traded Company Method
Common-Size Financial Statements

Financial Fundamentals	Saucony 1/3/04 %	Vans, Inc. 5/31/04 %	Weyco Group 12/31/03 %	Median %	Employer, Inc. 12/31/04 %
BALANCE SHEET					
ASSETS					
Cash & Equivalents	39.4	22.2	6.4	6.4	0.4
Accounts Receivable	17.7	10.8	22.0	21.7	8.5
Inventory	31.1	26.9	34.0	31.1	65.1
Other Current Assets	4.0	6.2	2.9	2.9	1.3
Total Current Assets	92.2	66.1	65.3	66.9	75.4
Fixed Assets (at Cost)	22.0	25.1	21.3	21.3	41.7
Acc. Depreciation	(15.5)	(14.6)	(6.1)	(6.1)	(18.0)
Net Fixed Assets	6.5	10.6	15.2	6.5	23.7
Intangible Assets	1.0	19.9	7.4	7.4	-
Other Assets	0.3	3.5	12.1	2.6	0.9
TOTAL ASSETS	100.0	100.0	100.0	100.0	100.0
LIABILITIES & EQUITY					
Accounts Payable	9.8	10.3	7.7	7.7	9.1
Accrued Expenses	8.9	5.6	5.8	5.5	4.8
Current Portion LTD	-	-	-	-	2.1
Other Interest-Bearing Debt	-	-	-	-	36.8
Other Current Liabilities	-	5.5	0.3	-	-
Total Current Liabilities	18.7	21.4	13.8	15.6	52.9
Long-Term Debt	-	1.1	25.9	1.1	16.7
Deferred Income Tax	2.1	1.0	2.3	1.1	-
Other Liabilities	0.7	0.7	-	0.7	-
Total Liabilities	21.5	24.2	42.0	23.5	69.5
Stockholder's Equity	78.5	75.8	58.0	75.8	30.5
TOTAL LIABILITIES & EQUITY	100.0	100.0	100.0	100.0	100.0
SIZE					
Assets ($Mill)	87.5	237.8	146.2	-	4.8
Revenues ($Mill)	133.5	330.2	181.2	-	11.8
MVIC ($Mill)	105.3	205.5	227.8	-	-
INCOME STATEMENTS					
Revenue	100.0	100.0	100.0	100.0	100.0
Operating Expenses	64.2	51.7	66.3	64.2	52.3
Gross Margin	35.8	48.3	33.7	33.7	47.7
General & Administrative Expenses	27.9	45.4	20.8	24.1	33.2
Depreciation Expense	1.2	3.2	1.2	1.2	2.6
Operating Profit	6.6	(0.2)	11.7	6.5	11.9
Interest Expense	0.0	0.1	0.7	0.1	0.6
Other Income (Expenses), Net	0.3	(5.1)	0.5	0.2	0.0
Pretax Income	6.9	(5.4)	11.5	6.1	11.3
Income Taxes	3.0	(0.5)	4.3	2.6	4.7
NET INCOME	3.9	(4.9)	7.2	3.5	6.7

LTD = Long-term debt

Sources: Forms 10-K and Exhibits 1, 2, 4, and Willamette Management Associates calculations.

Exhibit 8a

Employer, Inc.
Guideline Publicly Traded Company Method
Financial and Operating Ratios

Financial Ratio	Deckers Outdoor Co. 12/31/03	K-Swiss 12/31/04	Lacrosse Footwear 12/31/03	Maxwell Shoe Co. 10/31/04	Rocky Shoes &Boots 12/31/03
LIQUIDITY RATIOS					
Current Ratio	2.0	5.9	2.5	12.7	11.4
Quick Ratio	1.1	3.6	0.9	11.4	5.2
Working Capital ($Mill)	22.5	177.4	25.6	143.7	41.8
Cash to MVIC	0.0	0.1	-	0.4	0.0
ACTIVITY RATIOS					
Sales/Average Receivables	4.7	9.7	5.6	5.4	5.3
Days in Receivables	78	37	65	67	69
Cost of Sales/Inventory	3.1	3.7	2.4	10.1	2.4
Days in Inventory	118	98	152	36	151
Working Capital Turnover	3.1	2.8	3.7	1.7	2.1
Fixed Asset Turnover	25.7	50.4	16.0	57.3	4.5
Asset Turnover	1.0	2.1	1.4	1.4	1.2
COVERAGE/LEVERAGE RATIOS					
Interest Expense Coverage [a]:					
EBIT	24.0	260.6	(0.9)	NM	3.7
EBITDA	33.8	265.4	0.8	NM	6.6
Fixed Assets/Equity	0.1	0.0	0.1	0.0	0.4
Equity/Total Capital (%)	65.0	100.0	92.6	100.0	83.3
PROFITABILITY RATIOS (%) [a]					
Pretax Income/Average Equity	9.2	55.1	(8.8)	16.1	7.3
Pretax Income/Average Assets	5.8	42.0	(4.8)	14.9	5.3
Pretax Income/Sales	6.1	20.5	(3.5)	10.7	4.3
Net Income/Average Equity	5.3	33.7	(5.7)	10.0	5.5
Net Income/Average Assets	3.3	25.7	(3.1)	9.2	4.0
Net Income/Sales	3.5	12.5	(2.2)	6.7	3.2
Cash Flow/Average Equity	9.2	34.7	2.3	11.2	13.3
Cash Flow/Average Assets	5.8	26.5	1.3	10.3	9.6
Cash Flow/Sales	6.1	12.9	0.9	7.5	7.7
EBIT/Average Total Capital	7.6	55.3	(3.8)	16.1	7.9
EBDIT/Average Total Capital	10.7	56.4	3.5	17.4	14.1

Exhibit 8b

Employer, Inc.
Guideline Publicly Traded Company Method
Financial and Operating Ratios

Financial Ratio	Saucony 1/3/04	Vans, Inc. 5/31/04	Weyco Group 12/31/03	Median	Employer, Inc. 12/31/04
LIQUIDITY RATIOS					
Current Ratio	4.9	3.1	4.7	4.7	1.4
Quick Ratio	3.1	1.5	2.1	2.1	0.2
Working Capital ($Mill)	64.3	106.1	75.3	64.3	1.1
Cash to MVIC	0.3	0.3	0.0	0.0	NA
ACTIVITY RATIOS					
Sales/Average Receivables	8.8	12.3	6.8	5.6	26.8
Days in Receivables	41	30	53	53	14
Cost of Sales/Inventory	3.1	3.0	3.6	3.1	2.4
Days in Inventory	118	121	102	117.8	150
Working Capital Turnover	2.2	2.9	3.1	2.8	11.1
Fixed Asset Turnover	21.0	10.0	9.7	16.0	12.1
Asset Turnover	1.6	1.3	1.5	1.4	2.9
COVERAGE/LEVERAGE RATIOS					
Interest Expense Coverage [a]:					
EBIT	1,842.8	(47.1)	17.2	3.7	18.5
EBITDA	2,162.2	(19.2)	18.9	6.6	22.5
Fixed Assets/Equity	0.1	0.1	0.3	0.1	0.8
Equity/Total Capital (%)	100.0	98.6	69.2	92.6	64.6
PROFITABILITY RATIOS (%) [a]					
Pretax Income/Average Equity	14.0	(9.4)	26.3	9.2	93.2
Pretax Income/Average Assets	11.1	(7.3)	17.1	5.8	32.9
Pretax Income/Sales	6.9	(5.4)	11.5	6.1	11.3
Net Income/Average Equity	7.9	(8.4)	16.6	5.5	54.9
Net Income/Average Assets	6.3	(6.5)	10.7	4.0	19.3
Net Income/Sales	3.9	(4.9)	7.2	3.5	6.7
Cash Flow/Average Equity	10.3	(3.0)	19.4	10.3	76.4
Cash Flow/Average Assets	8.2	(2.3)	12.6	8.2	26.9
Cash Flow/Sales	5.1	(1.7)	8.5	6.1	9.3
EBIT/Average Total Capital	14.0	(9.0)	22.6	7.9	68.6
EBDIT/Average Total Capital	16.4	(3.7)	24.9	14.1	83.6

EBIT = Earnings before interest and taxes
EBITDA = Earnings before interest, taxes, depreciation, and amortization
Cash Flow = Net income plus Depreciation expense
Total capital = Equity plus LTD
NA = Not available
NM = Not meaningful
[a] Coverage and profitability ratios are based on pretax and after-tax income adjusted for nonrecurring items.

Sources: Forms 10-K and Exhibits 1, 2, 4, and Willamette Management Associates calculations.

Exhibit 9a

Employer, Inc.
Guideline Publicly Traded Company Method
Comparison of Operating Performance

PROFITABILITY

Company	LTM EBITDA Return on Revenue %	Company	5-Yr. Avg. EBITDA Return on Revenue %
K-Swiss, Inc.	21.0	K-Swiss, Inc.	19.3
Deckers Outdoor Corp.	15.6	*Employer, Inc.*	*16.8*
Employer, Inc.	*15.0*	Weyco Group, Inc.	13.3
Weyco Group, Inc.	13.8	Deckers Outdoor Corp.	11.5
Rocky Shoes & Boots, Inc.	12.3	Maxwell Shoe Co., Inc.	11.2
Maxwell Shoe Co., Inc.	11.5	Saucony, Inc.	9.7
Saucony, Inc.	10.9	Rocky Shoes & Boots, Inc.	7.8
Lacrosse Footwear, Inc.	8.6	Vans, Inc.	4.0
Vans, Inc.	(0.3)	Lacrosse Footwear, Inc.	3.3

SIZE

Company	LTM Revenue $000	Company	Total Assets $000
K-Swiss, Inc.	429,162	K-Swiss, Inc.	234,630
Vans, Inc.	341,533	Vans, Inc.	229,480
Maxwell Shoe Co., Inc.	225,012	Weyco Group, Inc.	148,793
Weyco Group, Inc.	215,380	Deckers Outdoor Corp.	121,570
Saucony, Inc.	134,032	Rocky Shoes & Boots, Inc.	109,895
Deckers Outdoor Corp.	111,090	Maxwell Shoe Co., Inc.	108,764
Rocky Shoes & Boots, Inc.	102,530	Saucony, Inc.	91,119
Lacrosse Footwear, Inc.	94,196	Lacrosse Footwear, Inc.	69,408
Employer, Inc.	*11,771*	*Employer, Inc.*	4,762

Exhibit 9b

Employer, Inc.
Guideline Publicly Traded Company Method
Comparison of Operating Performance

GROWTH RATES

Company	5-Yr. Avg. Annual Compound Growth in EBITDA %	Company	5-Yr. Avg. Annual Compound Growth in Revenue %
Employer, Inc.	*18.9*	*Employer, Inc.*	*36.3*
Maxwell Shoe Co., Inc.	16.8	Weyco Group, Inc.	11.8
Saucony, Inc.	14.1	Vans, Inc.	11.4
Weyco Group, Inc.	13.8	Maxwell Shoe Co., Inc.	10.6
K-Swiss, Inc.	11.5	K-Swiss, Inc.	10.6
Rocky Shoes & Boots, Inc.	9.4	Saucony, Inc.	5.1
Lacrosse Footwear, Inc.	(3.9)	Rocky Shoes & Boots, Inc.	2.9
Deckers Outdoor Corp.	NM	Deckers Outdoor Corp.	1.5
Vans, Inc.	NM	Lacrosse Footwear, Inc.	(7.1)

ASSET PRODUCTIVITY

Company	Days in Inventory [a]	Company	Asset Turnover [a]
Maxwell Shoe Co., Inc.	36.0	*Employer, Inc.*	*2.90*
K-Swiss, Inc.	98.3	K-Swiss, Inc.	2.05
Weyco Group, Inc.	102.2	Saucony, Inc.	1.61
Deckers Outdoor Corp.	117.8	Weyco Group, Inc.	1.48
Saucony, Inc.	118.3	Lacrosse Footwear, Inc.	1.39
Vans, Inc.	120.6	Maxwell Shoe Co., Inc.	1.39
Employer, Inc.	*150.4*	Vans, Inc.	1.34
Rocky Shoes & Boots, Inc.	151.0	Rocky Shoes & Boots, Inc.	1.24
Lacrosse Footwear, Inc.	151.7	Deckers Outdoor Corp.	0.95

Exhibit 9c

Employer, Inc.
Guideline Publicly Traded Company Method
Comparison of Operating Performance

COVERAGE / LEVERAGE

Company	Interest Expense Coverage (EBITDA) [a]	Company	Equity to Total Capital [a]
Saucony, Inc.	2,425.50	K-Swiss, Inc.	100.00
K-Swiss, Inc.	265.40	Lacrosse Footwear, Inc.	100.00
Employer, Inc.	*23.08*	Saucony, Inc.	100.00
Weyco Group, Inc.	19.08	Maxwell Shoe Co., Inc.	99.84
Rocky Shoes & Boots, Inc.	9.59	Vans, Inc.	99.12
Deckers Outdoor Corp.	7.41	Weyco Group, Inc.	73.22
Lacrosse Footwear, Inc.	6.61	Deckers Outdoor Corp.	70.25
Vans, Inc.	(3.65)	*Employer, Inc.*	64.62
Maxwell Shoe Co., Inc.	NA	Rocky Shoes & Boots, Inc.	56.91

EBITDA = Earnings before interest, taxes, depreciation & amortization
Total capital = Long-term debt plus Book value of equity
LTM = Latest 12 months
[a] As of latest fiscal year-end

Sources: Exhibits 7, 10, and Willamette Management Associates calculations.

Exhibit 10a

Employer, Inc.
Guideline Publicly Traded Company Method
Market Value of Invested Capital

Company Name	Mkt./Sym.	FYE	Lat. Qtr. TBV $000	Lat. Qtr. BV IBD $000	Lat. Qtr. TBVIC $000	Lat. Qtr. MV IBD [a] $000	As of or for Period Ending	Bid/Close Price Per Common Share 12/31/03 $	Common Shares Outstg.[b] 000s	MV Common Equity $000	MV Preferred Equity $000	MVIC $000
Deckers Outdoor Corp.	NNM/DECK	12/03	2,579	34,556	37,135	34,556	9/04	20.500	9,676	198,355	5,500	238,411
K-Swiss, Inc.	NNM/KSWS	12/04	172,226	-	172,226	-	12/04	24.100	35,438	854,058	-	854,058
Lacrosse Footwear, Inc.	NNM/BOOT	12/03	25,831	21,688	47,519	21,688	9/04	7.870	5,874	46,232	-	67,920
Maxwell Shoe Co., Inc.	NNM/MAXS	10/04	126,112	219	126,331	219	10/04	16.960	14,821	251,364	-	251,583
Rocky Shoes & Boots, Inc.	NNM/RCKY	12/04	52,213	41,278	93,491	41,278	9/03	22.390	4,213	94,330	-	135,608
Saucony, Inc.	NNM/SCNYA	1/04	75,821	-	75,821	-	10/04	17.154	6,141	105,348	-	105,348
Vans, Inc.	NNM/VANS	5/04	134,057	1,614	135,671	1,614	11/04	11.410	17,872	203,920	-	205,534
Weyco Group, Inc.	NNM/WEYS	12/03	84,736	34,962	119,698	34,962	9/04	33.649	5,732	192,867	-	227,829
Employer, Inc.	NA	12/04	1,451	1,807	3,257	NA	12/04	NA	1,000	NA	NA	NA

Definitions, sources, and footnotes are found at Exhibit 10l.

Exhibit 10b

Employer, Inc.
Guideline Publicly Traded Company Method
Earnings before Interest and Taxes

	Earnings before Interest & Taxes (EBIT)								
	Projected $000	Ending	LTM $000	Ending	2004/03 $000	2003/02 $000	2002/01 $000	2001/00 $000	2000/99 $000
Deckers Outdoor Corp.	18,473	12/04	15,546	9/04	6,336	5,103	12,687	6,622	(3,026)
K-Swiss, Inc.	182,360	12/04	88,330	12/04	88,330	53,140	41,424	35,140	56,836
Lacrosse Footwear, Inc.	NA	NA	6,019	9/04	(1,605)	(1,046)	(2,450)	389	5,654
Maxwell Shoe Co., Inc.	27,956	10/05	24,133	10/04	24,133	19,434	19,782	16,471	11,923
Rocky Shoes & Boots, Inc.	9,977	12/04	8,960	9/03	5,201	5,431	3,634	(4,942)	3,997
Saucony, Inc.	NA	NA	13,102	10/04	9,214	1,957	18,869	18,272	5,945
Vans, Inc.	14,788	5/05	(10,320)	11/04	(17,609)	249	28,318	22,528	15,035
Weyco Group, Inc.	NA	NA	27,569	9/04	22,153	14,729	17,038	17,636	15,516
MEAN									
MEDIAN									
STD. DEV.									
COEFF. VAR. (%)									
Employer, Inc.	2,209	12/04	1,453	12/04	1,453	1,570	1,232	651	830

Definitions, sources, and footnotes are found at Exhibit 10l.

Exhibit 10c

Employer, Inc.
Guideline Publicly Traded Company Method
Earnings before Interest and Taxes

	5-Yr. Avg.[c] EBIT $000	Projected EBIT Growth %	5-Yr. Avg. Annual Compound Growth[d] %	Coeff. of Var.[e] %	MVIC $000	MVIC/EBIT Projected	MVIC/EBIT LTM	MVIC/EBIT 5-Yr. Avg.
Deckers Outdoor Corp.	9,259	191.6	NM	49.5	238,411	12.9	15.3	25.7
K-Swiss, Inc.	54,974	106.5	11.7	37.5	854,058	4.7	9.7	15.5
Lacrosse Footwear, Inc.	261	NA	1.3	1,293.2	67,920	NA	11.3	NM
Maxwell Shoe Co., Inc.	18,349	15.8	19.3	24.6	251,583	9.0	10.4	13.7
Rocky Shoes & Boots, Inc.	3,657	91.8	18.5	141.8	135,608	13.6	15.1	37.1
Saucony, Inc.	12,283	NA	18.1	57.0	105,348	NA	8.0	8.6
Vans, Inc.	4,633	NM	NM	434.2	205,534	13.9	Df	44.4
Weyco Group, Inc.	19,825	NA	12.9	25.7	227,829	NA	8.3	11.5
MEAN		101.4	13.6			10.8	11.2	22.4
MEDIAN		99.1	15.5			12.9	10.4	15.5
STD. DEV.		72.0	6.8			4.0	3.0	13.8
COEFF. VAR. (%)		71.0	50.0			36.5	26.9	61.7
Employer, Inc.	1,147	52.0	15.0	34.5	NA	NA	NA	NA

Definitions, sources, and footnotes are found at Exhibit 10l.

Exhibit 10d

Employer, Inc.
Guideline Publicly Traded Company Method
Earnings before Interest, Taxes, Depreciation & Amortization

	Earnings before Interest, Taxes, Depreciation & Amortization (EBITDA)								
	Projected $000	Period	LTM $000	Period	2004/03 $000	2003/02 $000	2002/01 $000	2001/00 $000	2000/99 $000
Deckers Outdoor Corp.	20,241	12/04	17,314	9/04	8,920	8,680	15,627	9,748	(388)
K-Swiss, Inc.	184,360	12/04	89,972	12/04	89,972	54,769	43,062	36,671	58,210
Lacrosse Footwear, Inc.	NA	NA	8,081	9/04	1,491	3,188	1,541	4,728	9,771
Maxwell Shoe Co., Inc.	29,766	10/05	25,943	10/04	25,943	21,392	22,366	18,967	13,940
Rocky Shoes & Boots, Inc.	13,610	12/04	12,594	9/03	9,233	9,840	8,333	(1,105)	8,224
Saucony, Inc.	NA	NA	14,553	10/04	10,811	3,926	20,827	20,134	7,781
Vans, Inc.	14,788	5/05	(1,056)	11/04	(7,179)	8,429	36,009	28,580	20,063
Weyco Group, Inc.	NA	NA	29,800	9/04	24,384	16,338	18,528	18,877	16,142
MEAN									
MEDIAN									
STD. DEV.									
COEFF. VAR. (%)									
Employer, Inc.	2,648		1,761	12/04	1,761	1,734	1,353	759	881

Definitions, sources, and footnotes are found at Exhibit 10l.

Exhibit 10e

Employer, Inc.
Guideline Publicly Traded Company Method
Earnings before Interest, Taxes, Depreciation & Amortization

	5-Yr. Avg.[c] EBITDA $000	Projected EBITDA Growth %	5-Yr. Avg. Annual Compound Growth[d] %	Coeff. of Var.[e] %	MVIC $000	MVIC/EBITDA Projected	MVIC/EBITDA LTM	MVIC/EBITDA 5-Yr. Avg.
Deckers Outdoor Corp.	12,058	126.9	NM	33.9	238,411	11.8	13.8	19.8
K-Swiss, Inc.	56,537	104.9	11.5	36.5	854,058	4.6	9.5	15.1
Lacrosse Footwear, Inc.	3,806	NA	(3.9)	72.0	67,920	NA	8.4	17.8
Maxwell Shoe Co., Inc.	20,522	14.7	16.8	21.7	251,583	8.5	9.7	12.3
Rocky Shoes & Boots, Inc.	7,779	47.4	9.4	67.0	135,608	10.0	10.8	17.4
Saucony, Inc.	14,050	NA	14.1	49.8	105,348	NA	7.2	7.5
Vans, Inc.	12,957	NM	NM	144.3	205,534	13.9	Df	15.9
Weyco Group, Inc.	21,586	NA	13.8	25.3	227,829	NA	7.6	10.6
MEAN		73.5	10.3			9.7	9.6	14.5
MEDIAN		76.2	12.6			10.0	9.5	15.5
STD. DEV.		51.6	7.4			3.5	2.2	4.1
COEFF. VAR. (%)		70.2	72.0			36.0	23.2	28.4
Employer, Inc.	1,298	50.4	18.9	36.0	NA	NA	NA	NA

Definitions, sources, and footnotes are found at Exhibit 10l.

Exhibit 10f

Employer, Inc.
Guideline Publicly Traded Company Method
Net Income

	Net Income								
	Projected $000	Period	LTM $000	Period	2004/03 $000	2003/02 $000	2002/01 $000	2001/00 $000	2000/99 $000
Deckers Outdoor Corp.	9,192	12/04	8,062	9/04	3,459	2,887	7,015	2,884	(2,907)
K-Swiss, Inc.	111,276	12/04	53,792	12/04	53,792	31,813	24,305	21,059	34,284
Lacrosse Footwear, Inc.	NA	NA	3,117	9/04	(2,198)	(2,508)	(3,702)	(1,182)	2,204
Maxwell Shoe Co., Inc.	17,341	10/05	14,969	10/04	14,969	13,258	12,280	9,882	7,154
Rocky Shoes & Boots, Inc.	6,488	12/04	5,506	9/03	2,843	1,909	182	(5,130)	1,471
Saucony, Inc.	NA	NA	7,812	10/04	5,202	1,046	10,500	10,319	3,579
Vans, Inc.	13,047	5/05	(11,039)	1/00	(16,182)	52	15,593	12,087	8,484
Weyco Group, Inc.	NA	NA	16,403	9/04	13,110	9,328	10,583	11,148	9,737
MEAN									
MEDIAN									
STD. DEV.									
COEFF. VAR. (%)									
Employer, Inc.	1,297		785	12/04	785	870	667	353	460

Definitions, sources, and footnotes are found at Exhibit 10l.

Exhibit 10g

Employer, Inc.
Guideline Publicly Traded Company Method
Net Income

	5-Yr. Avg.[c] NI $000	Projected NI Growth %	5-Yr. Avg. Annual Compound Growth[d] %	Coeff. of Var.[e] %	MVE $000	MVE/NI Projected	MVE/NI LTM	MVE/NI 5-Yr. Avg.
Deckers Outdoor Corp.	4,861	165.8	NM	51.1	198,355	21.6	24.6	40.8
K-Swiss, Inc.	33,051	106.9	11.9	38.7	854,058	7.7	15.9	25.8
Lacrosse Footwear, Inc.	(1,295)	NA	7.6	(202.8)	46,232	NA	14.8	Df
Maxwell Shoe Co., Inc.	11,509	15.8	20.3	26.5	251,364	14.5	16.8	21.8
Rocky Shoes & Boots, Inc.	1,062	128.2	32.0	373.0	94,330	14.5	17.1	88.8
Saucony, Inc.	6,976	NA	17.9	56.7	105,348	NA	13.5	15.1
Vans, Inc.	102	(180.6)	NM	13,601.9	203,920	15.6	Df	NM
Weyco Group, Inc.	12,114	NA	11.6	22.8	192,867	NA	11.8	15.9
MEAN		47.2	16.9			14.8	16.4	34.7
MEDIAN		106.9	14.9			14.5	15.9	23.8
STD. DEV.		138.8	8.7			4.9	4.1	28.1
COEFF. VAR. (%)		294.0	51.7			33.4	25.1	80.9
Employer, Inc.	627	65.3	14.3	34.6	NA	NA	NA	NA

Definitions, sources, and footnotes are found at Exhibit 10l.

Exhibit 10h

Employer, Inc.
Guideline Publicly Traded Company Method
Revenue

	LTM		Revenue					5-Yr. Avg.[c]	5-Yr. Avg. Annual Compound	Coeff. of		MVIC/Revenue	
	Revenue $000	Ending	2004/03 $000	2003/02 $000	2002/01 $000	2001/00 $000	2000/99 $000	Revenue $000	Growth[d] %	Var.[e] %	MVIC $000	LTM	5-Yr. Avg.
Deckers Outdoor Corp.	111,090	9/04	99,107	91,461	113,738	111,099	103,534	105,299	1.5	9.1	238,411	2.15	2.26
K-Swiss, Inc.	429,162	12/04	429,162	289,593	237,252	223,102	286,856	293,193	10.6	27.8	854,058	1.99	2.91
Lacrosse Footwear, Inc.	94,196	9/04	97,785	125,301	138,161	124,328	133,405	115,954	(7.1)	16.4	67,920	0.72	0.59
Maxwell Shoe Co., Inc.	225,012	10/04	225,012	204,363	182,237	158,205	150,320	184,027	10.6	17.0	251,583	1.12	1.37
Rocky Shoes & Boots, Inc.	102,530	9/03	88,959	103,320	103,229	98,781	89,316	99,364	2.9	6.1	135,608	1.32	1.36
Saucony, Inc.	134,032	10/04	133,499	132,364	167,920	155,887	105,810	144,740	5.1	11.2	105,348	0.79	0.73
Vans, Inc.	341,533	11/04	330,197	331,443	340,150	276,247	210,113	323,914	11.4	8.4	205,534	0.60	0.63
Weyco Group, Inc.	215,380	9/04	181,200	131,693	148,155	132,905	126,576	161,867	11.8	22.2	227,829	1.06	1.41
MEAN									5.9			1.22	1.41
MEDIAN									7.8			1.09	1.37
STD. DEV.									6.6			0.58	0.82
COEFF. VAR. (%)									112.8			47.24	58.43
Employer, Inc.	11,771	12/04	11,771	10,552	7,859	4,941	3,408	7,706	36.3	46.2	NA	NA	NA

Definitions, sources, and footnotes are found at Exhibit 10l.

Exhibit 10j

Employer, Inc.
Guideline Publicly Traded Company Method
Revenue Performance Ratios

	LTM Return on Revenue		LTM Return on Revenue		5-Yr. Avg. Return on Revenue		5-Yr. Avg. Return on Revenue	
	EBIT %	EBITDA %	DFNI %	DFCF %	EBIT %	EBITDA %	DFNI %	DFCF %
Deckers Outdoor Corp.	14.0	15.6	8.5	10.1	8.8	11.5	5.1	7.8
K-Swiss, Inc.	20.6	21.0	12.6	13.0	18.8	19.3	11.4	11.9
Lacrosse Footwear, Inc.	6.4	8.6	4.2	6.3	0.2	3.3	0.1	3.2
Maxwell Shoe Co., Inc.	10.7	11.5	6.7	7.5	10.0	11.2	6.3	7.4
Rocky Shoes & Boots, Inc.	8.7	12.3	6.3	9.9	3.7	7.8	2.6	6.7
Saucony, Inc.	9.8	10.9	5.8	6.9	8.5	9.7	4.9	6.2
Vans, Inc.	(3.0)	(0.3)	(3.1)	(0.4)	1.4	4.0	0.3	2.9
Weyco Group, Inc.	12.8	13.8	8.1	9.1	12.2	13.3	7.8	8.9
MEAN	10.0	11.7	6.1	7.8	7.9	10.0	4.8	6.9
MEDIAN	10.3	11.9	6.5	8.3	8.6	10.4	5.0	7.1
STD. DEV.	6.8	6.1	4.5	3.9	6.1	5.2	3.8	2.9
COEFF. VAR. (%)	67.7	52.3	73.4	50.6	76.8	51.6	79.1	42.9
Employer, Inc.	12.3	15.0	7.0	9.7	14.9	16.8	8.5	10.4

Definitions, sources, and footnotes are found at Exhibit 10l.

Exhibit 10k

Employer, Inc.
Guideline Publicly Traded Company Method
Book Value of Invested Capital Performance Ratios

	MVIC $000s	MVIC/ Lat. Qtr. TBVIC Ratio	IBD/ TBVIC %	MV of IBD/ MVIC %	EBIT Return On TBVIC LTM %	EBIT Return On TBVIC 5-Yr. Avg. %	EBITDA Return On TBVIC LTM %	EBITDA Return On TBVIC 5-Yr. Avg. %	DFNI Return On TBVIC LTM %	DFNI Return On TBVIC 5-Yr. Avg. %	DFCF Return On TBVIC LTM %	DFCF Return On TBVIC 5-Yr. Avg. %
Deckers Outdoor Corp.	238,411	6.42	93.1	14.5	41.9	24.9	46.6	32.5	25.5	14.5	30.2	22.0
K-Swiss, Inc.	854,058	4.96	-	-	51.3	31.9	52.2	32.8	31.4	19.4	32.3	20.3
Lacrosse Footwear, Inc.	67,920	1.43	45.6	31.9	12.7	0.6	17.0	8.0	8.2	0.4	12.6	7.8
Maxwell Shoe Co., Inc.	251,583	1.99	0.2	0.1	19.1	14.5	20.5	16.2	11.8	9.1	13.3	10.8
Rocky Shoes & Boots, Inc.	135,608	1.45	44.2	30.4	9.6	3.9	13.5	8.3	6.9	2.7	10.8	7.2
Saucony, Inc.	105,348	1.39	-	-	17.3	16.2	19.2	18.5	10.3	9.4	12.2	11.8
Vans, Inc.	205,534	1.51	1.2	0.8	(7.6)	3.4	(0.8)	9.6	(7.9)	0.7	(1.1)	6.8
Weyco Group, Inc.	227,829	1.90	29.2	15.3	23.0	16.6	24.9	18.0	14.5	10.6	16.4	12.1
MEAN		2.63	26.7	11.6	20.9	14.0	24.1	18.0	12.6	8.3	15.8	12.3
MEDIAN		1.71	15.2	7.6	18.2	15.4	19.9	17.1	11.1	9.3	12.9	11.3
STD. DEV.		1.94	33.5	13.7	18.5	11.0	17.4	10.0	11.9	6.8	10.8	5.8
COEFF. VAR. (%)		73.69	125.6	117.5	88.4	78.6	72.0	55.5	94.8	81.0	68.3	47.1
Employer, Inc.	NA	NA	55.5	NA	44.6	35.2	54.1	39.9	25.4	20.1	34.9	24.7

Definitions, sources, and footnotes are found at Exhibit 10l.

Exhibit 10I

Employer, Inc.
Guideline Publicly Traded Company Method
Definitions, Footnotes, and Sources to Exhibits

BV = Book value
DF = Deficit
FYE = Fiscal year-end
IBD = Interest-bearing debt
IC = Invested capital
LTD = Long-term debt
LTM = Latest 12 months
MV = Market value
MVIC = LTD + ST interest-bearing debt + MV of preferred + MV of common equity
NA = Not available
NM = Not meaningful
ST = Short-term
T = Tangible
TBVIC = Stockholders' equity - goodwill + LTD + ST interest-bearing debt.

FOOTNOTES:
Financial information for publicly traded companies and Company Name have been adjusted for nonrecurring items.

[a] Book value if not publicly traded.
[b] Per most recently available data prior to the valuation date.
[c] Includes latest 12 months if at least six months beyond latest fiscal year-end.
[d] From earliest year on the table to the latest 12 months period.
[e] (Standard deviation/Mean) X 100.

Sources: SEC Forms 10K, 10Q, and S-1, Company financial statements, and Willamette Management Associates calculations.

Exhibit 11a

Employer, Inc.
Discounted Cash Flow Method
Value Summary

Present Value of Discrete Cash Flow:

Valuation Analysis	Projected Fiscal Years Ending December 31, 2005 $000	2006 $000	2007 $000	Adjusted 2007 $000
Debt-Free Net Income	1,297	2,598	3,153	3,153
Depreciation Expense [a]	439	512	419	419
Operating Cash Flow	1,736	3,110	3,572	3,572
Capital Expenditures [a]	(616)	(508)	(292)	(419)
Operating Working Capital Requirements [b]	(1,089)	(3,069)	(2,926)	(345)
Invested Capital Net Cash Flow (NCF)	31	(467)	354	2,808
Months in Initial Year	12.0			
	31			
Discounting Periods—Mid-Year Convention	0.500	1.500	2.500	
Discount Factor at 17.4% [c]	0.923	0.786	0.670	
Present Value of Discrete NCF	29	(367)	237	
Total Present Value of Discrete NCF	(101)			

Exhibit 11b

Employer, Inc.
Discounted Cash Flow Method
Value Summary

Present Value of Terminal Cash Flow:	
NCF—Fiscal Year 2008 [d]	2,920
Direct Capitalization Rate [e]	13.4
Terminal Value	39,132
Present Value Factor	0.670
Present Value of Terminal Cash Flow	26,204

Valuation Summary:	
Present Value of Discrete NCF	(101)
Present Value of Terminal Cash Flow	26,204
Indicated Value of Invested Capital	26,103
Less: Interest-Bearing Debt	(1,807)
Equals: Indicated Value of Common Stock (rounded)	24,300

[a] Depreciation expense and capital expenditures are projected to be equal in the long run.
[b] Based on management projections for 2005-2007. For terminal year, based on the Company's projected working capital requirements and the industry average working capital requirements.
[c] Based on the discounting periods and the 17.4% WACC as presented in Exhibit 14.
[d] Equals adjusted year 2007 NCF increased by the 4.0% expected long-term growth rate presented in Exhibit 14.
[e] Equals the direct capitalization rate presented in Exhibit 14.

Sources: As indicated above and Willamette Management Associates estimates and calculations.

Exhibit 12

Employer, Inc.
Discounted Cash Flow Method
Projected Balance Sheets

	Actual	Projected Fiscal Years Ending December 31,			Actual	Projected Fiscal Years Ending December 31,		
	2004	2005	2006	2007	2004	2005	2006	2007
	$000	$000	$000	$000	%	%	%	%
Assets:								
Current Assets:								
Cash & Marketable Securities	18	723	4,229	6,927	0.4	16.1	51.5	62.6
Accounts Receivable	407	543	814	1,021	8.5	12.1	9.9	9.2
Inventory	3,101	1,899	1,857	1,918	65.1	42.3	22.6	17.3
Prepaid & Deposits	62	15	15	15	1.3	0.3	0.2	0.1
Total Current Assets	3,589	3,180	6,915	9,881	75.4	70.9	84.1	89.4
Fixed Assets - Net	1,129	1,308	1,304	1,176	23.7	29.1	15.9	10.6
Other Long-Term Assets	44	-	-	-	0.9	-	-	-
Total Assets	4,762	4,488	8,219	11,057	100.0	100.0	100.0	100.0
Liabilities & Equity								
Current Liabilities:								
Accounts Payable	433	157	421	479	9.1	3.5	5.1	4.3
Income Taxes Payable	39	488	816	769	0.8	10.9	9.9	7.0
Accruals	191	275	349	378	4.0	6.1	4.2	3.4
Line of Credit	1,755	-	-	-	36.8	-	-	-
Total Current Liabilities	2,417	920	1,586	1,626	50.8	20.5	19.3	14.7
Long-Term Debt	894	804	714	624	18.8	17.9	8.7	5.6
Total Liabilities	3,312	1,724	2,300	2,250	69.5	38.4	28.0	20.3
Equity	1,451	2,764	5,919	8,807	30.5	61.6	72.0	79.7
Total Liabilities & Equity	4,762	4,488	8,219	11,057	100.0	100.0	100.0	100.0
Capital Expenditures	665	616	508	292				
Depreciation Expense	308	439	512	419				

Sources: Management-prepared projections and Willamette Management Associates calculations

Exhibit 13

Employer, Inc.
Discounted Cash Flow Method
Projected Income Statements

	Actual	Projected Fiscal Years Ending December 31,			Actual	Projected Fiscal Years Ending December 31,		
	2004	2005	2006	2007	2004	2005	2006	2007
	$000	$000	$000	$000	%	%	%	%
Revenue	11,771	15,035	21,883	25,809	100.0	100.0	100.0	100.0
Growth Rate	*11.6%*	*27.7%*	*45.5%*	*17.9%*				
Cost of Goods Sold	6,156	7,930	11,611	13,585	52.3	52.7	53.1	52.6
Gross Profit	5,615	7,105	10,272	12,224	47.7	47.3	46.9	47.4
Operating Expenses:								
Shipping & Distribution	340	532	771	1,309	2.9	3.5	3.5	5.1
Product Development	508	607	478	507	4.3	4.0	2.2	2.0
General & Administrative	1,236	1,248	1,397	1,429	10.5	8.3	6.4	5.5
Sales & Marketing	2,126	2,334	2,999	3,418	18.1	15.5	13.7	13.2
Total Operating Expenses	4,211	4,721	5,645	6,663	35.8	31.4	25.8	25.8
Operating Profit	1,404	2,384	4,627	5,561	11.9	15.9	21.1	21.5
Other (Income) Expense	71	109	69	30	0.6	0.7	0.3	0.1
Profit Before Tax	1,334	2,275	4,558	5,531	11.3	15.1	20.8	21.4
Growth Rate	*-12.8%*	*70.6%*	*100.4%*	*21.3%*				
Provision for Income Tax		978	1,960	2,378		6.5	9.0	9.2
Net Income		1,297	2,598	3,153		8.6	11.9	12.2

Sources: Management-prepared projections and Willamette Management Associates calculations

Exhibit 14a

Employer, Inc.
Discounted Cash Flow Method
Weighted Average Cost of Capital

Cost of Equity Capital:			**Source:**
Risk-Free Rate		5.10%	*Wall Street Journal,* as of December 31, 2004
			20-year Treasury bond
Plus:			
Long-Term Equity Risk Premium	7.00%		*Ibbotson Associates, Stocks, Bonds, Bills and Inflation*, 2004 Yearbook
Multiplied by: Beta	0.90		Based on the median beta of the selected guideline companies.
		6.30%	
Small Stock Equity Risk Premium		5.67%	*Ibbotson Associates, Stocks, Bonds, Bills and Inflation*, 2004 Yearbook
Company-Specific Equity Risk Premium		3.00%	Willamette Management Associates estimate
Total Cost of Equity (rounded)		20.10%	
Cost of Debt Capital:			
Cost of Debt (Pretax)		4.3%	Interest rate on the Employer line of credit
Income Tax Rate		43.0%	Based on management-prepared projections
After-Tax Cost of Debt (tax-affected/rounded)		2.4%	

Exhibit 14b

Employer, Inc.
Discounted Cash Flow Method
Weighted Average Cost of Capital

Weighted Average Cost of Capital (WACC):			
Cost of Equity Capital	20.1%		
Percent of Equity in Capital Structure	85%		Based on the Employer market value capital structure
Weighted Rate		17.09%	
Cost of Debt Capital	2.4%		
Percent of Debt in Capital Structure	15%		Based on the Employer market value capital structure
Weighted Rate		0.36%	
WACC (Rounded)		17.4%	Present value discount rate
Less: Expected Long-Term Growth Rate		4.0%	Willamette Management Associates estimate
Equals: Direct Capitalization Rate		13.4%	Direct capitalization rate

Sources: As indicated above

Exhibit 15a

Employer, Inc.
Guideline Merged and Acquired Company Method
Value Summary

Guideline Company Transaction Details:

Seller:	TEVA [a]
Buyer:	Deckers Outdoor Corp.
Closing Date:	11/25/02
Type:	Asset
MVE:	62,300
MVIC:	62,300
Seller Description:	Leading sport sandal brand in the footwear industry.

Financial Fundamentals:

	Projected 2004 $000	Actual 2003 $000	Actual 2002 $000	Three-Year Average $000
Revenue	NA	64,849	61,221	63,035
EBIT	NA	4,753	5,075	4,914
EBIT Margin	*NA*	*7.3%*	*8.3%*	*7.8%*
EBITDA	6,000	4,840	5,159	4,999
EBITDA Margin	*NA*	*7.5%*	*8.4%*	*7.9%*
Net Income	NA	3,090	3,298	3,194
Net Margin	*NA*	*4.8%*	*5.4%*	*5.1%*

Exhibit 15b

Employer, Inc.
Guideline Merged and Acquired Company Method
Value Summary

Value Summary:

Financial Fundamentals	Employer $000	Market-Derived Pricing Multiples: TEVA	Market-Derived Pricing Multiples: Selected Pricing Multiple	Indicated Invested Capital $000	Less: Long-Term Debt	Indicated Common Stock $000	Value Indication Weight	Weighted Value Indication $000
EBIT - LTM	1,453	13.1	11.5	16,710	(1,807)	14,904	0.15	2,236
EBITDA - Proj.	2,648	10.4	9.0	23,832	(1,807)	22,025	0.15	3,304
EBITDA - LTM	1,761	12.9	11.0	19,370	(1,807)	17,563	0.20	3,513
Net Income - LTM	785	20.2	17.0			13,341	0.50	6,670
							1.00	
Indicated Value of Common Stock (on a marketable, controlling ownership interest basis)								15,722
Less: Discount for Lack of Control at 15% [b]								(2,358)
Indicated Value of Common Stock (rounded) (on a marketable, noncontrolling ownership interest basis)								13,360

EBIT = Earnings before interest, taxes, and depreciation
EBITDA = EBIT + Depreciation and amortization
MVE = Market value of equity
MVIC = Market value of invested capital
NA = Not available

[a] Deckers has been selling TEVA sandals since 1985 under a license agreement. Sales of TEVA sandals accounted for approximately two-thirds of Deckers revenues in 2003.
[b] Willamette Management Associates estimate. Considers empirical evidence and existing relationship between Deckers and TEVA.

Sources: Deckers Forms 8-K and 10-K, Exhibit 4, and Willamette Management Associates estimates and calculations.

Section VIII

ESOP Bibliography

Chapter 30

Bibliography Regarding ESOP Valuation and Independent Financial Adviser Services

ARTICLES

The following recently published articles discuss issues related to ESOP feasibility, formation, valuation, financing, transaction pricing, transaction structuring, financial adviser due diligence, and trustee due diligence.

Ackerman, David. "Technical Issues under the New S Corporation ESOP Laws." *Journal of Employee Ownership Law and Finance*, Winter 1999, pp. 3–19.

Bonn, Karen. "Feasibility Studies Help Avoid ESOP Foibles." *The Tax Advisor*, February 1999, pp. 82–83.

Buckley, Allen, Lynda M. Crouse, and Greg Kniesel. "S Corporation ESOPs in Dispositive Sales and Reorganization Transactions." *Valuation Strategies*, January/February 2001.

Casciari, Mark, and Sari Alamuddin. "ESOP Valuation Firms and ERISA Fiduciary Status: Where Courts Draw the Line." *The Journal of Employee Ownership Law & Finance*, Summer 2003.

Crow, Matthew R. "The Basics on Fairness Opinions in Transactions Involving ESOPs." *CPA Litigation Service Counselor*, August 1999, pp. 9–10.

"ESOPs and S Corporations." *The Tax Adviser*, August 2004, pp. 493–495.

Hall, C. Wells III. "The S Corporation ESOP: Incentivised Employee Stock Ownership or Tax Gimmickry?" *Business Entities*, January/February 1999, pp. 14–19, 62.

Johanson, David R. "Direct Stock Purchases in Closely Held Companies." *Journal of Employee Ownership Law and Finance*, Winter 2004, pp. 47–64.

Julius, J. Michael. "ESOP Appraisals and Non-ESOP Shareholders." *CPA Litigation Service Counselor*, July 1998, pp. 9–10.

Knight, David L., and Robert R. Trumble. "ESOP Complexities: Financial Valuation Techniques and Strategies." *Valuation Strategies*, May/June 2001, pp. 42–47.

Kubersky, Andrew S. "Marketability Discounts and ESOP Acquisitions of Minority Share Interests." *Journal of Employee Ownership Law and Finance*, Fall 1998, pp. 97–103.

Leimberg, Stephan R., and Roland G. Thon. "The Advantages and Uses of ESOPs in Estate and Business Planning." *Estate Planning*, February 2003, pp. 59–66.

Long, Dennis J. "Creating an ESOP Distribution Policy." *The Journal of Employee Ownership Law and Finance*, Summer 1997, pp. 85–92.

Miller, Thomas D. "Demystifying the Lattice Model." *The Journal of Employee Ownership Law and Finance*, Fall 2004, pp. 79–83.

Regnitz, Timothy J. "Understanding the ESOP Repurchase Obligation." *The Journal of Employee Ownership Law and Finance*, Winter 1999, pp. 21–34.

Reilly, Robert F. "Current Issues in the Valuations of ESOP-Owned Securities." *Journal of Pension Planning & Compliance*, Winter 1996, pp. 47–60.

_____. "A New Study on Pre-IPO Discounts for Lack of Marketability." *The Journal of Employee Ownership Law and Finance*, Summer 2004, pp. 55–68.

_____. "Recent Daubert-Related Decisions and ESOP Valuation Expert Testimony." *The Journal of Employee Ownership Law and Finance*, Fall 1999, pp. 31–41.

_____. "Recent Research on Valuation Adjustments for Voting Rights." *The Journal of Employee Ownership Law and Finance*, Summer 2004, pp. 69–94.

"Repurchase Liability: What ESOP Companies Should Know About It." *The ESOP Newsletter of McBride Baker and Coles*, Winter 2000.

Sandquist, Andrew, and John J. Cresto. "Anticipating and Avoiding ESOP Financing Obstacles." *The Journal of Employee Ownership Law and Finance*, Summer 1999, pp. 63–72.

Suhre, Karen K. "Should the ESOP-Owned Company Elect to Become an S Corporation?" *Benefits Law Journal*, Spring 1998.

Titus, John W., and B. David Joffe. "Sarbanes-Oxley: What It Means for Private Companies and ESOPs." *The Journal of Employee Ownership Law and Finance*, Winter 2004, pp. 3–9.

Trumble, Robert R., Gregory Lawson, and Karen Hawkridge. "ESOP Valuation Techniques." *Valuation Strategies,* July/August 2002.

Van Horn, Brad, and Gregory K. Brown. "Terminating an ESOP: Valuation and Fiduciary Issues." *The Journal of Employee Ownership Law and Finance,* Winter 1999, pp. 69–94.

BOOKS

The following list of books covers all aspects of ESOP formation, administration, financial issues, regulatory issues, and legal issues.

Ash, Merri E., Virginia J. Bartlett, et al. *The ESOP Association Administration Handbook*. Washington, DC: The ESOP Association, 1996.

An Employer's Guide to Employee Stock Ownership Plans. St. Paul, MN: Minnesota Small Business Assistance Office, Minnesota Department of Trade and Economic Development, 1994.

ESOP Accounting Standards. Washington, DC: The ESOP Association, 1999.

The ESOP Reader. Oakland, CA: The National Center for Employee Ownership, 2003.

ESOP Valuation, 2d ed. Oakland, CA: The National Center for Employee Ownership, 2003.

Fisch, Robert A. *The ESOP Handbook: Practical Strategies for Achieving Corporate Financing Goals*. New York: John Wiley & Sons, 1994, supplemented 1998.

How the ESOP Really Works. Washington, DC: The ESOP Association, 1997.

An Introduction to ESOP Valuations. Washington, DC: The ESOP Association, 1997.

Kaplan, Jared, John E. Curtis Jr., and Gregory K. Brown. *ESOPs* (Tax Management Portfolio). Washington, DC: Tax Management Inc., 1991.

Regnitz, Timothy J. *How ESOP Companies Handle the Repurchase Obligation,* 2d ed. Oakland, CA: The National Center for Employee Ownership, 2000.

Report on Valuation Considerations for Leveraged ESOPs. Washington, DC: The ESOP Association, 1998.

Rodrick, Scott S., ed. *Leveraged ESOPs and Employee Buyouts*. Oakland, CA: The National Center for Employee Ownership, 1998.

_____. *ESOP Valuation*. Oakland, CA: The National Center for Employee Ownership, 1999.

Rosen, Cory. *Understanding ESOP Valuation*. Oakland, CA: The National Center for Employee Ownership, 2000.

Selling to an ESOP, 7th ed. Oakland, CA: The National Center for Employee Ownership, 2002.

Smiley, Robert W. Jr., and Ronald J. Gilbert, eds. *Employee Stock Ownership Plans: Business Planning, Implementation, and Law and Taxation*. New York: Warren, Gorham & Lamont, 1991, supplemented annually.

Structuring Leveraged ESOP Transactions. Washington, DC: The ESOP Association: 1999.

Valuing ESOP Shares. Washington, DC: The ESOP Association: 1994.

CONFERENCE PRESENTATIONS

This section lists presentations made at recent ESOP-related conferences and seminars.

The ESOP Association 2004 Two-Day Deal Conference, November 2004

Abello, Kim S., and Jeffrey M. Risius. "Fiduciary Review of Valuation Reports."

Bickley, Bruce F., and John Cresto. "Seller Financing."

Brown, Alexis, and Cindy Prodoehl. "Impact of Employee Ownership on Company Performance."

Dittmer, Nancy K., and Jeffrey M. Johns. "409(p) Testing: What the Company Needs to Know."

Eskind, Steven, and Riva T. Johnson. "Sarbanes Oxley and ESOPs."

Fisher, Tina, and Kevin P. Rettler. "Advanced ESOP Administrative Issues in an S-Corporation ESOP."

Frost, David J., and Rebecca J. Miller. "ESOP Accounting."

Grassi, Carl J., et al. "ESOPs as Acquisition Tools."

Hafner, Dawn, and Anne M. Johnson. "Basic Review of the Tests Needed to Ensure Compliance with ERISA."

Hector, Brian, and Brian Warpts. "Advanced 409(p) Testing Issues."

Hennessy, Nell, et al. "Tackling the Tough Issues of Being an ESOP Fiduciary: Monitoring, Valuation and Avoiding Pitfalls."

Hommel, John G., and Alexander P. Moss. "Voting Pass-Through."

Jackson, Kreg J., and Elyse S. Blah. "Post Transaction Drop in Value of ESOP Stock."

Jochim, Tim and Daniel Bell. "ESOP Committees: What Are Differences between an ESOP Fiduciary Committee and an ESOP Communications Committee?"

Josephs, Mary S., et al. "Advanced Financing Issues."

Karch, Gary R., and Kenneth E. Serwinski. "Current Financial and Capital Conditions and ESOPs."

Keans, Leslie, and Merri Ash. "401(k) and ESOPs."

Klingler, Carla, et al. "ESOP Reporting and Disclosure Requirements."

Mathews, Anthony I., and Susan Lenczewski. "Distributions."

McIntyre, G. William, and Susan Petrirena. "Diversification."

Morrison, Helen H., Karen D. Ng. "Review of Differences between S Corporations and C Corporation ESOPs."

Nelson, James R., et al. "Estate and Succession Planning."

Rodgers, Loren. "Initial ESOP Communications."

Shuler, Pete, and Brian Lehmer. "Advanced ESOP Administration Issues in C Corporations."

Walter, Wendy, et al. "Basic Administration Part I and II."

Wimer, Ruth, et al. "Executive and Equity Based Compensation."

The ESOP Association, 27th Annual Conference, May 2004

Karlsrud, Deborah, and Pete Shuler. "Basic Administration"

Ash, Merri, et al. "Fiduciaries: Who Are They and What Do They Do?"

Aspengren, Victor N. "Governance, with Focus on Board Membership Issues"

Morrison, Helen M. "The Impact of Corporate Governance Reforms on ESOP Companies"

Spagnolo, John, et al. "The Basics of ESOP Communications: Starting on the Right Track"

Dittmer, Nancy K., and Daren S. Bonn. "Advanced Administration"

Abrahamson, Peter J. Et al. "Valuing Synthetic Equity"

Kornfeld, Judith L., and Karen D. Ng. "Forecasting Repurchase Objections"

Ivancic, Cathy. "The Basics of an ESOP Employee Committee: Who, What, When, Where"

Kober, John A., and Robert W. Bolt. "Basic Financing"

Gross, Robert J., et al. "Valuation and Employee Stock Ownership Plans (ESOPs)"

Etkind, Steven. "Second Stage ESOP Decisions"

Diamond, Louis H. "Multi-Stage ESOP Transactions—A Recommended Way Out of the Woods"

Olson, E Van. "DOL and IRS Audits"

Moss, Alexander P. "Connecting Ownership to Company Performance"

Vanderslice, Virginia J., et al. "Leadership Challenges & Skills in an Ownership Culture"

Purcell, E.W., and Robert D. Grossman. "Advanced Financing Developments"

Ackerman, David. "Mergers and Acquisitions Involving ESOPs"

Eastman, Thomas P., and David J. Frost. "Accounting for Employee Stock Ownership Plans"

Johanson, David R., and Gregory K. Brown. "Legislative, Regulatory and Judicial Update"

Merten, William W. "Use of Executive Compensation in ESOP Companies: Looking beyond Section 409(p) and Synthetic Equity"

Gilbert, Ronald J. "Executive Compensation and ESOPs"

Bye, Robert C., and Timothy J. Regnitz. "Funding Repurchase Obligations"

ASSOCIATIONS

This section presents the contact information for the two national employee ownership membership organizations.

The ESOP Association
1726 M Street N.W., Suite 501
Washington, DC 20036
(202) 293-2971
www.esopassociation.org

The National Center for Employee Ownership
1736 Franklin Street, 8th floor
Oakland, CA 94612
(510) 272-9461
www.nceo.org

Willamette Management Associates Insights Articles—Willamette Authors

This section lists ESOP-related articles that appeared in Willamette Management Associates *Insights* during the last 10 years. These articles were all authored by Willamette Management Associates analysts.

Abello, Kim. "How to Identify Prospective ESOP Situations for Ownership Transition," Spring 1996

_____. "Identifying Prospective S Corporation ESOPs," Spring 1998

_____. "Transaction Structures Using Employee Stock Ownership Plans," Special Issue 2001

Abello, Kim, and David Ackerman. "S Corporation ESOPs—A New Opportunity, Autumn 1997

Abello, Kim, and Gregory Brown. "ESOPs and Security Design: Common Stock, Super Common, or Convertible Preferred?" Spring 1995

Barkman, Ken. "The Post-Transaction Value of Equity in Leveraged ESOPs," Spring 2000

Barkman, Ken, and Scott Levine. "Basic ESOP Valuation Issues," Spring 1998

Buettner, Jeff. "The Impact of Synthetic Equity on ESOP Valuations," Spring 2003

Christie, Deborah. "S Corporation Dividends on Allocated Shares: Can They Be Use to Pay ESOP Debt?" Spring 2000

Daly, Kathryn. "Valuation Considerations for the Mature ESOP," Spring 1995

Damiano, Karen. "Tax Considerations of Employee Stock Ownership Plans," Spring 2001

Gaffen, Greg, and Brian Swift. "Strategic Motivations for ESOP Formation," Spring 1999

Garber, Steve. "ESOP Valuations and the Regulatory Environment," Special Issue 1994

_____. "Valuing Convertible Preferred Stock Equity Interests in Employee Stock Ownership Plans," Spring 1995

Garber, Steve, and Jeffrey S. Tarbell. "Managing the ESOP Repurchase Liability," Spring 1998

Garland, Pamela J., and Ashley L. Reilly. "Assessing the Reasonableness of Retained Owner/Manager Compensation in ESOP Stock Purchase Analyses," Winter 2005

Garland, Pamela J., and Robert F. Reilly. "Reasonableness of Executive Compensation within an ESOP Context," Spring 2000

Gerber, Frank. "Valuation Issues in the IRS Audit Guidelines," Spring 1998

Gould, Susan E. "Letter Ruling 199906044: ESOP Counts as One Shareholder for S Corporation Purposes," Autumn 1999

Gould, Susan E., and Gregory Brown. "Fiduciary and Valuation Issues Arising from Eyler v. Commissioner," Spring 1999

Gould, Susan E., and Mike Hartman. "Experts Weigh in on Enron and ESOPs," Spring 2002

Gould, Susan E., and Robert S. Socol. "ESOPs and Control," Spring 2001

Hartman, Malcolm R. "An Overview of ESOP Feasibility," Spring 2001

_____. "Leveraged ESOP Candidate Criteria Guidelines," Spring 2003

_____. "Unique Factors Related to the Valuation of ESOP Stock," Winter 2005

Jacobson, Craig A. "Revenue Ruling 2004-4 Provides Guidelines to Classify Certain SESOP Transactions as 'Listed Tax Shelters,'" Winter 2005

Kimball, Curtis R. "Repurchase Liability: A Nexus for ESOPs and Family Shares," Special Issue 1993

_____. "ESOPs and Estate Planning," Special Issue 1994

Levine, Scott, and Ken Barkman. "The Role of the Financial Adviser," Spring 1999

Meinhart, Timothy J. "Champlain Enterprises, Inc.—Court Emphasizes Importance of Fiduciary Procedural Protocol," Winter 2005

Millon, Thomas. "The Role of the Financial Advisor in the Analysis of Tender Offers for ESOP-Owned Shares," Special Issue 1994

Moore, Sharon. "ESOP Dividends Must Be Included in Calculating Corporate ATM," Spring 1995

_____. "IRS Issues Proposed Examination Guidelines for Leveraged ESOPs," Spring 1996

Murray, William F. "Letter Ruling 200436015 Increases the Leveraged ESOP Contribution Deduction Limitation," Winter 2005

Rabe, James G. "Howard v. Shay Redux," Spring 1999

Rabe, James G., and Charles A. Wilhoite. "Ownership Control Issues in ESOPs," Spring 1998

Reilly, Robert F. "Beals Bros. Management Corp.-Appeals Court Disallows Scheme to Shift ESOP Benefits to Corporate Officers," Spring 2003

_____. "Current Issues in the Valuation of ESOP-Owned Securities," Spring 2003

_____. "Professional Practices with Regard to Private Equity Valuation Discounts and Premiums," Winter 2005.

_____. "Valuation Issues with Regard to Mature ESOPs," Special Issue 1994

Reilly, Robert F., and Steve Garber. "ESOP Valuation and Financial Advisory Due Diligence Checklist," Spring 1996

Reilly, Robert F., and Robert P. Schweihs. "Recent Letter Ruling Allows Rollover of S Corporation ESOP Stock," Spring 2002

Roosma, Jacob. "ESOP Cash and Stock Distributions and the Anti-Cutback Rules," Spring 2000

Schmidt, Leigh. "Structuring a Leveraged ESOP," Spring 2000

Schweihs, Robert P. "Financial Opinions for ESOP Fiduciaries," Special Issue 1994

_____. "Ownership Transition Alternatives," Spring 1995

_____. "Will an ESOP Work for Me?" Special Issue 1994

Schweihs, Robert P., and Robert F. Reilly. "EGTRRA Provisions Generally Enhance ESOP Attractiveness," Winter 2003

Socol, Robert S. "ESOPs—A Powerful Estate Planning Tool," Spring 1995

_____. "ESOP Termination Issues," Spring 1998

Socol, Robert S., and John Kober. "ESOP Contributions and Allocations," Spring 1999

Socol, Robert S., and William M. Merten. "Using ESOPs and Stock-Based Compensation to Facilitate Liquidity, Business Succession Planning, Intergenerational Wealth Transfer, and Employee Corporate Ownership," Spring 1999

Tarbell, Jeffrey S. "Fairness Opinions in ESOP Transactions," Winter 2005.

Tarbell, Jeffrey S., and David Ackerman. "ESOP Regulatory and Case Law Update," Spring 1996

Thompson, Eric, and Gary Korn. "Overview of Employee Stock Ownership Plans," Spring 1999.

Ward, Andy, and Susan Gould. "The ESOP Advantage in Acquisitions," Spring 1999

Ward, Andy, Damon Martin, and Robert Reilly. "Taxpayer-Friendly Letter Ruling Describes Estate Planning Strategy for Control Owners of ESOP Corporations," Spring 2003

Wilhoite, Charles, and Scott Levine. "The Valuation Statement Impact of Accounting for ESOPs," Spring 1997.

Willamette Management Associates Insights Articles—Non-Willamette Authors

This section lists ESOP-related articles that appeared in *Insights* during the last decade and that were authored by prominent ESOP professionals not affiliated with Willamette Management Associates.

Ackerman, David. "Recent Court Ruling Regarding Excess Compensation Paid to Officer and Trustee of ESOP Company: The Need for Fairness Opinions," Spring 2001

Bickley, Bruce F. "Leveraged ESOP Transactions Using Seller Financing," Spring 2002

Braun, Richard, and Jared Kaplan. "The Use of ESOPs in Corporate Financial Restructuring," Spring 1996

Brown, Gregory. "A Legal Perspective on Using Control Premiums in ESOP Transactions," Spring 2001

Butcher, Keith D. "ESOPs and Government Contractors: Planning Ideas and Pitfalls," Spring 2002

Goldberg, Laurence A. "Legislative and Regulatory Developments Affecting ESOPs in 2004," Winter 2005

Gordy, Vauhgn. "Acquisition, Sale, Tender, or Plan Termination of an ESOP," Spring 2001

_____. "Corporate Governance in ESOP Companies," Spring 2003

Henderson, Colin M. "The ESOP as the Majority Stock Holder," Spring 2003

Kober, John. "Behind Open Doors: Corporate Governance with Emphasis on Implementing a Financial Plan Is Not a New Concept for ESOP Companies," Winter 2005

_____. "ESOPs Often Overlooked as a Planning Tool for Corporations and Shareholders," Spring 2001

Kober, John, and David Ackerman. "ESOP Company Corporate Governance: Financing of an ESOP Transaction Affects Corporate Governance," Autumn 2003

Kornfeld, Judith L. "ESOP Repurchase Obligation Issues in S Corporations," Spring 2002

Marchetti, Marilyn H. "Fiduciary Duties of the ESOP Trustee," Spring 2000

_____. "The Insider ESOP Trustee's Dilemma: Responding to an Offer to Buy the Company," Spring 2001

Marchetti, Marilyn H., and James E. Staruck. "The Trustee's Duty to Monitor Sponsor Company Transactions," Winter 2005

Merten, William W., and Daniel L. Smith. "Stock-Based Compensation Techniques in ESOP Transactions," Spring 1996

Merten, William M., and Robert S. Socol. "Using ESOPs and Stock-Based Compensation to Facilitate Liquidity, Business Succession and Estate Planning, and Management Buyouts," Spring 2001

Miller, Michael S. "Plan Design and the Long-Term Success of Employee Stock Ownership Plans," Spring 2002

Prodoehl, Peter J. "Administrative Issues Relating to Merger and Acquisitions Involving an ESOP Company," Spring 2001

Smith, Stephen D. "Department of Labor Brief in Enron Litigation Holds Lessons for ESOP Fiduciaries," Spring 2003

_____. "Using an ESOP as an Acquisition Vehicle," Spring 2001

Smith, Stephen D., and Sharon B. Hearn. "Plan Drafting and Related Issues in the Wake of the "Breaux/Ramstad" Provisions of the Economic Growth and Tax Relief Reconciliation Act of 2001," Spring 2002

Williams, Peter. "Using COLI to Fund the ESOP Repurchase Liability," Spring 2003